Key Categories in the Study of Religion

NAASR Working Papers

Series Editor: Brad Stoddard, McDaniel College in Westminster, Maryland.

NAASR Working Papers provides a venue for publishing the latest research carried out by scholars who understand religion to be an historical element of human cognition, practice, and organization. Whether monographs or multi-authored collections, the volumes published in this series all reflect timely, cutting edge work that takes seriously both the need for developing bold theories as well as rigorous testing and debate concerning the scope of our tools and the implications of our studies. NAASR Working Papers therefore assess the current state-of-the-art while charting new ways forward in the academic study of religion.

Published

Constructing "Data" in Religious Studies: Examining the Architecture of the Academy
Edited by Leslie Dorrough Smith

Hijacked: A Critical Treatment of the Public Rhetoric of Good and Bad Religion
Edited by Leslie Dorrough Smith, Steffen Führding, and Adrian Hermann

Jesus and Addiction to Origins: Towards an Anthropocentric Study of Religion
Willi Braun
Edited by Russell T. McCutcheon

Method Today: Redescribing Approaches to the Study of Religion
Edited by Brad Stoddard

"Religion" in Theory and Practice: Demystifying the Field for Burgeoning Academics
Russell T. McCutcheon

Remembering J. Z. Smith: A Career and its Consequence
Edited by Emily D. Crews and Russell T. McCutcheon

Forthcoming

Discourses of Crisis and the Study of Religion
Edited by Lauren Horn Griffin

On the Subject of Religion: Charting the Fault Lines of a Field of Study
Edited by James Dennis LoRusso

Thinking with J. Z. Smith: Mapping Methods in the Study of Religion
Edited by Barbara Krawcowicz

Key Categories in the Study of Religion

Contexts and Critiques

Edited by
Rebekka King

SHEFFIELD UK BRISTOL CT

Published by Equinox Publishing Ltd.

UK: Office 415, The Workstation, 15 Paternoster Row, Sheffield, South Yorkshire S1 2BX

USA: ISD, 70 Enterprise Drive, Bristol, CT 06010

www.equinoxpub.com

First published 2022

© Rebekka King and contributors 2022

All rights reserved. No part of this publication may be reproduced or transmitted in any form or by any means, electronic or mechanical, including photocopying, recording or any information storage or retrieval system, without prior permission in writing from the publishers.

ISBN-13 978 1 78179 965 9 (hardback)
         978 1 78179 966 6 (paperback)
         978 1 78179 967 3 (ePDF)
         978 1 80050 182 9 (ePub)

British Library Cataloguing-in-Publication Data

A catalogue record for this book is available from the British Library.

Library of Congress Cataloging-in-Publication Data

Names: King, Rebekka, editor.
Title: Key categories in the study of religion : contexts and critiques / edited by Rebekka King.
Description: Sheffield, South Yorkshire ; Bristol, CT : Equinox Publishing Ltd., 2022. | Series: NAASR working papers | Includes bibliographical references and index. | Summary: "Key Categories in the Study of Religion builds upon the groundwork laid by previous NAASR Working Papers titles in order to bring us full circle to the symbiotic relationship between context and critique. This volume assembles diverse sets of data to consider pertinent categories in which critique occurs"—Provided by publisher.
Identifiers: LCCN 2022001170 (print) | LCCN 2022001171 (ebook) | ISBN 9781781799659 (hardback) | ISBN 9781781799666 (paperback) | ISBN 9781781799673 (epdf) | ISBN 9781800501829 (epub)
Subjects: LCSH: Religion—Study and teaching.
Classification: LCC BL41 .K455 2022 (print) | LCC BL41 (ebook) | DDC 200.71—dc23/eng20220315
LC record available at https://lccn.loc.gov/2022001170
LC ebook record available at https://lccn.loc.gov/2022001171

Typeset by JS Typesetting Ltd, Porthcawl, Mid Glamorgan

Contents

Introduction: Critique in Context   1
Rebekka King

Part I   Citizenship and Politics

1   Paper Terrorism: Religion, Paperwork, and the Contestation of State Power in the "Sovereign Citizen" Movement   9
Michael J. McVicar

2   The Rohingya, Buddhism, and the Category "Religion"   31
Tenzan Eaghll

3   Citizenship, Religion, and the Frailty of State Sovereignty   42
Daniel Miller

4   The Material Production of Otherworldly Citizenship: From Paper to Digital Files to Bodies   55
Lauren Horn Griffin

5   Paper Terrorism as Counter-Conduct   67
Michael J. McVicar

Part II   Race and Ethnicity

6   Signifying "Der Rassist" in Religious Studies and the Axes of Social Difference   73
Richard Newton

7   Of Dualisms and Doppelgängers: Mapping Ancient Minds and Bodies in Religious Studies   92
Robyn Faith Walsh

8   Dark S(k)in: Two Versions of Newton's *Crimen Oscuro*   100
Rudy V. Busto

9   Reworking our Schemes   104
Craig R. Prentiss

10   That's a Racist Question: Interrogating Racism in the Study of American Religions   112
Martha Smith Roberts

| 11 | The Trope Has Been Set: Race and Religion as Critical Entanglement
Richard Newton | 123 |

Part III Gender and Sexuality

12	This Field Which Is Not One/The Body Is Smart: Rethinking Theory in the Study of Religion Megan Goodwin	135
13	A Happy Headache Emily D. Crews	146
14	Addressing Gender Parity in Critical Pedagogy Tara Baldrick-Morrone	151
15	The "Muscle Jew" and Maccabean Heroism of the Jewish Legion during World War I Tim Langille	156
16	"There is No Place for the State in the Bedrooms of the Nation": The Case of Québec's Bill 21 Jennifer A. Selby	162

Part IV Class and Economy

17	Regulating Religion to Maintain the Status Quo Suzanne Owen	179
18	A Gramscian Inversion: Hegemony in Theory and in Practice Thomas J. Carrico, Jr.	187
19	The Druid Network as a Capitalist Success Story: or, Why The Druid Network's Charity Status is Beside the Point Neil George	197
20	Who's Afraid of Class Analysis? Rethinking Identity and Class in the Study of Religion James Dennis LoRusso	204
21	Definition, Comparison, Critique Johan Strijdom	213
22	The Public Good Requirement Suzanne Owen	220

| Index | 227 |

Introduction: Critique in Context

Rebekka King

What if you found a portal to a parallel universe? What if you could slide into a thousand different worlds—where it's the same year, and you're the same person, but everything else is different? And what if you can't find your way home?

Do you remember the American science fiction television series *Sliders*? Probably not. It was not very good—even within its genre of late-twentieth-century sci-fi dramas. Like many people, recent political upheavals, the global pandemic, and the general malaise that has settled in public discourse have made me reticent to leave the house. I have found myself aimlessly browsing television streaming services for shows that remind me of a simpler time. Pickings are slim for those of us who came of age in the late-1990s. And so, I found myself re-watching *Sliders*.

Running for five seasons from 1995 to 2000, the show featured four protagonists who used a special device or "timer" to "slide" between parallel worlds through a wormhole.[1] In this process, they found themselves moving into parallel universes while remaining temporally and spatially static. Passing through the wormhole, they would arrive in the same year and roughly the same location, but on a different earth, a premise that allowed for endless possible alternative histories and contemporary scenarios. For example, they found themselves on worlds where dinosaurs had not gone extinct, where nudity was the norm, where penicillin had not been discovered and a worldwide pandemic was raging, where there was an established matriarchy, and (perhaps unbelievable in the mid-1990s) Hillary Clinton, rather than Bill Clinton, was president.

As the series progresses, the seemingly endless possibilities for alternative realities are strikingly repetitive. In the pilot episode, they arrived in a world where the Cold War domino theory had come true, and the sliders joined the American resistance in their struggle against the Soviets. In the fourth season, they find themselves on a world where the enslavement of racialized migrants supported California's economy. Per the series' recurring trope, they fight against

---

1. This era saw a renaissance of sorts for science fiction. The popularity of shows like *Star Trek: The Next Generation*, *Stargate SG-1*, and *Babylon 5* meant that networks were looking to capitalize on similar trends such as futuristic technologies, space shows, and time travel. The producers, Tracy Tormé (who was one the story editors for the first two season of *Star Trek: The Next Generation*) and Robert K. Weiss introduced the idea of parallel universes as a new spin on the genre.

this system of oppression because, to quote one of the episode's protagonists, "it's not my America." Indeed, as the series progresses, each novel earth is examined through a lens of similarities and differences to the characters' original earth. In this way, each new parallel universe functions as a proximate other, reminding its protagonists (and presumably the series' audience) of the uniqueness of their own "home earth" (see Smith 2004).

With their home earth presented as standard, the show replicated something akin to the world religions paradigm (Owen 2011; Cotter and Robertson 2016). The characters slide from earth to earth without ever pausing to interrogate the category. They do not ask what makes each earth an earth, nor do they consider their own standpoints. Nor should they. It is, after all, a television show. But like the persistent question-asker at every academic conference, I could not shake the fact that it reminded me of my research. Or more specifically, it reminded me of my frequent sense of displacement in certain sectors of the academic study of religion. A foreboding sense that while the terms and categories are the same (e.g., it's the same the year and I am the same person), everything else is different.

Previous volumes in the NAASR Working Papers series have centered on theory (2017), method (2018), and data (2019) as venues through which our otherwise evasive efforts to pinpoint scholarship of religion can be taken up. This volume takes up the theme of categories—a venture which Richard Newton worries might result in a "fool's errand" (see Newton, Chapter 11, this volume). In considering categories, we find ourselves in a parallel universe with recognizably similar problems to those we have trained ourselves to articulate when studying religion. Like "religion," many people bring a priori assumptions to such endeavors. Whereas scholars might spend substantial energies delineating the boundaries of the field of religious studies and religious traditions,[2] the definitions and analytical frameworks within a given category are often presumed to be shared and not requiring in-depth explanation, let alone theorizing or debate. Our assumption that these categories are independent of religion has restricted us from interrogating their use and misuse as categories of the study of religion.[3] We allow ourselves to slide into them as if they are fully formed worlds that do not require the same attention or inquiry that we extend to our own.

Academia is not devoid of ritual. As Leslie Dorrough Smith (2019) recounts in her introduction to the previous volume in this series, perhaps most ubiquitous among the subsection of religious studies scholars who find their home in

---

2. Aaron Hughes astutely notes the predominance of religious traditions in job advertisements on the AAR's online employment database (Hughes 2017: 3). Employers are required to choose from a list of 56 options, which by my count consisted primarily of religious traditions (28), geographical regions (11), and proprietary conjunctions (e.g., religion and, religion in, religion of) (8) options. Of course, the idea that someone might employ search terms to limit their options to a given field seems unlikely given the current state of the higher education job market.

3. I am mindful of Tim Fitzgerald's point in his critique of Lincoln's "Theses on Method" in which he argues against seeing religion as possessing a distinct nature in contrast to other categories (Fitzgerald 2006: 398).

NAASR—and elsewhere—is the ritualistic evocation of Jonathan Z. Smith's adage that there is "no data for religion" (Smith 1982: xi). We use it is as a rejoinder in publications to denote affiliation and gesture wildly at maps in introductory religious studies classes to highlight the refrain "map is not territory." The elder Smith's point underscores the imaginative work that scholars assume in bringing together data for analysis. Work with a generative power to construct fields of study, consecrate systems of classification, and delineate disciplinary boundaries. Many others have noted an ironic failure on the part of scholars to consider the full implications of Smith's argument.[4] There remains an underlying sense that the evocation of Smith's critique atones for a failure to apply it. To restate Smith's observations serves as a protective amulet against accusations of abstraction, essentialism, and domestication. As if by sheer force of utterance and performative action, the field of religious studies might be realigned or corrected in a way that magically avoids the very real pitfalls of essentialisms.

Even rarer is the consideration of the ways that other terms are overlooked as objects of the scholar's creation. There are many ways to draw a map. The same terrain might be exposed differently depending on the type or details it intends to reveal. While some conscientiously follow Smith's directive "to show their work" in the classroom and elsewhere and expose their previously misaligned maps and charts to students and colleagues (Smith 2007), a closer examination is warranted. In the same way that religion has been shown to be devoid of data so too should we think about our deployment of certain categories, terms, and theoretical lenses as cartographic phenomenon.

This is not to say that categories remain unexplored in religious studies. In a 2007 review essay for the *Journal of the American Academy of Religion*, Russell McCutcheon interrogates our consumption of handbooks or guidebooks related to the academic study of religion. No doubt a cursory glance of bookshelves belonging to those engaged in the academic study of religion will reveal a collection of books dedicated to offering an "informative," "provocative," "revitalized," "accessible," and "authoritative guide" to the study of religion.[5] For example, Robert Orsi's *The Cambridge Companion to Religious Studies* (2005) is extolled as "both informative and provocative, introducing readers to key debates in the contemporary study of religion and suggesting future research possibilities." *The Oxford Handbook of the Study of Religion* (2016) edited by Michael Stausberg and Steven Engler comprises an "authoritative collection [that] will advance the state of the discipline and is an invaluable reference for students and scholars." Also "authoritative" and "interdisciplinary" is Robert Segal's *The Blackwell Companion to the Study of Religion* (2008). Likewise, Mark C. Taylor's *Critical Terms for Religious Studies* (1998), which

---

4. See for example the collection of essays in William Arnal and Russell T. McCutcheon's *The Sacred is Profane* (2012). Smith himself appears to bemoan the failure of scholars to comprehend his statement. In an interview, he noted that the quote is often used in ways that are unrecognizable to him (Braun and McCutcheon 2018: 71).

5. These terms come from the Amazon descriptions of readers or guidebooks that many of us—myself included—use to introduce concepts to students in undergraduate courses.

served as my introduction to Method and Theory as an MA student, is presented as providing "a revitalized, self-aware vocabulary with which this bewildering religious diversity can be accurately described and responsibly discussed."

In assessing representations of the handbook genre, McCutcheon (2007) finds them to be filled—at times arbitrarily—with both first and second order terms and categories presumed to be relevant to the study of religion. In those volumes that McCutcheon examines and others, there is significant crossover in terms of topics and themes. Some maintain a consistent theoretical or methodological bend, while others allow individual authors to pursue their own viewpoints without regard for an overarching message. A close reading of these guidebooks reveals less about the categories themselves and more about the means through which they reify given assumptions about religion and how its study should be arranged. To return to the metaphor of parallel universes from *Sliders*, it is the continuity rather than the differences that are noteworthy.

This volume considers four social categories prominent in religious studies: citizenship and politics; race and ethnicity; gender and sexuality; and class and economy. In doing so, it offers an opportunity to redescribe these categories. Like religion, they are not natural or self-evident categories, but they are often treated as such. A failure to adequately theorize them leaves us without any real starting point for analysis. Thus, this volume's premise is to establish an analytical framework in which the same redescription warranted to the study of religion might be likewise provided for critical categories qua the study of religion. Each section opens with a main essay that addresses the category's currency and its application within the author's research specialization. Michael McVicar, Richard Newton, Megan Goodwin, and Suzanne Owen each offer a redescription of the approach scholars of religion might take to their category. These opening chapters are followed by response chapters with an eye toward expounding the category. The respondents were asked to take up the themes of the chapter with special attention to category and show how it might be applicable in new contexts. Rather than repeating the category, they were asked to explore how it worked or did not when applied to divergent contexts. In doing so, we hoped to provide a multivocal conversation that might resonate with readers who could place their own potential contributions in conversation with the primary essays and the responses.[6]

While I will leave it to the reader to gauge each section's success, I would like to highlight the value of cojoined theorization and application in a "rinse and repeat" fashion. From Robyn Faith Walsh's Myers–Briggs results to Tenzan Eaghll's arguments with his robed-monk students about the ubiquity of religion, from Lauren Horn Griffin's analysis of the fluidity of Instagram posts to Martha Smith

---

6. Like religion, these categories do not exist in a vacuum. Indeed, as Tim Langille points out in his response to Megan Goodwin's paper, many of the responses might just as easily fit into other sections of this book. At the end of the day, Langille saw his chapter as more congruent with McVicar's discussion of citizenship over and against Goodwin on gender.

Roberts's evocation of Charles Long and signification, at every turn in this book, we find examples, case studies, or (as Newton so astutely puts it) "the tropes" where we "find our footing" that do the work of moving a category forward. This book serves as a stopping point in the continued project taken up by NAASR and those who position themselves within the rubric of method and theory in the study of religion. A project that takes serious not only the categories that are employed when studying religion but also their context and the criteria by which they are brought to light.

Rebekka King is Associate Professor of Religious Studies and Resident Faculty Fellow of the Honors College at Middle Tennessee State University. She currently serves as President of the North American Association for the Study of Religion. Her areas of expertise are North American religions, anthropology of religion, and contemporary biblical reception. Her first monograph, *The New Heretics: Skepticism, Secularism, and Progressive Christianity* is forthcoming with New York University Press.

References

Arnal, William, and Russell T. McCutcheon. 2012. *The Sacred is Profane: The Political Nature of "Religion"*. New York: Oxford University Press.

Braun, Willi, and Russell T. McCutcheon. 2018. *Reading J. Z. Smith: Interviews and Essay*. New York: Oxford University Press.

Cotter, Christopher R., and David G. Robertson (eds.). 2016. *After World Religions: Reconstructing Religious Studies*. New York: Routledge.

Fitzgerald, Tim. 2006. "Bruce Lincoln's 'Theses on Method': Antithesis." *Method and Theory in the Study of Religion* 18: 392–423. https://doi.org/10.1163/157006806778665521

Hughes, Aaron W. 2017. "Introduction: Theory in a Time of Excess." In Aaron W. Hughes (ed.), *Theory in a Time of Excess: Beyond Reflection and Explanation in Religious Studies Scholarship*. Sheffield: Equinox.

McCutcheon, Russell T. 2007. "Words, Words, Words." *Journal of the American Academy of Religion* 75(4): 952–987. https://doi.org/10.1093/jaarel/lfm082

Owen, Suzanne. 2011. "The World Religions Paradigm: Time for a Change." *Arts and Humanities in Higher Education* 10(3): 253–268. https://doi.org/10.1177/1474022211408038

Smith, Jonathan Z. 1982. *Imagining Religion: From Babylon to Jonestown*. Chicago, IL: University of Chicago Press.

Smith, Jonathan Z. 2004. "What a Difference a Difference Makes." In Jonathan Z. Smith, *Relating Religion: Essays in the Study of Religion*, 251–302. Chicago, IL: University of Chicago Press.

Smith, Jonathan Z. 2007. "Afterword: The necessary Lie: Duplicity in the Disciplines." In Russell T. McCutcheon, *Studying Religion: An Introduction*, 73–80. London: Equinox.

Smith, Leslie Dorrough. 2019. "'If I Had a Nickle for Every Time …: Thinking Critically about 'Data'." In Leslie Dorrough Smith (ed.), *Constructing "Data" in Religious Studies: Examining the Architecture of the Academy*, 1–6. Sheffield: Equinox.

Part I

Citizenship and Politics

Chapter 1

Paper Terrorism: Religion, Paperwork, and the Contestation of State Power in the "Sovereign Citizen" Movement

Michael J. McVicar

Citizenship, for all of its ideological and political entailments, is in many ways an aggregated, material phenomenon. That is, at its root, modern citizenship is predicated on the ability of a governed subject of state power to produce a complex secession of documentary traces that witness to the subject's entanglement with state and non-state bureaucratic agencies. From the birth certificate—the originary and essential document for most forms of modern citizenship—to the credit score—the documentary essence of *homo economicus*—the status of the modern citizen-subject is intimately entwined with myriad bureaucratic forms, files, and digital bits that register a citizen's competing and complimentary social, cultural, economic, and political characteristics.

Interest in paperwork, documents, bureaucracy, and filing techniques has increasingly captured the attention of historians, anthropologists, and literature scholars precisely because these topics have been largely overlooked in the past while, simultaneously, the material residue of official paperwork is an increasingly omnipresent modern phenomenon that a savvy researcher can exploit. Whether in the form of declassified (or illegally leaked) government dossiers, or corporate files released as part of an official public disclosure or delivered to the public through a bankruptcy filing, bureaucratic paperwork and its ubiquity make it an easy and essential source for researchers.[1] With some notable exceptions in the recent work of Sylvester Johnson (2015) and Judith Weisenfeld (2017), for example, scholars of religion have been slow to recognize the significance of the so-called "archival" or "bureaucratic turn" emerging in other areas in the humanities.

---

1. This chapter seeks to synthesize American religious historians' abiding interest in business practices and corporations with the so-called "archival turn" emerging in anthropology and cultural studies. The "archival turn" attends to the forms of information collected by states, corporations, and other systems of bureaucratic surveillance. Scholars operating in this mode study the material mechanisms and cultural practices used to create, preserve, and distribute these records. For introductory summaries of this trend see Hull (2012) and Edwards et al. (2011). Representative studies might include Latour (2013) and Gitelman (2014).

This chapter takes up the problem of paperwork and techniques of documentation practiced in religious movements to explore the complex relationship between the material production of citizenship and religious practice in the contemporary United States.[2] Specifically, it focuses on the "sovereign citizen" movement in the United States and its network of politically affiliated libertarian, anarchist, and antigovernment activists in the wider Anglophone world. A political movement with deep—and seemingly paradoxical—roots in both white right-wing racist theologies and separatist African American movements that broke with the Moorish Science Temple, sovereign citizens use sophisticated bureaucratic techniques to resist normative understandings of citizenship. Through alternative systems of record-keeping, counter-surveillance methods, combative litigation, and efforts to avoid generating paperwork in the first place, so-called sovereign citizens attempt to disrupt the state's ability to regulate their behavior, even as such resistance prompts more intensive and coercive actions on the part of state agencies. By focusing on the explosion of litigious and bureaucratic paperwork associated with the sovereign citizenship movement, this chapter ultimately challenges conventional attempts in religious studies to frame political resistance movements such as sovereign citizens in terms of their unique religious worldviews, and instead emphasizes how these movements may be productively understood as social objects that emerge from the imperative of state and corporate bureaucracies to keep records rather than autonomous manifestations of some deeper human search for religious or spiritual meaning.

Magical Strawmen

Although the sovereign citizen movement has been increasingly associated with violent antigovernment extremism in the form of aggressive resistance to federal

---

2. At the outset, I should note that I make no attempt in this chapter to offer any sort of stipulative or ostensive definitions for the terms "citizen," "citizenship," or "religion." While J. Z. Smith might have considered such stipulative definitions essential for any responsible study of the of the concepts at hand, I am persuaded by Bruno Latour's argument that students of social phenomena should not focus their attention on generating stipulative definitions for conceptual categories. Latour argues that scholars should instead focus on tracing the controversies associated with historically durable, but widely contested concepts. Rather than stipulative or ostensive definitions, Latour has insisted that scholars should pay as much attention to performative definitions of social objects that emerge as actors attempt to delineate the boundaries of social phenomena. Following this methodology, scholars do not generate a definition of "religion" or "citizen" to ground their research, but rather they track how others define and battle over such definitions. If social actors abandon a given concept or definitional battle, then scholars have nothing to track, or they have only the social traces of previous, now-extinct battles. For J. Z. Smith's reflections on the scholarly significance of stipulative definitions (and how he contrasts them with lexical definitions), see Smith (2004), especially the chapters "Manna, Mana Everywhere and /ˇ/ˇ," "A Matter of Class: Taxonomies of Religion," and "Religion, Religions, Religious." For Latour's discussion of performative definitions, see Latour (2005: 44–48).

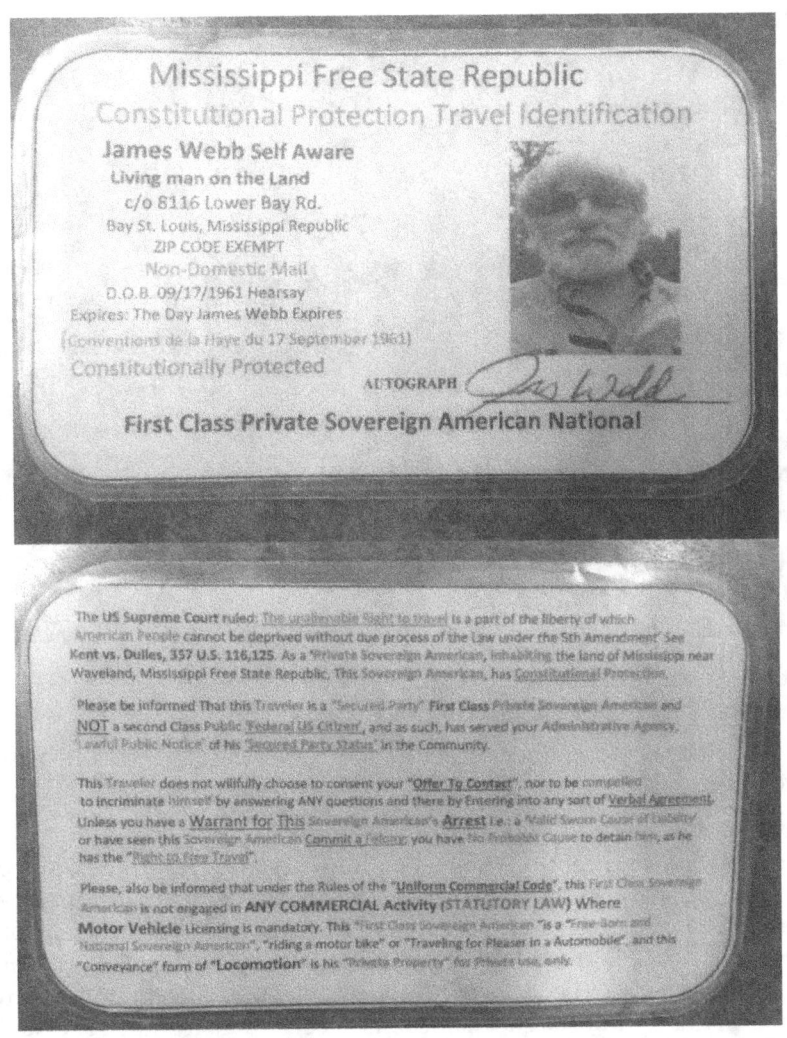

Figure 1.1 Example of a sovereign citizen "constitutional protection travel identification" driver's license, Slidell (Louisiana) Police Department, 2016.

Source: retrieved from www.facebook.com/SlidellPD/photos/pcb.1122423387803821/ 1122421221137371/?type=3&theater (image in the public domain)

land policy in the West and Moorish violence against (mostly) municipal and county law enforcement officers, this large, diffuse movement is still singularly associated with the nonviolent legal tactics authorities have dubbed "paper terrorism." Paper terrorism is generally marked by the issuance of property liens, the aggressive use of illegal or extralegal court filings, the printing of homemade or nongovernment-backed currencies, and the creation of personal diplomatic

Figure 1.2 Example of a sovereign citizen "private mode of travel" license plate, Washington County (Oregon) Sheriff's Office, 2017.

Source: retrieved from https://twitter.com/WCSOOregon/status/867483978801872896 (image in the public domain)

paperwork, drivers' licenses (Figure 1.1), license plates (Figure 1.2), and passports.[3] The rationale behind the issuance of all of this alternative legal paperwork is complex. Some sovereign citizens argue that in the years immediately following the Civil War, a new legal regime illegally usurped the English common-law system established by the Founding Fathers in the U.S. Constitution. Sovereign theorists in this tradition argue that federal Reconstruction of the South and the ratification of thirteenth, fourteenth, and fifteenth amendments to the constitution illegally impressed formerly free white citizens into the service of a secret government administered by Admiralty Law. The clandestine imposition of this maritime legal system effectively transformed all free whites into the property of the federal government. Other sovereign theorists, as legal scholar Charles E. Loeser summarizes, argue that the United States' departure from the gold standard in 1933 established a new legal and financial regime in which the federal government "began using its citizens as collateral in trade agreements with foreign nations" (Loeser 2014: 1121). To administer this shadow banking system, the U.S. Treasury established "an account for each citizen at birth and pledges

---

3. For a summary of "paper terrorism" as defined by federal attorneys and law enforcement, see Ihlo and Pulice (2013) and Federal Bureau of Investigation (2010).

some amount of money on that account. This securitization creates two separate identities—the corporate account, or 'strawman,' and the 'common-law,' or core identity" (ibid.). Sovereign theorists therefore reject all federal documentation as representations of their collateralized "strawman" identity, and they seek to "redeem" their "flesh-and-blood" identity, often by trying to claim the value of their "strawman" account through innovative tax filings and property liens, or by insisting on copyrighting their name and "flesh-and-blood" identity.

Both the "Admiralty Law" and the "Redemption" theories of sovereignty—or some combination of the two—have led to an explosion of resistive bureaucratic techniques designed to overwhelm courts, confuse banks, intimidate local officials, and clog federal agencies with clever, silly, and occasionally successful filings. In the wake of the 2008 financial crisis in the United States, the problem further expanded as sovereigns used liens and other tactics—including squatting and violence—to claim or retain foreclosed property.[4] By the close of the first decade of the twenty-first century, twenty-seven states had passed laws designed to curb sovereign citizens' "paper terrorism" tactics, and the number has only continued to increase as more and more states recognize sovereign filings as a threat to the United States' judicial, political, and financial systems (Chamberlain and Haider-Markel 2005: 452).

When scholars of religion have explored the bureaucratic tactics of sovereign citizens, they have tended to fall into two camps. First, following the work of political scientist Michael Barkun, scholars have tended to frame sovereign paper terrorism as an alternative, but nonetheless patently fraudulent legal framework designed to "monkey-wrench" the U.S. judicial and financial systems. "Conceptually," Barkun writes, sovereign citizens live "in a parallel legal universe, holding to the view that conspiratorial forces have highjacked the government and the legal system to strip Americans of their rights" (Barkun 2013: 197). Whether they act out of stubborn principled defiance, or naked financial opportunism, Barkun understands the activities of sovereign citizens in much the same way that law enforcement officials do: sovereign "paper terrorism" poses a legitimate threat to law and order and must be constrained by every mechanism possible through the American justice system.

In contrast to Barkun, religious historian Catherine Wessinger suggests a more complicated and generous understanding of the "paper terrorism" techniques of sovereign citizens. In her study of the sovereign-inspired Montana Freemen movement of the 1990s, Wessinger identifies sovereign citizen ideology as a nativist movement that "appropriate[s] the enemy's power by imitating their actions and their use of words possessing power" (Wessinger 2000: 196). Through Wessinger's comparative schema, sovereign citizens are best understood as nativists resisting encroaching colonial forces, not unlike Sioux Ghost Dancers on the

---

4. Anecdotal evidence of the explosion of sovereign "paper terrorism" tactics abounded in the wake of the 2008 financial crisis. Most of the media coverage "paper terrorism" has been in regional business journals that document local reality market conditions. See, for example, Chandler (2011: 1, 23), Collins (2012), and, for a national perspective, Goode (2013).

Great Plains during the 1880s or the cargo cults of the Pacific after World War II.[5] Religion scholar Spencer Dew has developed Wessinger's insights in his study of contemporary sovereign Moorish legal theory. For Dew, Moorish sovereign citizen legal theorists interpret "[i]nteractions in court or confrontations with police" through a magical "feedback loop" in which the law is understood as having the "transcendent efficacy" to shape reality (Dew 2016: 72).[6] Echoing Sir James George Frazer's classic theory of "sympathetic magic" both Wessinger and Dew argue that the magical efficacy of "paper terrorism" rests on, in Frazer's words, "the principle that like produces like" (Frazer 1966: 85). This magical model suggests that the sovereign activist engages in "deliberate imitation of the result he seeks to attain"—in this case a legally recognized and legitimate alternative political status—by mimicking or appropriating state bureaucratic techniques, and also by "scrupulously avoid[ing]" outcomes "which would really be disastrous" (ibid.), such as being enslaved by Admiralty Law or becoming legally synonymous with one's indebted "strawman."

Without completely dismissing Wessinger's and Dew's focus on the "magical thinking" of sovereign "paper terrorism," I want to suggest another route that avoids the temptation to read this movement as some *sui generis* autochthonous expression of human longing for freedom from colonial domination. Rather than cycling through a succession of well-worn comparative categories used in religious studies (such as nativist revivalism, magic, ritual, and so on), I would instead like to focus on the way state officials and court officers have responded to the "paper terrorism" tactics of sovereign citizens. I believe this is useful for two reasons. First, the "magical" paradigm (whether intended or not on the part of scholars) insists on a *prima facie* dismissal of the legal legitimacy of sovereign paperwork—an assumption that state agencies themselves do not and cannot make. Indeed, the problem with "paper terrorism" is not that it is always patently fraudulent. Instead, the issue is that "paper terrorism" forces state bureaucratic regimes to assess the questionable paperwork before drawing any particular conclusions about it. In many instances, such as in the case of property liens, even if the paperwork is fraudulent, the state must still assess it before rejecting its legal merits. This suggests that there is nothing homeopathic or sympathetic about "paper terrorism." In fact, the opposite is true: sovereign citizens deploy this paperwork because it works in a very practical way by *occasionally* yielding the very financial, bureaucratic, and legal outcomes they seek.

Second, and much more importantly, the magical paradigm is rooted in the temptation to see state agencies and their affiliates as the *real* sources of documentation, paperwork, and bureaucratic production. This is a deeply problematic assumption that allows the state-form to precede all other forms of political,

---

5. Rosenfeld (2016) develops and extensively elaborates on Wessinger's comparative system.
6. Dew (2019) significantly refines and revises this discussion of magic and the law. I have retained my original comments based on Dew (2016). But I must note that his 2019 work on this point is significantly different from the argument that I outlined in the original 2018 version of this paper.

social, cultural, and governing authority. Historically, state bureaucracies have simply been one among many competing issuers of authoritative public documents. Churches, corporations, benevolent societies, and other social and political bodies have all laid claim to the ability to issue authoritative paperwork. Sometimes this authority comes with the blessing of the state, while in other cases such paperwork generates conflict and friction with state agencies. In instances of legal ambiguity, it is the state that is frequently the aggressive appropriator of other bureaucratic forms as it seeks to make citizens and noncitizens legible for the purpose of governing them.

Before "Paper Terrorism"

Before turning to contemporary examples of "paper terrorism" and state responses to it, I want to look at what law enforcement might rightly regard as a proto-form of sovereign citizen paperwork tactics: the issuance of "Nationality and Identification Cards" by the Moorish Science Temple of America (MSTA). These cards provide an interesting entry point into sovereign citizen bureaucratic practices because, first, they underscore how the scholarly focus on white sovereigns has neglected the longer history of the phenomena and ignored the complex role Black activism has played in shaping contemporary forms of white nationalism and vice versa. Second, in the 1930s and the 1940s, federal authorities regarded the generation of alternative and resistive bureaucratic systems of recording, archiving, and using paperwork as one of the primary dangers of MSTA. For example, a number of scholars have pointed out that the Bureau of Investigation (BI), the predecessor agency of today's Federal Bureau of Investigation (FBI), originally identified the MSTA as a national security threat precisely because it promoted an alternative "olive" Asiatic Moorish ethnic and racial identity that undermined the ability of state agencies to regulate "black" African American bodies through Jim Crow-era segregation laws, Selective Service enrollment, and other legally required registration processes that collected and created information about race, religion, and ethnic identity (see Johnson 2015: ch. 6).

For the Bureau of Investigation, the MSTA's issuance of Nationality Cards represented the radical implications of the movement's racial politics. Why? Certainly not because the bureau's agents cared very much about the religious ideas underlying the cards.[7] Instead, the BI agents worried that the MSTA IDs might have their

---

7. In fact, bureau investigators were explicit about the fact they found nothing especially criminal about Moorish religious belief or practice. In a summary of federal efforts to prosecute MSTA members, the bureau concluded that, at best, federal agents only had authority to prosecute members on attempts "to evade the Selective Service Act," and they saw no grounds for persecuting anyone "on the basis of the teachings of the MSTA" (Federal Bureau of Investigation 1943b: 15).

The distinction developed in this BI report is significant because bureau memoranda barely manage to conceal the agents' contempt for MSTA members. Investigating personnel showed no interest in attempting to understand the racial and ethnic claims made by MSTA members

intended public effect and be viewed as an official document attesting to their non-negro status as U.S. citizens with full membership in the American body politic.[8] In the 1930s, agents from the BI took an interest in MSTA Nationality Cards because they represented a threat to local segregation laws and federal registration regulations, and because they might have the effect of encouraging the mixing of races.

A BI memorandum summarizing an interview with an MSTA recruiter identified only as "Bey" in the redacted documents summarized the purpose of the cards:

> These cards are supposed to identify the bearer as a descendant of the Moors and the writing thereon pays homage to Allah, Budda [sic], and the other divine prophets, refers to Mecca in reverent terms, and contains a statement concerning the equality of all races. Agent [redacted] learned that the members are assured that they can identify themselves with these cards at any hotel or eating place throughout the United States, and be assured every courtesy and equal privileges with other races.
>
> (Bureau of Investigation 1931a: 3)

The perplexed interviewing agent concluded, "Bey has all of the appearance and characteristics of a full blooded negro" (ibid.: 2). Further, he advised that Bey "is a fanatic on the subject of equality for all races, and is attempting to promote and carry on the Moorish Science Temple of America for propaganda purposes"

---

and recruiters. During interviews, federal agents and cooperating local officials did not hesitate to threaten MSTA members with arrest and prosecution based on dubious or nonexistent charges such as operating confidence games or swindling others out of money through the collection of membership fees or the selling of Moorish garb. These threats, however real their effect might have been in intimidating MSTA members, had no basis in federal law. Aside from Selective Service violations, agents could have only reasonably arrested suspects for violating federal rules related to mail fraud, tax evasion, interstate financial fraud, or similar violations of federal statue. Very few, if any, of the alleged confidence games or quotidian swindles the agents believed they uncovered would have risen to the level of federal crimes.

8. As Zareena Grewal has noted, "The Moor's nationality cards are a material assertation of their countercitizenship, encompassing their contradictory desire for inclusion and their embrace of their difference" (Grewal 2014: 88). "The nationality cards that members flashed when stopped by the police fused a politics of recognition and an assertion of American citizenship with a rejection of the American mainstream and the racial status quo" (ibid.: 90). In spite of the seeming radicalness of the MSTA members' assertion of their Moorish or Asiatic identity, Grewal points out that MSTA's claims "deflected but did not undermine the dominant biological claims for the racial inferiority of black" (ibid.). In some ways, the insistence on their "Asiatic" identity had unintended consequences for MSTA members. By swapping one ostensibly "inferior" racial status for another, MSTA members opened themselves up to other claims of subversion. The BI suspected MSTA members of working with the Pacific Movement of the Eastern World, a pro-Japanese organization that sought to build relationships with African Americans influenced by Garveyism and MSTA ideas to create a coalition between African Americans, white liberals, and Japanese nationalists. The MSTA's adoption of Asiatic nationality and some of its members reported positive statements regarding Japanese Imperial ambitions provided the BI with multiple opportunities to surveil the MSTA during the 1930s.

(ibid.: 3). Bey allowed the agent to inspect his card but refused to let him take it. In turn, the agent "managed to secure a description and exact copy of the wording" and produced a typescript replica of the card complete with hand-sketched crescent-moon-and-star insignia (Figure 1.3) (Bureau of Investigation 1931b).

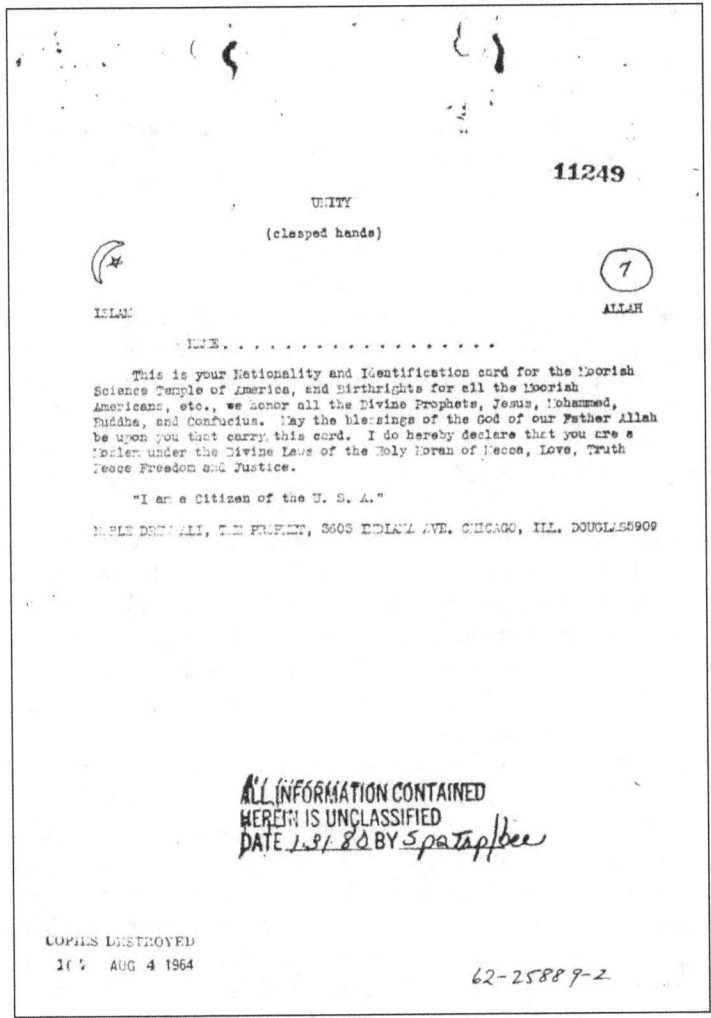

Figure 1.3 Bureau of Investigation reproduction of a Moorish Science Temple "Nationality Card."

Source: Appendix to memorandum from Rhea Whitley to [J. Edgar Hoover] Director of Bureau of Investigation, September 12, 1931, in Bureau of Investigation file number 62-25889, Subject: Moorish Science Temple of America (Noble Drew Ali), serial 2, released through the Freedom of Information and Privacy Acts and retrieved from The FBI: Federal Bureau of Investigation, "FBI Records: The Vault," https://vault.fbi.gov/Moorish%20Science%20Temple%20of%20America (image in the public domain)

The agent focused on the card because he believed it provided Bey and any MSTA member with a bureaucratic mechanism for challenging Jim Crow-era segregation laws, undermining Selective Service policies, and legitimizing claims to a Moorish or Asiatic ethnicity on official documents. MSTA recruiters and public speakers explicitly linked knowledge of one's true ethnic and racial identity with efforts to resist legal segregation during the 1930s and the 1940s. In notes from a January 10, 1943, meeting of the Moorish Temple in Hartford, Connecticut, a bureau informant recorded that one speaker proudly rejected his "negro" identity and asserted his Moorish heritage. The speaker concluded, "Man, know thyself! The truth will set you free! Yes, free from Jim-Crowisms, discriminations, and our most distasteful poll-tax" (Federal Bureau of Investigation 1943a: 10). By documenting the Moorish identity of their bearers, BI agents worried that MSTA Nationality Cards had the potential to subvert local segregation policies, undermine regulatory agencies' ability to document "accurate" racial categorization, and lead to conflict with governmental registering authorities.

More to the point, however, the BI specifically worried that claims of Moorish nationality could lead to a cascade of new paperwork and burdensome reissuing of identity documents as MSTA members sought to reconcile the information on their nationality cards with public records. "The Moors are urged," reported one internal bureau memo, "to 'tell other Negroes who they really are' and not to recognize the name Negro if applied to MSTA members. Accordingly, all public records in which may be found the given name of a MSTA member are to be changed to add the surname BEY or EL. For this purpose MSTA members regularly visit Social Security agencies, Selective Service Boards, Election Registration agencies, etc." (Federal Bureau of Investigation 1943b: 5). On occasion during World War II, MSTA members used their Nationality Cards to assert conscientious objector status before draft boards around the country, sometimes successfully petitioning for noncombatant service.[9]

While not "paper terrorism" as scholars, lawyers, and law enforcement agents understand the phrase today, the MSTA membership cards anticipated much of the contemporary angst over such alternative bureaucratic techniques for documenting one's identity. From law enforcement's perspective, these documents posed a threat because they *might* make citizens less knowable to state agencies.[10] Further, their issuance and acceptance *might* prompt a secession of changes to public records as their holders sought to reconcile one form of identification with another. As a consequence, the bureau and other federal and local agencies sought to regulate their use for identification purposes and to delegitimize

---

9. For a summary of the various conscientious objector status cases associated with the MTSA and their outcomes, see Weisenfeld (2017: 220–221).
10. On the state's need to "know" its citizens, see Igo (2018). There can be little doubt that law enforcement's anxieties about registering brown bodies under alternative racial and ethnic categories emerged from a long American history of making blackness visible through all manner of surveillance techniques. For a catalogue of these surveillance strategies and their racializing consequences, see Browne (2015).

any legal claims to equality their bearers might make. In this manner, MSTA Nationality Cards did not represent a battle between "magical" nativists and "legitimate" legal discourses. Nor did they mark a simplistic "appropriation" of state bureaucratic forms by religious adherents. Such distinctions presume the very boundaries the BI and the MSTA were fighting to create, not ones that pre-existed the bureaucratic conflict itself.

Anti-Tax, Anti-License

On July 17, 2016, Cosmo Ausar Setepenra (also known as Gavin E. Long), a 29-year-old former Marine and self-identified Moorish sovereign citizen, ambushed and shot six police officers outside a convenience store in Baton Rouge, Louisiana (Jansen 2016; Swaine 2016). Three of the officers died of their wounds. SWAT officers eventually surrounded the masked, black-clad, and heavily armed Setepenra and killed him. When law enforcement retrieved his body using a bomb squad robot, they discovered a Washitaw Nation membership card in Setepenra's possession (Stickney 2016). Although the Washitaw Nation condemned Setepenra's violent rampage, Setepenra's possession of the membership card linked him to the complex and ever-evolving sovereign citizen phenomenon.[11]

During the 1970s, the Washitaw Nation splintered from the Moorish Science Temple movement as a dissident group dedicated to asserting the sovereignty of Moors as a distinct Native American tribe in the United States. Unlike conventional MSTA teaching that insists on the U.S. citizenship of all Moors, the Washitaw Nation diverged sharply from Noble Drew Ali's ideas. Under the leadership of Empress Verdiacee Tiari Washitaw Turner Goston El-Bey (also known as Verdiacee Hampton Goston), Washitaw Moors insist that some African Americans are descendants of an ancient tribe of Africans that settled in the Americas and these descendants retain sovereign rights to an ancient homeland that comprises

---

11. Fredrix Joe Washington, the son of Washitaw Nation founder Verdiacee Hampton Goston, explicitly denounced Setepenra's actions and denied his association with Washitaw Nation. Washington told the *Wall Street Journal* that he could not account for everyone who claimed citizenship in the Washitaw Nation, insisting, "A lot of groups think they can come in use the name, use our family name, and use our book to get what they want" (Palazzolo 2016). Similarly, Azeem Hopkins-Bey, a spokesperson for the Moorish Science Temple, condemned Setepenra and forcefully rejected sovereign citizenship ideas in a press conference following the Baton Rogue shootings. As Spencer Dew has noted, any attempt to pin down Washitaw Nation members is especially difficult because of the dynamic nature of both sovereign citizen ideology and shifting religious identities: "There likely are only a few hundred Washitaw nationwide, though this estimate is complicated by schism within the movement and porous boundaries between Washitaw groups and other African American NRMs advancing similar claims to indigeneity and antiquity, be they Islamic, Moorish, African, Egyptian, Israelite, or Native American" (Dew 2015: 66). Given these facts and in spite of the best efforts of leaders like Washington and Hopkins-Bey to rein in the most radical fringes of the sovereign citizen movement, the combination of fluid, nomadic notions of citizenship, ethnicity, and religious identity are as problematic for religious groups as they are for governments.

modern Louisiana, Missouri, and Arkansas (Goston 1993). Washitaw sovereigns began using "paper terrorism" to issue property liens and "strawman" filings to secure, according to one press account, a 30-million-acre "empire" in the South (Reynolds 2014).

Some legal scholars have argued that members of the Washitaw Nation adopted tactics popularized by the most commonly cited "paper terrorism" innovators of the sovereignty movement: the Sheriff's Posse Comitatus (SPC) (see Loeser 2014). The SPC, a militant, white nationalist group, emerged in the American West in the 1970s as a complex, decentralized antigovernment movement protesting federal taxes, resisting federal management of Western lands, and dedicated to fighting the U.S. banking industry—especially mortgages and other financial instruments that they believed undermined private property. The FBI characterized the ideas behind the SPC as "a nameless, loosely organized network of anti-tax, anti-license proponents, who are self styled, 'tax patriots' and 'constitutionalists.'" (Federal Bureau of Investigation 1985: 3). Many of the key leaders of the SPC were influenced by the Christian Identity movement, a violently anti-Jewish Christian theology that teaches Jews are the offspring of Satan and all other nonwhite minorities are subhuman animals or demonic beasts (Barkun 1997). Identity Christians' view of white religious identity fed off a host of anti-Jewish ideas regarding the nature of the U.S. Federal Reserve system, and Identity beliefs helped fuel the rise of a number of white nationalist terrorist organizations, including the Aryan Nations, the Order, and the Covenant, Sword, and Arm of the Lord.

Leaders in the Posse Comitatus movement generated the core theories of sovereign citizen ideology—including the Admiralty Law and Strawman theories of the shadow U.S. government—that spawned many of the popular techniques of "paper terrorism" used today. Through the Citizen's Law Enforcement and Research Committee (CLERC), Henry L. Beach and a number of other early leaders in the SPC published documents calling for, in the words of one FBI memorandum, "the establishment of a posse in each county to assist the only legitimate law enforcement authority, the county sheriff, in combating the unlawful acts of others, particularly those of federal and state officials" (Federal Bureau of Investigation 1976: 2). These sheriffs' posses would arrest federal agents and local officials, try them in "common law courts," and reestablish the common law Christian Republic originally envisioned by the U.S. founders. Through a series of seminars, CLERC began teaching sovereigns how to issue tax liens on local officials, frequently targeting the homes and property of sheriffs, judges, and other law enforcement officials.

From the beginning, activists associated with the SPC and CLERC issued documents designed to either confuse law enforcement agents, or to assert rights they believed law enforcement agents might ignore or attempt to subvert. Similar to MSTA nationality cards, these early sovereign citizens created objects such as "Constitutional Arms Permit" cards (Figure 1.4) that "cit[e] federal laws written to help protect your rights" to carry a firearm (Federal Bureau of Investigation 1974: 73). The makers of these "Arms Permit" cards did not see them as talismans that, once presented to police, would magically intervene in the situation. Instead, the

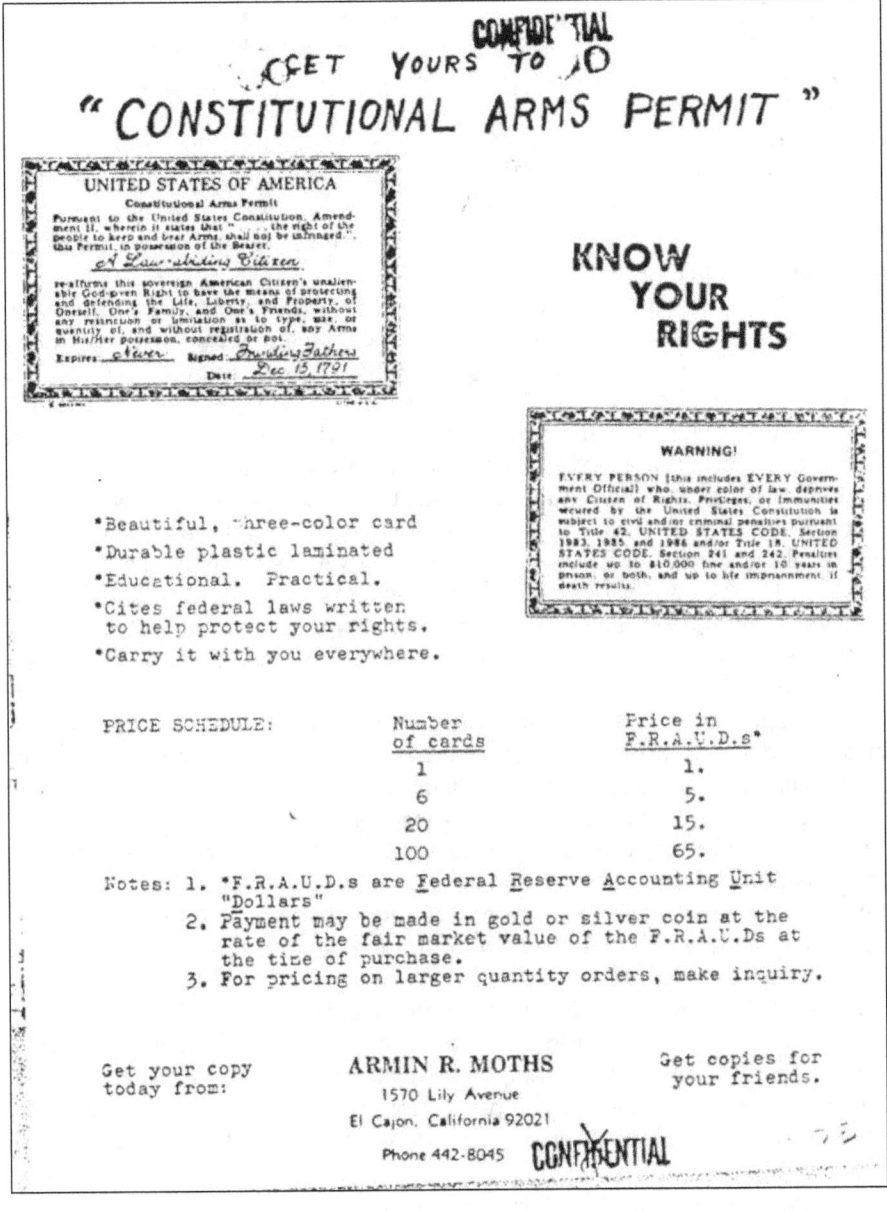

Figure 1.4 "Constitutional Arms Permit" advertisement reproduced in appendix to Federal Bureau of Investigation memorandum on "Sheriff's Posse Comitatus," November 7, 1974, Milwaukee, Wisconsin.

Source: Federal Bureau of Investigation Detroit Field Office file number 157-10687, serial 2, page 73, released through the Freedom of Information and Privacy Acts and retrieved from Internet Archive, "Ernie Lazar FOIA Collection," https://archive.org/details/Sheriffs PosseComitatusDetroit15710687/page/n101/mode/1up (image in the public domain)

purpose of the cards paralleled and inverted the use of *Miranda* warning cards used by police officers to inform citizens of their "right to remain silent."[12] The holder of an "Arms Permit" card presented these "[b]eautiful, three-color" "[d]urable plastic laminated" wallet-size cards to police officers or investigators to notify them of the presence of a firearm and to discourage any attempt on the part of law enforcement to confiscate the weapon or to escalate the situation (ibid.: 73). Over time, the market for alternative forms of documentation such as these "Arms Permit" cards metastasized into a cottage industry for alternative ID documents and licenses.

The need for alternative ID documents and licenses emerged from the traditional policing and investigative methods of federal and local law enforcement officers. In the 1970s and the 1980s, the FBI typically deployed conventional surveillance methods to trace the activities of SPC sympathizers. Most commonly, agents staked out meetings and recorded the license plate numbers of all vehicles present at an event. Through simple visual surveillance, the bureau built a large list of SPC-associated activists, tax-protestors, and fellow travelers. Many of the attendees made the bureau's job easier by affixing bumper stickers, decals, or logos that further associated their vehicles with the tax-resistance movement. Increasingly, as this weakness became obvious, SPC-affiliated organizers and activists, who had a long-stated hostility to federal and state licensing, began a systemic push to reject licensing procedures and to develop their own alternatives.

The "paper terrorism" associated with property liens and "strawman" tax filings frequently resulted in temporary bureaucratic victories of SPC-influenced sovereigns. When issued correctly, the liens could take years for law enforcement to recognize and then result in years of legal wrangling to remove, oftentimes destroying credit ratings and requiring expensive legal remedies for their targets (Goode 2013). More astoundingly, "strawman" tax filings regularly made it through Internal Revenue Service processing, with some sovereigns receiving hundreds of thousands of dollars in tax refunds before audits recognized the error (Weir 2015: 830–834).

By the 1990s, sovereign citizens of all persuasions not only issued liens and other financial documentation, but they also generated their own diplomatic papers, licenses, and other forms of identification. In contrast to the sometimes-successful slow-burn of procedural "paper terrorism" techniques, the emergence of alternative licensing and identification mechanisms has proven

---

12. Following the landmark, 1966 U.S. Supreme Court ruling in *Miranda v. Arizona* police officers began carrying *Miranda* cards outlining the rights established in the case. The cards present people taken into police custody with their *Miranda* rights outlined into a short, clear list of four or five rights (that is, the right to remain silent, the right to counsel, the right to public counsel if they cannot afford an attorney, and the interrogatee's ability to assert these rights at any point during their detention), and information about the consequences of waiving these rights (such as, their words can be used against them in court). The wording on these cards and the number of described rights might vary by jurisdictions and officers can purchase them in bulk in multi-lingual formats.

more likely to spark violent conflict with law enforcement agents. As early as the 1970s, FBI agents noted that antigovernment actors associated with the SPC had begun refusing to use state-issued identification documents and licenses to identify themselves during interactions with law enforcement.[13] The heightened tension produced by such refusal often escalated events like routine traffic stops into violent altercations.

By the 2000s, however, homemade licenses and IDs further confused such interactions and made them increasingly dangerous for both law enforcement and sovereigns—especially for Black sovereigns as the FBI would acknowledge. In a highly controversial 2017 threat assessment of "Black Identity Extremism," the FBI concluded—against the mountain of evidence to the contrary—that "although non-Moorish [i.e., predominately white Sovereign Citizen Extremists] have committed lethal violence against law enforcement in the past, this violence has typically occurred in response to encounters with law enforcement—for example, during traffic stops or the issuing of warrants—rather than through premeditated, targeted aggression" (Federal Bureau of Investigation 2017: 6). While the bureau's assessment neglected instances of large-scale premeditated violence perpetrated by white sovereigns, and people sympathetic to sovereign citizen ideology—events ranging from recent land disputes with the Bundy family of Nevada to Andrew Joseph Stack crashing a Piper Dakota aircraft into an Austin, Texas, IRS field office—the more basic point of the assessment was correct. Alternative citizenship documents can lead to more violent, defensive interactions with law enforcement agencies. Race could further complicate these interactions as agencies primed officers to see Black sovereigns as more aggressive than their white counterparts. But the cutting-edge of sovereign citizen bureaucratic innovation is no longer in "paper terrorism" but, instead, the total lack of the "paper" itself.

Without Papers

If there is anything "magical" about the sovereign citizen movement and the documentary practices driving it, it is that it underscores the essential fragility of citizenship in the contemporary United States. Whether read through the lens of contemporary battles over "illegal" immigration or through recent high-profile police shootings of African American men and boys, the sovereignty movement highlights that a growing number of Americans see little to no value in the legal framework and security bestowed by citizenship. Even if the movement has its roots in white men rejecting their citizenship as a backlash against the Civil Rights reforms of the 1950s and the 1960s and the economic downturn of the 1960s and the 1970s, today it is increasingly detethered from this context as white evangelicals, Moorish Americans, fundamentalist Mormons, and any number of other dissidents seek sovereign status for themselves and their children.

---

13. Examples of efforts to refuse presenting licenses, creating alternative forms of identification, and the problems caused by such activities are documented throughout FBI file no. 157-33487.

As sovereignty has grown into an underground network of religious communities, political ideologies, and racially and ethnically motivated separatist groups, the "paper terrorism" that has troubled state agencies since the 1970s has begun to mutate. Suddenly, and almost wholly without precedent in contemporary society, a number of sovereign children have become legal, social, and political problems for state governments. No longer producers of alternative paperwork to attest to their sovereign status, these children have no state-produced bureaucratic traces of their existence. They are illegible to the state; unknown, uncountable, and potentially ungovernable. They are only recognizable when, by either accident or intention, they come before a state agency and contest their sovereign status.

Illustrative of this new problem is the case of Alecia Faith Pennington. Pennington, born on November 26, 1995, and raised in Texas, became a viral YouTube video sensation in 2015 when she used the streaming platform to ask viewers to help her prove her existence as a citizen and legal subject of the State of Texas and the United States of America (Pennington 2015). Pennington was born at home with the aid of a midwife. Her parents and the midwife never filed for her birth certificate. Further, her parents homeschooled her and her siblings; her father refused to allow her to be vaccinated or receive routine medical checkups; and, she never had a bank account, Social Security card, or any form of health or life insurance (Mikkelson 2015). When she left home at the age of eighteen, rejected her parents' fundamentalist Baptist faith, and sought to escape their sovereign-citizen-inspired political ideas, she was shocked to learn that she could not prove her citizenship status. Her parents had purposefully and skillfully made establishing her legal existence impossible.[14]

Within the homeschooling community, Pennington's case became a paradigmatic instance of "Identification Abuse," or "ID abuse" (Homeschool Alumni Reaching Out 2016: 18). Groups such as Coalition for Responsible Home Education, Homeschoolers Anonymous, and Homeschool Alumni Reaching Out define "ID abuse" as, "Not providing you with, withholding, or destroying any of your identification documents: driver's license, social security card, etc." Of the tiny number of homeschooling alumni self-reporting ID abuse, a Homeschool Alumni Reaching Out report concluded, "birth certificates were the document most commonly not possessed. 29% of respondents did not possess a birth certificate whereas 25% did not possess a Social Security card" (Homeschool Alumni Reaching Out 2015: 2).[15] Pennington's parents had pushed the "identification abuse" of their daughter

---

14. For an account of the Penningtons' relationship to sovereign citizen ideology, listen to "The Girl Who Doesn't Exist" (Young 2016).
15. It is worth noting at this point that the birth certificate itself began its history as a non-state-issued document. In the United States, the idea of registering and certifying births emerged from the American Progressive movement as a means of, in the words of historian Sarah Igo, "lowering infant mortality, ending child labor, ensuring compulsory education, and barring interracial mixing" (Igo 2018: 396 n.28). Over the course of the twentieth century, states and the federal government began to formalize and standardize the registration of births and use birth certificates to track the vital statistics of citizenship. See also Landrum (2014).

and her siblings to an extreme uncommon even in the most radical of homeschooling circles.

When Pennington sought to establish her status as a U.S. citizen, her lawyer determined that the State of Texas would recognize three different proofs of her birth in the state and use those records to establish her "natural born" status. Evidence could include records from religious rituals—baptisms, christenings, confirmations, and so on—or bank records, such as her name on a savings or checking account. Likewise, the state would consider dental records, vaccination certificates, or other medical reports that included some reference to her residence and an indication of her birth date. A notarized affidavit from a witness to her birth could also count as one of the three forms of proof of long-term residence in the state. In short, the state would allow Pennington to bootstrap her way into citizenship by cobbling together a host of non-state forms and records that collectively testified to her legal person-ness under Texas and, ultimately, federal law (Young 2016).

After a year of research, tireless work, and the application of official pressure on her parents to provide the missing documentation, Pennington petitioned for and received a delayed birth certificate attesting to her natural-born citizenship status. Her parents had refused to sign an affidavit attesting to their knowledge of her "date of birth, place of birth, and parentage." In 2015, Pennington's case led the Texas legislature to pass and Governor Greg Abbott to sign House Bill 2794. The law expanded the legal options for children like Pennington and it also made it a misdemeanor for parents to withhold the requested documentation from a child. Her case underscores the limits of the state's ability to register new citizens when parents or other interested parties actively seek to avoid its oversight and opt for alternative or resistive bureaucratic methods of record keeping.

Conclusion

Pennington's case and hundreds of others like it point to the relationship between religious attempts to resist state power by generating alternative bureaucratic regimes. While her parents' form of "paper terrorism" relied on denying the state the ability to name and claim their daughter through paperwork, their strategy did not completely reject paperwork. Throughout her life, she left documentary traces in church proceedings, homeschooling records, and in private voluntary societies. None of these records, however, met the state's minimum standards for making her a legible and regulatable citizen of Texas or the United States. The result was that Pennington was many things—a young woman, a Baptist, a student, child of her parents, and a legal problem—but her status as any one of these social objects fell short of the state's minimum threshold for establishing her desired status of *citizen*.

Whatever a *citizen* is, it is the product of material traces. Without these traces, there can be no subject of state power as we understand it today. This point is inspired by the Italian philosopher Maurizio Ferraris's modification of Derrida's infamous phrase: "nothing *social* exists outside the text" (Ferraris 2012). For Ferraris, *social* objects—including subject positions such as *citizen* and *noncitizen*—only exist as a function of material traces, typically in the form of written words or other material inscriptions. Social objects, in Ferraris's theory of social ontology, are therefore best understood as "inscribed acts." As one of his interpreters has summarized, "Through the performance of inscribing acts (acts of signing or of publishing an official document; acts of writing on a hard drive, or on a baby's forehead, or of impressing something upon someone's memory) we *change the world* by bringing into being social objects" (Smith 2012).

From this perspective, the social object at the heart of this chapter—namely the "sovereign citizen"—should not be viewed *prima facie* as illegitimate, illegal, or somehow magical or imaginary, especially if these latter terms are intended to imply that sovereigns are less *real* than other social objects. Instead, the "sovereign citizen" is a complex social object that emerges at the juncture of legal, political, and religious regimes of record keeping. Efforts by sovereign citizens to create alternative "performances of inscribing acts" to resist, redraw, and retrace the nature of their social reality as "citizens" require the very paperwork and bureaucracy that conjure them into being as "criminals," "tax resistors," "racial separatists," or other deviant social objects. In this manner, sovereign citizens develop alternative regimes of record keeping and inscribing that materialize one of the boundaries between citizen and noncitizen in contemporary society. That ostensibly "religious" mechanisms of inscription (rituals, church records, initiation rites, and so on) play such a significant role in contesting and redrawing the nature of citizenship should not therefore be surprising. The social objects related to "religion"—however one might define the term—have historically relied on a robust infrastructure of inscribing and recording. Witnessing to the simultaneous fragility of the "citizen" as a social object and the durability of scriptural systems, sovereign citizens have managed to pit bureaucratic regimes against each other to carve out new resistive subject positions.

In the end, the extreme expression of "sovereign citizenship" inscribed in Pennington's parents' actions, those of Washitaw Moors, and the activities of many other groups might be best conceptualized as forms of "autonomous citizenship." In contrast to state-sponsored and endorsed forms of "responsible citizenship," criminologist Les Johnston defines "autonomous citizenship" as, "a voluntary activity engaged in by 'active citizens' (private voluntary agents) without the state's authority or support" (Johnston 1996: 226; see also Reeves 2017). Through the resistive systems of inscribing and record keeping, "paper terrorism" emerges from an autonomous impulse to reject the material constraints of responsible citizenship and generate alternative bureaucratic regimes. The impulse is neither magical—especially not in any "sympathetic," Frazierian sense—nor is it necessarily or essentially rooted in nativist protest against colonial forces. Rather, it emerges from the structure and logic of record-keeping itself. Through the simple acts of observing and creating records of what one sees, individuals and groups collectively sort bodies, categorize actions, value certain behaviors over others, and collect and collate archives of information that through their very preservation conjure the societies in which we live (Lyon 2003). Sovereign "paper terrorism" is part and parcel of this inscribing process, not an outlier opposed to it.

Michael J. McVicar is Associate Professor in the Department of Religion at Florida State University. He teaches classes on American religious history and is the author of *Christian Reconstruction: R. J. Rushdoony and American Religious Conservatism* (2015).

References

Barkun, Michael. 1997. *Religion and the Racist Right: The Origins of the Christian Identity Movement*. Chapel Hill, NC: University of North Carolina Press.

Barkun, Michael. 2013. *A Culture of Conspiracy: Apocalyptic Visions in Contemporary America*, 2nd edition. Comparative Studies in Religion and Society 15. Berkeley, CA: University of California Press.

Browne, Simone. 2015. *Dark Matters: On the Surveillance of Blackness*. Durham, NC: Duke University Press Books.

Bureau of Investigation. 1931a. Memorandum from Rhea Whitley to [J. Edgar Hoover] Director of Bureau of Investigation, September 12, 1931, in Bureau of Investigation file number 62-25889, Subject: Moorish Science Temple of America (Noble Drew Ali), serial 1. Released through the Freedom of Information and Privacy Acts and retrieved from *The FBI: Federal Bureau of Investigation*, "FBI Records: The Vault," retrieved from https://vault.fbi.gov/Moorish%20Science%20Temple%20of%20America.

Bureau of Investigation. 1931b. Memorandum from Rhea Whitley to [J. Edgar Hoover] Director of Bureau of Investigation, September 12, 1931, in Bureau of Investigation file number 62-25889, Subject: Moorish Science Temple of America (Noble Drew Ali), serial 2. Released through the Freedom of Information and Privacy Acts and retrieved from *The FBI: Federal Bureau of Investigation*, "FBI Records: The Vault," retrieved from https://vault.fbi.gov/Moorish%20Science%20Temple%20of%20America.

Chamberlain, Robert, and Donald P. Haider-Markel. 2005. "'Lien on Me': State Policy Innovation in Response to Paper Terrorism." *Political Research Quarterly* 58(3): 449–460. https://doi.org/10.1177/106591290505800307

Chandler, Clay. 2011. "'Paper Terrorism': Squatters, Part of a National Movement, Descend upon Greenville." *Mississippi Business Journal*, September 12.

Collins, Jeff. 2012. "Sovereign Citizens Inspire Rise in Real Estate Filings." *Orange County (California) Register*, November 26. Retrieved from www.ocregister.com/2012/11/26/sovereign-citizens-inspire-rise-in-real-estate-filings.

Dew, Spencer. 2015. "Washitaw de Dugdahmoundyah: Counterfactual Religious Readings of the Law." *Nova Religio* 19(2): 65–82. https://doi.org/10.1525/nr.2015.19.2.65

Dew, Spencer. 2016. "'Moors Know the Law': Sovereign Legal Discourse in Moorish Science Religious Communities and the Hermeneutics of Supersession." *Journal of Law and Religion* 31(1): 70–91. https://doi.org/10.1017/jlr.2016.3

Dew, Spencer. 2019. *The Aliites: Race and Law in the Religions of Noble Drew Ali*. Class 200, New Studies in Religion. Chicago, IL: University of Chicago Press.

Edwards, Paul N., Lisa Gitelman, Gabrielle Hecht, Adrian Johns, Brian Larkin, and Neil Safier. 2011. "AHR Conversation: Historical Perspectives on the Circulation of Information." *American Historical Review* 116(5): 1393–1435. https://doi.org/10.1086/ahr.116.5.1393

Federal Bureau of Investigation. 1943a. "Address given by [redacted] Bey at Meeting of Moorish Science Temple of Hartford Conn. On Jan 10, 1943," quoted in "Report of Special Agent [redacted]," dated July 12, 1943, at New Haven, Connecticut, entitled, [redacted], Moorish Science Temple, Internal Security—J, Selective Service, Sedition," in Federal Bureau of Investigation file number 62-25889, Subject: Moorish Science Temple of America (Noble Drew Ali), serial 105. Released through the Freedom of Information and Privacy Acts and retrieved from *The FBI: Federal Bureau of Investigation*, "FBI Records: The Vault," https://vault.fbi.gov/Moorish%20Science%20Temple%20of%20America.

Federal Bureau of Investigation. 1943b. Report on "Colonel C. Kirkman Bey," Internal Security—J Sedition Overthrow or Destruction of the Government, March 3, 1943, in Bureau of Investigation file number 62-25889, Subject: Moorish Science Temple of America (Noble Drew Ali), serial 105. Released through the Freedom of Information and Privacy Acts and retrieved from *The FBI: Federal Bureau of Investigation*, "FBI Records: The Vault," retrieved from https://vault.fbi.gov/Moorish%20Science%20Temple%20of%20America.

Federal Bureau of Investigation. 1974. LHM [letterhead memorandum] on "Sheriff's Posse Comitatus," from Milwaukee, Wisconsin, Field Officer, November 7, 1974, FBI file no. 157-33487, Subject: Sheriff's Posse Comitatus, serial 24. Released through the Freedom of Information and Privacy Acts.

Federal Bureau of Investigation. 1976. NITEL [night teletype] from Portland, Oregon, Field Office, re: Sheriff's Posse Comitatus, May 1, 1976, Federal Bureau of Investigation file no. 157-33487, Subject: Sheriff's Posse Comitatus, serial 331. Released through the Freedom of Information and Privacy Acts.

Federal Bureau of Investigation. 1985. U.S. Justice department memorandum on the Sheriff's Posse Comitatus, Contra Costa County, California, February 8, 1985, Federal Bureau of Investigation file no. 157-33487, Subject: Sheriff's Posse Comitatus, serial 95. Released through the Freedom of Information and Privacy Acts.

Federal Bureau of Investigation. 2010. "Sovereign Citizens: An Introduction for Law Enforcement." Domestic Terrorism Operations Unit II. Retrieved from www.mschiefs.org/wp-content/uploads/2012/05/Sovereign_Citizens_Intro_For_LE.pdf.

Federal Bureau of Investigation. 2017. "Black Identity Extremists Likely Motivated to Target Law Enforcement Officers." Federal Bureau of Investigation Intelligence Assessment. Retrieved from https://privacysos.org/wp-content/uploads/2017/10/FBI-BlackIdentityExtremists.pdf.

Ferraris, Maurizio. 2012. *Documentality: Why It Is Necessary to Leave Traces*. Translated by Richard Davies. New York: Fordham University Press.

Frazer, James George. 1966. *The Magic Art and the Evolution of Kings*, 3rd edition, vol. 1. *The Golden Bough: A Study in Magic and Religion*. New York: St. Martin's Press. Retrieved from http://hdl.handle.net/2027/pst.000029417995.

Gitelman, Lisa. 2014. *Paper Knowledge: Toward a Media History of Documents*. Sign, Storage, Transmission. Durham, NC: Duke University Press.

Goode, Erica. 2013. "In Paper War, Flood of Liens Is the Weapon." *The New York Times*, August 23. Retrieved from www.nytimes.com/2013/08/24/us/citizens-without-a-country-wage-battle-with-liens.html.

Goston, Verdiacee Washitaw-Turner. 1993. *Return of the Ancient Ones: (The True History Uncovered) of the Washitaw de Dugdahmoundyah Empire*. Chicago, Washitaw Province, IL: Washitaw Pub. Co.

Grewal, Zareena. 2014. *Islam is a Foreign Country: American Muslims and the Global Crisis of Authority*. New York: NYU Press.

Homeschool Alumni Reaching Out. 2015. "Identity as Means of Control: Results from the 2015 Survey of Identification Abuse Within Homeschooling." Retrieved from https://hareachingout.files.wordpress.com/2015/02/results-from-the-2015-survey-of-identification-abuse-within-homeschooling.pdf.

Homeschool Alumni Reaching Out. 2016. "A Complex Picture: Results of a 2014 Survey of Adult Alumni of the Modern Christian Homeschool Movement—Installment 9: Abuse." Retrieved from https://hareachingout.files.wordpress.com/2016/04/haro-installment-9-abuse.pdf.

Hull, Matthew S. 2012. "Documents and Bureaucracy." *Annual Review of Anthropology* 41: 251–267. https://doi.org/10.1146/annurev.anthro.012809.104953

Igo, Sarah E. 2018. *The Known Citizen: A History of Privacy in Modern America*. Cambridge, MA: Harvard University Press.

Ihlo, Jen E., and Erin B. Pulice. 2013. "Prosecuting Tax Defier and Sovereign Citizen Cases—Frequently Asked Questions Tax Enforcement I." *United States Attorneys' Bulletin* 61: 45–57.

Jansen, Bart. 2016. "3 Police Officers Fatally Shot in Baton Rouge; Dead Suspect Identified." *USA Today*, July 17. Retrieved from www.usatoday.com/story/news/2016/07/17/reports-baton-rouge-police-officers-shot/87218884.

Johnson, Sylvester A. 2015. *African American Religions, 1500-2000*. New York: Cambridge University Press.

Johnston, L. 1996. "What Is Vigilantism?" *British Journal of Criminology* 36(2): 220–236. https://doi.org/10.1093/oxfordjournals.bjc.a014083

Landrum, Shane. 2014. "The State's Big Family Bible: Birth Certificates, Personal Identity, and Citizenship in the United States, 1840–1950." Ph.D. dissertation, Brandeis University.

Latour, Bruno. 2005. *Reassembling the Social: An Introduction to Actor-Network Theory*. Clarendon Lectures in Management Studies. New York: Oxford University Press.

Latour, Bruno. 2013. *The Making of Law: An Ethnography of the* Conseil d'état. Malden, MA: Polity.

Loeser, Charles E. 2014. "From Paper Terrorists to Cop Killers: The Sovereign Citizen Threat Comment." *North Carolina Law Review* 93: 1106–1139.

Lyon, David. 2003. *Surveillance as Social Sorting: Privacy, Risk, and Digital Discrimination*. New York: Routledge.

Mikkelson, David. 2015. "Help Me Prove It." *Snopes*, February 12. Retrieved from www.snopes.com/news/2015/02/12/show-me-my-papers/.

Palazzolo, Joe. 2016. "Black Separatist Group Denies Connection to Baton Rouge Gunman; Washitaw Nation Spokesman Says He Had Never Heard of Gavin Long before Sunday's Shooting." *Wall Street Journal*, July 18. Retrieved from http://search.proquest.com/docview/1805061068/abstract/80E5C3CEDD7F417EPQ/1.

Pennington, Alecia. 2015. "19 Year Old Girl Can't Prove Her American Citizenship." YouTube, February 9. Retrieved from www.youtube.com/watch?time_continue=8&v=CPtpKNyaO0U.

Reeves, Joshua. 2017. *Citizen Spies: The Long Rise of America's Surveillance Society*. New York: NYU Press.

Reynolds, Matt. 2014. "Recalling the FBI Raid of Late Washitaw Nation Leader's Home." *The Franklin (Louisiana) Sun*, March 2. Retrieved from www.hannapub.com/franklinsun/recalling-the-fbi-raid-of-late-washitaw-nation-leader-s/article_de819b14-d233-11e3-91b9-001a4bcf6878.html.

Rosenfeld, Jean E. 2016. "Nativist Millennialism." In Catherine Wessinger (ed.), *The Oxford Handbook of Millennialism*, 89–111. New York: Oxford University Press.

Smith, Barry. 2012. "How to Do Things with Documents." *Rivista Di Estetica*, 50 (July): 179–198. https://doi.org/10.4000/estetica.1480.

Smith, Jonathan Z. 2004. *Relating Religion: Essays in the Study of Religion*. Chicago, IL: University of Chicago Press.

Stickney, Ken. 2016. "Baton Rouge Shooter May Have Embraced Bizarre Outlook." *The (Lafayette, Louisiana) Daily Advertiser*, July 17. Retrieved from www.theadvertiser.com/story/news/2016/07/17/baton-rouge-shooter-may-have-embraced-bizarre-outlook/87234938/.

Swaine, Jon. 2016. "Baton Rouge Suspect Gavin Long Was Marine with Alias Cosmo Setepenra." *The Guardian*, July 18. Retrieved from www.theguardian.com/us-news/2016/jul/17/baton-rouge-gunman-gavin-e-long-cosmo-setepenra-marines.

Weir, Joshua P. 2015. "Sovereign Citizens: A Reasoned Response to the Madness." *Lewis & Clark Law Review* 19(3): 830–868.

Weisenfeld, Judith. 2017. *New World A-Coming: Black Religion and Racial Identity during the Great Migration*. New York: NYU Press.

Wessinger, Catherine. 2000. *How the Millennium Comes Violently: From Jonestown to Heaven's Gate*. New York: Seven Bridges.

Young, Alexandra Leigh. 2016. "The Girl Who Doesn't Exist." *Radiolab*. NPR. Retrieved from www.wnycstudios.org/story/invisible-girl.

Chapter 2

The Rohingya, Buddhism, and the Category "Religion"

Tenzan Eaghll

In Michael McVicar's analysis of the "sovereign citizenship movement," he argues that we shouldn't use essentialist notions of religion "to frame political resistance movements," suggesting that we should instead emphasize "how these movements may be productively understood" as by-products of state and corporate activities, "rather than autonomous manifestations of some deeper human search for religious or spiritual meaning." I fully agree with this sentiment: In the attempt to theorize the role of "religion" in modern public life, scholars often underemphasize the relationship between citizenship and politics in the formation of group identity. There is a tendency to reify religion as a particularly unique or distinct phenomena, and this obscures the fact that what is really at stake in most events has nothing to do with religion, *per se*, but with the ways in which societies and groups of people organize membership in political communities, and the power dynamics contained therein.

Over the course of the past several years, one event outside of America that clearly illustrated this scholarly tendency was the response to the Rohingya genocide in Myanmar. Between August and October 2017, more than 500,000 Rohingya Muslims were forcibly and brutally expelled from the country, a tragic event that garnered a considerable amount of media and scholarly attention around the world. One trend in this coverage was to call for an end to the peaceful romanticization of Buddhism and a realistic assessment of the relationship between religion and violence in south and southeast Asia. For example, the prominent scholar Michael Jerryson wrote an article for Aeon titled, "Buddhism can be as violent as any other religion," in which he traces out the religious origins of the violence by drawing attention to various "foundational principles" in Buddhism (Jerryson 2017). Though well intentioned—and valuable for critique of the old cliché that Buddhism is a thoroughly non-violent religion—scholarship which attempts to account for the role of religion in public life by improving how we define Buddhism or other religious groups conceals the fact that what is really at stake in places like Myanmar is the way that political communities include, exclude, and marginalize others. It obscures the fact that the violence in Myanmar over the past year has more to do with the various social and historical conflicts between specific ethnic groups in the region, than it does with any specific religious influence. By searching for foundational religious principles that cause violence rather than the ethnic, militaristic, and state-sanctioned causes of violence, scholars obscure the political source of the conflict.

In this chapter, I will respond to McVicar's paper by elaborating upon this scholarly tendency to obscure political causes with invented religious causes by using the media and scholarly response to the Rohingya genocide as an example. The Myanmar conflict will help me demonstrate how the attempt to theorize religion as a particularly unique or distinct phenomenon that causes violence conceals the deeper relationships between citizenship and politics that are at play in such conflicts. By drawing upon popular and scholarly academic publications on the conflict, I will argue that understanding the role of religion in modern public life requires a fine-grained analysis of how different groups include, exclude, and marginalize others in their respective communities. In particular, I will stress that in places like Myanmar, what is needed to understand conflicts is less focus on Buddhism and its foundational principles, and more attention to the historical, ethnic, and political tensions at play.

Now, before I get into any specifics, I want to start with a little back story explaining why I am even discussing the Myanmar crisis of 2017. This is relevant because Buddhism and southeast Asian studies are not my usual area of academic focus. My academic research is typically focused on topics more related to method and theory in the study of religion, so why I am I even writing about southeast Asia at all? Well, it just so happens that I work at the College of Religious Studies at Mahidol University, which is located in Bangkok, Thailand. This gives me a front seat to the political events in the region, as well as to the local and international response to events that transpire nearby. Moreover, in 2017, at the precise time that the Myanmar government was forcibly expelling hundreds of thousands of Rohingya from the country, I happened to be teaching an M.A. course on "Core Concepts in the Study of Religion" to a group of monks from Myanmar. At Mahidol University, our B.A. students are generally all Thai, but many of our M.A. and Ph.D. students come from Myanmar, Indonesia, China, etc., and the particular group of M.A. students I was teaching during the conflict in Myanmar were all monks from Myanmar who were heavily influenced by Myanmar state ideology, which, as I will discuss below, has justified the disenfranchisement of the Rohingya. Because of this, the class I was teaching at the time of the crisis allowed for lots of discussion about the intersection of method and theory in the study of religion and politics in southeast Asia. And it also allowed me to witness first-hand how the history, ethnic tensions, and current hyper-nationalist rhetoric of Myanmar informs the practice and understanding of Buddhism in the region.

So, flashback to September/October 2017 when the brutal expulsion of 500,000 Rohingya from Myanmar was taking place. I would often wake up in the morning, sit and watch the horrific news stories over breakfast on Al Jazeera about the expulsion of the Rohingya from Myanmar, and then teach a three-hour seminar to seven Myanmar monks about some of the deep theoretical issues in our field. Long story short, all this led to some intense classroom discussions and made me very self-conscious about how we, as religious studies professors and scholars, tend to approach events like the Myanmar crisis when "religion" is involved. It gave me first-hand experience of how it is often we academics who create the problems, as we often assume that religion is at play in some social issue or conflict. It gave me first-hand experience of J. Z. Smith's well-cited adage that "Religion is solely the creation of the scholar's study" (Smith 1982: xi). Additionally, it made me realize the monks from Myanmar have opinions about Muslims that are akin to Donald Trump's opinions about people from Mexico. In fact, teaching these monks was kind of like hanging out with seven little Donald Trumps in ochre robes, as they were each hyper-nationalistic and said that any journalism that suggested that the Rohingya were being persecuted by the Myanmar government was "fake news"; they said the conflict was not the government's fault, but the "terrorist" Rohingya. Blind to any evidence to the contrary, the monks were extremely committed to the brand of nationalism espoused by their government and insisted that the expulsion of the Rohingya from the country was justified. Obviously, this means that having these conversations with the monks was not always easy, as it was difficult to read stories in the *New York Times* and *Al Jazeera* about mass graves being uncovered, rape, and ethnic cleansing, and then to try and have reasonable theory conversations with students who deny that the violence is even occurring.

My first approach to this conflict in the classroom was what I might call the "angry critical theory approach," or what on the internet might get me called a social justice warrior (SJW). I would often arrive to class, my head fresh with brutal images from the news, and ask bluntly, "what the (insert expletive!) is going on in your country? Why are all the Buddhists in your country persecuting the Rohingya and how do you justify it?" This approach was obviously confrontational, but my aim at the time was to try to make the monks recognize how Buddhism was being used to justify violent action against the Rohingya. My aim was to use the events to challenge the stereotype of the peaceful Buddhist monk who only wants to meditate and pray. Clearly, I would often stress to them, the Buddhist community in Myanmar bears some responsibility for this ethnic cleansing.

The response of the monks to this angry interrogation was always kind of the same, and basically boiled down to a version of the true vs. false religion dichotomy that is often used by politicians and in popular discourse. This dichotomy is usually used to separate violent social acts from the so-called "true nature of religion." This dichotomy suggests that real religion is about peace, salvation, or some other platitude, and that the conflict in question ultimately has nothing to do with religion because true religion is about peace. The monks seemed to be using this dichotomy because they argued that since the Rohingya were themselves using violence, they weren't even Muslims, really, just terrorists who weren't worthy of the "religion" classification. Moreover, they would argue that the Rohingya are an invented ethnic group—as if there are ethnic groups that aren't invented at some point!—that is native to Bangladesh, and therefore don't deserve Myanmar citizenship. In this manner, they denied the Rohingya the right to religion and citizenship, linking both together with notions of ethnicity and nationalism. As one monk quipped one morning, "this has nothing to do with Buddhists hating Muslims, all over Myanmar Buddhists and Muslims live in peace together, the Rohingya are just Bengali terrorists who want to steal our land. This is why they have to be kicked out of Myanmar."

Although the attempt to disqualify the Rohingya from any claim to citizenship, land, and religious identification was disturbing, I was not really shocked by it or their attempt to disqualify them from having a religion. The reasons for this are twofold: one, as I will detail below, the systematic rejection of Rohingya claims to citizenship on ethnic grounds is standard government policy and propaganda;[1] two, the appeal to the "true religion is about peace" cliché is a fairly typical argument whenever violent events threaten to besmudge the sanctity of the category, and is used at times by politicians and even academic scholars (see Eaghll 2015; Sheedy 2017). Moreover, the attempt to defend Buddhism from charges of violence by appealing to this cliché was also occurring in print at the time of our class. For instance, the Buddhist-leaning online magazine *Lion's Roar* published an article by Randy Rosenthal not long after the conflict trying to make a distinction between Buddhism and the violence. The article was titled, "What's the Connection between Buddhism and Ethnic Cleansing," and it tried to distance Buddhism from the conflict by suggesting Buddhist scripture doesn't encourage the use of violence. Rosenthal cites the *Dhammapada*, "All tremble before violence. All fear death. Having done the same yourself, you should neither harm nor kill," and the *Metta Sutta*: "Toward the whole world one should develop loving-kindness, a state of mind without boundaries—above, below, and across—unconfined, without enmity, without adversaries," in order to illustrate its point (Rosenthal 2018). In this manner, the article opens by suggesting that the principle of non-violence is foundational to the Pali canon and Buddhism as a whole, and concordantly, that any violence that occurs in Myanmar has nothing to do with Buddhism.[2]

However, if the monks attempt to defend Buddhism from charges of violence—or disqualify the religious identity of the Rohingya—by appealing to the "true religion is about peace" cliché, it must also be said that my "angry critical theory" response to the monks' defense is also fairly typical for how scholars of religion responded to the crisis in Myanmar. The typical response by contemporary critical Buddhist scholars—particularly those who specialize in religion and

---

1. Although "Rohingyan writers hold that the Rohingya are descendants of mixed Asian and Arab identities and have been present in Arakan since the 9th century" (Yusuf 2018: 2), the government maintains that these claims are lies invented to steal Myanmar land, and that the Rohingya are in fact Bengali in origin, and therefore have no right to citizenship. The fact that this is accepted rather unquestioningly by monks who have been educated in Myanmar is not that surprising.

2. Ironically, the argument in this article defended this claim by appealing to much of the same evidence I appeal to below in order to point out how the conflict actually lies in political, historical, and ethnic tensions in the region. In fact, in this chapter, I even cite some of the same sources cited in this *Lion's Roar* article. However, the difference between their argument and mine is that I am not attempting to isolate Buddhism, or religion more generally, as a distinct sphere of meaning independent of the conflict. Rather, I am merely arguing that doing the inverse—locating the source of the violence in Buddhism or religion specifically, doesn't teach us much about the conflict on the ground.

violence—was to point out how Buddhist history and literature is also tainted by violence. For instance, Michael Jerryson—who used to teach at my College of Religious Studies in Thailand—has written extensively on this subject and repeatedly pointed out the history of violence in Buddhist majority countries, as well as how Buddhist scripture has been used to state political violence (e.g., Jerryson 2011). In the above-cited article, Jerryson wrote for *Aeon* titled, "Buddhism Can be as Violent as any Other Religion," he explicitly traces the cause of religious violence in Thailand, Sri Lanka, and Myanmar to the apocalyptic idea of cosmic time in Buddhist thought. As Jerryson notes, many Buddhist scriptures have a cyclical notion of time that revolves around four *kalpas*, or eons, which ultimately end in the deterioration of the Dharma and the arrival of a new Buddha. This has, at times, led Buddhists to take up arms for one reason or another. As he writes, "Today, monks in Thailand, Burma and Sri Lanka continue to fight—violently—for their religion and to call their followers to action. The cycle of violence continues in this final stage of the cycle of time: the Kali Yuga, the Age of Destruction." Jerryson's ultimate point is much different than that of Rosenthal's article cited above, as he argues that "no religion has a monopoly on 'violent people', nor does any one religion have a greater propensity for violence" (Jerryson 2017). Rather, he suggests, all religions contain the same potential for violence because humans make of religion for what they want, in response to their social conditions.

Now, in terms of Buddhist studies scholarship, this latter critical approach is obviously better than the former protectionist approach that seeks to define Buddhism and religion as peace. If we have to pick between the two, it is better to challenge the essentialistic protection of religion from political conflict and show how it can be used for different ends and purposes. From a critical perspective, this is a valuable move because it challenges the cliché of monks as peaceful all-knowing sages who would never hurt a fly. As Donald Lopez recently argued in an interview for *Buddhistdoor Global*, the former position reflects the romanticization of Buddhism that dominated Western scholarship on the subject since the nineteenth century, and so I acknowledge that this critical work is important (Menon 2018).

However, after going through this experience of teaching Myanmar monks method and theory in the study of religion during the height of the Myanmar conflict, I think there is a third more nuanced approach that is perhaps more appropriate when dealing with crises of this nature. In short: I don't think we should use tragedies like this to look for new "religious causes" to violence at all. Although I think tracing how Buddhists have justified violence with their Pali texts and sutras, as well as with their political commitments, is perhaps useful for Buddhist or South Asian studies more generally, I don't think we should be looking for some Buddhist cause to the violence. Rather, Like McVicar's suggested in his paper, I would suggest that instead of looking for "some deeper human search for religious or spiritual meaning," we should instead emphasize how these conflicts—and in terms of southeast Asia this observation could be extended to conflicts in the entire region—are perhaps best understood as by-products of ethnic, political, and state-sanctioned violence.

To be clear, my solution to emphasize the historical, political, and ethnic issues surrounding the question of citizenship, not religion, is not because I want to preserve Buddhism or the category religion as peaceful transcendental objects, but simply because I don't think that there are any normative Buddhist principles that can be identified as the cause of violence one way or the other. Certainly, people may act in the name of this or that interpretation of ideas that scholars deem as Buddhist or religious, but this doesn't prove a causative link between some essentialistic definition of these categories and the violence. Rather, all it shows is how the religious studies categories are being used to describe the action in a particular situation.[3] Following Russell McCutcheon's thesis in *Manufacturing Religion*, I would suggest religion is manufactured by scholars in ahistorical terms and imposed upon phenomena (McCutcheon 1997: 14), and that issues on the ground in specific regions, whether in America or Myanmar, must be examined in relation to their specific context and the power dynamics contained therein. In such situations, the category religion might be useful for a scholar if they are using it in a functional manner, to understand certain phenomena from specific context, but it has no real independent determining power in the situation.

In relation to Myanmar, we find lots of evidence to support this, both in its history, politics, and regional ethnic tensions. Indeed, in Myanmar, the complex confluence of colonial, imperial, nationalist, militaristic, economic, and regional conflicts are so inextricably linked to different religious claims and actors in a web of complex political and ethnic tensions that it is impossible to extricate "religion" or "Buddhist" actions in any distinct, clear sense. For instance, take a look at a map of the different ethnic groups in Myanmar. As one of my monk students pointed out to me, the ethnic groupings in Myanmar are extremely diverse and look like a jumbled Rubik's cube when color-coded.

The Burman ethnic group is the most dominant in Myanmar but there are at least nineteen other major ethnic groups within Myanmar vying for influence in the country. In fact, the Myanmar government recognized 135 different ethnic groups in the latest census. Moreover, despite the fact that the Burman majority controls the military and government, they have always struggled to foster a sense of national unity to hold the country together. Since Myanmar achieved independence in 1948, it has experience eleven armed struggles within its tumultuous post-colonial borders, and almost all of these can be directly linked to different groups claiming a common ethnicity.

At the bureaucratic level, the country was specifically run by the Burman military Junta from 1962 to 2011, and despite various attempts by different ethnic groups to separate from the state during this period—such as the Lahu

---

3. In fact, I would go so far as to argue that all this shows is how "religion" or "Buddhism"—or other related religious studies categories—are used as "operational acts of identification," which is a phrase that comes from Jean-François Bayart. In *The Illusion of Cultural Identity*, Bayart claims there is no such thing as identity, *per se*, only operational acts of identification (Bayart 1996), and this claim can be extended to "religion" because there is also no such thing as religion, *per se*, only its use in operational act of identification.

people in the Shan territory in 1973—the military managed to keep the countries post-independence borders intact. The government's solution to the various conflicts and rebellions that emerged during its near forty-year rule is well documented and includes reports of murder, rape, theft, arbitrary arrest, relocation, and forced labor in deliberate and systematic ways, and it is necessary to view their current treatment of the Rohingya in this context (Lee et al. 2006; Hessey and Hurst 2012).

International observers had hoped that all this would change with the transition to democracy that began in 2011 and the rise to power of Nobel Laureate Aung San Suu Kyi, but so far, the old tactics of repression and abuse at the hands of Burman elite continue. In the past, Suu Kyi had been praised by the United Nations Commission on Human Rights for her desire to "bring about social and political changes which will guarantee a peaceful, stable and progressive society where human rights, as outlined in the Universal Declaration of Human Rights," but her silence on the recent ethnic cleansing of the Rohingya shows that she is either unable or unwilling to stop the repression of minorities by the majority (Rosenthal 2018).[4]

The persecution of the Rohingya is, therefore, the worst example of a horrible situation. Like other ethnic minorities in the country, they have suffered at the hands of the majority, but their persecution has led to ethnic cleansing because it has included their systematic disenfranchisement at the state level. As is well documented, the Rohingya were originally granted National Registration Certificates in the 1947 legislation, but this was slowly stripped away in five government acts that were passed between 1970 and 2015.

This process of disenfranchisement can be summed up in five governmental acts: First, in 1974, a new Constitution of the Socialist Republic of Myanmar was drawn up that laid the basis for ethnic citizenship; this change invalidated the National Registration Certificates previously issued to the Rohingya. Second, in 1982, a citizenship law was passed that prevented Rohingya from becoming new Myanmar citizens. Third, in 1989, the name of the state of Arakan where the majority of Rohingya lived was changed to "Rakhine state," legally identifying it as an exclusively Rakhine Buddhist state. Fourth, in 1994, General Than Shew's government stopped issuing birth certificates for Rohingya children. And fifth, in 2015, the Thein Sein government invalidated the identity cards held by all Rohingya (Yusuf 2018: 3). As Imtiyaz Yusuf notes in his article on this subject, the end result of all these acts was that the 2015 nationwide census "declared that Myanmar had a population of 51 million people and 135 official ethnic groups," and "the Rohingya were not included in this list." Instead, they were declared "outsider 'Bengalis' from Bangladesh, making them the only stateless people in Southeast Asia" (ibid.; see also Zan and Chan 2005).

---

4. According to the 2008 Constitution, the military must hold a quarter of the seats in Parliament and always retains the power to veto any legal changes, so perhaps this is the reason for Suu Kyi's silence on the issue of the Rohingya.

Taking these acts into consideration, it is clear that the persecution of the Rohingya in Myanmar is primarily the by-product of state activities and the power politics contained therein, rather than any so-called religious causes.

Of course, some scholars might want to counter my argument by pointing out that Buddhist or Muslim groups have specifically instigated acts of violence, but I think this ignores how even these groups are influenced by state activities. For instance, many scholars have pointed out that Ma Ba Tha, or 969—the ultra-nationalist conservative Buddhist Association for the Protection of Race and Religion—directly pressured the Thein Sein government to formally strip the Rohingya of citizenship by invalidating their identity cards (Yusuf 2018; Jerryson 2017). Ma Ba Tha has received considerable attention in the media and news organizations for this because it repeatably incites bigotry and violence against Muslims. The group's leader, the radical monk Ashin Wirathu—who fashions himself the "Buddhist Bin Laden"—was even featured on the cover of Time magazine in 2013, next to the caption, "The Buddhist face of Terror." This group is frequently used by critical scholars to point out how Buddhist groups have incited bigotry and violence against Muslims. As Jerryson writes:

> This movement and the Ma Ba Tha (the Patriotic Association of Myanmar) retain significant influence over the Buddhists of Myanmar. They distribute pamphlets and taped sermons that warn about the threat of Islam. Their work to foment fear of Muslims helps to propel Burmese Buddhists toward violence, as in the murderous anti-Muslim riots in the central city of Meiktila in 2013, where at least 40 people died.
>
> (Jerryson 2017)

As noted above, Jerryson connects the numerous violent acts that can be linked to this group to certain Buddhist notions about the cyclical decline of cosmic time. The monks believe that the longer they can preserve the Buddhist integrity of Myanmar and neighboring regions, the longer they can stave off the end of the world (Jerryson 2011, 2017).

Now, I don't want to deny that there is some connection between the use of certain Buddhist ideas or principles by Ma Ba Tha and the violence committed against the Rohingya, but I think the real cause of the violence, in this case, is the government and the military, and there are various sources which support this observation. For instance, as Azeem Ibrahim suggested in his 2016 book, *The Rohingyas: Inside Myanmar's Hidden Genocide*, the supposed conflict between Buddhists and Muslims is fueled by government and military actors who are specifically using Buddhist monks to advance their own interests. On the news, the conflicts between Buddhists and Muslims are often portrayed as spontaneous local skirmishes that get out of hand; a Muslim burns down a Buddhist home or a group of Buddhists attack a Muslim person in the street, and then an escalation of violence occurs. However, as Ibrahim notes, "there is growing evidence that the Ma Ba Tha Buddhist extremist organization was set up by the military as an alternative power base." According to research, Ma Ba Tha is a "front organization" for the military. Moreover, "the military is directly backing two different groups in contemporary Myanmar," the USDP (their political party) and "its own organization of Buddhist extremists who both offer the means to channel electoral support to the USDP and to create violence that can later be used to justify a military intervention" (Ibrahim 2016: 29).

Similar evidence was also provided in the 2015 *Foreign Policy* article, "Monks, PowerPoint Presentations, and Ethnic Cleansing: Damning New Evidence Shows the Myanmar Government's Role in Promoting Anti-Muslim Hatred" (Stoakes 2015), as well as by the 2015 Al Jazeera investigative documentary "Genocide Agenda." In particular, the latter details the general persecution of the Rohingya in explicit images and shows how Ma Ba Tha is directly used by the military to stir up conflict between different ethnic groups and solidify their own control of the country. As a Myanmar monk notes in an interview during the documentary, "Ma Ba Tha is controlled by the military. When it wants to start a problem at any time, it's like turning on a tap. They will turn it on or turn it off when they want" (Al Jazeera 2015).[5]

Now, I could go further with this and document how the categories of race and religion are used in conjunction in Myanmar and neighboring countries—not to mention the modern world as a whole—and how the very attempt to isolate some kind essential Buddhist ideas that are common to all the conflicts and violence is erroneous, but I don't have space for that here.[6] As noted at the outset, all I want to stress in this short chapter is that using tragedies like the conflict in Myanmar to understand something essential about how Buddhism can cause violence—or even religion more generally—is just as problematic as trying to suggest that Buddhism is really all about peace and not implicated in the violence. Moreover, as I have noted in the main body of this chapter, contemporary critical work on Buddhism tends to fall victim to this error by trying to find some essential religious traits that are at work in social and political events. Such observations are perhaps valuable for Buddhist studies scholars but they tend to conceal the fact that what is at stake in places like Myanmar is the way that political communities include, exclude, and marginalize others, and the power politics contained therein; it obscures the fact that the violence in Myanmar over the past year has more to do with the various social and historical conflicts between specific ethnic groups in the region than it does with any so-called religious influence. Again, following McCutcheon, I would suggest that whenever religion is invoked as a

---

5. It should be noted that the sources referenced in the last several paragraphs of this chapter were also cited in the *Lion's Roar* article cited at the outset of this chapter (see Rosenthal 2018). However, whereas the *Lion's Roar* article uses these data to suggest that Buddhism is ultimately a religion of peace and not implicated in the violence and ethnic cleansing, I am suggesting that very attempt to locate and define the role of religion in the conflict—whether to absolve religion of guilt or blame it for its contribution—misses the deeper theoretical point: religion is constructed through and through and exist solely within the imaginative acts of the scholar.
6. For a recent study detailing how religion and race are connected in Myanmar see *Myanmar's Enemy Within: Buddhist Violence and the Making of a Muslim "Other"* (Wade 2017). Or, more broadly, for a recent study on how religion is a racialized category through and through, and how the two are always linked in the modern world, see *Modern Religion, Modern Race* (Vlal 2016).

causative force to explain the conflict, it is that scholarly act itself that should be interrogated. In other words, it is the very mode of inquiry that should itself be the object of inquiry.

In sum, what I am suggesting is that instead of trying to use events like the crisis in Myanmar to define "Buddhism" or "religion" in some particular manner, the focus should be on how religion is imagined for various political ends in different contexts. Following McVicar, I would suggest that we shouldn't use essentialist notions of religion to frame political contemporary events or movements—to see them as "autonomous manifestations of some deeper human search for religious or spiritual meaning"—but instead emphasize how they are the by-products of larger political forces, whether they be state, military, bureaucratic, or corporate. Our primary goal shouldn't be to reify religion or related categories as particularly unique or distinct phenomena, but to detail how individuals, societies, and groups organize membership in political communities and the acts of identification with which they associate such terms.

Tenzan Eaghll is an independent academic and author based in Hong Kong. His research focuses on the intersection of the film studies, method, and theory in the study of religion, continental philosophy, and History of Religions. He is the co-editor of *Representing Religion in Film* and the creator and co-host of the podcast *Fascism in Cinema*.

References

Al Jazeera. 2015. "Genocide Agenda." *Al Jazeera Investigates*, season 3, episode 5. Retrieved from www.aljazeera.com/program/investigations/2015/10/26/genocide-agenda.
Bayart, Jean-François. 1996. *The Illusion of Cultural Identity*. Chicago, IL: University of Chicago Press.
Eaghll, Tenzan. 2015. "Religious Clichés." *Bulletin for the Study of Religion* 44(1): 33–38. https://doi.org/10.1558/bsor.v44i1.26746
Hessey, Jay, and Jill C. Hurst. 2012. "Democracy in Burma? Life for the Ethnic People of Burma." *Social Policy* 42(4): 40–44.
Ibrahim, Azeem. 2016. *The Rohingyas: Inside Myanmar's Hidden Genocide*. London: Hurst.
Jerryson, Michael. 2011. *Buddhist Fury: Religion and Violence in Southern Thailand*. Oxford: Oxford University Press.
Jerryson, Michael. 2017. "Monks with Guns: Buddhism can be as Violent as any Other Religion." *Aeon*. Retrieved from https://aeon.co/essays/Buddhism-can-be-as-violent-as-any-other-religion
Lee, Thomas J., Luke C. Mullany, Adam K. Richards, Heather K. Kulper, Cynthia Maung, and Chris Beyrer. 2006. "Mortality Rates in Conflict Zones in Karen, Karenni, and Mon States in Eastern Burma." *Tropical Medicine and International Health* 11(7): 1119–1127. https://doi.org/10.1111/j.1365-3156.2006.01651.x
McCutcheon, Russell. 1997. *Manufacturing Religion: The Discourse of Sui Generis Religion and the Politics of Nostalgia*. Oxford: Oxford University Press.
Menon, Harsha. 2018. "Buddhist Studies, Past, Present, and Future: An Interview with Dr. Donald Lopez." *Buddhistdoor Global*. Retrieved from www.Buddhistdoor.net/features/Buddhist-studies-past-present-and-future-an-interview-with-dr-donald-lopez-part-one

Rosenthal, Randy. 2018. "What's the connection between Buddhism and ethnic cleansing in Myanmar?" *Lion's Roar*. Retrieved from www.lionsroar.com/what-does-Buddhism-have-to-do-with-the-ethnic-cleansing-in-myanmar/?utm_source=Lion%27s+Roar+Newsletter&utm_campaign=f209c6b04a-WR-July-20-2018&utm_medium=email&utm_term=0_1988ee44b2-f209c6b04a-23241525&goal=0_1988ee44b2-f209c6b04a-23241525&mc_cid=f209c6b04a&mc_eid=7d79f8d4d7

Sheedy, Matt. 2017. "Religions are Intrinsically Violent." In Craig Martin and Brad Stoddard (eds.), *Stereotyping Religion: Critiquing Cliches*, 23–39. New York: Bloomsbury.

Smith, Jonathan Z. 1982. *Imagining Religion: From Babylon to Jonestown*. Chicago, IL: University of Chicago Press.

Stoakes, Emanuel. 2015. "Monks, PowerPoint Presentations, and Ethnic Cleansing: Damning New Evidence shows the Myanmar Government's Role in Promoting Anti-Muslim Hatred." *Foreign Policy*. Retrieved from https://foreignpolicy.com/2015/10/26/evidence-links-myanmar-government-monks-ethnic-cleansing-rohingya.

Vlal, Theodore. 2016. *Modern Religion, Modern Race*. Oxford: Oxford University Press.

Wade, Francis. 2017. *Myanmar's Enemy Within: Buddhist Violence and the Making of a Muslim "Other"*. London: Zed Books.

Yusuf, Imtiyaz. 2018. "Three Faces of the Rohingya Crisis: Religious Nationalism, Asian Islamophobia, and Delegitimizing Citizenship." *Studia Islamika* 25(3): 503–541. https://doi.org/10.15408/sdi.v25i3.8038

Zan, U Shw, and Aye Chan. 2005. *Influx Viruses, The Illegal Muslims in Arakan*. New York: Arakanese in the United States.

Chapter 3

Citizenship, Religion, and the Frailty of State Sovereignty

Daniel Miller

Introduction

In "Paper Terrorism: Religion, Paperwork, and the Contestation of State Power in the 'Sovereign Citizen' Movement," Michael J. McVicar (Chapter 1, this volume) opens a discussion of a range of complex issues and their interrelation. His specific focus is the "sovereign citizen" movement, a disparate and "somewhat paradoxical" cluster of libertarian, anarchist, and anti-government movements with representation on both the racist White right and among separatist African American movements. His primary focus is these movements' shared practice of what has been termed "paper terrorism," consisting of the "nonviolent legal tactics" employed by sovereign citizen groups in opposition to the federal and state governments in the U.S. Paper terrorism, as McVicar summarizes it, "is generally marked by the issuance of property liens, the aggressive use of illegal or extra-legal court filings, the printing of homemade or nongovernment-backed currencies, and the creation of personal diplomatic paperwork, drivers' licenses, and passports."

McVicar is critical of two broad approaches that scholars of religion have taken to the sovereign citizen movement. The first approaches the movement as a fraudulent legal framework intended to disrupt the US judicial and financial systems, while the second understands it as "nativists resisting encroaching colonial forces." The latter of these approaches draws on James Frazer's classic account of "sympathetic magic" to develop an account of the "magical efficacy" of paper terrorism. McVicar critiques these approaches (the second in particular) for succumbing to "the temptation to read this movement as some *sui generis* autochthonous expression of human longing for freedom from colonial domination" (8), thereby ignoring or overlooking the complex ways in which these movements are entangled in considerations of state sovereignty, the material constitution of citizenship, and the interests of the state in categorizing and tracking those subject to its dictates. Related to this, McVicar contests the degree to which such approaches uncritically view "state agencies and their affiliates as the *real* sources of documentation, paperwork, and bureaucratic production."

In contrast to such approaches, McVicar sees these movements as opening up the space to question such presumptions of naturalized state authority and to explore "the complex relationship between the material production of citizenship and religious practice in the contemporary United States." He argues that these approaches miss the significance of the "sovereign citizen" as social object, an object that "should not be viewed *prima facie* as illegitimate, illegal, or somehow magical or imaginary, especially if these latter terms are intended to imply that sovereigns are less *real* than other social objects." As he suggests, "if there is anything 'magical' about the sovereign citizen movement and the documentary practices driving it, it is that it underscores the essential fragility of citizenship in the contemporary United States." This issue, as revealed in "religious attempts to resist state power," drives McVicar's essay.

In this essay, I pursue some of these points further, pressing beyond McVicar's proximate focus on the sovereign citizen movement to consider some of the broader issues onto which his reflections open. I want to focus, in particular, on some of the "historically durable, but widely contested concepts" around which his essay takes shape. I agree with his theoretical rationale for avoiding "stipulative" or "ostensive" definitions for some of the key concepts considered in his essay (e.g., "religion," "citizenship," "state"). I share his expressed interest, following Bruno Latour, in attending to the "performative definitions of social objects that emerge as actors attempt to delineate the boundaries of social phenomena." While the specific concepts McVicar singles out are "religion" and "citizen," I want to consider a concept that, in its modern articulation, is enmeshed with both of these: political sovereignty. The sovereign citizens movement, particularly in the specific case of Alecia Faith Pennington, reveals the frailty at the heart of political sovereignty and, in so doing, highlights the contingency of one of the defining features of modernity itself: the political state.

The Sovereign State

Christopher W. Morris suggests that "philosophers often take the state for granted" (Morris 2011: 544), a point which is certainly not limited to philosophers. The state is a ubiquitous fact of modern social and political life, in more senses than one. As Morris notes, "today virtually the entire land mass of the globe is the territory of one state or another" (ibid.), and Richard Bellamy points out that it is virtually impossible in the present global order *not* to live in a state, such that it is, in this sense, virtually impossible to be "stateless" (Bellamy 2008: 53; see also Morris 2011: 545).[1] States have "swept the world," both conceptually and literally (Morris 2004: 206).

The ubiquity of the state, and the taken-for-grantedness that comes with it, occludes the reality that the contemporary state system, the only political system

---

1. This is not to deny, of course, the reality of groups and individuals who are denied citizenship status within any state. While such people are effectively denied the "right to have rights" (see below) granted by a state, they nevertheless typically remain within the borders of a state, and so remain subject to its authority.

to have become truly global in scope (Philpott 2011: 564), is distinctly modern, representing a marked departure from prior historical forms of socio-political organization (Morris 2011: 545). Two related features of the modern state are central to this point: territoriality and sovereignty. Philpott defines political sovereignty as "supreme authority within a territory" (Philpott 2001: 16; see also Philpott 2011: 561; Morris 2004, 198), which applies to the population and resources of that territory (Diener and Hagan 2012: 7).

As a form of authority, Philpott (2011: 561) notes that sovereignty implies legitimacy or right, not the mere exercise of force or power. If authority is understood as "the right to command and correlatively, the right to be obeyed" (Wolff 1990, quoted in Philpott 2011: 561), then "the holders of sovereignty do not just prod, coerce, assert their will, or force their way, but rule according to natural law, divine mandate, a communal law or tradition, or international law," which serve as "sources of sovereignty" (Philpott 2001: 16). Sovereignty, then, implies "some sort of consensually conferred authoritative sanction," which, in the contemporary world, typically takes the form of law (Philpott 2011: 561) representing the rule of the constitutionally defined people (ibid.: 563). "Authority," then, carries a normative sense. As Morris (2004: 199) suggests, "something is an authority ... only if its directives are (and are intended to be) action-guiding," distinguishing authority from "justified force." This is why Morris distinguishes between authority, on the one hand, and coercion or the exercise of force, on the other, as they relate to the exercise of law within the state. The sovereign exercise of law is such that it is obeyed because of a respect for its authority. While "we should, of course, expect that laws will be backed by the threat of sanctions and that force may be needed" (ibid.: 201), were the explicit threat or force or coercion the sole basis for obedience to the law, this would demonstrate a *lack* of full authority, not its exercise, thereby indicating the absence of sovereignty. As Philpott (2011: 561) suggests, claims to sovereign authority must correspond to actual practice, such that the naked exercise of coercion to enforce law, should it become the normal and sole reason for obedience, would represent a breakdown in authority.

The specifically sovereign exercise of authority is also supreme in nature. Developing this point in terms of "ultimacy," Morris (2004: 199) points out that "an authority may be ultimate if it is the highest in a hierarchy of authorities." As Philpott (2001: 16–17) puts it, "in the chain of authority by which I look to a higher authority, who in turn looks to a higher one, the holder of sovereignty is highest." To insist on the supremacy or ultimacy of sovereignty, however, is not to claim that sovereignty is necessarily absolute. The sovereign may be the highest authority in matters over which sovereignty is effectively exercised, but this does not mean that the scope of sovereignty is all-encompassing; there may be elements of social or political life that are deemed not be subject to sovereign authority (ibid.: 18–19).

Modern state sovereignty, and the exercise it entails, is premised on a distinctively geographical conception of territoriality, reflected in the modern notion of borders. As Alexander C. Diener and Joshua Hagan (2012: 4, 54) note, modern state borders tend to take on a sense of permanence and timelessness. This sense is, however, deeply misleading. In contrast to this static view, they argue that "borders are essentially evolving practices and institutions subject to the influences of contingent events and ideas" (ibid.: 67). Taking seriously the insight that "human spatial thinking has manifested in very different ways over time" (ibid.: 6), they advance a constructivist conception, noting that territoriality "results from historical contexts, practical needs, and geopolitical contingencies" (ibid.: 67). On such a view, a defined territory is less a fixed object than the outcome of an active and always ongoing process of territorialization, a twofold process, involving "the division of land between social entities and assigning specific meanings to the resultant places" (ibid.: 59). Territoriality "results from historical contexts, practical needs, and geopolitical contingencies" (ibid.: 6), and the enactment of the borders between states is no different in this regard. With the rise of the modern state, "territoriality has become institutionalized in the modern era with the effect of naturalizing the overtly social processes of bordering (ibid.: 6).

Modern bordering practices express a distinctively geographical form of territoriality. Stated succinctly, within the state geographical location takes precedence over society or shared culture. As Philpott (2011: 562) notes, within the state system, "people are members of a political community … by virtue of their residence within a set of geographical borders." The subjection to the state's exercise of authority on the part of all those inhabiting its geographical territory grants a historically new significance to geography (Morris 2004: 197). The distinctiveness of this territorial conception comes into view through a consideration of alternative conceptions of territoriality (e.g., the nation) and governance (e.g., that of medieval Europe).

While often used interchangeably, or simply combined (as in "nation-state") in popular usage, the terms "nation" and "state" actually reflect very different conceptions of territoriality, legitimacy, and social order. As Morris (2004: 205) notes, "a nation is a society whose members are linked by sentiments of solidarity and self-conscious identity based on a number of other bonds (e.g. history, territory, culture, race, 'ethnicity,' language, religion, customs)." As Steven Grosby (2005: 22) suggests, "the legal and political relation of the state is analytically distinct from the cultural community of the territorial relationship of kinship, the nation." Reflecting this distinction, "a group of humans will constitute a nation in this sense in so far as the members share certain properties and in so far as they are conscious of this shared condition" (Morris 2004: 205; see Morris 2011: 547). Within the national form, in contrast to that of the state, the social has priority over legal, political, or territorial relations (Grosby 2005: 27).

Grosby (2005) points out that the English "nation" is derived from the Latin noun *natio*, itself a derivation of the verb *nasci*, "to be born from." This also leads to the Latin derivation *nativus*. Reflecting these considerations, "nation" reflects a dual sense of origins, having to do with place of origin (one's "native" place) and lines of birth or descent (as in "nativity"). Thus, "while familial descent … is different from territorial descent, these two forms of kinship are neither mutually exclusive nor historically demarcated" (ibid.: 44). Belonging to a nation is therefore a matter of these two lines of descent: "descent in the territory of the nation *and* descent from parents who are members of the nation" (ibid.: 13, emphasis added).

While the concept of the nation clearly involves a sense of territory, this sense of territoriality is coded according to culture and (real or perceived) kinship, not geography narrowly considered. Thus, "the term 'nation' implies the continuation over time of a relatively uniform territorial culture" (Grosby 2005: 20). In contrast to the state, then, "the boundaries of a territory are never merely geographical; they indicate the spatial limit to many of those traditions that are passed from one generation to the next." Grosby continues, "the individuals who dwell within a territory do not merely interact with one another; they participate in territorially bounded traditions" (ibid.: 47).

Within the state system, by way of contrast, geography takes priority over shared culture or perceived kinship. While the territorial scope of the nation is determined by shared culture or kinship, whatever commonality exists among those living within the state is determined by geographical boundaries alone. Reflecting such considerations, Philpott (2011: 562) notes that "territoriality often does not succeed in defining membership so as to correspond with the identity of a 'people' or 'nation'." These very different conceptions of territoriality demonstrate why there is generally not a one-to-one correspondence between nations and states. As Morris (2004: 205–206) notes, "since the entire land mass of the globe is now the territory of some state, we do not find any nation that does not overlap with a state." The common term "nation-state" is best reserved for those examples of political states with a single nation, or favoring a particular nation, while most states are best described as multinational states (see Morris 2011: 547). To these considerations, we can add those cases in which nations are divided among multiple political states (common in the case of former colonies) or those nations that are denied the status of belonging to any state (e.g., the Palestinians or Rohingya). It is also possible to imagine states that develop a strong enough and pervasively shared sense of civic identity as to represent a kind of "civic nation," as in idealized presentations of shared French republican identity or the mythology of the U.S. as a cultural "melting pot."[2]

The unique character of the modern state, then, is given in its specifically geographical territoriality. But the modern state system also reflects a historically unique form of governance, which comes into view when contrasted with medieval governance, which was not primarily territorial in nature (Philpott 2001: 78; Morris 2004: 197). At the macro-level, medieval governance relied, in keeping with the logic of shared cultures we have just considered, a widely shared "normative world," namely Christendom. Thus, in contrast to the modern state system, "the various realms of Christendom were not separate, self-sufficient juridical domains (Morris 2004: 197). As Philpott (2001: 77) suggests, "the Pauline

---

2. I describe these as "idealized" presentations because there is little basis to support a universally shared sense of "Frenchness" or "Americanness" in either respective state. For the case of the U.S., see Kaufman (2000) and Theiss-Morse (2009); for the French case, see Scott (2007).

metaphor of the Body of Christ, which publicists, philosophers, theologians, and holders of power used to describe politics and society, renders the [medieval] era well. All believers in the true faith were members of a single organism ..."

Governance in the medieval period also differed from that of the modern state system at the micro-level. Morris usefully highlights five distinct differences between political and social governance in the medieval period as compared to that within the modern state system:

> First, most people were governed by rulers whose practices and institutions were not likely to survive their deaths or those of their sons. The realms governed by these rulers would not have precise boundaries, and the lands in their possession often would not be contiguous ... Second, their rule was largely personal; the allegiance of their subjects was owed to their person, not them qua holder of an office ... Third ... rule was largely indirect or mediated ... Fourth, people might find themselves the subject of several different rulers or systems of rule. The authority of kings competed with that of lords and princes, independent towns, popes and bishops, and the emperor ... Lastly, a person's allegiance or loyalty to a ruler would not exclude similar allegiance to others.
>
> (Morris 2011: 553-554)

By way of contrast, "governance in the modern state is relatively centralized, unified, uniform, hierarchical, direct, impersonal, and territorial" (ibid.: 554; see also 546). Emphasizing the impersonal and independent nature of the state, Morris emphasizes that the sovereign state represents "a unitary public order distinct from and superior to both ruled and rulers, one capable of agency," exercised through various complex institutions, which are themselves not the state, but its agents (ibid.: 546). The state is a "legally recognized personality" (ibid.: 554), granting it a kind of "transcendence" of both ruler and governed that is historically unique (Morris 2004: 199). Given such considerations, Philpott (2001: 80) is correct in suggesting that "in the Middle Ages, virtually nobody was sovereign" in the modern sense of the term.

The modern system of sovereign states therefore marks a significant historical and conceptual development. Formalized in the 1648 Treaty of Westphalia, the system attained European dominance with the defeat of those (primarily Catholic) polities that opposed it, and was eventually "exported" globally through colonization and former colonies' subsequent attainment of independence.[3] As I suggested above, the sovereign state has become the ubiquitous form of political

---

3. As Philpott (2001: 77) suggests, the Treaty of Westphalia represented a decisive consolidation of developments in European statehood that had been going on for centuries. While it does not represent a sole source of the international system of sovereign states, Philpott nevertheless makes a strong case that, had it not been for the Treaty, which formally ended the Thirty Years' War, the emerge of a system of sovereign state in Europe would have occurred much later if at all (ibid.: 75-96). At any rate, Westphalia is commonly noted as the event that formalized the emergence of the sovereign state system in Europe, effectively inaugurating the common international system of sovereign states (see Diener and Hagan 2012: 3; Thomas 2005: 54; Steger 2013: 61-63). For a full discussion of the significance of Westphalia for the constitution of the

governance insofar as it is global in scope. From the perspective of international relations, states possess "external" sovereignty, meaning that they are free to manage their own affairs without intervention from other states. This concept of sovereignty was first applied to religion, ensuring that states would not intervene against one another to enforce religious orthodoxy or conformity, and later became the basis for non-intervention more broadly construed, representing the "external" dimension of political sovereignty (see Thomas 2005: 25–26; Philpott 2001: 147–149).

But state sovereignty also involves, as we have seen in our discussion of authority, an "internal" dimension, which has to do with its exercise of sovereignty *within* its own borders. The state is omnipresent not only in a global sense, but in the lives of those who live within its borders as well. As Morris (2004: 195) suggests, "it is hard to ignore the state or government—'You may not be interested in the state, but the state is certainly interested in you,' to adapt Trotsky's quip about war. Almost everywhere we find ourselves today, we find government." There is virtually no aspect of individual life that is not impacted by the state's exercise of authority and, as we have seen, the sovereignty of the modern state is such that all who dwell within its borders are subject its authority. When Philpott (2011: 562) describes the modern sovereign state as a "political community," then, he is only partially correct. While it may be the case that all who dwell within the borders of the state are subject to the state's authority, this is *not* to say that all such people are granted equivalent status within the state. While differences in status should not, in normative liberal terms, be based on such issues as culture, religion, kinship, etc., they *are* based on law itself.

Stated somewhat differently, not all who dwell within the borders of the state are recognized as members of the political community. The name for such membership, of course, is "citizenship." While citizenship is often defined in terms of rights, Richard Bellamy (2008: 80) suggests the citizenship be understood in even more fundamental terms, as the "right to have rights." This formulation effectively highlights the significance of state sovereignty within the state itself. Determinations of citizenship are a high-stakes affair, determining who, within the state's territory, is not only *subject to* its pervasive exercise of authority, but who, we might say, *subjects it to* authority. While it may sound straightforward enough to suggest that sovereignty lies with the constitutionally-defined "people,"[4] it remains the prerogative of the state to make the final determination who "counts" as "the people," insofar as this has to do with citizenship.[5]

---

international system of sovereign states, including its global expansion, as well as the historical significance of the Protestant Reformation, see Philpott (2001).

4. Though we can't address the issue here, this notion of "the people" as constitutionally defined is deeply paradoxical in nature. This is because, on the one hand, any constitution is considered legitimate only to the degree that it is affirmed as such by "the people" while, on the other hand, the constitution is what determines the legitimate bounds of "the people." For a discussion of these and related paradoxes, see Honig (2009: 12–39).

5. I'm only dealing with an institutional/legal determination of citizens as "the people" here. For a more robust theoretical account of the constitution of the people, see Miller (2016).

The Sovereign Citizen Challenge to State Sovereignty

As McVicar (Chapter 1, this volume) correctly reminds us, there is an irreducibly material dimension to the state's ubiquitous authority to determine who has the right to have rights. These two dimensions, authority and materiality, are co-constitutive. As McVicar writes, "citizenship, for all of its ideological and political entailments, is in many ways an aggregated, material phenomenon. That is, at its root, modern citizenship is predicated on the ability of a governed subject of state power to produce a complex succession of documentary traces that witness to the subject's entanglement with state and non-state bureaucratic agencies." The sovereign authority of the state, with all of its pervasive effects, is enacted in and through the materiality of documentation and bureaucratic agencies.

Determining who, within its borders, has the right to have rights represents one of the most fundamental performances of sovereign authority on the part of the state. This, then, is precisely why something like the sovereign citizen movement represents such a challenge to its authority. What unites this disparate movement is the deployment of "sophisticated bureaucratic techniques" to "resist normative understandings of citizenship" (McVicar, Chapter 1, this volume). The description of these techniques as "paper terrorism" could reasonably elicit a cynical response. At first blush, such actions hardly seem to represent the kind of danger popularly associated with "terrorism." While there is no agreed-upon definition of terrorism (see Townshend 2018: 4–5), Jackson (2009: 75) suggests that a "relatively uncontroversial" definition within the field of terrorism studies would be "violence directed towards or threatened against civilians which is designed to instill terror or intimidate a population for political reasons." Working with such a definition, the practices employed by those within the sovereign citizen movement appear rather anodyne in nature. While McVicar (Chapter 1, this volume) notes that the tactics of the sovereign citizen movement are occasionally effective in attaining their ends, the most typical effect is the tying of red-tape knots that gum up the effective bureaucratic functioning of the state apparatus. While certainly representing an expense of time and money, when compared to the many dangers confronting the contemporary state, the sovereign state movement, which directly involves a very small number of people, might seem inconsequential overall.

Yet, as scholars of critical terrorism studies correctly note, "it can be argued that terrorism is not a causally coherent, free-standing phenomenon which can be identified in terms of characteristics inherent to the violence itself (Jackson 2009: 75). As Jackson et al. (2011: 112) suggest, "terms such as terrorism should not be thought of as neutral words we employ to refer to an independent realm of existence. Rather, they are lenses that shape or co-construct the world around us, giving it order and meaning *as* we engage in the act of observation." As Rom Harré (2004: 92) notes, "the category attributions [of terrorism or terrorist] are not simple descriptions but psychologically potent labels," going on to pose the centrally critical question: "What is their import?"

Jackson (2009: 67) captures this import succinctly: Labelling a group or movement as "terrorist" "functions ideologically to reinforce and reify existing structures of power in society, particularly that of the state." As the very name implies, the sovereign citizen movement represents a denial of state sovereignty, specifically its authority to determine questions of citizenship. The challenge to state sovereignty represented by the movement does not lie in its relative success (or lack thereof). As we have noted above, a defining feature of state sovereignty is the *effective* exercise of territorially defined authority. The exercise of state authority lies not only on the side of the state, in the passage of laws, the leveling of demands, the imposition of regulations, etc., but in the willingness of those subject to those laws, demands, and regulations to assent to their perceived authority. As suggested above, the effective exercise of sovereignty is threatened to precisely the extent that this assent is not freely given, but must be explicitly coerced. This is even more the case when it comes to a refusal to acquiesce to state determinations of citizenship, arguably the most fundamental contemporary expression of "internal" state sovereignty. Whether understood as a challenge to the state's assignation of citizenship or its ability to protect its citizens from violence, terrorism represents a challenge to state sovereignty and, by extension, legitimacy (Townshend 2018: 5).

The enactment of the sovereign state challenge to state sovereignty through the appropriation of the material means by which the state establishes citizenship heightens this challenge. Insofar as terrorism is typically understood to be undertaken by non-state actors (Jackson 2009: 70), it typically represents a form of asymmetrical conflict involving the employment of powerful states' resources against them to their own detriment. This redeployment of resources reveals the frailty at the heart of state sovereignty. Modifying the application of Jacques Derrida's (2003) term, terrorism therefore represents an autoimmunitary threat to state sovereignty. Application of the term "terrorism" to the sovereign citizen movement reflects a dis-ease on the part of the state and its apparatuses of sovereignty.

Religion and the Reassertion of Sovereignty?

The act of defining the sovereign citizen movement as a form of "paper terrorism" represents an attempt on the part of the state to reassert its fundamentally contested authority. Given the nature of the movement's attempts to contest state sovereignty, the primary state means of reasserting its authority lies in the exercise of its various bureaucratic and juridical institutions. But, as McVicar (Chapter 1, this volume) illustrates with his discussion of Alecia Faith Pennington, whose parents were Christian fundamentalists adhering to sovereign citizen ideas, such means may prove insufficient. Born in Texas in 1995 without a birth certificate, Pennington was prevented from receiving vaccinations or regular medical check-ups and never had a bank account or social security card. When she left her parents and their sovereign citizen lifestyle behind, she discovered that she had no means of proving her US citizenship. She possessed none of the material means so central for demonstrating citizenship within the contemporary US.

Pennington's case illustrates contradictory points. On the one hand, it would seem to represent a victory (albeit a small-scale one) on the part of the sovereign state, insofar as it revolves around a citizen's formal recognition of state authority, and concomitant repudiation of those rejecting it (at least with regard to citizenship). On the other hand, the apparent reassertion of state sovereignty is rendered a pyrrhic victory, insofar as the paradoxical effect of the state's assertion of sovereignty is the revelation of sovereignty's frailty and fundamental contingency. A consideration of this point brings us back to McVicar's earlier discussion regarding "performative definitions of social objects that emerge as actors attempt to delineate the boundaries of social phenomena" (Chapter 1, this volume), specifically the explicit juxtaposition of "religion" and the sovereign state.

In Pennington's case, the determination was made that, in the absence of recognized state documentation, she could "bootstrap her way into citizenship by cobbling together a host of non-state forms and records that collectively testified to her legal person-ness under Texas and, ultimately, federal law" (McVicar, Chapter 1, this volume) . Of particular note, these bootstrap documents included "records from religious rituals," such as baptisms, christenings, and confirmations. This allowance is noteworthy insofar as modern "religion" was born with the modern state. The establishment of the sovereign state system required, by definition, the subordination of all potential rivals to state authority within its territory. One of the chief historical rivals to secular, which is simply to say non-ecclesiastical, political authority was the Church. The establishment of the sovereign state system therefore required the subordination of church to state. This was accomplished through the constitution of "religion" as privatized and, in an important sense, de-materialized. As Scott Thomas (2005: 25) writes, "for the state to be born, religion had to become privatized and nationalized." Thus, "'religion,' as a set of moral and theological propositions, had to be made compatible with the power and discipline of the new monarchies of Europe, by detaching them from the virtues and practices embedded in the religious tradition embodied in the ecclesial community" (ibid.).

As William T. Cavanaugh (2009) makes clear, the contours of modern "religion" are both familiar and radically different from the religious expression of the medieval period. Cavanaugh highlights a number of distinctions between the medieval *religio*, the etymological root of the English "religion," and the modern sense of the latter term. First, he notes that *religio* explicitly referred to Christian worship, and was not considered universal (thereby encompassing non-Christians) in scope (ibid.: 65). *Religio* also "was not ... a system of propositions or beliefs," "a purely interior impulse secreted away in the human soul," or "an 'institutional force' separable from other nonreligious, or secular, forces" (ibid.: 66–67). The privatization of religion and delimitation of it to specified social institutions and spheres was a function of the institution of sovereign state authority within its territorial bounds. Thus, "the state used the invention of religion to legitimate the transfer of the ultimate loyalty of people from religion to the state as part of the consolidation of its power—the process of state-building and nation-building, which we have come to call internal sovereignty" (Thomas 2005: 25).[6]

The exercise of internal sovereignty therefore necessitated the emergence of the modern conception of religion as a set of individual (i.e., private) beliefs having to do with spiritual salvation. Brent Nongbri (2012) notes the contribution of thinkers such as Jean Bodin and John Locke in the development of such a notion. Tracing Locke's own formulation of religion in his well-known "Letter Concerning Toleration" (1689), he notes that what emerges is a conception of "religions as groups of individuals who freely choose to associate with each other and adhere to a particular set of writings for the purpose of salvation, and who ideally operate in ways that *do not interfere or overlap with the concerns of the state*" (Nongbri 2012: 103, emphasis added).

This latter point is key for understanding the complexity of the Pennington case with regard to the exercise or reassertion of state sovereignty. The effective exercise of the sovereign state's authority within its territorial borders is premised on the non-coincidence of religion and its areas of authority. It is only to the extent that religion remains marginalized vis-à-vis state concerns that the state can be said to effectively exercise its authority. Sovereign state authority requires the banishment of religion from the designated sphere of state authority.

In the case of Alecia Faith Pennington, the state reasserts its authority, effectively designating her as a citizen, only through appeal to religious documentation. But this means, of course, that the reassertion of state authority *required* the coincidence of state and religious authority. The apparent reassertion of state authority therefore comes only at the expense of its ultimacy, rendering the "sovereign" state dependent on the very institution against which its ultimacy has been constituted.

Conclusion: The Frailty of State Sovereignty

In terms of overall numbers or social effect, the sovereign citizens movement is not expansive. Nor is the case of Alecia Faith Pennington typical of the assignation of citizenship on the part of the state. They are, nonetheless, revelatory, insofar as they bring to light the frailty at the heart of modern state sovereignty

---

6. The privatization of religion therefore represented the nationalization of religion as well. A key feature of the Westphalian settlement, anticipated in the Treaty of Augsburg a century earlier, was the principle *cuius regio, eius religio*, "the ruler determines the religion of his realm." This principle served as the basis of non-intervention between sovereign states: "External" sovereignty was such that states would not interfere with one another on the basis of religious belief, effectively establishing the principle of religious pluralism between states (Thomas 2005: 55; Philpott 2001: 81). It is also worth clarifying that "religious pluralism" here does not signify a recognition of religious pluralism *within* the states in question. What emerged following the Westphalian settlement was a system of confessional states, not religiously diverse liberal pluralist states in a contemporary sense.

and the definition of citizenship, as McVicar suggests (Chapter 1, this volume). While the sovereign state and the concept of religion concomitant with it have been so thoroughly hegemonized as to seem natural and immutable, we have seen that they are, in fact, historically contingent social and political accomplishments. Crucially, the effective exercise of state sovereignty depends on precisely this air of immutability or naturalness. As we have seen, sovereign authority is most effectively exercised when those subject to the state's authority recognize it *as* authoritative and respond accordingly. An element of this is the requirement that religion remain in its properly designated sphere, separate from the state's exercise of sovereign authority. The sovereign citizen movement and the Pennington case illustrate just how fragile these complex social structures and practices actually are.

Daniel D. Miller is Associate Professor of Religion and Social Thought and Chair of the Department of Liberal Studies at Landmark College. His research interests include religion, political theory and American politics, gender and embodiment, 20th century Continental philosophy, and theory and method in the study of religion. He is the author of two books: *The Myth of Normative Secularism: Religion and Politics in the Democratic Homeworld* (Duquesne University Press, 2015) and *Queer Democracy: Desire, Dysphoria, and the Body Politic* (Routledge, 2022). He also co-hosts the podcast *Straight White American Jesus* and works as a coach for individuals working to resolve the effects of religious trauma.

References

Bellamy, Richard. 2008. *Citizenship: A Very Short Introduction.* Oxford: Oxford University Press.
Cavanaugh, William T. 2009. *The Myth of Religious Violence.* Oxford: Oxford University Press.
Derrida, Jacques. 2003. "Autoimmunity: Real and Symbolic Suicides—A Dialogue with Jacques Derrida." Translated by Pascale-Anne Brault and Michael Naas. In *Philosophy in a Time of Terror: Dialogues with Jürgen Habermas and Jacques Derrida*, edited by Giovanna Borradori, 85–136. Chicago, IL: University of Chicago Press.
Diener, Alexander C., and Joshua Hagan. 2012. *Borders: A Very Short Introduction.* Oxford: Oxford University Press.
Grosby, Steven. 2005. *Nationalism: A Very Short Introduction.* Oxford: Oxford University Press.
Harré, Rom. 2004. "The Social Construction of Terrorism." In Fathali M. Moghaddam and Anthony J. Marsella (eds.), *Understanding Terrorism: Psychological Roots, Consequences, and Interventions*, 91–102. Washington, DC: American Psychological Association. https://doi.org/10.1037/10621-004
Honig, Bonnie. 2009. *Emergency Politics: Paradox, Law, Democracy.* Princeton, NJ: Princeton University Press.
Jackson, Richard. 2009. "Knowledge, Power, and Politics in the Study of Political Terrorism." In Richard Jackson, Marie Breen Smyth, and Jeroen Gunning (eds.), *Critical Terrorism Studies: A New Research Agenda*, 66–83. London: Routledge.
Jackson, Richard, Lee Jarvis, Jeroen Gunning, and Marie Breen Smyth. 2011. *Terrorism: A Critical Introduction.* New York: Palgrave Macmillan.
Kaufman, Eric Peter. 2000. "Ethnic or Civic Nation?: Theorizing the American Case." *Canadian Review of Studies in Nationalism* 27(1–2): 133–154.

Miller, Daniel D. 2016. *The Myth of Normative Secularism*. Pittsburgh, PA: Duquesne University Press.

Morris, Christopher W. 2004. "The Modern State." In Gerald F. Gaus and Chandran Kukathas (eds.), *Handbook of Political Theory*, 195–209. London: Sage. https://doi.org/10.4135/9781848608139.n15

Morris, Christopher W. 2011. "The State." In George Klosko (ed.), *The Oxford Handbook of Political Philosophy*, 544–560. Oxford: Oxford University Press. https://doi.org/10.1093/oxfordhb/9780199238804.003.0031

Nongbri, Brent. 2013. *Before Religion: A History of a Modern Concept*. New Haven, CT: Yale University Press.

Philpott, Daniel. 2001. *Revolutions in Sovereignty: How Ideas Shaped Modern International Relations*. Princeton, NJ: Princeton University Press.

Philpott, Daniel. 2011. "Sovereignty." In George Klosko (ed.), *The Oxford Handbook of Political Philosophy*, 561–572. Oxford: Oxford University Press. https://doi.org/10.1093/oxfordhb/9780199238804.003.0032

Scott, Joan Wallach. 2007. *The Politics of the Veil*. Princeton, NJ: Princeton University Press.

Steger, Manfred B. 2013. *Globalization: A Very Short Introduction*. Oxford: Oxford University Press.

Theiss-Morse, Elizabeth. 2009. *Who Counts as American? The Boundaries of National Identity*. Cambridge: Cambridge University Press.

Thomas, Scott M. 2005. *The Global Resurgence of Religion and the Transformation of International Relations*. New York: Palgrave.

Townshend, Charles. 2018. *Terrorism: A Very Short Introduction*. Oxford: Oxford University Press.

Wolff, Robert. 1990. "The Conflict Between Authority and Autonomy." In Joseph Raz (ed.), *Authority*, 20–55. Oxford: Basil Blackwell.

Chapter 4

The Material Production of Otherworldly Citizenship: From Paper to Digital Files to Bodies

Lauren Horn Griffin

In 2019, a U.S. citizen was detained by U.S. Customs and Border Protection and Immigration Customs Enforcement. He was eventually released after languishing for weeks in CPB and ICE facilities while authorities sought to confirm his paperwork, which they wrongly suspected were fake (Flynn 2019). This happened the same month that four congresswomen were told to go back to where they came from, despite their U.S. citizenship (Pengelly 2019). Being born here, living here, serving here, even having the right paperwork—sometimes those facts are not enough to secure the benefits of "citizenship." Michael McVicar's "Paper Terrorism: Religion, Paperwork, and the Contestation of State Power in the 'Sovereign Citizen' Movement" (Chapter 1, this volume) offers a thoughtful analysis of the material production of citizenship to emphasize, as in the examples above, what he terms "the fragility of citizenship in this country." Indeed, citizenship can be fragile in part because the records and papers needed to prove it can be lost, faked, or nonexistent (as McVicar's examples demonstrate). But the fragility also stems from a sovereign state acting to govern a nation, or an imagined community, that is framed and formulated in relation to ideas of shared history and values.[1] This necessarily involves the need to categorize difference; therefore, discourses of citizenship are often discourses of race, culture, and religion. Even with the right materials to mediate it, "citizenship" can remain elusive.

There are several ways to engage McVicar's main arguments, but here I will present two separate but related issues. Both revolve around the realization that discourses on identity are always inextricable, and that these intersecting identities are written no more clearly than on our own bodies. From the Black men who created alternative national ID cards to subvert Jim Crow laws to the contemporary FBI using facial recognition to verify citizenship, placing these examples next to each other highlights the body as material mediator. First, I show how

---

1. In using Benedict Anderson's concept of imagined communities, I am (as he did) highlighting that all of these nations, including the United States of America, are imagined, constructed entities. I am not, therefore, arguing that the "alternative" nations created by the bureaucracies are less "real" that the United States, though they lack a powerful regime like the state to enforce any imagined order.

these groups are looking for a sort of dual citizenship, with the imagined community created by the alternative bureaucracy taking primacy. In an analysis of how citizenship is mediated by records and materials, McVicar notes how other types of non-state materials can still carry weight with the state. McVicar's main point, in the end, is that sovereign "paper terrorists" are not outliers of the bureaucratic system so much as they are generating *alternative* bureaucracies, mirroring the processes of the state and creating similar regimes of paperwork. The ideologies and worldviews that accompany the bureaucracies do not emerge from a vacuum, but rather as a response to perceived state overreach. I appreciate McVicar's contextualization, and certainly bringing different groups (e.g., MSTA, sovereign citizens, and religious fundamentalists) together under this framework reveals the similarities in the alternative bureaucracies that get created despite their disparate circumstances and social situations. What a religious studies lens can offer to this analysis, then, is a teasing out of exactly what alternative "nations" or "worlds" get imagined through these regimes of paperwork, and how those imagined communities shape the discourses on identities and either challenge or maintain normative conceptions of American national identity.

In the second section, I refocus the analysis from the discursive worlds created by materials back to the materials themselves, exploring the move from paper to digital files as mediators of citizenship. As so much of material culture becomes digital, I am interested in digital artifacts and how the digital material they produce mediates various acts of identification. To explore these questions, I look at my own work on the digital material culture of devotion and consider what that might have to offer those considering the material phenomenon of citizenship. I discuss the performative aspects of material artifacts and raise questions about the changes digitization might bring in society's relationship to identity formation and to memory. I then explore another imagined otherworld, the virtual world.[2] Analyzing each of the "alternative nations" together as part of an expansive category of imagined communities avoids any reification of "religion" and "nation" as separate categories.

Dual Citizenship

Several individuals and social networks have contested state power through imitating state paperwork, using religion, ethnicity, or birthplace (i.e., nativist claims) to legitimize alternative nationalities. One of the groups McVicar analyzes is the Moorish Science Temple of America (MSTA), an organization that promotes an alternative national identity in an effort to challenge segregation and discrimination against Black Americans by state agencies. Islamic in faith, "Moorish" or

---

2. During my research for this chapter I found a article that also employs the term "otherworldly" to refer to a variety of imagined communities in the hopes of avoiding any reification of "religion" and "nation" as separate categories, though the author's and my usage are not exactly the same (see Webb 2018).

"Asiatic" in ethnicity, and claiming to be descendants of the "Moroccan empire," MSTA uses ethnicity, religion, and ancestry to legitimize an alternative nation, or imagined community. In the 1930s and 40s, the MSTA began to issue their own "Nationality and Identification Cards," and federal agents worried that such official-looking documents might be taken seriously by local authorities and fellow citizens. But in addition to alternative paperwork produced by groups like the MSTA, McVicar describes another, opposite tactic: some sovereign citizens have completely avoided paperwork for their children, leaving no birth certificate, no social security card, no medical records—basically no bureaucratic trace of their existence. Within the homeschooling community, this is referred to as identification abuse. Ryan Stollar, the Executive Director of Homeschool Alumni Reaching Out (HARO) and editor of the blog, Homeschoolers Anonymous, explains that one reason homeschool parents avoid documents is "a belief that any form of government-issued identification is a 'mark of the Beast'" (a reference to a biblical prophecy describing a powerful leader and his government as the Antichrist) (Turner 2015). In the case of Alecia Faith Pennington, a Texas teen who had no documents to prove her citizenship, her parents adhered to a fundamentalist Baptist ideology. Pennington says in an interview that her father rejected a state-issued birth certificate because it was a "paper of ownership," and he viewed his daughter as belonging to God (Young 2016). Indeed, the Penningtons seem to reject U.S. citizenship and participation in the nation as being "not of this world," invoking the gospel of John, which is why her parents allowed baptism and a baptismal certificate, but not a government-issued birth certificate.

These Christian homeschoolers provide an interesting and extreme example of the hierarchies of citizenship (i.e., earthly versus heavenly citizenship) that accompany even mainstream American Christian groups. But most American Christians are not antistatist, per se. Indeed, Christianity is often seen by its practitioners as associated with national identity, and the vast majority of people holding state power are avowed Christians. While there may be an overlap (especially among American evangelicals) between Christians and a "small government" political ideology, the majority of Christianities in America are notably patriotic, and some explicitly espousing Christian nationalism (PRRI 2011). While there are a number of fundamentalist Christian families or communities (like that of the Pennington family) that take extreme actions to avoid the authority of the state, the vast majority do not. Yet, the majority of Christian communities seem to share this idea of the primacy of heavenly citizenship. Applying McVicar's framework to my own research, which examines digital media and religion, I want to address two issues. First, I want to explore the notion of alternative citizenship in Christian communities where they are not looking to directly challenge state paperwork. Second, I want to ask to what extent these creations of alternative citizenships can be viewed as byproducts of state actions in the first place.

Life.Church is a self-described evangelical megachurch based in Oklahoma City, and (as of this writing) is actually the largest church in America. The Church is comprised of over 30 campuses (20 in Oklahoma and the others sprinkled across 11 other states), including an "online campus." The church's weekly attendance across its campuses nationwide regularly exceeds 100,000 people, and its "online church" weekly attendance at least doubles that, making it the most successful of their campus sites, numbers-wise. A sermon given by the senior pastor is broadcast live in each of the satellite campuses each Sunday as well as online from their very own platform, Church Online, which can also be accessed through their mobile app. In Oklahoma and north Texas, hundreds of thousands of people are exposed to their media on a weekly basis, making them anything but fringe. Indeed, the materials produced by Life.Church are meant to connect the individual to the local Church community, but there is an even larger emphasis on connection to the larger Life.Church, to Christians globally, and, most importantly, to God and the divine realm. This more united or universal depiction of the Church highlights the heavenly realm and eternity, a distinction that causes the relationships between confessional, political, and national boundaries to recede into the background, foregrounding heaven as the most significant territory of Christendom. The leadership of the church tries very hard to (as they see it) rise above political division, but when political conflicts are alluded to a bit more explicitly, they are always connected to a cosmic battle between Christ and Antichrist and they situate current political leaders (vaguely) as part of this long historical cosmic fight. This strategy—connecting the temporal political history of the earthly realm with the cosmic time of the heavenly realm—has become the default for Life.Church in framing citizenship. Earthly society both imitates and is a part of the cosmic story, but heavenly citizenship overrides any national or regional citizenship. For example, an Instagram post immediately leading up to the 2016 presidential election featured a black background with stark white words depicting the phrase "we are loyal to our country, but we worship a different King."[3] Another post was a quote from a sermon, highlighting the phrase "You're an ambassador. We represent God every single day. We're sent from heaven."[4] This, of course, is an inherited narrative used by many Christian communities throughout history. But, *why* did Life.Church invoke it in this context? Indeed, this framing, though used throughout the centuries, is not deployed in a vacuum. What sorts of actions (or reactions or inaction) are they legitimizing with this argument about a "dual citizenship"?

I think it is both interesting and fitting to place this more common Christian framing next to McVicar's "paper terrorists"; indeed, as I have shown, the phrases, scriptural invocations, and framework of earthly versus heavenly citizenship is consistent between extreme homeschool parents like the Penningtons and mainstream Protestant Christianity in America. One might assume that the same alternative citizenship framework applied by less extreme groups would result in a less extreme, but still palpable, antistatism. But that is not what happens. Indeed, when looking at the Instagram posts put out by the leadership of Life.Church in the days immediately *after* the 2016 presidential election, they are

---

3. See www.instagram.com/p/BMMWOTlg0yG.
4. See www.instagram.com/p/BMUj-zGAA7C.

explicitly pacifying. One post immediately following the election featured the same black background with white letters, reading "Be known for what you're for, not who you're against."[5] A few days later, another post reminded practitioners, "We don't have time to fight among ourselves. *Our* mission is too important, and our time is too short."[6] This message explicitly directed followers to direct their attention and loyalty upward, to the "mission" as citizens of heaven, and to avoid any conflicts about the state (i.e., the less important "earthly" citizenship). Thus, rather than use their alternative citizenship to subvert state authority, it is actually working to uphold it. In other words, the Instagram posts function to legitimate the power of the state by implying that the earthly nation is less real and less worthy of attention than the otherworldly nation.

My application of McVicar's arguments to my own work on a contemporary digital megachurch reveals a few issues, both about the Life.Church community and about the sovereign citizen groups. McVicar uses the Pennington example to underscore the limits of the state, implicitly arguing that the lack of any citizenship materials is more effective at combating state authority than ideas of an alternative national citizenship. However, when put side by side with the Life.Church example, we can see that the "rejection of citizenship paperwork" approach actually *does* create and reinforce an alternative citizenship: a heavenly one. Rather than resisting "normative understandings of citizenship," many of these groups are employing a very consistent framework of citizenship to other imagined communities. Indeed, the very fact that Alecia Faith Pennington was able to eventually prove her citizenship by using her baptismal certificate even legitimizes, in some sense, her heavenly citizenship. Her baptismal certificate operated as a birth certificate, with Heaven being the analogous "nation." McVicar also argues that we can best understand the creation of alternative citizenships as "by-products of state actions" that "disrupt the state's ability to regulate their behavior." This is clearly the case for the sovereign citizens and the MSTA, but when thinking about the heavenly citizenship prioritized by more mainstream groups, this framework breaks down. The Instagram posts of Life.Church, while made in preparation for a contentious election, were not reacting against state authority. Rather than reacting to any specific state actions, Life.Church explicitly promotes political inaction. To employ a Marxist lens, Life.Church indeed preserves the political status quo by explicitly promoting a message that urges practitioners to "look upward," or look away from the body politic, and focus instead on another nation: the heavenly kingdom that awaits. Furthermore, scholars like Brent Nongbri have shown that it is precisely the development of the modern nation-state that gave rise to religious pluralism as a means of subduing citizens. The different creeds that emerged during the Reformations became a matter of the private sphere existing under a single dominating state government. Paraphrasing John Locke, Nongbri explains that any church gathering "ought to be tolerated by the civil

---

5. See www.instagram.com/p/BMwgljgAzsw.
6. See www.instagram.com/p/BM2MZ0FgxIh.

authorities provided that the participants played by the rules of the game, the most important of which was, do not disturb the functions of the state" (Nongbri 2013: 102). Far from promoting some sort of religious nationalism, this rhetoric of otherworldly citizenship in no way threatens the citizenship authorized by the state because it is based on an imagined *private* community without direct political relevance.

Each of these groups uses alternative imagined communities to legitimize a citizenship apart from or in addition to their U.S. citizenship. Sometimes this upholds the status quo and sometimes it challenges it, but eschewing the categories of "religious" and "national" in favor of a more comprehensive framework puts the spotlight on their processes of identity formation and allows us to see how they might be shaping other conversations about American identity. At the end of the chapter, McVicar notes that the state is not the only arbiter of documentation, even as it relates to citizenship: "through the simple acts of recording events, we sort bodies, categorize actions, value certain behaviors over others, and collect information that through their very preservation conjure the societies in which we live." Indeed, all types of records can be mobilized to legitimize various aspects of identity or function as acts of identification themselves. But under the vast majority of circumstances in which citizenship is materially produced, it is done so through documents and IDs provided by said state. After all, recognizing that nations are imaginary does little to curb the state's authorizing power. Perhaps the central concern, then, is not so much about the relationship of non-state records to citizenship, but rather the implications of such a thorough paper mediation of relationships among people and national governments. We could even ask if there is anything distinctive about the U.S. political economy of paper that shapes how citizenship is constructed and regulated. Further, how does this change when the paperwork goes digital? What about when one's very body is the material through which citizenship is mediated? It is to these questions I turn in the next section.

The Digital World

Beyond the transfer of documents from paper to digital form, digitization opens up a whole new and otherworldly location: cyberspace. Typically, when people talk about "digital citizenship" they are thinking of online behavior: protecting privacy, behaving civilly, understanding the rights and responsibilities under copyright, and just generally being aware of one's digital footprint. But seeing oneself as a "digital citizen" is more than being nice online; it adds another imagined community to the mix. As discussed in the previous section, Christian material culture has long been used to connect earthly and heavenly identities, but there is now another spatial identity—another citizenship—to negotiate. While I do not have the space here to go into detail, I want to show how the digital artifacts produced by Life.Church actually participate in the construction of a virtual world that is imagined as separate from "real life," which in turn is but a shadow of the heavenly realm.[7]

Just as culture is written onto architecture, geography, and the landscape, so it is written onto the digital landscape. Just as a medieval peasant might wake up to the sound of church bells and walk past a holy healing well and a church on their way to work, a modern person might wake up to the alarm on their smartphone and read their emails and social media feeds on their way to work. Images from that digital landscape now fill our brains, and there is so much to consume. The goal for many groups and individuals—from companies to churches to activists to influencers—is to litter the digital landscape with as much content as possible. The marks left on the digital landscape are both reflections of and shapers of culture, and the more marks they can leave, the more influence they can have.

The amount of digital media produced by Life.Church is astounding. They even have their own technology branch, YouVersion, which produced the Bible App and the Bible App for kids (with almost 400 million installs worldwide). It employs dozens of software engineers, product designers, copyrighters, social media specialists, and more. Digital media is so central to their identity that their very name, Life.Church (updated from Lifechurch.tv in 2012) reflects this. Because of the sheer amount of digital devotional material produced by Life.Church, I want to focus on just one: Instagram. Their main account has almost 400 thousand followers and the main pastor has almost a million followers. While they utilize Instagram's Stories, Live, and IGTV functions, I'll focus on just the posts to the feed. The majority of their Instagram posts fall into one of two genres: church service (worship, preaching, or lobby greeting) and the inspirational or biblical quote displayed over an image of a person's face or body.

One subgenre of the inspirational quote that appears many times is (what I call) the digital communication image, or a post that depicts the quote itself as a form of digital communication. For example, the post will display the quote in a text message bubble, or as the reminder function on a smartphone, with a face or body in the background.[8] These images visually make the connection between a perceived digital world (the digital communication image), a "real life" (the physical body), and a spiritual life (usually highlighted in the content of the quote). They show an awareness of how we perform embodied identities in virtual worlds. Christian material culture has long employed constructions of earthly and heavenly citizenship, but now there is another realm to include in this negotiation of (sometimes conflicting) identities. The Church's digital name, their posts, and their commentary on many posts exhibits an awareness of the ways in which

---

7. This analysis could go even further by exploring the ways in which many digital citizens are thinking about the virtual world as a post-human future, transcending mortal life and the structures (like the contemporary state) that regulates it (see Geraci 2014).

8. For example, "When the voices tell you that you can't, remember that with Christ, you can," www.instagram.com/p/B0d2PnclqAf; "The longer we view ourselves through a distorted lens, the more likely we are to believe the distorted truth," www.instagram.com/p/B0bKtFelfae; "Mark 9:37," www.instagram.com/p/B0TcNZxjrho.

digital material—a new kind of material culture—dominates modern life. Thus the virtual world is now another imagined community that brings with it another world and digital identity, to which you also need the right material to belong (see, for example, Leung 2018). This digital identity, however, is contrasted with the physical body and with the soul. The Life.Church Instagram posts imply that we have a real life on earth and another, less real, virtual life online that is something to be escaped, overcome, or at least attenuated. In fact, senior pastor Craig Groeschel wrote a book, *#Struggles: Following Jesus in a Selfie-Centered World*, that builds on this theme of overcoming the online world. It is paradoxical for a digital church, indeed with its web address as its very name, to take this stance. Yet it is understandable, as the widespread conception of cyberspace as an intangible otherworld leads to superficial distinctions between physical, surrogate, and virtual. Even McVicar, citing recent research on the sovereign citizens movements, notes how many scholars also view "otherworldly" materials and identities as less "real" than the state-issued ones, despite the general consensus and ubiquity of Anderson's concept of imagined communities.[9] I think the construction of these hierarchies, demonstrated by both the sovereign citizens and the mainstream evangelical megachurch, is worthy of further exploration—what makes certain identities, or acts of identification, acceptable and normative? What causes these norms to shift?

Digital Citizenship in a Material World

McVicar's chapter examines citizenship as a material phenomenon, exploring the ways in which modern citizenship is comprised of a subject's ability to produce the right paperwork. The MSTA created national identification cards, sovereign citizens created license plates, and religious fundamentalists created baptismal certificates. In these examples, the material was not only a record but also an artifact meant for display. Showing the alternative identification card, for instance, was a symbolic performance of power meant to discredit the federal government's identifiers and reinforce a new identity. Indeed, McVicar notes how sometimes (though not often) these alternative citizenship materials caused confusion among local authorities and attracted the attention of the Bureau of Investigation. The materials had the weight to legitimize another identity—whether as citizens of another nation or sovereign American nationals. To what extent would the digitization of the paperwork and artifacts affect the "material production of citizenship"? For example, if something like identification cards were digitized, would they be available for display? Could one pull up the ID card on a phone? Given that so much record-keeping is now digital, to what extent can we analyze it as paperwork? On the one hand, digital records (like paper records) can have the same function of shaping our behaviors, memory, and narratives. Records prove that you have a life, or a narrative attached to you. But, if

---

9. McVicar notes, for example, Barkun (2013: 197).

the records aren't physically tangible, it might not have the performative ability that material records could have. Ultimately, McVicar points to the importance of documentation for identity formation. But, since documentation shapes identity, how much does the *material* itself have to do with this, and how much is about the *act* of documentation? Or the performance of displaying it? Or the narrative created when we do these things? Some people, for example, keep their old driver's licenses or ID cards from former schools and jobs as mementos. Those objects are more meaningful than a record of attendance stored in a database, for example. Materials are not created equal when it comes to making meaning for people. Researchers have been looking at the different effects of material versus digital in relation to books, photographs, and even advertisements, exploring how the digital alters society's relationship to memory.[10] Applying this to citizenship materials would not only be fruitful in further understanding the consequences of such a thorough material mediation of citizenship as it relates to national identity, but also to understanding the ways in which the performance of display is affected by digitizing our material artifacts.[11] Of course, this is not to say that digital artifacts are not displayed. Indeed, as we saw in the previous section, many people view the digital world created from all of our digital materials as an entirely other realm distinguishable from the "real," physical world.

As we have seen, the transfer of data (names, numbers, and even images) from paper to a digital file or database already includes a shift in the verification of citizenship, but the uses of digital technology go far beyond that. Using digital recognition tools, our actual bodies can (and have) become the material mediators of that citizenship. From microchips implanted underneath the skin to advanced technological biometric verification, the digital and the material are combined in an intimate way when our bodies are, literally, our IDs. Far beyond fingerprints, the technology now exists to recognize an individual based on unique identifiers like hand or earlobe geometry, retina and iris patterns, voice waves, DNA, facial patterns, and even body movement (including gait). The storage of this data (and the digitization of analog data) in databases makes for nearly immediate personal identification. Obviously, there are many ethical concerns, including privacy, conflicts with personal beliefs about biometric data collection, and the protection/(mis)use of the data. Not to mention that these scans can fail or be fooled.

Indeed, any study of the contemporary mediation of citizenship will have to address new technologies, just as studies of contemporary material culture will likely involve digital materials. However, while not underestimating the impact biometric identification will have on both the conception and verification of

---

10. Regarding books, see Baron (2015); regarding photos, see Hostetler and Green (2016); and regarding advertisements, see Dooley (2015).
11. Another aspect of the of the relationship between the digital and the material is the materiality of the hardware and software itself. Digital forensics is analogous to the activities of book historians and bibliographers working with manuscript/print who analyze the physical characteristics, handwriting styles and inks, printmaking, illustration, and bookbinding. For more on how digital materiality is captured in metadata, interfaces, and time-stamped information processing, see Shep (2016).

citizenship, our bodies are already texts that store ethnic, gender, religious, and even ideological information in interesting ways. McVicar's discussion of the MSTA and their adoption of an alternative "Moorish" identity in an attempt to subvert Jim Crow laws brings the implications of embodied identity to the fore. Of course, racial, religious, and national identity are not separate discourses. To take a contemporary example, Ilhan Omar, a congresswoman from Minnesota, further demonstrates the ways in which intersecting identities are written on bodies. Like many black and brown citizens, she has been told to return to another nation—another community—despite her American citizenship (Davis 2019). She is the first person in congress to wear a hijab, highlighting her religious/cultural affiliations. Even her political ideology gets mapped on to her body, as her (perceived) leftist political ideology is inseparable from her Blackness. Indeed, many have written about how racialized discourse is used to reinforce political projects of anti-communism or anti-socialism (see, for example, Woods 2003; Lewis 2004). For the MSTA and Omar, then, "religion" is not an isolated discourse, but one that speaks to race, birthplace, and nation. Ethnic, religious, and even ideological identities are already stored on our bodies, but the inseparability of these intersecting identities create unique experiences for people and, in the case of Omar, become central in conversations about American national identity. In other words, acts of identification are already a result of our interactions with the world with and through our bodies, and more consideration of intersecting identities are necessary in analyses of embodied identity.

Conclusion: Categorizing Difference

These examples of negotiating, legitimizing, or authorizing citizenships do not just "bring together" various aspects of identity (e.g., race, religion/culture, birthplace, nationality), they instead reveal their inextricable connectedness, highlighting the ways in which the state and others (e.g., scholars, and anyone in the business of constructing and using these categories) still tend to perpetuate a framework born of colonial definitions and analyses. As many scholars have now shown, religion is not a natural category, but is implicated in regimes of control and, as such, can play a role in the process of identity construction, creating (in some of the cases discussed in this chapter) national "others." In the sixteenth and seventeenth centuries, the state contributed to the creation of the modern liberal idea of religion as personal belief by situating (newly multiple) churches as the private counterpart to a single governing secular state. Mainstream protestant groups like Life.Church, even with their higher heavenly loyalty, can easily operate under this categorization. Groups that challenge national norms due to racial, ideological, or cultural difference attempt to challenge the state (who authorizes those norms) by creating otherworldly "nations." Every now and then, these groups will succeed in subverting the authority of the state, but their larger success comes in their contribution to changing normative understandings of the nation, of national identity, and of citizenship.

Considering McVicar's and my examples side by side emphasizes three issues in thinking about citizenship as a key category in the study of religion: first, analyzing each of the "alternative nations" together as part of a more expansive framework (as opposed to the "religious" versus "national/secular" binary) is necessary to understand what is going on in the creation of these alternative bureaucracies and materials. Second, material records and objects are fundamental to acts of identification, and the mediation of identities have, are, and will be further complicated by both digitization/the virtual world and by considering bodies as part of the material culture of citizenship. Finally, discourse on religion is often discourse on national identity, and vice versa. Looking not only at how these discourses overlap but also at the unique positions of groups and individuals with intersecting identities can reveal key conversations in which normative ideas of citizenship and national identity are continuously (re)constructed.

Lauren Horn Griffin is Assistant Professor in the Religious Studies Department at Louisiana State University. Her work focuses on religion, politics, media, and technology.

References

Anderson, Benedict. 1983. *Imagined Communities: Reflections On the Origin and Spread of Nationalism*. New York: Verso.

Barkun, Michael. 2013. *A Culture of Conspiracy: Apocalyptic Visions in Contemporary America*, 2nd edition. Comparative Studies in Religious and Society 15. Berkeley, CA: University of California Press.

Baron, Naomi S. 2015. *Words Onscreen: The Fate of Reading in a Digital World*. Oxford: Oxford University Press.

Davis, Julia Hirschfeld. 2019. "House Condemns Trump's Attach on Four Congresswomen as Racist." *The New York Times*, July 16. Retrieved from www.nytimes.com/2019/07/16/us/politics/trump-tweet-house-vote.html (accessed July 19, 2019).

Dooley, Roger. 2015. "Paper Beats Digital In Many Ways, According To Neuroscience." *Forbes Magazine*, September 16. Retrieved from www.forbes.com/sites/rogerdooley/2015/09/16/paper-vs-digital/#25d0cc6e33c3 (accessed July 29, 2019).

Flynn, Meagan. 2019. "U.S. Citizen Freed after Nearly a Month in Immigration Custody." *The Washington Post*, July 24. Retrieved from www.washingtonpost.com/nation/2019/07/23/francisco-erwin-galicia-ice-cpb-us-citizen-detained-texas/?utm_term=.bc0ddcc8fb60 (accessed July 26, 2019).

Geraci, Robert. 2014. *Virtually Sacred: Myth and Meaning in World of Warcraft and Second Life*. Oxford: Oxford University Press.

Hostetler, Lisa, and William Green. 2016. *A Matter of Memory: Photography as Object in the Digital Age*. Rochester, NY: George Eastman Museum.

Leung, Linda. 2018. *Technologies of Refuge and Displacement: Rethinking Digital Divides*. Lanham, MD: Lexington Books.

Lewis, George. 2004. *The White South and the Red Menace: Segregationists, Anticommunism, and Massive Resistance, 1945–1965*. Gainesville, FL: University of Florida Press.

Nongbri, Brent. 2013. *Before Religion: A History of a Modern Concept*. New Haven, CT: Yale University Press.

Pengelly, Martin. 2019. "'Go Back Home': Trump Aims Racist Attack at Ocasio-Cortez and Other Congresswomen." *The Guardian*. July 15. Retrieved from www.theguardian.com/us-news/2019/jul/14/trump-squad-tlaib-omar-pressley-ocasio-cortez (accessed July 19, 2019).

PRRI. 2011. "'Teavangelicals': Alignments and Tensions between the Tea Party and White Evangelical Protestants." Retrieved from www.prri.org/spotlight/fact-sheet-alignment-of-evangelical-and-tea-party-values (accessed Jun 23, 2019).

Shep, Syndey J. 2016. "Digital Materiality," In Susan Schreibman (ed.), *A New Companion to Digital Humanities*, 322–330. Chichester: John Wiley & Sons. https://doi.org/10.1002/9781118680605.ch22

Turner, Matthew Paul. 2015. "Homeschool Teen Can't Prove She's an American." *The Daily Beast*, February 14. Retrieved from www.thedailybeast.com/homeschool-teen-cant-prove-shes-an-american (accessed June 23, 2019).

Webb, C Travis. 2018. "'Otherworldly' States: Reimagining the Study of (Civil) 'Religion'." *Journal of the American Academy of Religion* 86(1): 62–93. https://doi.org/10.1093/jaarel/lfx040

Woods, Jeff. 2003. Black Struggle, Red Scare: Segregation and Anti-Communism in the South, 1948–1968. Baton Rouge, LA: LSU Press.

Young, Alexandra Leigh. 2016. "The Girl Who Doesn't Exist." *Radiolab*, WNYC Studios, August 29. Retrieved from www.wnycstudios.org/story/invisible-girl (accessed January 30, 2019).

Chapter 5

Paper Terrorism as Counter-Conduct

Michael J. McVicar

I must begin by expressing my deep appreciation to Tenzan Eaghll, Lauren Horn Griffin, and Daniel Miller for their thoughtful, smart, and all-too-kind engagement with my chapter.[1] Both in the form of their original, oral comments at the Denver meeting of NAASR, and now in these revised and expanded written contributions, they have forced me to think carefully about just what exactly I am trying to do with the concepts of *citizenship* and *religion* as they converge in the so-called sovereign citizen movement in the United States and elsewhere in the anglophone world. I am amazed—and humbled—by their ability to pull off such preceptive pieces and engaging contributions from the messy chapter I submitted to the conference program. At minimum, they have forced me to acknowledge how half-baked and inchoate the entire project is in its current form.

Next, and somewhat surprisingly, given the range of topics, geographies, and forms of citizenship discussed by each of the commenters, the contributions are largely consistent in homing in on a key concept that I mostly neglected to address in my original chapter: the nation-state. While I wrote about the state and its effects on creating and managing the raw bureaucratic material of citizenship; and, while I elliptically wrote about *nation* by referring to the Nationality Cards used by American Moors in the 1930s, I said next to nothing about the complex relationship between *nation*, state, religion, and citizenship. I would like to be able to claim that this oversight emerged from some deep theoretical or methodological consideration on my part, but it did not. I simply neglected the subject even as I wrote around it—blissfully ignorant of its centrality to the topics at hand. The result was an omission that I cannot quite fully address in this brief response, but I must acknowledge.

Eaghll's essay on the relationship between hyper-nationalist responses to the Rohingya crisis in Myanmar (Chapter 2, this volume) opens up this problem of the nation-state through his insistence on refusing to reduce that crisis to some

---

1. And, while I'm doing the whole acknowledgements thing, I should also thank Brad Stoddard for inviting me to present in the first place, and Rebekka King for shepherding this volume to publication. Also thanks to Jessica Radin who offered a response during the 2018 conference in Denver, but that could not be included in this volume. Finally, at FSU, Dan Wells, Taylor Dean, and the faculty and graduate students in the American Religious History track of the Religion Department offered feedback on an earlier version of my original chapter.

essentialized conflict between Muslims and Buddhists. Instead, as he points out, "what is really at stake... is the way that political communities include, exclude, and marginalize others." In this sense, boundary formation by a modern state such as Myanmar—or the United States for that matter—emerges at the juncture of military force, state-supportive media outlets, religious leaders' support for the use of violence, and long-established notions of sovereignty and territorial integrity that allow regimes to execute violent campaigns within their boundaries. For Eaghll, religion and the nation-state are intimately interconnected but neither one reducible to the other.

Unlike the monks from Eaghll's essay who refuse to imagine a Burmese nation with Rohingyas in it, Griffin (Chapter 4, this volume) describes how U.S. evangelicals associated with Life.Church aspire to a different form of heavenly citizenship in which they imagine themselves to be in the nation, but not of it. By harkening to this ancient tension in Christian political thinking Griffin's contribution encourages us to turn our attention to the *imaginative* work of citizenship in which some members of the U.S. body politic—especially white, predominately middle-class, status-quo-supportive evangelicals—have the material and spiritual luxury of "looking upward" toward a form of heavenly citizenship imagined within the context of a newly emerging digital culture. As Griffin notes, by "digitizing our material artifacts," we are likely to reshape not only the ways we document and perform citizenship in the future, but digitization will also open up ways of imagining new forms of citizenship and counter-citizenship. But, as Griffin concludes, no matter how digitized the bureaucratic materials of citizenship become in the twenty-first century, the materiality of the citizen's (or noncitizen's) body is likely to become even more significant "as part of the material culture of citizenship." As biometric data increasingly become intimately entwined with crossing borders, consumer activity, and gaining access to state-sponsored services, the body will become a contested site upon which states, corporations, and those individuals who resist the power of both will revise what it means to be a citizen and how such a status is imagined.

Miller's essay (Chapter 3, this volume), in many ways, synthesizes the themes of my chapter with the comments and criticisms of the other responders. Through his elegant exploration of the concept of sovereignty and its relationship to the nation-state, Miller crystalizes a point hinted at in Eaghll's, Griffin's, and my contributions. Namely, Miller succinctly observes, "'religion' was born with the modern state." Regardless of whether we are considering the legitimacy of Myanmar's claims regarding the "illegal" status of the Rohingya people or if we are pondering how white, middle-class evangelicals can insist on the un-political nature of their very politicized religion, Miller forces us to return the 1648 Peace of Westphalia. The treaty, which birthed the modern nation-state, also helped to create what we understand as "religion" today. As Miller makes clear, whatever "religion" is today, it is what it is because emerging European nation-states decided its shape, fixed its boundaries, tolerated it, and, when necessary, excluded it. Thus, "stateless Muslims" only become possible as a by-product of centuries of international agreements and disagreements between Southeast Asian states and their interface with Western colonialism. Likewise, American evangelicals who appeal to heavenly citizenship might envision some timeless, essential resonance with their ancient persecuted forerunners, but they make their current appeals within the context of a system of mostly bloodless "tolerance" shaped by the Westphalia compromise and the sort of multi-Christian pluralism it created.

Miller's comments pushed me back to the lectures by Michel Foucault on sovereignty and territory and their relationship to modern practices of governance. So, as I round up this response, I want to linger on Foucault for a moment and his reading of the significance of Westphalia to the practice of religion, nationality, and citizenship. In his later lectures on "governmentality" (or "governmental rationality," to avoid his jargon) from the late 1970s and early 1980s, Foucault resisted the idea then common in both left- and right-wing circles to argue that states inevitably expand by gobbling up techniques of power and governance as some inherent, timeless function of their nature. Furthermore, he also resisted attempts to develop a general theory of the state as such. Instead, according to Colin Gordon, Foucault thought the "nature of the institution of the state" is "a function of changes in practices of government" (Gordon 1991: 4). Foucault attempted to uncover the deep structure of modern government through his study of the "micro-physics of power" (Foucault 1995) in clinics, hospitals, barracks, prisons, libraries, and other "environments of enclosure" (Deleuze 1988: 60) in early modern Europe. He focused his attention on practices of government—that is, on strategies for conducting the conduct and structuring the behaviors, compartments, and ways of thinking of individuals and groups of individuals—rather than studying specific state institutions (see Foucault 2007: 190–226).

In his study of Western, early modern societies, he argued that a network of new practices emerged from the fusion of older forms of Christian pastoral governance—concerned primarily with the care and cultivation of an individual's soul—and the emergence of "a diplomatic-military technique" in the wake of the Treaty of Westphalia. At one poll stood the individualizing processes of the care and cultivation of individual selves; at the other, a totalizing system of sovereignty that subordinated and frequently demanded the sacrifice of individuals to the new territorial system of the nation-state. At the juncture of these two polls, the police emerged as a new system for governing populations through a network of practices that synthesized the individualizing features of the pastoral regime with the totalizing demands modern states made on these individual subjects. Through the police function, states could come to know their populations (and the populations of their rivals) and develop an endless proliferation of governing practices for administering and conducting the behavior of individual citizens. Through the fusion of the police powers of surveillance (counting, recording), institutional discipline (shaping conduct), and discourse (classifying, naming), a modern state could maximize its population and develop a new "governmental rationality" of biopolitics through which it could focus on the growth and development of its own population through territorial protection and expansion.

If government is, as Foucault defined it, the "conduct of conduct," then it conversely becomes possible to write counter histories that highlight the "revolts of conduct" or "counter-conducts" that offer alternative practices that resist the biopolitical prerogatives of modern nation-states (Foucault 2007: 200–202). Also, if "life" is the focus of the state, then individuals can begin, in the words of Gordon, "to formulate the needs and imperatives of that same life as the basis for political counter-demands. Biopolitics thus provides a prime instance of what Foucault calls here the 'strategic reversibility' of power relations, or the ways in which the terms of governmental practice can be turned around into focuses of resistance" (Gordon 1991: 5). In this sense, for the sovereign citizens I highlighted in my original essay, "counter-conduct" takes the form of insisting on one's ability to be a "citizen" outside of the contours of the Westphalian compromise. Sovereigns forefront pastoral practices as tools for resisting the diplomatic-military territorial modes developed in the wake of 1648. They are "living men [and women] on the land:" autonomous agents unbounded by the territorial constraints of the nation-state whose very political, social, and cultural identities are impossible to image without the existence of the very state from which they seek emancipation. By developing alternative practices of surveillance and rejecting the structure of the Westphalian nation-state, they reject citizenship as a product of state bureaucratic institutions—and they have all the homemade paperwork, licenses, and certificates necessary to prove it.

Michael J. McVicar is Associate Professor in the Department of Religion at Florida State University. He teaches classes on American religious history and is the author of *Christian Reconstruction: R. J. Rushdoony and American Religious Conservatism* (2015).

References

Deleuze, Gilles. 1988. *Foucault*. Translated by Seán Hand. Minneapolis, MN: University of Minnesota Press.
Foucault, Michel. 1995. *Discipline and Punish: The Birth of the Prison*, 2nd edition. Translated by Alan Sheridan. New York: Vintage Books.
Foucault, Michel. 2007. *Security, Territory, Population: Lectures at the Collège de France, 1977-78*. Edited by Michel Senellart, François Ewald, Alessandro Fontana, and Arnold I. Davidson. Translated by Graham Burchell. Lectures at the Collège de France. New York: Palgrave Macmillan.
Gordon, Colin. 1991. "Governmental Rationality: An Introduction." In *The Foucault Effect: Studies in Governmentality*. Edited by Graham Burchell, Colin Gordon, and Peter Miller. Chicago, IL: University of Chicago Press.

Part II

Race and Ethnicity

Chapter 6

Signifying "Der Rassist" in Religious Studies and the Axes of Social Difference

Richard Newton

> The important point is that those in such a school's subsequent generations are never characterized as merely doing derivative work and failing to think for themselves. Instead, we reverentially talk about such people's intellectual predecessors and identify their *Doktorvater*—saying it in German, as many English speakers whom I've met tend to do, makes this imprimatur and thus lineage seem all the more profound and thus legitimate (as does the Latin term imprimatur itself, no?).
> —Russell McCutcheon (2015: 136)

The task of constructing a history—let alone a history of religions—lends itself to the cultivation of tropes. These tropes are the familiar talking points that ease the labor of those working in a field of study. They are "a displacement of the facts onto the ground of literary fictions or, what amounts to the same thing, the projection onto the facts of the plot structure of one or another of the genres of literary figuration" (White 1987: 47). Tropes are the commonplaces, touchstones, and signposts that give subsequent students an opportunity to find their bearings within our field's vast intellectual terrain. In times of unsureness, they are the moments where we can find our footing in registering similarity and difference.

That distinction is paramount, for it is in that metric called comparison that we ultimately chart knowledge. In the juxtaposition of heretofore singular instances, the cunning scholar derives meaning befitting that auspicious and yet austere title, the "science of religion," *Religionwissenschaft*.[1] It is auspicious because of our modern genuflection to all things "scientific"; austere, on account of science's calibration toward the disprovable rather than the provable. In this our fieldwork is nothing more than degrees of observation. And so to a significant extent, strengthening our assertions depends on the finding of precedent until our own observations can *take precedent*.

As we, scholars of religion, pay attention to the plowlines, we would do well to ask whether we tread where those who came before had gone or venture to the places they did not or could not reach. It is a question that prompts us to

---

1. On this point, I commend Reinhard Pummer's (1972) exploration of the conflicting ways scholars have signified their specific intellectual branches and conceptions of the field with this sign.

acknowledge our dependence upon previous workers and their work, for how we narrate this intellectual heritage—its call and our response—makes a harrowing difference. At the very least, it distinguishes the *Doktorvaters* and *Doktomaters* that we effigiate from the ones we eulogize to subsequent generations (McCutcheon 2015: 136).

At its most honest, the history of religions is a chronicle of legacies and the sowing and reaping necessary to be remembered. This account of the academy is by no means unique to Religious Studies, and yet on this point Jorge Luis Borges might regard our field as a setting ripe for reflection. In *Three Versions of Judas* (1944), the Argentine writer entreats readers to a fantastic short story in the guise of an erudite, footnoted article about the life's work of Nils Runeberg. Runeberg, we are told, was an early-twentieth-century Swedish scholar whose work centered on the figure of Judas Iscariot.

Runeberg could not abide the simplistic plot device of the secret betrayer, reading it as unnecessary in light of Jesus's provocative, counter-cultural behavior. In his first book, *Kristus och Judas* (1904), he opined that Judas was motivated by obedience to God's cosmic plan rather than animus toward his teacher. God's plan preordained Judas's premeditated action so as to demand an equal and opposite reaction from Christ. Judas's sin required an ascetic piety equal to Christ's glorious sacrifice, making the one a Doppelgänger of the other. Runeberg developed this thesis further in the second edition of the book (1909), arguing that the burden of Judas's task—and its associated infamy—was more virtuous than the renown enjoyed by Jesus.

By this point Runeberg had failed to sway his colleagues away from convention at great risk to his own career. He wondered whether the majesty of God's incarnation was realized more in the rejection of Judas or in the orthodox exaltation of Christ. Runeberg then hazarded that the mystery of faith was not God becoming Jesus, but God becoming Judas, for the suffering servant must have been the figure of illest repute. Runeberg revealed his identity in a final book, *Den hemlige Frälsaren* (1909), "The Secret Savior."

At the start of Borges's essay, Nils Runeberg plays agent provocateur, inviting us into the heresy of daring to ask the unquestioned. But Runeberg dies a true believer, the faithful devotee whose piety gains him no renown (save for God's sake). His conclusions, thrice rejected by his colleagues, lead him out of academic discourse and into obscurity. Presumably his own mental probing caused a sudden aneurism, though history hinted to him his fate.

> He felt that ancient, divine curses were met in him ... Saul, whose eyes were blinded on the road to Damascus; the rabbi Simeon ben Azai, who saw the Garden and died; the famous wizard John of Viterbo, who went mad when the Trinity was revealed to him; the Midrashim, who abominate those who speak the *Shem Hamephorash*, the Secret Name of God. Was it not that dark sin that he, Runeberg, was guilty of?[2]
> (Borges 1998 [1944]: 167)

---

2. In my original manuscript, delivered at the 2018 annual meeting of the North American Association for the Study of Religion, I miswrote Andrew Hurley's English translation of Borges's

The nature of "the dark sin" presents a paradox. Is it to discover the undiscovered—the very name of God, as it were—or is it to challenge the presumed realities cultivated in the field?

From this integral question we can derive another view of the perimeter within which we work—the place where we "can read our titles clear." The British hymnist Isaac Watts wrote "When I Can Read My Title Clear" (1707) to triumphantly describe seeing "paradise." But its intonation in the Black Church music setting of "Doctor Watts" hymnody, popularized by Charles Dorsey and others, became a multivalent acknowledgment of what happens when the wrong body "doth protest too much."[3] Whatever we may say about "religion," it is nothing if not a regulated space of vying, where some are more free to dare than others.

I wager that the racial and ethnic dimension to religion's "dark sin" would not be lost on Borges. In the one story, we already see that the dark sin is not a matter of volition. It is the defeating inertia exuded from a social topography. Already in the one story Borges shows interest in the way humans determine the place, utility, and potential of other humans. On this he was wont to leave no stone unturned, providing a map of the racial terrain in an earlier 1941 short story called *The Garden of Forking Paths*.

The Garden of Forking Paths is a hypertextual tale set against the backdrop of World War I-era spy games. To be fair, a summary of the story on account of a single protagonist or antagonist would do a disservice to the literary experiment alluded to in its title. And it would undersell the rich execution of the author's employ of Doppelgänger, frame story, symbolism, and *in media res*. *The Garden* is a narrative labyrinth wherein one could begin at any number of plot points and presumably enjoy the same story. Cloak and dagger espionage and literary riddles infuse the story's agents with a postcolonial irony as whimsical as Oscar Wilde's *The Importance of Being Earnest* (1895) and as tragic as Erich Maria Remarque's *All Quiet on the Western Front* (1929).

Readers learn that in 1916, Captain Richard Madden—an Irish officer working for the British—had apprehended and killed Viktor Runeberg—a German spy. Runeberg's associate, Dr. Yu Tsun (a Chinese English teacher spying for Germany), had been on the phone with Runeberg, heard an altercation happening in German, and recognized Madden's voice—surmising that he would come for him next. In an effort to flee Madden and complete his mission of reporting

---

phrase, "*crimen oscuro*," as "dark skin" rather than "dark sin." Respondent Rudy Busto rightly pointed out my typographic error and challenged Hurley's translation of the Spanish phrase. I will leave the matter to Busto to discuss this in his published response. For now, I will say, in Borgesian fashion, that one might take my Freudian slip as a "forking path" to a reading of race present in the themes and details of the short story I discuss later, *The Garden of Forking Paths* (Borges 1998 [1941]). In this, race is the obscure crime for which those on the wrong side of the colorline are guilty on spec in the eyes of a culpable jury.

3. To hear an example of this hymn performed, listen to Rev. Lonnie Weaver "line-out" the celebratory dirge for antiphonal singing on the live album recording Take Me Back to the Old Landmark, available at www.youtube.com/watch?v=wVw_ncYU8wc. Read Current (1982) for further history about the wider Black Church music tradition of which this hymn is a part.

the location of a British artillery base, Tsun visited and killed Dr. Stephen Albert, a British missionary turned Sinologist who, Tsun learns, had solved a maddening riddle called "The Garden of Forking Paths," written by one of Tsun's ancestor. The family had wished the story to die with their ancestor, but it had been published by the estate's executor—"a Taoist or Buddhist monk." When Madden happened upon Tsun and Albert discussing the riddle, Tsun killed Albert, whose otherwise mysterious death was soon recorded in British newspapers. Meanwhile, Tsun was hung, but not before being deposed by a British court. Borges presents these events in the form of Tsun's affidavit, the dictation of which is missing the first two pages and accounts for most of Borges's *Garden*.

Borges's *Garden* also includes three other grafs. The first is an epigraph that introduces the near-complete affidavit with an editorial note calling into question the explanation given by military historian and World War I veteran Captain Liddell Hart regarding why British forces were delayed in their attack against Germany at the Serre-Montauban pass in France. In his *A History of the World War*, Hart maintained that "torrential rains" were to blame. The affidavit implies that Hart only told half the truth, for it was the rain of German bombs upon *Albert*, France that was to blame for the Allies's protracted advancements on the Western Front (otherwise recorded as a series of conflicts commonly called the "Battle of Albert"). The second graf is an editorial footnote to the affidavit that revealed, contra Tsun, that Viktor Runeberg was the alias of a Prussian spy named Hans Rabener who was shot for resisting arrest from Captain Madden. The third graf is the larger essay's address or dedication to Victoria Ocampo, an avant-garde Argentine writer and publisher whose literary magazine featured the works of Borges and others— arrogating Borges's *Garden* with that of Albert and Tsun's ancestor.

Like "religion," Borges theorizes "race" as a bounded, contentious, and determining space of human striving. The labyrinth that is *The Garden of Forking Paths* turns around at least two clear axes—which are in fact one and the same. The first is that the desired knowledge (that is, riddle) is shrouded in darkness. For instance, the "Battle of Albert" is never explicitly mentioned, though a reader familiar with European geography and history can extrapolate the central event from the epigraphic reference to "Serre-Montauban" and "the World War." As Dr. Albert explains to Dr. Tsun, "'To *always* omit one word, to employ awkward metaphors and obvious circumlocutions, is perhaps the most emphatic way of calling attention to that word'" (Borges 1998 [1941]: 126).

Second, the rising conflict results from a person of one race killing someone of another in an attempt to prove their allegiance to a colonizer—always resulting in a calamitous result. Tsun interpreted the Irish Madden as having to shake the shadow of British doubt, just as he was trying to placate his German "Leader." Tsun's raison d'être was the "sens[e] that the Leader looked down on the people of my race—the countless ancestors whose blood flows through my veins. I wanted to prove to him that a yellow man could save his armies" (Borges 1998 [1941]: 121). The Doppelgänger never see each other—but understand each other—because of their mutual situatedness in "darkness." This darkness was not simply about the ontology of their melanin (Anderson 1995), but "the imperative of running for life to a zone of discursive and ideological marronage ... [o]n account of forced place-ment in a zone of nonsubjectivity" (Wimbush 2011: 23). Madden was "obliged" to work relentlessly even though he could never be enough for his colonial overlords (Borges 1998 [1941]: 119). Tsun lived out his last day in spite of his endless cunning performance in the European theater (ibid.: 120). Thus, Borges describes both Tsun and Madden as "implacable" in their desire to read—and not be read— their titles clear.

Race—like gender, citizenship, or class— is shorthand for some of the authoritative and authorizing social forces that justify, as Frantz Fanon put it, "*comparaison,*" the constant preoccupation with self-assertion and the ego ideal," "the self-positioning or self-fixation [that] maintains a relationship of dependence on the collapse of the other," that which "build[s] its virility" upon "the ruins of [one's] entourage (Fanon 2008 [1952]: 185–186)." The dark sin is forgetting how little "the self" has to do with one's formation and confusing the novelty of content with the determinance of form. Is this trope not the heroic genius and grotesqueness of race (Anderson 1995: 120–131)?

To me, Borges's oeuvre is convincing enough to suggest that scholars of religion—particularly those who see themselves as part of the critical or "Copernican turn" toward theorizing—could have a lot to say about race (Newton 2017a: 461; King 2013). And indeed they have. Despite employment trends in our wider field, departments are reconstituting programs and resources to establish faculty lines committed to the study of race and religion. I myself have enjoyed now a number of gainful positions on account of institutional interest in subjects like "African American Religions" and most recently "Social Theory of Race and Religion in the U.S." I include this detail on account that, if historicized, betrays an acknowledgment of the exceptions and rules at play in the landscape of higher education.

My sense is that while viable, prescient Religious Studies programs have wagered the importance of discussing race in unprecedented ways, it is unclear what those discussions could and should entail. Is it the work of an area specialist? Is it the purview of the generalist who sees the forest for the trees? What are we to make of the often conjoined term "ethnicity" let alone the categories of "race" and "religion?" Truth be told, I fear that the prospect of critical work on religion and race too often confounds scholars like a Borgesian garden because we try—as best we can or know how—to leave unsignified the sign that is "race." For we know something of the dark truth that there is power in mystifying definition (Newton 2018).

I take Borges's work as an intimation that Religious Studies scholars have tools to contribute to the study of race, but the riddle requires us to come to terms with the legacy of race in the field. In this chapter, I return to models in the studies of race and religion that frequently fetishize rather than explain the making of human social difference. I then qualify and retrofit them to create a framework for charting how humans map desire upon bodies (i.e., "race") especially in relation to land (i.e., ethnicity). The chapter discusses how some of the nineteenth-century (and some would say obsolete) tools from our field can be effective in naming—that is, signifying—the axes by which humans mark social difference—particularly social actions, environments, and ideological orientations.

Race as Modern Riddle

Given our prior study of so-called axial social movements, I hypothesize that we can narrate some of the ways humans take precedent over others while qualifying and quantifying the cost-benefits associated with this body-language game. Despite the rise of Critical Race Theory or race consciousness, "race" persists as a modern riddle, in part because of the tempting gains that come with essentializing it. Much of the jargon now present in public discussions of racism obscure the social features that by which cultural critics have identified race at work.

Take for instance the designation "people of color," frequently abbreviated as POC in written form. Today the term is synonymous with non-white, but three decades ago, Donna Haraway argued that the coining of phrases such as "women of color" and "people of color" were not designed to champion "relativisms and pluralisms" but to produce what Chela Sandoval called an "oppositional consciousness," a rendering of identity premised on its composition of "contradictory locations and heterochronic calendars" (Haraway 1991 [1985]: 155–156). In fact, as a "self-consciously constructed space built solely on the basis of conscious coalition, of affinity, [and] of political kinship," these phrases arose as a mechanism for eschewing rhetorics of naturalist identification, of which I would count the latest in vogue phrase, "diverse persons." With each of these names, cultural critics have attempted to signal pervasive power dynamics—albeit through specific discursive circumstances (i.e., race, ethnicity, gender, and sexuality). But somewhere, these terms were elided into euphemisms for missing the mean quantum of Whiteness, whatever it may be.[4]

To be clear, I am not arguing for the jettison of identity politics, but a return to the savvy of signifiers like the Combahee River Collective, a Black Feminist and Lesbian Socialist collaborative that challenged the precedent taken by the presumably aracial Second-Wave Feminist movement (Combahee River Collective 2017 [1977]: 19). Because discourses of identity built upon being better than or for an other can justify oppressive acts done under the veil of ignorance, the Collective set out to conscientiously develop an identity politics attentive to its own self-interests by realizing and limiting them. Far from the objectivist claims of Ayn Rand or the myopia of subjectivity, this is a framework that considers the human propensity for stratification and dares to construct a limit on the self. In the words of their 1977 "Statement," "We reject pedestals, queenhood, and walking ten paces behind. To be recognized as human, levelly human, is enough" (ibid.). They rejected "biological determinism" as "a particularly dangerous and

---

4. "Whiteness" is a term that has been signified in a variety of ways, a history that has led to its allure, ephemerality, and connotation of power (Driscoll 2015). Foley (1999), Jacobson (2008), and Baker (2011) provide histories of the changing parameters of Whiteness within North America.

reactionary basis upon which to build a politic" (ibid.: 21). Among their other pronouncements, they suggested that all politics are identity politics and defined power as the extent to which the unnamed dictates the discourse of naming.

Theorizing about the ramifications of identity politics in this way requires an intersectional sensitivity attuned to the complex and compounding ways differences shape one's potential for being read as human. This is not the "intersectionality" of the headline-skimming, newsfeed scrolling pundit, but that of an astute observer of social struggle. Legal scholar and critical race theorist Kimberlé Williams Crenshaw posits that part of the reason why identity politics falls or resorts to oppressive actions is because of structures that occlude mechanisms of enforcement.

> The problem with identity politics is not that it fails to transcend difference, as some critics charge, but rather the opposite—that it frequently conflates or ignores intra group differences ... this elision of difference is problematic, fundamentally because the violence that many women experience is often shaped by other dimensions of their identities ... Moreover, ignoring differences within groups frequently contributes to tension among groups.
>
> (Crenshaw 1991: 1242)

Intersectionality is not simply a quality of the various identity markers one finds worthwhile, like the school boy errand of Stephen Dedalus recounting his place in the world for homework in Joyce's *A Portrait of an Artist as a Young Man*:

> Stephen Dedalus
> Class of Elements
> Clongowes Wood College
> Sallins
> County Kildare
> Ireland
> Europe
> The World
> The Universe
>
> That was in his writing: and Fleming one night for a cod had written on the opposite page:
>
> Stephen Dedalus is my name,
> Ireland is my nation.
> Clongowes is my dwelling place
> And heaven my expectation.
>
> (Joyce 1916: 11–12)

It is signifying the exponential rather than arithmetic costs and benefits accrued from deriving value from the integral of difference.

One need not identify with the ends of Haraway, the Combahee River Collective, or Crenshaw to appreciate their significations on race. After all, when compared, they disagree on the significance of the discourse itself. But their work is an admission—if not, concurrence—of the disorienting nature of theorizing about race. What I find commendable is that they still commit to mapping the axes of social difference that it represents. And whereas Borges imagined the scholar of religion as having something worthwhile to say about human conditioning, I think a riddling silence on social difference is taking precedence in our field.

Signifying Theory and Excess in Society

The field of Religious Studies is in a moment in which neither budding nor seasoned scholar need to search for precedent in order to bandy oneself as "theorist." In fact, the importance—and even self-importance—of theory has taken precedent to the extent that one can find no shortage of applications of the term. In a "time of excess," the question is no longer whether one is a theorist but the right kind of theorist (Hughes 2017: 2; Hermann 2018: 8–9). This need to align oneself with job ads and department goals and guild partisanry is what leads Michael J. Altman to opine that, "It's hard out here for a theorist" (Altman 2017: 32). Altman's declaration suggests that there is a social complexity behind the glitz of the title worthy of exploration. One way of further exploring these complexities is to signify the wordplay further.

In the tradition of African American thought, "signifying" or "signifyin'" plays with the boundaries of a discursive form by bending a literal expression to speak about the context and assumptions that give it shape. It is to watch how, as anthropologist Zora Neale Hurston did of Eatonville, Florida's "Negro" population (Hurston 1942: 11), people can "hit a straight lick with a crooked stick," or Susan E. Meisenhelder elaborates in her study of Hurston, "assess power relations" from those who had to learn "when to fight and when to negotiate or dissemble, when to specify and when to signify, when to be a 'tiger' and when to be a trickster" (Meisenhelder 1999: 143).

So were we to continue the wordplay begun by Altman's allusion to the Three 6 Mafia and Cedric Coleman's 2005 rap lyric and song title, "It's hard out here for a pimp," we could more deftly redescribe the social politics of theorizing in the field of Religious Studies. In the domain of the song, the referent sign of "pimp," as a figure of repute who sexually exploits the bodies of others for economic gain, is also revered in light of the prestige that comes with power over others—whether demonstrated physically (e.g., "the pimp hand" used to regulate the behavior of his prostitute) or economically (e.g., the "bling" or other capital used to showcase his status over poorer persons in a shared scenario). And while I shudder to think anyone would want to extend the comparison to this length, does it not reveal a critical reality, regardless of our willingness to face it? Among the most convenient ways for a theorist to present their bona fides is through their dejecting of another theorist.

For those more familiar with the argot of so-called "classical" rhetoric, the *ad hominem* attack, is a serviceable example. At some point, a critique becomes so conventional that it pierces through an already torn argument and into the strawperson thought to hold it.[5] We only care to repent of this dark sin when we acknowledge that the holder is akin to us. One would think that recognizing someone like ourselves would be easy enough, but to quote the musical lyricist Ira Gershwin's own signifyin', "It ain't necessarily so." I maintain that the critical turn in Religious Studies has yet to complete a revolution toward the self-aware or self-reflective critique frequently decried as navel-gazing (Newton 2017b: 37). On the issue of race, the field appears satisfied with distancing ourselves 180 degrees from unsavory pasts, unfavorable rhetorics, and unseemly totems.

In terms of theorizing in Religious Studies, it is far more convenient to say "das racist" of an other's theory or to signify a theorist as "der Rassist" in our intellectual heritage than it is to recognize (1) that our difference is probably less than we may be ready to acknowledge and (2) that such figures might have said something by way of explanation (i.e., as useful commentary) or description (i.e., as data for our further study) to help us map social difference. On this point I appreciate Richard King's poignant synopsis of one such debate in the field:

> To what extent, such diverse thinkers ask, is the modern liberal acceptance of the constructed nature of cultures built upon a much older legacy of historicist thought that derives from the European Enlightenment and its critique of tradition, and which, in the field of the study of religions has been most strongly expressed in terms of naturalistic accounts of religion (European thinkers such as Hume, Kant, Nietzsche, Feuerbach, Marx and Freud)? To what extent do "secularist" accounts of religion offer an account that is unfairly "reductive" of the object of study (in this case the reputed object "religion")? An earlier rendition of such concerns about the implications of "naturalist reductionism" precipitated the rise of the phenomenological approach to the study of religion which gained prominence in the late twentieth century (under the leadership in North America of figures such as Joachim Wach and Mircea Eliade) and in institutional terms helped

---

5. Rather than thinking about *ad hominem* in terms of volition, the Combahee River Collective might have us read the *Journal of the American Academy of Religion* as a domain that benefits off the impasse of contentious signs. For example, see the debate over the concept of "justice" between which Kavka and McCutcheon (2017) and Esack and Mahomed (2017). On one level it is an exchange over how a sign such as "justice" should be signified in scholarship (the former, as an object of study rigorously interrogated; the latter, a telos to be painstakingly perfected); on another, the parameters of Religious Studies and the laborers in the field of religion. I would not characterize the conversation as resorting to *ad* hominem, however were the exchange to continue further in the volume, one could likely read where contributors understood themselves to be misread and even attacked by the other side. My interest here, however, is not to the authors but to the journal as a document of ambivalence. Who ultimately benefits from the contest over amorphous terms? If the debate over our field's operational terms does not matter that much, how do we appraise our work, those who come before us, and those who come after us? Put differently, what would we make of the Religious Studies scholar were we to read the *Journal of the American Academy of Religion* as "a Garden of Forking Paths" or a Gospel of Judas? The Combahee River Collective's affirmation of the value of limits might be a way forward and the tragic body count in Borges's work, a cautionary tale. My sense is that there is much to learn by reading through the field's "darkness" (cf. Wimbush) to consider the crises being faced (or not faced, as the case may be).

spawn the rise of autonomous "Religious Studies" departments in the US and UK in the late 1960s and early 1970s.

(King 2013: 139)

In this short summary, I see a reminder of how the progenitors of many social theorists are connected to a particularist cultural paradigm—that is, the European Enlightenment—and that anti-reductionists as well could be understood as laboring toward a more ethnological (or perhaps "inclusive"), multicultural data set so far as the postulated phenomena in question is globally accessible. Given my own work in the area of social theory, my point is not to advocate a particularist "whataboutism" except to say that the discourses in which our interlocutors are engaged are more complicated than we often want to acknowledge.

However, today's scholars of religion, King goes on to write, either "will place themselves (or be placed by their academic peers and readers)," somewhere between these two concerns (King 2013: 139). My concern is that it has become a chore to do so with precision to too many and that we are too often satisfied with signifying our own virtues at the expense of the merits of an argument or the people arguing them. When this is the case, we scholars have replicated the very politics we might otherwise abhor, but more importantly, have become (or more clearly become) exemplars of the social dynamics that we want to explain. And the latter is only of issue in proportion to the extent that we have become disciplined to accept that state as given rather than curious.

Take for instance the popular concept of cultural appropriation. In recent years, it has become a choice phrase for naming the use of a subaltern group's expressions by representatives of a more powerful group in a manner disapproved or disavowed by members of the subaltern group. Religious Studies scholars are likely no stranger to the proliferation of "yoga" or "meditation" in the "West" and the chasm between everyday contemporary practice and ancient origins.[6] Instances like these are where one might hear "cultural appropriation" invoked.

I am not sure that racism is best imagined in terms of proximity to a set of actions, where one's distance from the epicenter determines whether one is guilty, guilty by association, or innocent. Analytically, I am more intrigued in the way racism is the map, the rule, and the law in a cultural space. What I am calling for here is an investigation into the social conditions and productions that a group uses to signify culture—theirs and others—and the boundaries of propriety—which I have argued elsewhere is rootinized and routinized—as significant (Newton 2018 [2013]). In Michel de Certeau's terms, the scholar of Religious Studies is expert in observing many of the ways so-called enlightened and revolutionary groups signify, that activity "that transforms nature by inscribing itself on it." And we are witnesses, signatories, and even co-signers of "that scriptural project" that "produce[s] *a new history (refaire l'histoire)* on the model of what it fabricates (and this will be 'progress')" (de Certeau 1988 [1984]: 135).

---

6. See Jain (2014) for alternative explanations regarding the politics of orientalism and appropriation as it pertains to yoga.

Though he and I arrive at this conclusion via different paths, I agree with Malory Nye's conclusion in "Race and Religion: Postcolonial Formations of Power and Whiteness":

> Thus, in the end it is not really a matter of determining whether religion is (or is not) different from race, but rather how the categories are distinguished as different, as though the distinction matters. This can be distinguished in terms of creed and skin, belief and attributes, or traditions and geographies. The differences themselves are not the causes of the distinction, they are the means by which the distinctions are policed and enforced. Racialization does particular political work, and so does "religionization", by attributing difference or similarity on the basis of the category of religion.
>
> (Nye 2019: 232)

But where I believe Nye is moving on to greener pastures in the theorizing of religion and race, I am inclined to continue with an askew view toward the recesses of the "scholar's study" (Smith 1982: xi), for I think there may still be lessons to learn in the sketchy "workrooms" we have abandoned (ibid.: 44).

Like Yu Tsun fleeing Captain Madden, we can critique "der Rassist" and the social formations by which we trace his constitution. But how long is it before we realize that for all our progressive "words and things" (cf. Foucault's *Les mots et les choses*, published in English as *The Order of Things* 1994 [1966]), for all our best intents and purposes, we may have more in common with "die Rassisten" than the resistance in so far as we are subject to the dizzying garden of historical tropes by which we construct our comparisons? Just as American anthropologists must reckon with a heritage of CIA collusion (Price 2016) or American psychologists assisting with "enhanced interrogators" in the War on Terror in the Middle East (Marks 2018), is "der Rassist" not the name of the albatross or scarlet letter worn around the necks of those tilling the field of *Religionwissenschaft*? I take Borges's Nils Runeberg as a lesson for us, that we might dare to continue along the arc of critical reflection toward a picture that better reveals, better names, better maps the work of race—even if its radical gleanings bring to trial our *vitae*.

Revisiting Old Maps

Religious Studies is nothing if not a disciplined commitment to chart the cultural cartography taking precedent over territories such as land and bodies—nay, our views of lands and bodies.[7] As Mark Quentin Gardiner and Steven Engler clarify

---

7. My interest in bodies and lands is a part of a move away from "culture" as a fixed, static entity and toward a study of delineating processes of identification. To quote Kamala Visweswaran's work in *Un/Common Cultures: Racism and the Rearticulation of Cultural Difference*: "Culture is thus not something merely acted upon by globalization, nor is it primarily a bounded set of social interactions constituting social space. Culture as it travels through, but also shapes the world system, is about tracking shifting logics through of culturalist explanation across and within multiple sites of circulation that destabilize the distinction between life world and analytic

(2011: 11), "the map is not a representation of reality but a guide to research." It is a record of prior observations that have one time taken precedent as a product of social relationships. And on this, maybe we can use the furled maps of our predecessors, discarded somewhere in the recesses of our study. Having just signified on Jonathan Z. Smith's well known *bon mots*, we might do better to imagine how much he gleaned from finding the scores on which Frazer's *The Golden Bough* was wanting (Smith 1973). Do we not owe it to them—our past and future selves—to ask precisely where lies the fork in the questions we ask and the lesson we can harvest before we cry folly?

As much as we in the field of Religious Studies may decry the ethnological amnesia regarding the Americas, Africa, and the "indigenous" populations the world over (Tsonis 2012, 2016), Jaspers's epochal narrative was also highly critical of the Third Reich and Germans' acceptance of that calendaring (Clark 2002).[8] While Friedrich Max Müller's *Sacred Books of the East* did not exactly decenter Eurocentric philological or historical concerns, it reflected at least a utilitatrian awareness of "enlightenment" beyond the West (Masuzawa 2005). Perhaps Tiele's read of certain "religions" as having transcended ethnic boundaries appears too naturally selective, specifically since it assumes those religions to be discrete phenomenon (i.e., traditions) in contrast to the supposedly looser social configurations bound by tribalism (Molendijk 1999: 242). But at least the idea of a "world religion" as a social aim would not be unwelcome in those fond of the Frankfurt School's ideals, especially in justice-oriented interpretations of their work. All of this to say, to reject these or any other figures as Judas without realizing how they are Jesus for another cause is to leave unnamed and unmapped the axes of social difference humans use to draw power.[9]

---

system" (Visweswaran 2010: 8). Given the variety of ways race and ethnicity have been constituted (Sussman 2016), I appreciate Visweswaran's call for "an affiliative interdisciplinarity" whose focus would be not on ethnic studies versus area studies, but "the potential to read cultural displacements, transpositions, and reversals between community and the state, and between disciplines" (Visweswaran 2010: 14). I see the mutuality and divergences of studies on race (as a focus on signifying the body's ability to claim, among other things, land) and ethnicity (as centering an anthropology upon land claims) as part and parcel of this work. As I will discuss, the critical thrust of social theory in Religious Studies is primed to intervene.

8. From what I gather, Jack Tsonis's work argues that "the Axial Age narrative reproduces stereotypes about the intellectual and moral capacities of colonized people" (Tsonis 2016). He calls for the complete rejection of the Axial Age framework by critical scholars of religion. Tsonis's work on this history is much needed in the field, and I look forward to reading more as it is published. What I hope is clear in my narration of the study of religion and race is not a disagreement, but a laboring of the point that to not speak about the Axial Age out of rote is to overlook a historical trope that we may have not yet escaped and a piece of data that can prompt us toward sharper critical reflection on social difference.

9. For examples of different yet related ways of signifying on religion, see Brent Nongbri's work on the historicity of the term "religion" in the so-called classical "West" (Nongbri 2013) and David Chidester's reading of "religion" as colonial classification in Southern Africa (Chidester 1996).

My point is that the question of race is one where these Religious Studies tropes such as the Axial Age, the World Religions Paradigm, and the study of scriptures (also known as Sacred Texts and Great Books) can assist us not in signifying the territories of land and bodies, but the maps that have sought do so in an effort to construct and demarcate social difference. To adopt this signifying worldview regarding race is to open oneself up to the historiographic irony that it is in retracing the faux pas of our disciplinary predecessors, and not simply our intellectual heroes' journeys, that we have the most to learn.

Sociologist Stephen Sharot models a way forward (or rather, back) in his framing of the Axial Age (Sharot 2001). For Sharot, the concept's takeaway is its observation of pivotal social actions that shape authorizing and authoritative views of the world. His emphasis is not so much on when religion began but on observing the "social actions" effective for forcing and reinforcing the direction of groups (ibid.: 4). His analysis counterposes two types of action—change and maintenance—each distinguished further in terms of the theater of discourse (understood emically): "transformative" change and "nomic" maintenance versus "thaumaturgical" change and "extrinsic" maintenance. Sharot's synthesis of Durkheim (i.e., nomic), Marx (i.e., extrinsic), and Weber (i.e., transformative/thaumaturgical) presents an analytical framework for redescribing "patterns" of behavior on comparative terms (ibid.).

These patterns take place in three observable "environments." Sharot argues that social actions effect a group's values, organization, and socioeconomic and political concerns. And all of these significations are informed by ideological orientations characterized as rationalization or disenchantment; concerns for transcendence or the supramundane; and most notably, universalization (Sharot 2001: 8-9). Sharot attempts to hold in analytical tension the diversity of discourses and the social boundaries in flux.

In his ethnological study of "religious action in the world religions," he focuses on the volatile power dynamics between the stratification of persons, which he delineates as elites (both virtuosi and hierocrats) and the popular masses. Perhaps his greatest contribution to sharpening the Axial Age conversation is that rejection of the complexity thesis, that is, the idea that elites of a community practice a pure, complex form of religious action that is diffused into syncretic, simpler, and often passive concessions on the part of the popular class. In regard to economic archetypes—or tropes, as I prefer—he writes, "the extent to which the religion of the elites and the religion of peasants overlap, differ, and conflict, and the extent to which these dimensions vary from society to society, are subject to empirical investigation, comparisons, and explanations" (Sharot 2001: 14). The scholar's task becomes narrating the levels of complexity at work in a historical moment (ibid.: 19).

Religious Studies theorists who have read Sharot's work will probably have no problem finding points of contention. Grand histories (or sociology) are fodder for any number of specialist critiques. Sharot readily responds to Timothy Fitzgerald's critique of the World Religions Paradigm, agreeing "that a world religion is not an abstraction contained in its texts or an essential entity that is only contingently associated with particular social group" (Sharot 2001: 10). Nevertheless, he insists, for instance, that the difference between "a societal-bound religion" and a "world religion" is not that the world religion is an empirical object of study that transcends social groups but rather that group carriers of a world religion espouse a tradition that they claim is available to people who belong to societies and cultures other than their own" (ibid.). While I suspect that I am not alone in finding this response wanting (Cotter and Robertson 2016: 1–20), I think Sharot's rejoinder has analytical use when the sign "carriers" is subordinate to the signification that is espousal, or as said previously, when we examine the social configurations where people are so bold or unassuming as to take precedence over and above and underneath some other.[10]

After all Sharot acknowledges Religious Studies scholars' dismissal of much of this vocabulary given its fraught history of valorizing or essentializing "world religions," but the sociologist is also quick to reiterate that his focus is on the social features that foster domination rather than the actual rightness or morality of a group (Sharot 2001: 7). In studying the interactions between the cast of actors, one can note appeals to orthodoxy and authenticity—that is to say, the claim to being exemplars of the "great," whole, or essence of a group in contrast to a "little" variety, sect or denomination. Relatedly, Sharot gives heed to popular negotiations or unofficial practices that elites tolerate for the sake of social cohesion. All of this—the social action, the environments, and the orientations—he constitutes as the site of culture formation. I am not sure whether such an argument can help us enumerate how groups left Plato's cave, entered enlightenment, and found religion. But it gives us clues as to how people convince others they are in the dark.

Traditionally, the study of religion has done the former by ranking the sophistication and literacy of groups. And for Sharot, this is understandable given that "the development of literacy was integrally linked to the spread of world religions; in contrast with nonliterate religions, whose boundaries are identical with the boundaries of the societies in which they are embedded, the written word can be said to have created and defined boundaries of literate religions" (Sharot 2001: 16). But this is all the more reason for us to be careful in not confusing maps for territory.

Sharot's project spurs my attention toward the myriad ways groups bureaucratize and restrict those charisms like literacy that are used to define difference. So where he rightly acknowledges literacy as "an important locus of inequality in agrarian societies," we should remember that the impact and complexity of canonical engagement in less bureaucratized or non-literate societies should not

---

10. Bruce Lincoln's distinction between maximalist and minimalist discourses is a more promising Weberian dialectic than the notion of great and little except to reiterate the axial presumption being made (i.e. Sharot's "change") or reinforced (i.e. Sharot's "maintenance") in a historical moment (Lincoln 2006: 58–59). In light of Sharot's interest in "the ends, means, and conditions" of social actions (Sharot 2001: 21), Lincoln's heuristic on the intended extent of discursive claims avoids a scenario of explanatory *post hoc ergo propter hoc*.

surprise us (lest we be like the various *authorities* in Borges's *Garden*). Like J. Z. Smith in his redescription of canons as cultural productions, we would do well to pay heed to "the necessary concomitant of exegetical ingenuity which ought to prevent our applying terms such as 'closed,' 'static,' or 'cool,' to societies which possess canons—even those we classify as non-literate" (Smith 1982: 44). I agree with Sharot that "the written word can be said to have created and defined the boundaries of literate religions" (Sharot 2001: 16). However, "the process of arbitrary limitation and of overcoming limitation through ingenuity recurs" regardless of the signs used (Smith 1982: 50).

For scholars of religion, the distinction frees us to both avoid repeating the mistake of measuring sophistication in zero-sum terms (i.e., civilization v. primitivity) while daring us to present redescriptions attuned to the creativity groups use in their exploits of signification, especially human differentiation. So Jared Diamond's daring historical explanation aside, the power of social difference is not just identifying who has "guns, germs, and steel" (Diamond 1977). It is, as the historian of religion Charles H. Long examined of African Americans and others, the ambi-valent, transcendent, and transgressive signification of signs through which we come to know our "historical beginnings" and are reminded of our "involuntary presence" often against the backdrop of some place (Long 1999 [1986]: 190). There we will see people reading—and being read—their titles clear. And it is between those coordinates that the scholar's work is to be done.

Conclusion

The study of religion is an exercise in comparison, but it does not have to be one in Fanon's *comparaison*. As we look forward for what is next in the study of religion and race, I hope we can side step the trope of asserting that "race" does not historically exist in this or that data domain. In signifying *Der Rassist*, I hope to have pivoted our inquiry toward how social difference is configured within a framework of social actions, environments, and ideologies. Who is so bold as to impress their reading of the terrain upon others? And what are the processes by which shared perspectives become map legends, master texts, and cultural canons? *Religionwissenschaft* has something to say not because it has always given a straight account of human history, but because historically its laborers are not in the dark on how to hit a straight lick with a crooked stick. It is all we have ever done.

We know that race does not exist at the level of essence but discourse. It is a categorization of similarity and difference, inflected through any number of signs—though I have focused here on bodies and lands as two noteworthy sites for of observation. Thinking with Sharot, we are prepared to watch for social actions—significations—that result in change and maintenance. These dynamics are at play in personal evaluation, the varied level of community organization, and the socio-politics and economics of a broader system. And Sharot's work helps us highlight some of the tensions of signification. The need to make intelligible (i.e., rationalization/disenchantment) cultural assumptions is tempered by appeals to abstraction (i.e., notions of transcendence/supramundane). And in efforts of expansion—even, universalization—we see conspicuous significations, not only in the form of literacy, but in renderings of all manner of signs, including people. Race is a symbol system.

Again, one need not subscribe to Axial Age histories, sign off on the World Religions Paradigm, or devote study to the philological complexity of civilizations to find utility in Sharot's work. In fact, it is at this fork where my own interests in race and ethnicity diverge. For I think in examining the allegiances and negotiations between elites and the popular folk, maximalist and minimalist claims, and official prescriptions and tolerated variations, the question of human origins becomes moot. What is at stake in these formations are the very terms by which people are signified as at home, out of place, and even members of the human race.

What more might we say about religion and race? Quite a bit, I hope. For now, I will proffer that the meaning of such work will yield in proportion to our willingness to reckon with the visage and vestiges of *Der Rassist aus der Religionwissenschaft*. Borges, in his own signifyin' way, maps a path for us to learn a valuable lesson from those who came before us in the field: to remain complacently riddled by religion and race is a luxury some cannot afford.

Richard Newton is Assistant Professor of Religious Studies at the University of Alabama, where he serves as Undergraduate Director in the Department of Religious Studies. Newton's research focuses on scriptures as sites of identity formation, the politics of comparison, and the legacy of the New Testament. He is the author of *Identifying Roots: Alex Haley and the Anthropology of Scriptures* (Equinox 2020), Editor of the *Bulletin for the Study of Religion*, and founding curator of the social media professional development network, Sowing the Seed: Fruitful Conversations in Religion, Culture, and Teaching (SowingTheSeed.org).

References

Altman, Michael J. 2017. "It's Hard Out There for a Theorist." In Aaron W. Hughes (ed.), *Theory in a Time of Excess: Beyond Reflection and Explanation in Religious Studies Scholarship*, 32–36. Sheffield: Equinox.

Anderson, Victor. 1995. *Beyond Ontological Blackness: An Essay on African American Religious and Cultural Criticism*. New York: Continuum.

Baker, Kelly J. 2011. *Gospel According to the Klan: The KKK's Appeal to Protestant America, 1915-1930*. Lawrence, KS: University Press of Kansas.

Borges, Jorge Luis. 1998 [1941]. "The Garden of Forking Paths." In Jorge Luis Borges, *Collected Fictions*, trans. Andrew Hurley, 119–128. New York: Penguin Books.

Borges, Jorge Luis. 1998 [1944]. "Three Versions of Judas." In Jorge Luis Borges, *Collected Fictions*, trans. Andrew Hurley, 163–167. New York: Penguin Books.

Chidester, David. 1996. *Savage Systems: Colonialism and Comparative Religion in Southern Africa*. Charlottesville, VA: University of Virginia Press.

Clark, Mark W. 2002. "A Prophet without Honour: Karl Jaspers in Germany, 1945–48." *Journal of Contemporary History* 37(2): 197–222. https://doi.org/10.1177/00220094020370020301.

Combahee River Collective. 2017 [1977]. "The Combahee River Collective Statement." In Keeanga-Yamahtta Taylor (ed.), *How We Get Free: Black Feminism and the Combahee River Collective*, 15–27. Chicago, IL: Haymarket Books.
Cotter, Christopher R., and David G. Robertson. 2016. "The World Religions in Contemporary Religious Studies," In Christopher R. Cotter and David G. Robertson (eds), *After World Religions: Reconstructing Religious Studies*, 1–20. New York: Routledge.
Crenshaw, Kimberle. 1991. "Mapping the Margins: Intersectionality, Identity Politics, and Violence against Women of Color." *Stanford Law Review* 43(6): 1241–1299. https://doi.org/10.2307/1229039
Current, Gloster B. 1982. "'Precious Lord Take My Hand' ... Black Church Music—How Sweet It Sounds," November 22. *The Crisis* 89(9). 422–429.
De Certeau, Michel. 1988 [1984]. *The Practice of Everyday Life*. Trans. Steven F. Rendall. Berkeley, CA: University of California Press.
Diamond, Jared. 1977. *Guns, Germs, and Steel: The Fates of Human Societies*. New York: W. W. Norton.
Driscoll, Christopher M. 2015. *White Lies: Race and Uncertainty in the Twilight of American Religion*. New York: Routledge.
Esack, Farid, and Nadeem Mahomed. 2017. "A Rejoinder to 'Justice, That Fraught Idea,' by Martin Kavka and Russell McCutcheon." *Journal of the American Academy of Religion* 85(1): 255–260.
Fanon, Frantz. 2008 [1952]. *Black Skin, White Masks*. Trans. Richard Philcox. New York: Grove Press.
Fitzgerald, Timothy. 1997. "A Critique of 'Religion' as a Cross-Cultural Category," *Method and Theory in the Study of Religion* 9(2): 91–110. https://doi.org/10.1163/157006897X00070
Foley, Neil. 1999. *The White Scourge: Mexicans, Blacks, and Poor Whites in Texas Cotton Culture*. Berkeley, CA: University of California Press.
Foucault, Michel. 1994 [1966]. *The Order of Things: An Archaeology of the Human Sciences*. New York: Vintage Books.
Gardiner, Mark Quentin, and Steven Engler. 2010. "Charting the Map Metaphor in Theories of Religion," *Religion* 40(1): 1–13. https://doi.org/10.1016/j.religion.2009.08.010
Haraway, Donna. 1991 [1985]. "A Cyborg Manifesto: Science, Technology, and Socialist-Feminism in the Late Twentieth Century," In Donna Haraway, *Simians, Cyborgs and Women: The Reinvention of Nature*, 149–181. New York: Routledge.
Hermann, Adrian. 2018. "A Call for Permissable Plurality Within Theory-Building in a Time of Excess," *Method and Theory in the Study of Religion* 30: 487–497. https://doi.org/10.1163/15700682-12341442
Hughes, Aaron W. 2017. "Introduction: Theory in a Time of Excess," In Aaron W. Hughes (ed.), *Theory in a Time of Excess: Beyond Reflection and Explanation in Religious Studies Scholarship*, 1–12. Sheffield: Equinox.
Hurston, Zora Neale. 1942. *Dust Tracks on a Road: An Autobiography*. Philadelphia, PA: Lippincott.
Jacobson, Matthew Frye. 2008. *Roots Too: White Ethnic Revival in Post-Civil Rights America*. Cambridge, MA: Harvard University Press.
Jain, Andrea. 2014. "Who is to Say Modern Yoga Practitioners Have it All Wrong?: On Hindu Origins and Yogaphobia, *Journal of the American Academy of Religion* 82(2): 427–471. https://doi.org/10.1093/jaarel/lft099
Joyce, James. 1916. *A Portrait of the Artist as a Young Man*. New York: Huebsch.
Kavka, Martin, and Russell T. McCutcheon. 2017. "Justice, That Fraught Idea: A Response to "The Normal and Abnormal," *Journal of the American Academy of Religion* 85(1): 244–254. https://doi.org/10.1093/jaarel/lfw085

King, Richard. 2013. "The Copernican Turn in the Study of Religion," *Method and Theory in the Study of Religion* 25: 137–159. https://doi.org/10.1163/15700682-12341280

Lincoln, Bruce. 1999. *Theorizing Myth: Narrative, Ideology, and Scholarship*. Chicago, IL: University of Chicago Press.

Lincoln, Bruce. 2006. *Holy Terrors: Thinking About Religion After September 11*, 2nd Edition. Chicago, IL: University of Chicago Press.

Long, Charles H. 1999 [1986]. *Significations: Signs, Symbols, and Images in the Interpretation of Religion*. Aurora, CO: The Davies Group.

Marks, David F. 2018. American Psychologists, the Central Intelligence Agency, and Enhanced Interrogation: *Health Psychology Open* 2018: 1–2.

Mahomed, Nadeem, and Farid Esack. 2017. "The Normal and Abnormal: On the Politics of Being Muslim and Relating to Same-Sex Sexuality." *Journal of the American Academy of Religion* 85(1): 224–243.

Masuzawa, Tomoko. 2005. *The Invention of World Religions: Or, How European Universalism was Preserved in the Language of Pluralism*. Chicago, IL: University of Chicago Press.

McCutcheon, Russell T. 2015. "Orthodoxies in the Field of Production," *Religion and Theology* 25: 133–152. https://doi.org/10.1163/15743012-02201006

Meisenhelder, Susan E. 1999. *Hitting a Straight Lick with a Crooked Stick: Race and Gender in the Work of Zora Neale Hurston*. Tuscaloosa, AL: University of Alabama Press.

Molendijk, Arie L. 1999. "Tiele on Religion." *Numen* 46(3): 237–268. https://doi.org/10.1163/1568527991209015

Newton, Richard. 2017a. "Locating Value in the Study of Religion," *Method and Theory in the Study of Religion* 29: 459–478. https://doi.org/10.1163/15700682-12341407

Newton, Richard. 2017b. "Signifying 'Theory': Toward a Method of Mutually Assured Deconstruction," In Aaron W. Hughes (ed.), *Theory in a Time of Excess: Beyond Reflection and Explanation in Religious Studies Scholarship*, 37–46. Sheffield: Equinox.

Newton, Richard. 2018 [2013]. "Reading Alex Haley's *Roots*: Toward an Anthropology of Scriptures," *Postscripts: The Journal of Sacred Texts and Contemporary Worlds* 9(1): 1–26. https://doi.org/10.1558/post.27507

Newton, Richard. 2018. "The Spooky Politics of Dark Truth Claims," *Religion and Theology* 25: 1–21. https://doi.org/10.1163/15743012-02503007

Nongbri, Brent. 2013. *Before Religion: A History of a Modern Concept*. New Haven, CT: Yale University Press.

Nye, Malory. 2019. "Race and Religion in the Post-Colonial Formations of Power and Whiteness." *Method and Theory in the Study of Religion* 31(3): 210–237. https://doi.org/10.1163/15700682-12341444

Price, David H. 2016. *Cold War Anthropology: The CIA, The Pentagon, and the Growth of Dual Use Anthropology*. Durham, NC: Duke University Press.

Pummer, Reinhard. 1972. "Religionswissenschaft or Religiology?" *Numen* 19(2-3): 91–127. https://doi.org/10.2307/3269740

Sanderson, Stephen K. 2017. *Religious Evolution and the Axial Age: From Shamans and Priests to Prophets*. New York: Bloomsbury.

Sharot, Stephen. 2001. *A Comparative Sociology of World Religions: Virtuosi, Priests, and Popular Religion*. New York: New York University Press.

Smith, Jonathan Z. 1973. "When the Bough Breaks." *History of Religions* 12(4): 342–371. https://doi.org/10.1086/462686

Smith, Jonathan Z. 1982. *Imagining Religion: From Babylon to Jonestown*. Chicago, IL: University of Chicago Press.

Sussman, Robert Wald. 2016. *The Myth of Race: The Troubling Persistence of an Unscientific Idea.* Cambridge, MA: Harvard University Press.
Tsonis, Jack. 2012. "Review of *The Axial Age and its Consequences*, by Robert N. Bellah and Hans Joas." *Alternative Spirituality and Religion Review* 3(2): 253–258. https://doi.org/10.5840/asrr2012329
Tsonis, Jack. 2016. "The 'Axial Age': Problematising Religious History in a Post-Colonial Setting." *The Religious Studies Project*, May 30. Interview by Breann Fallon. Retrieved from www.religiousstudiesproject.com/podcast/the-axial-age-problematising-religious-history-in-a-post-colonial-setting (accessed October 1, 2018).
Visweswaran, Kamala. 2010. *Un/Common Cultures: Racism and the Rearticulation of Cultural Difference.* Durham, NC: Duke University Press.
White, Hayden. 1987. *The Content of the Form: Narrative Discourse and Historical Representation.* Baltimore, MD: The John Hopkins University Press.
Wimbush, Vincent. 2011. "Interpreters—Enslaving/Enslaved/Runagate." *Journal of Biblical Literature* 130(1): 5–24. https://doi.org/10.2307/41304184

Chapter 7

Of Dualisms and Doppelgängers: Mapping Ancient Minds and Bodies in Religious Studies

Robyn Faith Walsh

I am totally an INTP. My husband claims I am more of an ESFJ but he would; he's an ISTP. Our son is only nine weeks old, but we are pretty sure he's INFJ. To loosely quote George Harrison, something in the way he reaches for his Regenbogenbälle mobile—you know, the one we bought in Germany—or the way he insists on breaking out of his swaddle tells us that he is idealistic yet focused. I have been chronicling these early milestones on Instagram to show his future partner one day. I hope they are an ESFP.

The Myers–Briggs so-called "personality test" has reportedly made and broken marriages, hired and fired employees from Fortune 500 companies to colleges and government agencies, and has offered fodder for many an awkward professional or family dinner conversation. In the roughly fifty years since it gained acceptance, this Jungian off-shoot has been taken by an estimated fifty million people (Cunningham 2012). The conceit of the Myers–Briggs Type Indicator (MBTI) is that each of us falls into one of sixteen possible personality types, measured according to four axes with binary options such as "introvert/extrovert" and "sensing/intuition," according to the Myers & Briggs Foundation website (myersbriggs.org). In combination these pairs offer a map of one's tendencies and potential. Find out you are an extroverted/thinker/judge and you might be upper management material. Your job candidate is an introverted/feeler? Forget it. It will never work out. This pseudo-science is now so entrenched in certain pockets of American popular culture and its workforce, *The Washington Post* writer Lillian Cunningham once quipped of its influence: "Corporate America has its own religions, and one of them is Myers–Briggs" (Cunningham 2012).

Devotees of the MBTI might be surprised to learn that the test was devised by a mother and daughter team of amateur Jungian enthusiasts in the early-to-mid-twentieth century. Katharine Cook Briggs was a homemaker with no formal training in psychology or psychiatry who read Jung's 1921 *Psychologische Typen* and saw in his taxonomies confirmation of her own intuitions (Menand 2018). Her daughter, Isabel Briggs Myers, continued to promote her mother's work after her death. What the Mmes. Briggs lacked in expertise they made up for in determination. They had benevolent intentions; one of their objectives was for personality assessments to be used post-War to help women obtain professional positions, for instance. Personality characteristics acting as a stand-in for professional experience. Very meta.

These dubious origins do not appear to have had an adverse effect on the popularity of Myers–Briggs. In truth, I have no experience with any of these tests, but I have certainly fought through more than one awkward conversation about their perceived accuracy. The invented story with which I began this response serves to demonstrate precisely how persuasive the language of the MBTI can be. It is tempting to suppose that many of its contemporary advocates are unaware of its history. The literary scholar Merve Emre calls it "among the silliest, shallowest products of late capitalism" (Emre 2018: 259; cited in Menand 2018: 97). To discover that its basis is the inexpert musings of a pair of nineteenth-century analytic psychology fans may, indeed, give some pause. But Myers–Briggs is ultimately a case study in three areas touched upon by Richard Newton's engrossing essay (Chapter 6, this volume): the fetishization of knowledge, bodies, and expertise. The test, arguably by virtue of its longevity, has an air of authority. Its results, ably and tidily classifying predilections as attributes, maps certain expectations onto bodies. And those who wield it are able to point to its history, popular acceptance, and ubiquity to justify its use and its claims.

The MBTI also represents one among a number of "theory of mind" tools we have inherited from the nineteenth-century that require reconsideration and revision. While I cannot speak for the Academy writ large, my area of Religious Studies—the study of the New Testament and early Christianity—has done little to contend with the persistent racist and nationalist viewpoints inherited from the eighteenth- and nineteenth- century founders of our field. While largely studied and credentialed for their time (with some notable exceptions), thinkers like Johann Gottfried Herder (1744-1803), the Grimm Brothers (1785-1863), Ludwig Feuerbach (1804-1872), and Max Müller (1823-1900) advanced highly speculative theories on so-called Aryan history, the origins of language, and the moral-psychology of the ancients. Whether out of ignorance or out of what Newton acknowledges is the field's apparent satisfaction "with distancing ourselves 180 degrees from unsavory pasts, unfavorable rhetorics, and unseemly totems," what follows is a survey of certain lines of thought we have uncritically adopted pertaining to race, ethnicity, and cognition through the rhetorics of language and myth (Newton, Chapter 6, this volume).

* * *

Studies on German intellectual history and historical imagination, understandably, have long been occupied with how to make sense of the nationalist politics that animated so much of the twentieth century.[1] From the Frühromantik forward, scholars have lamented the "peculiarly German cultural disorder" that privileged nature, nostalgia, and warfare over rationalism (Williamson 2004: 3). The ready

---

1. I make a similar argument in Walsh (2015). I also discuss the history of oral tradition theory in New Testament studies and its relationship to German Romanticism in my recent monograph *The Origins of Early Christian Literature* (Walsh 2021).

and collective acceptance of such narratives signaled a marked enthusiasm for "myth"—a somewhat amorphous term used in reference to the aesthetics (literature, art), practices, and cosmologies of "pre-modern" societies. Reclaiming certain myths (or forging new ones) was a preoccupation in Germanic thought as early as the Renaissance as a variety of artists, academics, writers, and other intelligentsia sought cultural artifacts that expressed the unique and "essential spirit" of the German people or *Volk*. Chronically insecure about the authority and influence of "Rome" (both in the ancient and contemporary sense), the questions, methods, literature, so-called "folklore," and material culture developed or considered in this period were transparently aimed at uncovering and reclaiming any wisps of a perceived-as-lost past Germania (see Marchand 1996, 2009).

Indeed, there was a profound interest among eighteenth- and nineteenth-century German intellectuals in using language and myth as markers of *Völker*. In Rorschach fashion, these unique, "forgotten" narratives had the power to reveal the homeland gods of a unified Germany, not to mention the possible origins of humankind itself. With the book of Genesis as a guide, certain philologists sought the inaugural point of all language and *Völker*. The same de-constructive methodologies that guided the search for earlier and earlier layers of the (now) formative narratives of the German people were liberally applied to linguistics. Through the efforts of men like Herder, F. Schlegel, and, crucially, Sir William Jones (1746–1794), the consensus grew that the common origin for all human language was central Asia. These speculative etymological investigations argued that a family of "Indo-European" or Aryan languages (as well as Indo-European/Aryan gods) emerged from the cradle of India and extended out into Egypt, Persia, Greece, Rome, and on through northern Europe.[2] This colonialist rhapsodizing on the clichéd "East" also led enthusiasts like the Grimm Brothers and Adalbert Kuhn (1812–1881) to perform great feats of logic in order to link seemingly disparate linguistic and cultural elements together; Kuhn, for example, argued that the language of the *Rig Veda* etymologically prefigured terms later found in Greek and, ultimately, German (e.g., "pramantha" for "Prometheus").[3] Through this approach, one could associate common and long-held German practices like the "fire-wheel" celebrations at St. John's Day to a Vedic predecessor (rubbing wood together produces fire, Prometheus steals fire from above, the fire-wheel descends a hill) (see Williamson 2004: 215–219). Linguistic expressions of perceived cultural and even "natural" elements (e.g., the "solar mythology" that characterizes the *Rig Veda*) anticipated Müllerian comparative mythology and, in many respects,

---

2. These lists of Indo-European languages and territories often changed to suit the (scholarly) conversation. Take, for example, Jones's discussion of Jacob Bryant's *Analysis of Ancient Mythology* (1774–1776): "We shall, perhaps, agree at last with Mr. Bryant, that *Egyptians, Indians, Greeks,* and *Italians,* proceeded originally from one central place, and that the same people carried their religion and sciences into *China* and *Japan*: may we not add, even to *Mexico* and *Peru*?" (Jones 1807: 387).

3. "Pramantha" (प्रमन्थ) meaning "stick" used for producing fire. The Greek Prometheus (Προμηθεύς) is the "fire-bringer." The linguistic and broad topical similarities shared by these terms were enough for Kuhn and others to draw this specious association.

mirrored the parallel assessments of philosophers and theologians like Herder on language and peoples (e.g., Herder's position that the active verbs and sensory metaphors characteristic of Hebrew are a reflection of an essential nature of its "*wilder Völker*").[4]

Increasingly, a line of logic developed among "linguistic" thinkers that each individual Indo-European language fundamentally represented the earliest cultural expressions and "memories" of its ancient *Völkerwanderungen*—the migrations of *Volk* throughout the western hemisphere and into their present homelands (Lincoln 1999: 55).[5] Conceptually allied to the emerging phrenology movement of the period, even the physical differences between nationalities and races were viewed as a reflection, at least in part, of the material landscape of their respective *Vaterland*. Herder's *Ideen zur Philosophie der Geschichte der Meschheit* (1786), for instance, argued that the environment of a region (e.g., landscape and temperature) determined qualities of a people's oral traditions and poetry (*Volkspoesie*), as well as their skin color, skeletal structure, and so forth (Herder 1786: 2.7.1–5, 2.8.1). Unified by language and an essential *Geist* or Spirit, these individual *Volk* represented a holistic body and, as discrete individuals, physically manifested aspects of the same *Geist*. That said, culture—not biology *per se*—remained the primary driver of difference. "Race" remained a question of species or kind (*Stämme*) and origins; because human beings emerged from the same discrete region "in the beginning," they were fundamentally the same creatures. In an oft-cited passage (usually taken out of context as an apologetic), Herder declares, contra Kant, that to categorize people by race is ultimately faulty given that "the colors fade into one another" (Herder 1786: 13.257–258). Of course, measured against modern sensibilities, such a declaration might seem relatively liberal for its time; but this polemic should not be confused as evidence of a proto-egalitarianism. Such aspirational statements did not dissuade Herder from frequently making racist judgments about the *Volk* (primarily in Asia and Africa) he considered somehow inferior to his own.[6] Moreover, Herder and his Romantic sympathizers and interlocutors were debating issues that were nonetheless indicative of a greater trend towards obsessing over origins and the fetishization of the racialized body—and always allied to acute nationalist concerns.[7]

---

4. The phrase "*wilder Völker*" is found throughout Herder's *Vom Geist der ebräischen Poesie* (1825).
5. Two notable books that treat the larger questions of the historical Jesus and nationalism are William E. Arnal's *The Symbolic Jesus: Historical Scholarship, Judaism and the Construction of Contemporary Identity* (2014) and Halvor Moxnes's *Jesus and the Rise of Nationalism: A New Quest for the Nineteenth-Century Historical Jesus* (2012).
6. For more on Herder's perspectives on race and different ethnic groups, see Vicki A. Spencer's *Herder's Political Thought: A Study of Language, Culture, and Community* (2012), esp. 134–144.
7. One competing viewpoint, for example, was the *Völkerpsychologie* movement, championed by Heymann Steinthal (1823–1899) and Moritz Lazarus (1824–1903) who understood the *Volksgeist* as a "mental phenomenon" expressing elements of culture (language, religion, law, and so on) and not some kind of implicit "biological entity" or "ontological ideal" (see Williamson 2004: 219–221).

These early forays into comparative mythology tacitly accepted the ineffable or divine at the center of all cultural development—what George S. Williamson describes as "a Schleiermacherian feeling for the divinity that inspired the primitive Aryans to burst out in song at the sight of the dawn" (Williamson 2004: 217). Herder's tendency to wax-poetic about the "ancient cymbals and kettle-drums" of the *wilder Völker* of the Hebrew Bible and "David dancing in front of the Ark of the Covenant ... the prophet summoning [a minstrel] to inspire him" certainly stands as a composite example of the fetishization of both race/ethnicity and the past (Herder 1825: ch. 11, line 224).[8] Generally framed in terms of the ancient or "primitive" body, this "science of religion" traded on very specific ideas of what constitutes the civilized body, language, and belief (see also Williamson 2004: 217). The imagined, primitive Aryans were a "race of poets" crafting lyrical verses on nature that functioned as multi-layered and complex metaphors (Williamson 2004: 218). Later corrupted by the incursion of character and myth by the likes of Homer and Hesiod, the original meaning of the Indian or Hebrew poet was considered accessible solely to linguists like Müller or Kuhn with the tools of Wilhelm von Humboldt and Franz Bopp. Aesthetically, the language of the Greeks remained a critical and cherished inflection point in this perceived evolution of Aryan history, reflecting the moment the inspired musings of ancient minds advanced beyond the simplest expressions of the *Geist*. Selectively identifying a through line of origins and culture, the notion of the Aryan helped delineate what peoples and methods were worthy of consideration, up to and including the folktales of (what came to be known as) the German people. Yet, conspicuously and effectively excluded from this lineage were Judaism, Hebrew, and *its* people.

Romantic perspectives on race and ethnicity extended to the development of what Newton refers to as a "Borgesian garden" for scholars. While languages like German symbolized a rich and multi-layered history of human development, migration, and thriving, many deemed languages like Arabic and Hebrew to be outliers that lacked the refinement and "sublimity" of the *Ursprache* Sanskrit. Nationalistic and anti-Semitic prejudices unquestionably animated many such spurious theories about Aryan history and philology. Increasingly, the nineteenth-century found Feuerbach and Müller arguing for implicit contrasts between Aryan and Semitic history. While Müller named Vedic India and Homeric Greece worthy members of the Aryan family tree, languages like Hebrew were utilitarian—"less creative and more rigid"—and reflected concern for law and ritual (Lincoln 1999: 67). These fallacious observations extended to other facets of defining *Volk*, such as debating whether or not post-*Völkerwanderungen* peoples had succumbed to foreign influence. The Germans, for instance, celebrated the material spaces and natural features of their homeland in folktales about forests, springs and mountains; the Jews, by contrast, had abandoned their *Vaterland* long ago and were now a burden on other nations: "a race of crafty brokers throughout almost the whole World, who, in spite of all oppression, have nowhere longed for their own honor and dwelling" (Herder 1786: 3.12.3). Displaced, the Jews were

---

8. For more on this passage, see Walsh (2021): 91–92.

arguably not even proper *Volk*, unable to properly preserve a continuing record of their homeland and kinship community. Christianity, on the other hand, was considered a great unifier—with a cohesive community at its center "holding all things in common" (Acts 2:44)—acting as a culmination of Aryan antiquity.[9]

The Romantic dichotomy between Aryan and Jewish history holds disturbing yet important implications for later developments in New Testament studies. Of the many lines of thought I might discuss, allow me to focus on one in particular: the so-called Judaism/Hellenism divide. In short, the Judaism/Hellenism divide represents the tendency among scholars to treat Judaism not as one among a number of religions of the ancient Mediterranean, but as a wholly "other" set of practices, texts, and practitioners in what amounts to cultural isolation from the rest of the Greek and Roman world. Critiques of this approach have been rather thoroughly addressed in scholarship over the last twenty or so years, yet it persists when we see monographs and articles published marveling at the "Jewishness" of Jesus, failing to detect lines of Platonic or Stoic thought in Paul or the Gospel of Matthew, attributing certain tropes or teachings in the collected books of the New Testament to an "original" (e.g., "Palestinian") oral tradition, and so on. Long understood to be derivative of the *religionsgeschichtliche Schule* and the theological interests of Tübingen, when the Divide is acknowledged by scholars, more often than not it is in the context of pointing out that our predecessors in the field were overly concerned with identifying the Jewish roots of early Christianity, or that the terms "Judaism" and "Hellenism" were so ill-defined by the Romantics in practice that they were effectively, conceptually empty (Engberg-Pedersen 2001). This level of critique may be valid, but it also lacks teeth. To what extent does the field adequately attend to the racist and anti-Semitic discourse that informed the *religionsgeschichtliche Schule*, beyond the passing recognition of German Nationalism? As I have discussed, many of these methods were informed by discourse and reasoning from linguistics, comparative mythology, and so forth that are far more pernicious and wide-ranging than we perhaps generally acknowledge. It has also made the study of the New Testament an outlier, in many respects, from the rest of the Academy in how we approach our texts and how we reconstruct history, notably in the way the field imagines "the author."

By way of conclusion, allow me to draw one further observation on the latter point above concerning authorship and the New Testament. Pressing political interests continued to inform methodological developments in how Romantic scholars read ancient texts, particularly those that attributed authorship to communities rather than individual writers. Because language was alleged to contain the "preserved memories" of various *Volk*, comparative philology of the eighteenth and nineteenth centuries (including etymology, morphology, and so on) became increasingly aligned with the emerging fields of memory studies and the critical interpretation of ancient sources. As specific works became tightly associated with the history, national pride, and self-identification of various peoples,

---

9. On the British construction of Aryan identity see Trautmann (1997). For a wider-ranging discussion on philology and constructions of anti-Semitism see Maurice Olender (1992).

critics attempted to align these texts with an idea of "collective individuality"—that even a sole author is ultimately little more than a redactor of collective ideas (Williamson 2004: 63). This approach is strongly resonate with our long-standing ambition in New Testament studies to recover the folklore of the illiterate, "primitive Christians" embedded in the gospels, letters, Revelation, Acts, Q, and so forth. To the extent we continue to treat authors as spokespersons for their "communities" instead of creative writers, or treat Paul as the proto-orthodox spokesman of something called Pauline Christianity, we uncritically reify these Romantic leanings.

Through this sketch of my discrete corner of the field, I hope I have demonstrated how essential it is to take Newton's recommendation to reconsider "how we narrate … intellectual heritage." He reminds us that: "At its most honest, the history of religions is a chronicle of legacies and the sowing and reaping necessary to be remembered." Perhaps we have attended to some of these legacies and memories too selectively. Because whether it is a personality test or a particular assumption about our ancient sources, our uncritical acceptance of certain means and methods ultimately reveals more about us than it does about the ideas we cite or the history we seek to remember.

Robyn Faith Walsh is Associate Professor of the New Testament and Early Christianity at the University of Miami, Coral Gables. An editor at the Database of Religious History, her articles have appeared in Classical Quarterly and Jewish Studies Quarterly, among other publications. Her first monograph, *The Origins of Early Christian Literature: Contextualizing the New Testament within Greco-Roman Literary Culture* was recently published with Cambridge University Press.

Acknowledgments

A hearty thank you to Stephen Young for reading an earlier draft of this paper on my behalf at the "Critique in Context" Session at the 2018 American Academy of Religion annual conference in Denver, Colorado. All translations below are my own, unless otherwise noted.

References

Arnal, William E. 2014. *The Symbolic Jesus: Historical Scholarship, Judaism and the Construction of Contemporary Identity*. Sheffield: Equinox Publishing.
Cunningham, Lillian. 2012. "Myers–Briggs: Does it Pay to Know Your Type?" *The Washington Post* (December 14). Retrieved from www.washingtonpost.com/national/on-leadership/myers-briggs-does-it-pay-to-know-your-type/2012/12/14/eaed51ae-3fcc-11e2-bca3-aadc9b7e29c5_story.html (accessed October 9, 2018).
Emre, Merve. 2018. *The Personality Brokers: The Strange History of Myers-Briggs and the Birth of Personality Testing*. New York: Doubleday.
Engberg-Pedersen, Troels. (ed.). 2001. *Paul beyond the Judaism/Hellenism Divide*. Louisville, KY: Westminster John Knox.

Herder, Johann Gottfried. 1786. *Ideen zur Philosophie der Geschichte der Menschheit*. Leipzig: Erscheinungsjahr.
Herder, Johann Gottfried. 1825. *Vom Geist der ebräischen Poesie: eine Anleitung für die Liebhaber derselben, und der ältesten Geschichte des menschlichen Geistes*. 2 vols. Leipzig: J. A. Barth.
Jones, William. 1807. *Works of Sir William Jones*, vol. 3. London.
Lincoln, Bruce. 1999. *Theorizing Myth: Narrative, Ideology, and Scholarship*. Chicago, IL: University of Chicago Press.
Marchand, Suzanne L. 1996. *Down from Olympus: Archaeology and Philhellenism in Germany, 1750-1970*. Princeton, NJ: Princeton University Press.
Marchand, Suzanne L. 2009. *German Orientalism in the Age of Empire: Religion, Race, and Scholarship*. Washington, DC: German Historical Institute; New York: Cambridge University Press.
Menand, Louis. 2018. "Can you Type? The Use and Abuse of Personality Tests." *The New Yorker* (September 10): 94–97.
Moxnes, Halvor. 2012. *Jesus and the Rise of Nationalism: A New Quest for the Nineteenth-Century Historical Jesus*. New York: I. B. Tauris.
Olender, Maurice. 1992. *The Languages of Paradise: Race, Religion, and Philology in the Nineteenth Century*. Trans. Arthur Goldhammer. Cambridge, MA: Harvard University Press.
Spencer, Vicki A. 2012. *Herder's Political Thought: A Study of Language, Culture, and Community*. Toronto: University of Toronto Press.
Trautmann, Thomas R. 1997. *Aryans and British India*. Berkeley, CA: University of California Press.
Walsh, Robyn Faith. 2015. "The Influence of the Romantic Genius in Early Christian Studies," *Relegere* 2015: 31–60. https://doi.org/10.11157/rsrr5-1-647
Walsh, Robyn Faith. 2021. *The Origins of Early Christian Literature: Contextualizing the New Testament within Greco-Roman Literary Culture*. New York: Cambridge University Press.
Williamson, George S. 2004. *The Longing for Myth in Germany: Religion and Aesthetic Culture from Romanticism to Nietzsche*. Chicago, IL: University of Chicago Press.

Chapter 8

Dark S(k)in: Two Versions of Newton's *Crimen Oscuro*

Rudy V. Busto

One of the questions posed in Richard Newton's sprawling essay (Chapter 6, this volume) is what to do with the "legacy of race in the field," especially by those scholars of religion who "see themselves as part of the critical 'Copernican turn' toward theorizing" about race. Moving through a warehouse of texts and thinkers, Newton wrestles with how to move forward in a discipline that continues to "cultivate" the tropes of *Religionswissenschaft*, the World Religions paradigm, the lemming-drive for theory, overcoming "zero-sum" perspectives and, quoting at length Richard King, the European Enlightenment. Quite the wrestling match indeed.

I appreciate Newton's appeal to speculative fiction and especially his deployment of Borges's *Three Versions of Judas* to make the point that heretic scholars meet their final fate as blasphemers and obscure footnotes in the academy. Borges's parable asks whether the enigmatic theologian Nils Runeberg changed his conclusions about the true nature of Judas Iscariot through honest scholarly effort, or because he longed for academic recognition. Newton suggests Runeberg's miscarriage is having discovered the undiscovered and suffered the consequence of his rejection, thrice, by his academic peers. Borges asks: "Was it not that dark sin that he, Runeberg, was guilty of?" In Borges's Spanish, that sentence is not so clear. Whereas the English translation chosen by Newton suggests that the "dark sin" is an unintended consequence of Runeberg's honest labors, the Spanish can be read as an accusation. That is, Runeberg probably knew exactly what he was doing: "¿No era él, acaso, culpable de ese crimen oscuro?" That is, "Was he not, *perhaps*, guilty of this dark [or possibly "sinister" or "shady] *crime*?"[1] Perhaps Runeberg's scholarship is intentionally heretical, intentionally criminal? If so, as with Judas, he is disgraced in his death. Nothing is discovered. The status quo remains. I note here a tantalizing typographical error: In translation the phrase "dark sin" is in Newton's manuscript, "dark skin" a wry error very much in the spirit of Borges's tale. Is Newton's chapter a "crimen oscuro"? Is his account of race in the study of religion akin to Runeberg's betrayal of the status quo? As Newton rewrites Borges's "crimen oscuro" let me read Newton's "dark s(k)in" on race and religion.

---

1. In the Spanish: ¿No era él, acaso, culpable de ese crimen oscuro? (Was it not he, perhaps, guilty of this dark/obscure/shady/uncertain/sinister crime?) downloaded at https://ciudadseva.com/texto/tres-versiones-de-judas.

Let's call it the "Two Versions of Newton's dark s(k)in"—that is, two ways to assess Newton's assessment on the problem of race and religion.

Version 1: Race and Religion from the perspective of Religious Studies

I agree with Newton that "Religious Studies scholars have tools to contribute to the study of race," but not in the way that he sees it. That is, he defines Religious Studies' core task as "com[ing] to terms with the legacy of the field," that "on the issue of race, the field appears satisfied with distancing ourselves 180 degrees from unsavory pasts, unfavorable rhetorics, and unseemly totems." Newton's solution is to "signify" on the tropes of the discipline, such that, perhaps, we can retrieve something useful from, for example, "the Axial Age" or the fetishization of the text, or something from the "exercise of comparison."

I like this move but doubt that re-signifying the tropes of the discipline dig deep enough to root out established scholarly habits and/or escape the comfortable appeal to a science of religion or some such fiction of the power and influence of objective data and its responsible interpretations. As Philip K. Dick writes about the futility of making sense of an impossible situation, "sometimes it is an appropriate response to reality to go insane." That is, I would argue that the field of religious studies cannot adequately address theoretical, and power issues because its history, rules, and structures around race do not allow for substantive transformation. Philip K. Dick would liken this predicament to a "Chinese finger trap, where the harder you pull to get out, the tighter the trap gets" (Dick 1981: 10). Yes, it is true that there is more coverage of "race" in religious studies. When I was a young assistant professor in the early 1990s, I distinctly recall the feeling of isolation because I came into the discipline specifically to teach and research race and religion, only to have the dean tell me a few years later that my tenure possibilities were nil because, in his words, what I studied "was not important." Yes, there is more interest in the place of race in the study of religion, but my experience reveals that it has become a fashion accessory to the real substance of the discipline, a trend, an add-on; what one of my Americanist colleagues refers to as an example of "Religion and Lipstick." Writing about religion and race should be a transformative action. Writing about race and religion must be disruptive. Writing about race and religion should overturn the theory-changers tables in the temple. When race is a trend or trope like "materiality," or "lived religion," it eventually gets shelved as an "extra" or at its worst, as a value-added plus in otherwise traditionally construed academic job advertisements.

I refer to Philip K. Dick's metaphor of the Chinese finger trap to emphasize the mechanism of increasing resistance within the structures and apparatuses of the academic study of religion when one attempts to escape its disciplinary regimes. Whether accidental or intentional, Victor Runeberg fails to secure the laurels of academic recognition or the notoriety of heresy and in the end his works are forgotten because he dared to reveal the truth (God) through betrayal (Judas).

Version 2: Race and Religion from the perspective of Ethnic Studies

This leads me to the second reading of Newton's chapter from an ethnic studies perspective. I was struck by what seemed to be a reticence in the chapter's various arguments to move directly to a critique of power in the discipline even after invoking Fanon and noting "those who see themselves as part of a 'Copernican turn' towards theorizing." I was then surprised to find "race" described as a "riddle" that gets complicated by issues of essentialism, identity politics, intersectionality, and eventually gets pushed into representing a broader matrix of "axes of social difference." Newton writes that there is a "riddling silence on social difference [that is] taking precedence in the field." There is an error here if I'm reading the chapter correctly. Race can, indeed, stand as a "sign" for various types of social differences—as Omi and Winant have described projects of racialization (Omi and Winant 2015: 109ff). However, I do not find it defensible to cast race as a master category for "axes of social difference." That is, as "old school" ethnic studies scholars argue, race operates in specific historically and locatively contingent cultural superstructures in clear relationship to substructures of political economy and institutions and agencies of control.

Translated into religious studies, we can account for the discipline's allergy to honest accounts of race by acknowledging the legacy and perpetuation of white and Christian supremacies in the development of the discipline. We see this clearly, for example, in the rise of *Religionwissenschaft* out of European colonialism and in Protestant categories for what makes a religion a "real" religion, a world tradition. Every spring in my 200+ student "Introduction to Asian American Religions" course, I ask students to help me build a list of "world religions" on the chalkboard. And after the list of usual "-isms" (Hinduism, Buddhism, etc.)—and sometimes Scientology, or Jedi-ism—I ask them to explain the absence of a "world religion" from Africa or the Americas. But why, then, is the list from Asia? And why do students struggle with the fact that Christianity originates in Asia?[2] This exercise opens the door to the history of centers and peripheries, colonialism, uninterrogated assumptions, and especially the coalescing of the concept of discrete world religions correlative with the rise of concepts around discrete racial types.

While I agree that race is one of the axes of social difference (along with gender, class, sexuality, ethnicity, region, ableness, language distinctiveness, etc.), and that race may, indeed, have historical salience as a type human difference, I would argue that race is not a riddle, solved, perhaps by signification. Rather, race remains a thorn on the flesh of a discipline that refuses to "come to terms with the legacy of race" (for example, in its perpetuation of Orientalist scholarship and fetishizations of the exotic), but can contradictorily promote itself as champion of

---

2. Later in the course I quote Samuel Hugh Moffett that "the church began in Asia. Its earliest history, its first centers were Asian. Asia produced the first known church building, the first New Testament translation, perhaps the first Christian King, the first Christian poets, and even arguably the first Christian State" (Moffett 2003: xiii).

anti-racist pedagogy.³ This un-easy contradiction is not so subtle in the language of Newton's chapter, for even as he struggles to find a way to unlock and answer the riddle that he poses, I'm struck by the Nordic," dare I say Aryan hauntings in his chapter: "Religionswissenschaft, "Doktorvaters and Doktormaters," the Swede Nils Runeberg , and in another story another Runeberg (Viktor), a German spy, Karl Jaspers, Max Müller, and even the summing up phrase, "Der Rassist aus der Religionswissenschaft"—as if the weary ghost of Max Müller possessed his laptop. This is not a denunciation so much as it is a curious example of the very legacy which I thought we were trying to overcome. Finger traps everywhere. Thirty pieces of silver refused by the priests for the betrayal wrought by the *crimen oscuro*.

Rudy Busto is an Associate Professor and Director of Graduate Studies in the Religious Studies Department at the University of California, Santa Barbara. His research interests include: American religion, race and religion, and religions and science fiction. He authored the book *King Tiger: The Religious Visions of Reies Lopez Tijerina*, *The Gospel According to Rice: The Next Asian American Christianity* (2005) and has published articles for many journals including the Amerasian Journal and The Religious Studies Project.

References

Borges, Jorge Luis. "Tres versions de Judas." Retrieved from https://ciudadseva.com/texto/tres-versiones-de-judas.
Dick, Philip K. 1981. *Valis*. London: Bantam Books.
Jacoby, Sarah, et al. 2018. "Teaching Religion as Anti-Racism Education." *Religious Studies News* (November 5). Retrieved from http://rsn.aarweb.org/spotlight-on/teaching/anti-racism/editors-introduction.
Moffett, Samuel Hugh. 2003. *A History of Christianity in Asia (Volume 1): Beginnings to 1500*. New York: Orbis.
Omi, Michael, and Howard Winant. 2015. *Racial Formation in the United States*, 3rd edition. New York: Routledge.

---

3. See, for example, Jacoby et al. (2018).

Chapter 9

Reworking our Schemes

Craig R. Prentiss

First, I would like to thank Richard Newton for writing an insightful essay (Chapter 6, this volume) with original takes on the intersection of religion and race. There are several potential lines of response one could take, but I would like to build on Newton's reference to the Combahee River Collective, because I think the Collective's strategy for re-imagining the prevailing classificatory model for personhood may be instructive in pointing us toward reconstituting the relationship between religion and race as schemes for social ordering.

Newton highlights the Collective's "savvy" application of signification in their refusing to hold markers of identity in isolation. Instead, their strategy involved reworking old discourses of liberation that operated from the vantage points of race, gender, sexuality, and class to speak to their distinctive position as African American women confronting oppression on nearly every front imaginable, including white supremacy, patriarchy, capitalism, and in many cases, heterosexism. Their 1977 Statement summed up their location in the American social landscape by marshalling the words of Michele Wallace's *Village Voice* essay, "A Black Feminist Search for Sisterhood," published two years earlier. Wallace declared that "...being on the bottom, we would have to do what no one else has done: we would have to fight the world." (Combahee River Collective 1977; Wallace 1975). And fighting the world demanded reworking the categories the world handed them, as it was clear to them that when considered in isolation, each category left out significant data.

Newton observes that "their work is an admission ... of the disorienting nature of theorizing about race," yet this admission did nothing to blunt their commitment "to mapping the axes of social difference." As he astutely notes, the Combahee River Collective "suggested that all politics are identity politics and [they] defined power as the extent to which the unnamed dictates the discourse of naming." It is precisely this reference to "the unnamed" that interests me here and I would like to spend the remainder of my paper touching on the implications of this claim for the categories of religion and race. In recent years we have seen a growing awareness that these two categories should be understood as co-constituting. At least as early as Henry Goldschmidt and Elizabeth McAlister's 2004 *Race, Nation, and Religions in the Americas*, many scholars have theorized the underlying processes of category formation and linked them to discrete historical moments in which power dynamics were marked through the application of "race" and "religion" as co-constituting signifiers.[1]

But as Jared Hickman points out in *Black Prometheus: Race and Radicalism in the Age of Atlantic Slavery*, much of our scholarship on the relationship of religion to race "seems to conceptualize this co-constitution as the merging of preexistent categories" (Hickman 2016: 50). Hickman continues:

> It is no mistake that "polytheism" enters the English language in Samuel Purchas's modern compendium of European encounters with non-European peoples, and no mistake that it becomes a key term in racialized histories of civilizational development that make monotheism the high-water mark of human intellectual and spiritual achievement. In sum, "religious" and "racial" othering are inseparable, a point we are conditioned to miss because modern academic disciplines have parsed "religion" and "race" into "parallel" objects of inquiry. But perhaps more fundamentally, as Frederick Cooper has pinpointed, the problem lies in thinking in terms of *identities* rather than processes of *identification*.
>
> (Hickman 2016: 50–51)

Hickman's observations are valuable and point us in the direction of Newton's reference to the "Unnamed" that "dictates the discourse of naming." Though I would be more cautious than Hickman in attributing our being "conditioned to miss" the intimate relationship between the categories of "religion" and "race" solely to the fact that "*modern academic disciplines*" treat the terms as "'parallel' objects of inquiry." Why? Because we are not simply scholars of religion, nor do our own classificatory schemes spring from participating in our academic disciplines alone. We are, instead, individuals interpellated through a broad array of discursive fields in which we have operated from the day we were born, and presumably, all of us were handed the terms "race" and "religion" in non-academic venues. Moreover, what we imagined these terms to signify likely drew many of us toward our interest in the academy in the first place.

Notably, it is precisely our positions within a *range* of discursive fields that present obstacles to speaking of "race" and "religion" as classificatory fruits of the same vine instead of as "'parallel' objects of inquiry." Whether we are trying to attract students to our courses by utilizing a term like "religion" that they have some prior recognition of, and then *satisfying* them when they sit in the seats of our classrooms by speaking about things that align, somewhat, with what they assumed they would be learning about; whether we are trying to justify our value to our academic institutions when speaking with administrators or faculty colleagues possessing no academic knowledge of our field, and often resorting to shorthand explanations of our utility that include the need to know about the "religions of the world" in an age of globalism; whether we are trying to speak to journalists about a topic that they take to be about "religion" or "race" as they

---

1. For examples of scholars pointing to religion and race as co-constituting categories, see Goldschmidt (2006), Harvey (2017), Nye (2018), Delgado and Moss (2018), Jacobsen and Wadsworth (2012), Goetz (2012), Weisenfeld (2017), Johnson (2004), and Lum (2014, esp. ch. 2).

understand it—which is why they contacted us in the first place—knowing full well that we will be lucky if they use more than one quote or five seconds of footage, and that if we dive too much into challenging the categories they have presented us with, they will simply ignore what we have to say altogether; whether we are speaking to publishers who have a strong catalog in "African American religion" or "Indigenous religion" or "East Asian religion" and long mailing lists of readers interested in revisiting well-trodden source material with some new and insightful spin that still leaves the major classificatory schemes in-tact; whether its speaking to our family members, our friends from high school, or the person we sit next to on the flight back home after this conference, we fall back on simplistic and often troubling shorthand for categories like "religion" and "race" both because we rarely have the time to go in to a deep dive on these terms, *and* because we ourselves became fluent in the use of these categories in ways that resonated with people outside of academics long before we set foot in our first college classroom. And as such, we ourselves are implicated in preserving the parallel categorization of religion and race in both academic and non-academic ways (this is, after all, a session whose task was to reflect upon the intersection of two discreet categories, religion and race). In essence, the preservation of these as discreet categories points to a Foucauldian object lesson of how power operates through subtle daily practices according situational logic to reconstitute the outlines of those categories as they are negotiated in the most mundane of encounters.

But if this is the case, I think it is important that we begin asking what interests are being served in treating "religion" and "race" as separate, parallel categories? Newton warns against the prospect of leaving "unnamed and unmapped the axes of social difference humans used to draw power." But I am reminded of Bruce Lincoln's claim in *Discourse and the Construction of Society* that

> In practice there always exists potential bases for associating and for dissociating one's self and one's group from others, and the vast majority of social sentiments are ambivalent mixes in which potential sources of affinity are (partially and perhaps temporarily) overlooked or suppressed in the interests of establishing a clear social border, or conversely, potential sources of estrangement are similarly treated in order to effect or preserve a desired level of social integration and solidarity.
>
> (Lincoln 2014: 10)

I take Lincoln to be reminding us that the axes of social difference are brought into being through discourse (and sometimes force), and that while we use those differences to draw power, it is also power that produces the axes in the first place. When we frame these categories as means of explaining difference, we must attend to the fact that what we choose to highlight as "difference" itself is constituted through historically situated power dynamics.

Newton is right to call for a return to the classic texts of our field to retrace "the faux pas of our disciplinary predecessors." One of the questions we should be asking of these works, and the work of our contemporaries, and our own work, is what interests were and are being served in the maintenance of "religion" and "race" as discreet categories? How does scholarship, and the institutional structures in which we participate, work to naturalize these categories? Are there measurable consequences to carving up the world as a collection of discreet "religious" and "racial" identities and—even if we reject essentialist understandings of the terms—treating these categories as the fruit of profoundly different narratives.

It is fair to note that we can distinguish "religion" discourse from other discourses, including racial discourse, and the prevailing pattern is to do just that. For instance, Bruce Lincoln's working definition of "religion" is "that discourse whose defining characteristic is its desire to speak of things eternal and transcendent with an authority equally transcendent and eternal." He distinguishes religious discourse from historical discourse by identifying the latter as that which speaks of things "temporal and terrestrial" in a human and fallible voice while still staking its claim to authority on rigorous and critical practice (Lincoln 2012: 1). That Lincoln positions these discourses in the "sharpest possible contrast" (ibid.), could be read as lending credence to the notion that "racial" discourse is clearly distinguishable from religious discourse for similar reasons. After all, racial discourse invokes the body and biology, which one might take to be the opposite of the eternal and the transcendent, the key markers of religious discourse. Bodies are measurable, material, and subject to decay. Bodies are, like historical discourse, "temporal and terrestrial." So on the surface, suggesting these terms are the fruit of the same vine might seem confounding.

Yet while racial discourse has come to be paired with bodies—and little could be counted less eternal than our bodies—it projects an essential, unchanging quality onto those bodies. In the American context in particular, where the "one drop rule" emerged as the codified marker of race, all outward aspects of bodily appearance gave way at the first hint of evidence (or even rumor) of one's descent from an African ancestor to a social imaginary that would, from that point on, read "blackness" on to one's body (Davis 1994: 4–6). This classification, in turn, was the only thing necessary to deny an individual's civil rights. While the body may be temporal and terrestrial, racial classification operated as a permanent marker that could inform the public's understanding of our identities long after our bodies had decayed.

Perhaps, then, the hidden link between religion and race has to do with the fact that both discourses operate to fasten positionality to permanence. If fluidity and impermanence are the hallmarks of our encounter with the world, then authority, status, and other manifestations of power require a stable, fixed peg on which to hang their hats. Religion and race discourses may serve as such stabilizers through their capacity to evoke imaginings of permanence. In turn, both serve to authorize social hierarchies far more effectively than discourses rooted in things we all recognize as the fruit of human labor.

Take law, for instance. Social hierarchies can be modified through mundane acts of legislation as resources are redistributed. In addition, laws can have a direct bearing on the way social responsibilities are distributed among both individuals and groups. Laws, when implemented within the framework of a stable political structure, can be quite impactful for the transformation of social order. But nearly everyone recognizes the law as contingent. The efficacy of laws depends not on their permanence, but upon a state apparatus of enforcement. Laws can be reconfigured by legislative bodies charged with rescinding them, transforming them, and introducing new laws at any time. In recent years we have seen shifting legal (and, consequently, social) status for individuals in same-sex realtionships as the path to legally recognized marriage has been opened up through legislation and legal challenges in the courts. Another example may be seen in the legal (and, consequently, social) status of individuals who use marijuana. A few states have even taken steps to expunge prior criminal records of those convicted of marijuana possession or distribution. Laws may be authoritative, but we tend to be acutely aware of their mutability.

Authorizing positionality in the social matrix by appeals to religion and race bypass the self-evident contingency of legislation. Religious discourse, for instance, may be used to ground status in divine will, which is taken to be eternal. The "calling" to preach or the exemption from military service for "religious" reasons are mundane examples of this, as each is recognized as resulting from a person's claiming a relationship to transcendent authority. In the same way, discursive appeals to imagined essentialized racial classification in a social order where such classification impacts social hierarchies, as it has in the United States, impacts positionality. Thanks to systems of ideological production in which we participate, both consciously and subconsciously, appeals to religion and race have historically presented themselves as natural.

One might reasonably object by pointing out that history has shown great variation in the ways both religious claims and racial imagination have been understood. Even claims codified in "sacred" texts are subject to countless interpretations. There is no disputing this. Yet I contend that the difference rests in the discursive frameworks in which these vehicles for social control operate. In the current debate over a "border wall" proposed by President Donald Trump, for instance, Christian advocates for Trump's wall are fond of citing Deuteronomy 32:8, "When the Most High apportioned the nations, when he divided humankind, he fixed the boundaries of the peoples ...," or Luke 11:21, "When a strong man, fully armed, guards his castle, his property is safe," to authorize their position. When Christian opponents of Trump's wall attempt to authorize their views, they turn to the dozens of biblical passages commanding that we welcome "the stranger," or Matthew's eschatological narrative of Jesus claiming one's position at divine judgment will depend upon the treatment of "the least of these" in their time of need (25:31-40). Still, while conclusions about the righteousness of "the Wall" will vary and can be shown to be historically contingent, the discursive strategies both sides employ to insist on the "rightness" of their positions are grounded in appeals to *eternal truths* expressed in their common "sacred" book—a status the book enjoys through centuries of mundane verbal, symbolic, and at times even legal instantiations serving to produce the effect of regarding the book as the central transmitter of transcendent authority rooted in divine will.

The rules of racial discourse operate according to a similar logic. Take the case of Rachel Dolezal (whose legal name is now Nkechi Amare Diallo; Associated Press 2017) the president of the Spokane, Washington chapter of the NAACP who was "outed" as being "white" after years of presenting herself as an African American woman. The NAACP, of course, has a long history of white membership and even white presidents, but in this case Dolezal's offense was convincing others that she was African American, resulting in her expulsion from the organization. Though the episode provided an entryway for countless academic interventions aimed at dispelling the notion that race was anything other than a social construct with profound political consequences, the fate of Ms. Dolezal hinged on the question of whether she was "really" a black woman. Months after the scandal erupted, Dolezal would insist "If somebody asked me how I identify, I identify as black. Nothing about whiteness describes who I am" (McGreal 2015). Yet having two biological parents who identified as "Caucasian," coupled with a trail of photographs revealing her application of techniques aimed at darkening her skin and styling her hair in a manner common to African American women, along with filing a lawsuit against Howard University over a decade earlier on that grounds that it discriminated against her for being white when selecting artwork for a display (Svrluga 2015), proved enough "evidence" to not only lose her position with the NAACP, but to lose her job as an art instructor and be ostracized by nearly all of her friends and coworkers. Their sense of betrayal cannot be separated from the countless social mechanisms by which ideology produces racialized selves and renders those selves convinced that something essential differentiates "whiteness" from "blackness." For those who recognized intellectually that this distinction was not rooted in biology, the perception that Dolezal had the agency necessary to actually choose to position herself in alignment with racialized power in a white supremacist culture functioned as an essentialist reading of her racial identity.

In light of these examples, I contend that one angle from which to approach the relationship of "religion" to "race" is to conceive of them as *positioning instruments*. If we begin by observing that societies, from the smallest to the largest, exhibit various forms of stratification rooted largely in the division of labor which impacts access to resources, then we can also identify discourses that emerge to rationalize, authorize, maintain, or even challenge that division of labor. These very discourses become instruments for re-configuring access to resources as changes in material conditions emerge. And as we look closer at any society and recognize its complexity, we can expand our understanding of what constitutes a "resource" to include not only material resources, but also non-material, yet still measurable, resources in culture that impact status—mapping on to what Pierre Bourdieu identified as "cultural capital" (see Bourdieu 1977, 1986). The recorded history of the species suggests that at any given point in time, access to material and cultural resources has been unevenly distributed across any given social order, and this uneven access manifests itself in a fine, elaborate web of social arrangements that result in hierarchies. As the Combahee River Collective discerned, an individual may occupy innumerable points on multiple hierarchical scales connected to different material and cultural resources. So I would argue that looking at the classifications of religion and race as *positioning instruments* which we actively utilize to situate ourselves with respect to others, in the most mundane way possible through common distinctions made with words and practices, enables us to not only avoid the trap of essentializing these categories, but also helps us avoid the risk of treating observable social axes of difference as being static realities. Seeing them as positioning instruments also addresses Frederick Cooper's concern that we think too often in terms of *identities* when we should be thinking in terms of *identification*.

The Combahee River Collective set out to re-map our classification schemes as a means of liberation from profound oppression and to not only reconfigure their position on social hierarchies, but to use their insights to level the hierarchies altogether. As such, the Collective points the way to an invaluable strategy: when your classification scheme is not allowing you to tell your story the way you want to tell your story, it's time to imagine a new scheme.

Craig R. Prentiss is a Professor of Religious Studies at Rockhurst University in Kansas City, Missouri. He is the author of *Staging Faith: Religion and African American Theater from the Harlem Renaissance to World War II* (NYU 2014), and editor of *Religion and the Creation of Race and Ethnicity: An Introduction* (NYU 2003).

References

Associated Press. 2017. "Disgraced NAACP Leader Rachel Dolezal Now Struggling to Get By." March 27. Retrieved from www.kshb.com/news/national/disgraced-naacp-leader-rachel-dolezal-now-struggling-to-get-by (accessed February 18, 2019).
Bourdieu, Pierre. 1977. "Cultural Reproduction and Social Reproduction." In Jerome Karabel and A. H. Halsey (eds.), *Power and Ideology in Education*, 487–511. New York: Oxford University Press.
Bourdieu, Pierre. 1986. "The Forms of Capital." In John Richardson (ed.), *Handbook of Theory and Research for the Sociology of Culture*, 241–258. New York: Greenwood Press.
Combahee River Collective. 1977. "The Combahee River Collective Statement." Retrieved from http://circuitous.org/scraps/combahee.html (accessed February 22, 2019).
Davis, F. James. 1994. *Who is Black? One Nation's Definition*. University Park, PA: Penn State University Press.
Delgado, Jessica, and Kelsey C. Moss. 2018. "Religion and Race in the Early Modern Iberian Atlantic." In Paul Harvey and Kathryn Gin Lum (eds.), *The Oxford Handbook of Religion and Race in American History*. New York: Oxford University Press. Retrieved from www.oxfordhandbooks.com/view/10.1093/oxfordhb/9780190221171.001.0001/oxfordhb-9780190221171-e-32.
Goetz, Rebecca. 2012. *The Baptism of Early Virginia: How Christianity Created Race*. Baltimore, MD: Johns Hopkins University Press.
Goldschmidt, Henry. 2006. *Race and Religion Among the Chosen People of Crown Heights*. New Brunswick, NJ: Rutgers University Press.
Harvey, Paul. 2017. *Bounds of Their Habitation: Race and Religion in American History*. Lanham, MD: Rowman & Littlefield.

Hickman, Jared. 2016. *Black Prometheus: Race and Radicalism in the Age of Atlantic Slavery*. Oxford: Oxford University Press.

Jacobsen, Robin Dale, and Nancy D. Wadsworth. 2012. "Introduction: Intersecting Race and Religion." In Robin Dale Jacobsen, and Nancy D. Wadsworth (eds.), *Faith and Race in American Political Life*, 1–21. Charlottesville, VA: University of Virginia Press, 2012.

Johnson, Sylvester. 2004. *The Myth of Ham in Nineteenth Century American Christianity: Race, Heathens, and the People of God*. New York: Palgrave Macmillan.

Lincoln, Bruce. 2012. "Theses on Method." In Bruce Lincoln, *Gods and Demons, Priests and Scholars: Critical Explorations in the History of Religions*. Chicago, IL: University of Chicago Press.

Lincoln, Bruce. 2014. *Discourse and the Construction of Society*. New York: Oxford University Press.

Lum, Kathryn Gin. 2014. *Damned Nation: Hell in America from the Revolution to Reconstruction*. New York: Oxford University Press.

McGreal, Chris. 2015. "Interview: Rachel Dolzal: 'I Wasn't Identifying as Black to Upset People. I Was Being Me.'" *The Guardian* (December 13). Retrieved from www.theguardian.com/us-news/2015/dec/13/rachel-dolezal-i-wasnt-identifying-as-black-to-upset-people-i-was-being-me (accessed February 18, 2019).

Nye, Malory. 2018. "Race and Religion: Postcolonial Formations of Power and Whiteness." *Method and Theory in the Study of Religion* (July): 1–28.

Svrluga, Susan. 2015. "Rachel Dolezal Sued Howard for Racial Discrimination. Because She Was White." *The Washington Post* (June 15). Retrieved from www.washingtonpost.com/news/grade-point/wp/2015/06/15/rachel-dolezal-sued-howard-for-racial-discrimination-because-she-was-white/?utm_term=.5c04bc28ab03 (accessed February 18, 2019).

Wallace, Michelle. 1975. "A Black Feminist's Search for Sisterhood." *The Village Voice* (July 28): 6–7.

Weisenfeld, Judith. 2017. *New World A-Coming: Black Religion and Racial Identity during the Great Migration*. New York: NYU Press.

Chapter 10

That's a Racist Question: Interrogating Racism in the Study of American Religions

Martha Smith Roberts

Introduction

At a White House press conference following the 2018 midterm elections, there was one exchange that stood out to me as particularly relevant to the conversation about race and ethnicity in the field of religious studies. *USA Today* summarized the exchange between Yamiche Alcindor and President Trump:

> Yamiche Alcindor, a White House correspondent for PBS NewsHour, questioned whether the president's use of the word "nationalism" at several rallies ahead of the midterm was a dog whistle for "white nationalism," as many of his critics have suggested. "That's such a racist question," Trump said. "What you just said is so insulting to me. It's a very terrible thing that you said."
>
> (Fritze and Jackson 2018)

Specifically, Alcindor pointed out to Trump that "on the campaign trail you called yourself a nationalist, some people saw that as emboldening white nationalists" and that "there are some people who think that Republican Party is seen as supporting white nationalism because of your rhetoric, what do you make of that?" (ibid.).[1] Trump's response was to first claim that he had "high poll numbers" among African Americans, and then to quickly accuse Alcindor of asking a "racist question." Trump, rather than addressing the very real ways in which nationalist identity is tied to white supremacy in the U.S., simply denied the validity of the question itself. For Trump, racism is not to be found in his rhetoric of nationalism, but in the question about it.

There is something about this exchange that I found both problematic and instructional for a discussion of the ways in which the academic study of religion deals with questions about race and racism. The idea that asking a question about racism, about white nationalism and white supremacy, in particular, could be dismissed as a racist act by the president is actually not out of the ordinary at all. While perhaps we may want to respond with incredulity and shock at the president's (1) clear use of racist tropes, (2) his personal offense at the accusation,

---

1. The video of the longer exchange is also available online at www.youtube.com/watch?v=Kbg4zOascEs.

and (3) his manipulation of the question to turn the charge of racism back onto the reporter; I think these tactics are actually not surprising at all. That is because this exchange stands out not for its exceptional nature, but for its ordinariness. It is an example of a common kind of avoidance of dialogue on racism in the U.S. The exchange is instructional in its combination of effectiveness and banality. Instead of simply illustrating how insufficient the president's answer was, this example also sheds light on how difficult it is to even ask a question about race in the U.S.; how difficult it is, and has been, to reveal racist tropes (like the use of "nationalism" vs. "globalism" that Trump uses at his rallies); and how quickly the accusation of being a racist can silence and disempower those trying to dismantle, or even simply point out, the ways that race is deployed by those in positions of power.

Richard Newton's chapter took on a certain significance in light of this exchange. I read it with an eye toward the contemporary American political realities that continue to make it possible to blatantly disrespect and accuse a black woman of racism because she dared to ask the question—she dared to point out that the president's discourse was empowering white nationalists. To then turn to the racial dynamics of power in the academic study of religion, I see Newton as also interrogating this critical tension around the "dark sin" of "challenging the presumed reality of the field." How has the concept of race been constructed and utilized in the field of religious studies? How do we ask questions of race? And how do we respond to them without re-inscribing white supremacy?

Excavating our field's past will inevitably bring us the question of what to do with what we uncover. I see Richard Newton as calling for two main things in his chapter: (1) recognition of the racist past of religious studies (or the ways in which the category of race has been a part of the discursive construction of the field itself), and (2) a productive reckoning with that past (and this is not simply to say "we are not that," but also to ask "how are we also that?"). To do this, we must recognize the ways the field has historically reproduced structures of racism and think critically about our own roles in the use and perpetuation of those structures via the category of race.

Excavating American Religious History

In my own subfield of American Religions, the racist past of scholarship is very much the reality. Colonialism, slavery, nativism, and nationalism—these are historical realities that we study and out of which the study of American religions emerged. Some of the earliest versions of "American religious history" were white Protestant church histories written by white Protestant men (Robert Baird and Philip Schaff remain two of the primary examples). These histories excluded or minimized the role and existence of minority traditions. This approach to the study of American religions is referred to as the *consensus* model, and it dominated the field well into the twentieth century. Catherine Albanese provides a concise description of this model:

> Consensus historiography writes the Anglo-Protestant past at the center of U.S. religious history. It sees processes of religious and ethnic blending—the proverbial "melting pot"—strongly at work in the nation's history, and it minimizes any narrative of religious pluralism. Likewise, it minimizes the impact of social, cultural, and religious change over time and stresses a religious culture of continuity with Anglo-Protestantism.
>
> (Albanese 2002: 5)

Early church histories are representative of the beginnings of the consensus approach to American religion, both in what they include and exclude, but also in how they represent groups in terms of the categories of religion, race, and ethnicity. Robert Baird's 1844 volume was titled *Religion in America*, but the subtitle tells us more: *Religion in America: Or, an Account of the Origin, Relation to the State, and Present Condition of the Evangelical Churches in the United States. With Notices of the Unevangelical Denominations.* For Baird, "religion in America" referred to evangelical churches in the U.S. His brief acknowledgment of the unevangelical churches reveals that the breadth of the term religion was limited to its ability to encompass a variety of Christian denominations.

Baird's history created boundaries around what counted as religion at all. These limits on the category of religion cannot be separated from racial categories. This is clearly evidenced in Baird's section on the "Aborigines of North America" where indigenous peoples are categorically described as uncivilized, barbarous, and leading wretched lives. While Baird acknowledges that the indigenous population may have had notions of good and evil, he described them as mostly "like children" in their religious concepts. Baird also had lengthy descriptions of the physical appearance of indigenous peoples, his chapter cataloged their skin color, stature, hair, eyes, cheekbones, and general phrenological profiles. This nineteenth-century text on American religious history, in other words, is drawing upon a Protestant template for cataloging and granting "religious" status, and it is also utilizing racial biological essentialism to connect particular bodies to that status. Baird's work was creating an indigenous population that needed to be missionized, to be saved from themselves—a race with no religion (Baird 1844).

In addition to Robert Baird's often cited text, another early consensus history was Philip Schaff's *America: A Sketch of Its Political, Social, and Religious Character*, which first appeared in the U.S. in 1855, translated from the original German (Albanese 2002: 5). Schaff was a Protestant theologian, church historian, and professor, and his work on the American religious landscape was an ecclesiastical history that centered on Protestant denominations. Schaff also comments at length on the national character of Americans, arguing that

> The Anglo-Saxon and Anglo-American, of all modern races, possess the strongest national character and the one best fitted for universal dominion, and that, too, not a dominion of despotism but one, which makes its subjects free citizens ... In them—and this is the secret of their national greatness and importance—the impulse toward freedom and the sense of law and order are inseparably united, and

> both rest on a moral basis ... I doubt whether the moral influence of Christianity and Protestantism has more deeply and widely affected any nation, than it has the Anglo-Saxon.
>
> (Schaff 1855: 55)

Here, just as in Baird's work, the category of religion was tied to racial and ethnic identity. Anglo-American culture was Christian, free, and moral. But Schaff himself noted in several places that the "dreadful curse of American slavery" was present in this new land, and so when he refers to freedom and citizenship, he was acknowledging that these freedoms were not available to everyone, though his hope was that slavery could be turned into "an incalculable blessing to the pagan savages of Africa" when Christianity eventually conquered Africa itself (ibid.: 52). When he described the makeup of the American "national character and social life" he clearly delineated which racial and ethnic groups were able to take part in this project. "The United States present, in the first place, a wonderful mixture of all nations under heaven... English, Scotch, Irish, Germans of all provinces, Swiss, French, Spaniards, Italians, Swedes, Norwegians, Poles, Magyars... have peaceably settled down together in political and social equality" (ibid.). These "representatives of European nations" were able to assimilate into the dominant American culture of white Protestant Christianity.

Distinct from these Americans, Schaff also described those who could not participate. "The red aborigines of the country, who are constantly retreating further into the forests and prairies of the West, and, in spite of all attempts to Christianize and civilize them, are steadily approaching the tragical fate of self-extermination by intestine wars, contagious diseases, and the poison of rum" (Baird 1844: 53). He similarly described "the black sons of Africa, rejoicing in the childlike cheerfulness of their nature, and even in freedom bowing instinctively before the superiority of the whites" and "the yellow immigrants from the Celestial Empire, attracted by the gold of California, and bringing with them their oblong eyes, their quiet disposition and mechanical culture, their industry, avarice, and filthy habits" (ibid.: 53). For Schaff, the ethnic makeup of America was intimately tied to religion. However, this notion of national identity or ethnicity was also inseparable from the biological essentialism that dominated early race science and the broader colonialist and racist views of the era. In other words, these early histories were clearly centering white Christian identity as the epitome of American cultural reality.

Baird and Schaff were reproducing the ideas about race and religion that dominated nineteenth-century American and European thought. But to recognize this bias as simply representative of the historical moment and therefore separable from the field that it produced would be irresponsible. The consensus model of American religious history remained entangled with these notions of racial and ethnic identity for the next century, long after scholarship had abandoned the overt biological essentialism of race science. It was only in the second half of the twentieth century that the consensus model would be challenged by the *conflict* and *contact* models, which emphasize the contentiousness of religious conflict as well as the broader exchanges between religious groups in the American context (Albanese 2002: 6; see also Albanese 1988, 1995; Marty 1986). The new models attempted to be more expansive and inclusive of religious diversity outside of the Anglo-Protestant narrative; however, these models also reveal the entanglements of the categories of race and religion in scholarship.

As the twentieth century developed, race science developed along with it, and terminologies of biological essentialism were replaced in scholarship with social-constructionist formulations of race. In regard to religion, this would mean an adoption of a sense that race was not "real" it was "cultural" and thus, especially following World War II, the notion of a biologically essentialized, racialized religion became something to distance oneself from. There is a rise in the use of "ethnicity" to describe cultural differences (what Omi and Winant 2015 call the "ethnicity paradigm"), and as scholars tried to maintain this new neutrality, they found themselves struggling to make sense of the intersections of race and religion. Often the solution was to simply ignore these intersections or to equate them to an "ethnic experience" like that of European immigrants. Even as progress was made in countering racial science and overt racism, scholarship on American religion and race continued to develop in relation to a unifying consensus history that highlighted similarity over difference, and it continued to privilege the white Protestant experience, slowly expanding it to a common European immigrant experience, and even, as Will Herberg argued in the mid-1950s, a Protestant–Catholic–Jewish American identity.

By the time, in the mid-1980s, when Lawrence Moore wrote his *Religious Outsiders and the Making of America*, this trend of consensus history had only just begun to be challenged (Moore 1986). Moore argued that "the discipline had long been shaped by a 'historiography of desire': governed by providential narratives and bias toward New England Protestantism, nineteenth- and twentieth-century historical writing was fundamentally motivated by the desire to preserve an 'American national character' that was pervasive enough to construct unity out of diversity and consensus amidst religious conflict" (Davis 2018: 2). Moore's response to this consensus narrative was to attempt to take religious diversity seriously by telling the story of traditions outside of the mainline Protestant center: Mormons, Catholics, Jews, Christian Scientists, Black churches, and civil religion. Moore's work exemplifies the struggles of each group and their roles in the construction of American identity. His additive approach seeks to fill in the gaps of past histories, though outside of a chapter on Black culture and Black churches, Moore does not engage with the category of race as constitutive of American religions.

The additive approaches of conflict histories are important in diversifying the consensus narrative of Anglo-Protestant American religion. The question of how to signify "outsider" identities (those outside of the consensus) and recognize difference in real ways needs to be answered with attention to the role of "race" and "religion" in the construction and maintenance of what Moore called an "American national character" or what Charles Long called an "American cultural language." Instead of silence around the ways in which race and racialization of marginalized groups is inherent in the history of American religious studies, we need to recognize and try to signify race, to, as Newton suggests, "admit to its disorienting nature" and to "commit to mapping the axes of social difference that race represents" (Newton, Chapter 6, this volume). This means going further than an additive approach that highlights historical diversity; it means thinking beyond pluralism as a solution to the white Protestant bias of the field.

This kind of excavation is not about denigrating Baird or Schaff as racist; rather, it is about recognizing their roles in the construction of a racist body of work. It is about asking questions about their language and contexts, and then asking ourselves if we are perpetuating the structures of inequality that they helped to create. Perhaps most importantly, excavation is about uncovering the ways in which early scholarship reverberates in contemporary scholarship. Newton points out a need to move beyond a focus on the content of the self and the Fanonian *comparaison* that it demands, and into a critique of the darkness itself. In American religion, that darkness is the historical elision and erasure of racialized groups, and that erasure happens not simply in the past, but in the present as well. Excavation is also about critiquing the darkness not only in content, but in forms—in ways of knowing, writing, speaking—that covertly perpetuate power structures and dominant narratives without simply mimicking their content. To excavate the field's history, one must dig into the long-reigning consensus model as a rich site where the beginnings (and not the end) of a unifying narrative of American religion can be found. Scholars must also ask themselves how this consensus model is perpetuated, even in later conflict and contact approaches that attempt to disrupt it, as well as in contemporary scholarship that utilizes a pluralist framework to uncritically erase difference.

It is highly unlikely that contemporary scholars will use the derogatory and racist descriptions of minority groups quoted above from Baird and Schaff. However, not being overtly racist does not mean that other racist structures are not being replicated.[2] In addition to their elision of Native American versions of religious history and their overt denigration of Native American people, culture, and religion; Baird and Schaff also described the disappearance of indigenous peoples as an inevitable phenomenon. This narrative of a "vanishing Indian" culture that was to blame for its own demise and inferiority to Christianity is one that continued well into the twentieth century (and beyond), in a variety of forms (Deloria 1999: 64–66). Baird and Schaff's language names indigenous racial and religious inferiority as the cause of the destruction of Native American culture, effectively erasing the colonial violence and genocide that was actually to blame, while also attempting to erase indigenous people from contemporary life. Baird and Schaff's overt racism may be abandoned, but a more insidious racism persists in narrative form, through descriptions of unassimilable indigeneity that romanticize pre-contact cultures as the only authentic forms of Native American identity and those that simply erase Native American experience from American identity all together. Natalie Avalos discusses these latter elisions in her recent

---

2. See the special forum on the study of American Religions in *Religion* volume 42, including Curtis (2012) and Lofton (2012).

article, "We Are Not all Immigrants," which argues that even the most progressive pluralist claims for expanding American identity to include more diversity, such as the "we are all immigrants" mantra, rely on the erasure of non-immigrant, indigenous identities (Avalos 2018).

Expanding the scholarship of American religions beyond Baird and Schaff's consensus model requires more than simply a rebuke of or supplement to their work. It requires examination of the ways their ideas of race persist despite attempts to move past them. This kind of work can take many forms. In her recent dissertation, Alison Tyner Davis takes a deep dive into the texts of Baird, Schaff, and others, to analyze the spatio-temporal logics of these nineteenth-century American religious histories and illustrate the ways in which "representations of American national religion rely upon the coordination of both spatial and temporal logics in order to create a narrative of American religious history that both gestures to the extensive diversity of religions, cultures, and sectarian 'seed plots' and, at the same time orders its account into a complete and coherent story of Protestant exceptionalism" (Davis 2018: 156). Davis concludes her work by looking for these spatio-temporal logics in contemporary historical work as well, examining the ways in which texts like Sidney Mead's *The Lively Experiment* and Catherine Albanese's *America: Religions and Religion* replicate and disrupt these early models (ibid.: 161–171).

Form is just as important as content in excavations and revisions of American religious history. To attempt to remedy historical elision by simply adding more diversity to American religious history can itself be a continuation of Protestant consensus structures in the form of pluralism. The reverberations of consensus history are felt in a myriad of ways. What does all of this mean for a field that continues to point to Baird and Schaff as its progenitors even as it claims to move beyond their racism? To cite them can perpetuate these axes of race and religion, particularly when these citations continue to point to consensus narratives as accurate histories, disavow their bias as socially contextualized and thus understandable, and then replicate their racist structures with the overt racist content edited out. Scholars of American religion must find ways to move the conversation toward recognition of the structural racism that pervades the field and stop simply citing the omission of overt racism as a victory and the final word on the subject.

Signification and An-Other Way Forward

Charles Long's notion of signification invites us to imagine or re-imagine American religious histories that respond to silences or narrative elisions without simply supplementing a central storyline. Long has written extensively about the silence in American religious history that continues to render minority religious groups invisible. That silence is perpetuated through both the wholesale adoption of consensus narratives and the ignorance of counter-narratives that already exist alongside of and in tension with consensus histories. Juan M. Floyd-Thomas notes that "even as white historians were steadily documenting the grand historical narrative of the United States during the late eighteenth and early nineteenth centuries, African American writers faced the particular task of piecing together a *counterhistory*, an approach to history that would present both the necessity of and the means for the liberation of the oppressed" (Floyd-Thomas 2018: 12). For Long, counternarratives offer the content and the form for the re-shaping of American religious histories and futures. The tools to reconstruct scholarly forms already exist, though they remain peripheral, uncited, untaught, and unengaged in many ways. According to Long, counterhistories must be thoughtfully incorporated:

> It is no longer possible for us to add the "invisible ones" as addenda to a European-dominated historical method, for such a procedure fails to take into account the relationships of the ones omitted throughout the history of religion in America. Nor is it possible for us, simply in imitation of the historical method and historiography we are criticizing, to begin the project of writing history in which the ideological values of blacks or American Indians dominate.
> (Long 1995: 162)[3]

Instead of serving as supplements or replacement narratives, counterhistories have the potential to radically refigure the dominant forms in American religious history.

In Richard Newton's chapter, there are several parallels with Charles Long's theory of signification and his critique and corrective of the American cultural language. Long calls for a recognition that involves investigating the languages of hegemony in order to move beyond them, not just repeat them. Using the Civil Rights Movement as an example, Long proposes that a three-part process must happen: (1) those who are attempting to create a new narrative must really see each other—that is recognize and affirm each other's common humanity; (2) they must learn the nuances of the American cultural language, or come to "know the Man;" and (3) they must intentionally create another reality, a knowledge and experience of "reality not created or given by the Man" (Long 1995: 166).

In Newton's work, there is an explicit call to move outside of self-centered individualism, to recognize the limits of the self by forging relationships with "others" (like he illustrates with the examples of Combahee collective or Crenshaw's intersectionality). This seems to mean moving away from a conception of identity as a sort of neoliberal individual responsibility and toward a recognition of the power of social categories (like race, religion, nation) in identity construction. Newton also calls for a certain recognition of a "patriarchal" form of critique/theorizing seen in the ad hominem attack, what Long might call learning and recognizing the language of the Man. And finally, Newton suggests that signification is a way to dissemble reality and to reconstruct it (not just to talk around the thing, but to get to the heart of it). In this sense, Newton amplifies Long's call to action.

---

3. See also Rolsky (2012).

A Longian re-making of the dominant narrative moves us from searching for "the racist" in our history toward searching for "race and racism" as social axes, as constructed/constructing categories that we need to recognize. And by doing so, Long suggests, we can create an-other reality. Long's *Significations* begins the work of taking seriously the constructive power of race in the field of religious studies. Long does this not by trying to replace or displace American religious history, but to instead to use "signification" to get to the heart of it, to reveal the ways in which histories of classifying and controlling indigenous and black bodies have always been a part of the American cultural language. Reconstructing American religious history means recognizing that the original compromise of American language established freedom only through denying freedom on the basis of racial and religious categories.

Conclusion

I want to come back to the Alcindor–Trump press conference exchange. I think it is instructive because it might be a sort of "performance" of these tropes that Newton brings up in the field, that often by asking the question about the discursive construction of the field, the questioner becomes the maligned figure. The attempt (here by Alcindor) to get at the ways in which language can create national and nationalist identities, for example, is a question *about* race and racism, but is it a racist question? In fact, it is the case that calling it a racist question is simply to perform, enact, and perpetuate one version of reality and to try to silence those that seek to map these social axes—to illuminate the intersections of race, religion, and nation. It shifts the inquiry toward the personal, and away from the structural. It looks for someone to malign and move past, without actually questioning the systemic replications that are not so easy to distance oneself from. As Sara Ahmed notes, "Describing the problem of racism can mean being treated as if you have created the problem, as if the very talk about divisions is what is divisive" (Ahmed 2012: 152). If the study of American religions is to shift its paradigms, it cannot simply call its progenitors racist, and then ignore the questions about its own perpetuation of racist forms. It must truly hear the questions about racism and pay attention to who is asking those questions. As a field, why do we still have so much trouble asking, and answering these questions? Why is it that those doing this work are still seen as somehow marginal to the real work of the field of American religions?

In the examination of discursive narrative structures of racialized power and knowledge, we must not forget to excavate the material realities of race that reverberate in our institutional structures and continue to work against the possibilities of recognizing the work of scholars that embody these racialized identities. Scholars whose bodies are racialized are structurally disadvantaged at every stage of the academic process, from undergraduate education, graduate school, the job market, to the tenure process. Voices and bodies that attempt to disrupt the field's narratives are consistently and unwavering told that they are "asking racist questions" instead of recognizing the invisible racist structures that are the foundations of pluralist rhetoric. Sara Ahmed's work on institutional realities of racism offers insight on "the paradox between, on the one hand, the ubiquitous use of diversity as an official language by institutions and, on the other, how practitioners experience those institutions as resistant to their work" (Ahmed 2012: 17). The field must be wary of this as well. The above excavations of American religions should not be mistaken as the isolated problems of a sub-field. The academic study of religion as a whole must consider the ways in which our forms, theories, histories, and institutional frameworks need not only excavation, but thoughtful attention to the present. To dismiss questions as racist is a form of power that we cannot afford to continue to replicate.

Martha Smith Roberts is Assistant Professor of Religious Studies at Fullerton College. Her primary research is a critical analysis of post-racial and post-ethnic theories of American religious pluralism and extending this analysis to critical pedagogies of religious studies. Roberts is also working on a co-authored manuscript analyzing the various spiritualities emerging within the hula hooping subculture.

References

Ahmed, Sara. 2012. *On Being Included: Racism and Diversity in Institutional Life*. Durham, NC: Duke University Press.

Albanese, Catherine L. 1988. "Religion and the American Experience: A Century After." *Church History* 57(3): 337–351. https://doi.org/10.2307/3166577

Albanese, Catherine L. 1995. "Refusing the Wild Pomegranate Seed: America, Religious History and the Life of the Academy." *Journal of the American Academy of Religion* 63(2): 205–229. https://doi.org/10.1093/jaarel/LXIII.2.205

Albanese, Catherine L. 2002. *American Religious History: A Bibliographical Essay*. Currents in American Scholarship Series. Washington, DC: U.S. Department of State.

Avalos, Natalie. 2018. "We are Not all Immigrants: The White Liberal Nostalgia of Immigrant Life." *Sociological Imagination* 54(1): 57–65.

Baird, Rev. Robert. 1844. *Religion in America, or, An Account of the Origin, Progress, Relation to the State, and Present Condition of the Evangelical Churches in the United States: With Notices of the Unevangelical Denominations*. New York: Harper and Brothers.

Curtis, Finnbar. 2012. "The Study of American Religions: Critical Reflections on a Specialization." *Religion* 42(3): 355–372. https://doi.org/10.1080/0048721X.2012.681875

Davis, Alison Tyner. 2018. "Troping Protestant Desire: Patterns of Time and Space in Nineteenth-Century American Religious History." ProQuest Dissertations Publishing.

Deloria, Philip Joseph. 1999. *Playing Indian*. New Haven, CT: Yale University Press.

Floyd-Thomas, Juan M. 2018. "Towards a Religious History of the Black Atlantic: Charles H. Long's *Significations* and New World Slavery." *Journal of Religious History* 42(1): 3–24. https://doi.org/10.1111/1467-9809.12409

Fritze, John, and David Jackson. 2018. "Trump Accuses Reporter of Asking 'Racist' Question after She Presses Him on Nationalism." *USA Today* (November 7). Retrieved from www.usatoday.com/story/news/politics/elections/2018/11/07/election-results-donald-trump-accuses-reporter-asking-racist-question/1920331002 (accessed November 12, 2018).

Lofton, Katherine. 2012. "Religious History as Religious Studies," *Religion* 42(3): 383–394. https://doi.org/10.1080/0048721X.2012.681878

Long, Charles H., 1995. *Significations: Signs, Symbols, and Images in the Interpretation of Religion.* Aurora, CO: The Davies Group.

Marty, Martin E. 1986. "The American Religious History Canon," *Social Research* 53(3): 513–528.

Moore, R. Lawrence. 1986. *Religious Outsiders and the Making of America.* New York: Oxford University Press.

Omi, Michael, and Howard Winant. 2015. *Racial Formation in the United States*, 3rd edition. New York: Routledge.

Rolsky, Louis Benjamin. 2012. "Charles H. Long and the Re-Orientation of American Religious History." *Journal of the American Academy of Religion* 80(3): 750–774. https://doi.org/10.1093/jaarel/lfs045

Schaff, Philip. 1855. *America: A Sketch of the Political, Social, and Religious Character of the United States of North America: In Two Lectures.* New York: Scribner.

Chapter 11

The Trope Has Been Set: Race and Religion as Critical Entanglement

Richard Newton

The trope has been set ... As my essay suggests (Chapter 6, this volume), the scholar should not simply take narrations of origin and intention as gospel truth but as provocations for greater theorizing. But my truth be told, I had ambivalent feelings when members of the 2018 NAASR Program Committee invited me to present an orienting paper on theorizing the category of race in the academic study of religion. That my colleagues thought of me and my scholarship as up to the task was encouraging, yet I also wondered the extent to which I had been summoned for a fool's errand. The methodological and political histories evoked by race appear to be a sort of "third rail" in the academic study of religion. Nevertheless, as screenwriter Eli Attie wrote, "the third rail's where all the power is" (Hébert 2004). In that spirit I seized the welcome extended me to go there and bring NAASR along ... *but to where?*

The destination for this paper was foreshadowed in a previous NAASR paper that I titled "Signifying 'Theory': Toward a Mutually Assured Deconstruction" (Newton 2017: 37–46). I suggested that theory prompts us to "take note of the constructed self—especially the scholarly self—and to welcome the inevitable deauthorization of our own methodological regimes" (ibid.: 38). In the face of those who would critique the reflexive turn as an aimless exercise in navel-gazing, I argued that the work is "at least a nod toward a self-awareness that recognizes the scholar's interest in the construction and maintenance of an evaluative system that assigns meaning and worth to persons" (ibid.: 41). The rationale underlying this orientation is that I find the very framing of categorical indices of social difference—like those discussed in this volume—too conveniently deployed in the academic study of religion. "For all we know, our heuristic distinctions may be in service of aims unbefitting of a self-proclaimed 'observer'" (ibid.: 41). On the matter of race, I think the parameters by which the discourse is critically invoked are far too narrow. And it is that narrowness that locates the field in the very predicament that necessitates the preceding set of essays.

In this paper, I wanted to clarify the coordinates for analysis in a way that would surface the methodological and political tensions that adjoin—at least, what I take to be—a more self-aware approach to the examination of race from the purview of the academic study of religion. To me this amounts to understanding the way in which the discourse that is "race" ensnares the racialized and the racist alike. Because many historically characterize *Religionswissenschaft* as historically steeped in the trappings of racism (Murphy 2007; Nye 2019), I suspected that using it as a case study in "Signifying Der Rassist" would capture a significant haul on this occasion. Discussion of the paper did not disappoint. I am honored, challenged, and intrigued by the engagement of all who responded. They took my own thinking in directions that move the conversation to vantages suited for deeper reflection.

First, I want to speak to Rudy Busto's sharp reading of my essay (Chapter 8, this volume) and the ways that I see it both cutting the theoretical tensions of the larger conversation while tightening the hold on the political dynamics I intended to capture. I will then turn toward Craig Prentiss's discussion of race and religion as "schemes of social ordering" (Chapter 9, this volume), as I think the points he raised help enumerate some key methodological concerns facing the field. Robyn Walsh's critical history of biblical studies (Chapter 7, this volume) exemplifies how I hoped scholars would reassess their particular subfields' assumptions by way of critically mapping race and religion. To this I will add my own thoughts on possible futures for biblical studies. Finally, as Martha Smith Roberts considers the implication of my Longian theorizing for her own subfield of American Religious history (Chapter 10, this volume), I want to both echo her thesis and reflect on why the work of signification continues to elude many. This I will accomplish by using the axial framework that I discussed at the end of my paper to think about the mystification of racism in U.S. political life.

Two (A)versions of Busto

Busto rightfully notes that I made a typographical error in my presentation of the Borgesian phrase "crimen oscuro." In my hands the translation "dark sin" became "dark skin"—a misread akin to the corrupted and yet illuminating riffs on Marshall McLuhan's definition of "the message": "*Message* and *Mess Age*, *Massage* and *Mass Age*" (McLuhan n.d.). Busto's discussion of my paper considers two interpretations of my thesis on the manner in which a critical history of the academic study of religion can help scholars better understand race. I very much appreciate Busto's challenge, but rather than seeing the interpretations presented as forking paths, I understand them as exceptions demonstrative of the rule, explications of the circular logics that comprise the "Chinese finger trap" to which he likened race. And it is in gripping that tension that I see myself as actually less fatalistic than the Borgesian Doppelgänger when it comes to race, albeit for more sobering reasons.

In Version 1, Busto questions my premise about religious studies as having something worthwhile to contribute to examinations of race. He is pessimistic because the "history, rules, and structures" of the discipline often work in tandem with "racecraft" (Fields and Fields 2014). I do not disagree. When race becomes a value-additive to flavor-stale scholarship on religion, then we need to question the endeavor. Furthermore, when the institutions where we work discipline us for our disruptive scholarship on race and religion, then we need to take a moment to consider what these institutions are encouraging us to maintain. The pushback Busto has received in regard to his own presence and work in the academy is evidence of the racism that in so many ways defines the field. I take that very seriously and recommend NAASR do the same.

At the same time, the endurance—and, dare I say—success of Busto's work also has forced openings for the occasion of this panel to take place—not in the suspiciously trendy and self-congratulatory employ of the "anti-racist" banner, but with a forthright skepticism about the implications of our own work. I read Busto as reminding us that this is not grounds for celebration. For if we have truly heard and amplified the voices of those who have been disruptive, then we have all but prophesied our own end. To this I say, so be it.

Version 2 seems to suggest that I have not done my due diligence in listening to those voices, particularly as they have been echoed through "old school ethnic studies." In actuality, I think I am closer to Busto than was clear to him. I am content joining Omi and Winant in talking about racialization, just as I think scholars should name and historicize the superstructures where race is operationalized. This is why I concur with their most recent considerations of race as a master category whose effectiveness has defined other discourses of difference in the American project (Omi and Winant 2015: xi, 64, 106–131). This is why I am okay with using analysis of racecraft to understand other matters of social difference—though one must always recalibrate for context. For instance, in the case of Ireland, one might set the debate over Christian identity as analog to race in America. Or in the case of the Hakka and Hokkien in Taiwan, the analog may be the place of a contested land belonging to certain bodies rather than the phenotypic assumptions that are rampant in the U.S. case. As Craig Prentiss makes clear, the definition of terms is paramount, and I think Robyn Walsh's analysis of the German roots of biblical studies showed how this can be done to great effect.

The "riddling silence" to which I am pointing is the recognition that people operationalize race in ways with which they are not aware. And while we may think that goes without saying, evidence to the contrary can be found in the ironic ways in which popular anti-racist efforts have fetishized race as an essence possessed or an intersection of one's being. To use Omi and Winant's terms, appeals to anti-racism can be part of a "racist project" (Omi and Winant 2015: 109). What kind of scholars of religion wouldn't have something to say about this? Martha Smith Roberts' discussion of a black woman being labeled as racist fills such an analytical void. And I understand that as the responsibility of good religious studies scholarship.

I am not ready to talk about anti-solutions within the academy because I think we first need to talk about the aforementioned superstructures and histories. I don't trust the methods of the academy to rid racism. But I do think we can use its methods to help explain it. In this I concur with my old school ethnic studies colleagues in recognizing how racism has served as a blueprint for the construction of other (dis)orienting ways of marking difference. Perhaps our paths fork in so far as I am also interested in comparing the variety of ways people make and manage difference, as well as coming to understand the relationship between those ways. Having worked in and alongside a department of "ethnic and women's studies," I am privy to the institutional histories and politics that make such inquiries disruptive. Lest we forget, these lauded interdisciplinary housings are often the product of brokered deals for the scraps under institutional tables. Recasting that sublimation into synergy requires a fair amount of mythmaking. But as scholars of religion—and students of classification—we know how this happens. And as Busto said, scholarship on race and religion should be disruptive, even of the narratives with which we are most comfortable. Truer words may have never been spoken. I trust the argument laid out by Busto will keep us honest in more ways than we currently know.

Doing the (Re)work after Combahee and Prentiss

All of that said, I am not optimistic about the academic study of race and religion. But given what we know about the work people do with race and religion, I am realistic about the possibility for reworking our understandings of these categories and what people have done with them. As Craig Prentiss aptly outlines in his study of the Combahee River Collective, scholars would do well to interrogate the very terms on which we have come to work with these classificatory models. He explains, "fighting the world demanded reworking the categories the world handed [the Collective], as it was clear to them that when considered in isolation, each category left out significant data." With this in mind, scholars of race and religion can move to a conceptualization built upon the analytical disassembly of these classificatory models rather than the political replication of them. Prentiss offers two clarifying steps for those committed to this on-going project.

First, we need to be clear about our observational limits. Prentiss says that "when we frame these categories as means of explaining difference, we must attend to the fact that what we choose to highlight as 'difference' itself is constituted through historically situated power dynamics." What I appreciate here is that the difficulty in studying race and religion lay not in the further essentializing of the categories but in our theoretical imaginations. Maybe we would be better off thinking about race and religion not as phenomenological riddles but as epistemological labyrinths of our human design. (In this way, Busto's reference to the Chinese finger trap does make sense to me.) Furthermore these constructs are built upon social facts that impact us "within a range of discursive social fields" such that they demand the attention of those committed to making sense of the human.

Prentiss's elaboration would have us recall that we work with what we have received historically, and yet that does not make the scholar's work a matter of fate, just the opposite. His perspective puts the onus on us to confound the dictates of the past—our academic forebears, the bureaucracies from which we benefit, and our very sense of complacency. The Combahee River Collective was revolutionary in its political ambitions. Scholars will disagree on how far to follow them. But were scholars to wrestle with the implications of what the Collective presented, our treatment of the data on race and religion would be far more astute.

For those interested in how human beings map meaning onto the world, Prentiss's discussion of race and religion as "positioning instruments" is where I suggest scholars interested in method and theory might give more attention. Doing so requires care to recognize how our study—Müller's German workshop comes to mind here—was built with the tools of people who located themselves with the very positioning instruments we are examining. That does not mean we stop working. It does mean we take the time to look at the chips on the floor and ask what we are cutting.[1]

Walsh and the Quest for Critical Historiography

Without explaining the punchline of my title, I wanted it to do the double duty of sending up the fad of highlighting someone as racist while doubling down on the insidious workings of race as a discourse. Robyn Walsh's redescription of biblical studies within the wider frameworks the history of racism and the *religionsgeschichtliche Schule* uses a similar humor to bring us to some serious business. She begins with a deconstruction of a modern lingua franca—namely, the Myers–Briggs Type Indicator—and transitions into a discussion of a prior one—the *Geistesgeschicthe* or study of cultural or intellectual history. In so doing, Walsh lays out some of the positioning instruments that moved the *Volk* into locales that would so greatly determine the course of history, not only by way of the world wars, but by the work of those in our field. By observing how German Romantics mapped ancient minds and bodies, she underscores how racism is a most peculiar logic, inviting us to ask where else we see that logic at work.

Like a number of other subfields, biblical studies scholars have tried to unshackle themselves from a dominant German Romantic tradition. Perhaps no other tactic has been as effective as the liberationist project. Given that its proponents often find themselves at odds with each other, the proposition of unreading normative and normalizing texts has enticed a number of parties. The academy has seen increases in representation on a number of indices as a diversity of people are

---

1. For those wanting to engage my signifying on the metaphor further, the student of the field could learn a lot from pairing Müller's *Chips from a German Workshop* (1867–1875) and Jonathan Z. Smith's "When the Chips are Down" (Smith 2004: 1–60). The former has Müller charging forward with his project, the science of religion. The latter has Smith reflecting on his career in the history of religions by way of something akin to anthropologist Stanley Brandes's method of "ethnographic autobiography," a first-person attempt to historicize one's interests by situating them in relation to wider cultural themes, trends, patterns, and problematics (cf. the psychological focus of many of the researchers who employ autoethnography). For further discussion of this method, I commend Harry F. Wolcott's "The Ethnographic Autobiography" (2004) and "The Art of Discretion" (2005).

working through their questions and hypotheses about the world through these texts. Biblical studies, among other subfields, is trying to determine the place of representation in scholars and scholarship. But what if we were to assume that the politics are always and already at play in the work of scholars, and it is the job of our scholarship to help lay bare not only our best and most detailed analyses, but also the political influences and ramifications of our findings?

This is not an original suggestion, but it is different than simply talking about presence as "problematic" without explanation. The "problematic" could then be the riddles, puzzles, and conundrums that we examine rather than a dismissive trump card to be played in debate. For example, Walsh discusses how "pressing political interests continued to inform methodological developments in how Romantic scholars read ancient texts, particularly those that attributed authorship to communities rather than individual writers." What if the historical-critical method were an analysis that compared examples of both attributional tactics (the historicizing of the scholar and the scholar's historicizing) to understand what they do for communities? How are those referential techniques similarly and differently employed in positioning people in a mutual social plane? In this way, biblical studies scholars would have much to offer to the humanistic scholarship beyond fluency with a text or set of languages.

This suggestion also comes with the recognition that the texts that we scholars write are also primary sources for others' analysis. And as such, we should discursively analyze what people are doing with their bibliographies. This is why I have mixed feelings about some of the ways scholars will apply the citation practices that Megan Goodwin advocates for in her paper in this volume. After all, despite my citation of a number of minoritized thinkers (especially black women), someone on Twitter considered maligning the patriarchal normativity of my paper and those who responded to it based upon a photograph of the originating panel, one whose optics obscure how participants identify and are identified. And while Busto is correct to pick up on the "Nordic," even "Aryan hauntings" among the names mentioned my paper, I would have thought that the rationale for this choice was rather obvious. I see neither myself nor my scholarship as imprisoned by the West. In the words of the character Rorschach from *Watchmen*, "None of you seem to understand. *I'm* not locked up in here with *you*. *You're* locked up in here with *me*" (Moore and Gibbons 2008 [1986–1987]). To Walsh's point, let us help each other critically work through the traditions by which we have been—especially those "pertaining to race, ethnicity, and cognition through the rhetorics of language and myth."

Signifying American Religion

If Robyn Walsh's paper demonstrates how we might reconsider the constitution of our various subfields, Martha Smith Roberts's paper fleshes out how we might move beyond a fixation on *Homo religiosus* as apart from culture and instead approach our selected data as a reflection, even refraction of those aspects of culture that constitute our routine practices and "rootinized" assumptions (Newton 2020). Bringing to my mind the work of historian Hayden White (1987), she frames our task as an "excavation" of "content" and "form." Smith Roberts, furthermore, points out how this entails a reframing of how our methods can be imbricated in the work of discourses like race and religion. Both she and I take a cue from Charles H. Long in wanting to "investigat[e] the languages of hegemony in order to move beyond them, not just repeat them" (1999 [1986]: 166).

One way we could make good on this project is by experimenting with the model of axial signification that I present toward the end of my paper. We could use this critical framework—derived from some of the key offerings of *Religionswissenschaft*—to redescribe and explain the evocative vignette with which Smith Roberts begins her own excavation. In this story, Haitian-American journalist Yamiche Alcindor challenged President Trump to consider the ramifications of the patently "nationalist" language he used during the 2018 midterm election rallies. He rebuffed any insinuation that his diction implied a condoning of white nationalism or racism—refusing to acknowledge, as Smith Roberts put it, "the very real ways in which nationalist identity is tied to white supremacy in the U.S." I agree with her that this story is "an example of a common kind of avoidance of dialogue on racism in the U.S." I would also add that it is also a demonstration of racism's work as a shibboleth or cipher of belonging.

The place to start is in observation that the sign, "racism," is signified with a negative, even caustic valence at our present moment in history. This is a value—regardless of the social actions whose consequences may suggest otherwise—that seems as definitive as the belief in the potential of the United States as a nation. And it is this notion of nationhood that is being debated at the level of ideology or in Freudian terms, *Weltanschauung*, "an intellectual construction which solves all problems of our existence uniformly on the basis of one overriding hypothesis, which, accordingly, leaves no question unanswered and in which everything that interests us finds its fixed place" (Freud 2017 [1933]: 358). Far from shifting the conversation away from race, I think a discussion of nation brings race into view such that we can more convincingly explain the President's use of the term "racist."

As the official state executive, the President simultaneously claims to change and maintain America. In terms of change, he says that he is privileging American self-interest in a way that his predecessors did not, abbreviated in his slogan "America First." This does not necessarily appear self-centered because he and his predecessors have thoroughly laid the ground for an exceptionalist orientation. In particular, he has reiterated this orientation in the face of a globalist threat, an empty signifier used to denote an enemy, historically in anti-Semitic terms (Zimmer 2018). That history is important because it fuels the engine of his post-racial agenda. In his conceptualization, American greatness transcends racial difference and racist history. Hence he doubles down against any claim that would mar this vision.

The stakes of his racial play are high, as indicated by the organizations and methods he is attempting to handle in his argument. When Alcindor remarks that the public had debated the linkage between white nationalists (with whom he shares rhetoric) and the Republican Party (of which he is the leader), he responds with an appeal to favorable poll numbers among African Americans. Rationalizing a connection he has to racists or racism becomes more difficult because of the cognitive dissonance between white nationalist conviction and black support.

One could argue that the President's African American support is fabricated, but that plays directly into his patterned authenticity claims—namely, the vaunting of favorable news coverage as the *vox populi* and the rejection of critique as "fake news." To me, the President calling Alcindor's question "racist" is an attempt to affirm his authorial right to the nation-state. He is using the stage of a press conference to cast a journalist as an enemy of the state by casting her free exercise in the imagined community of the nation as contra its presumed ideals. If she can be placed as the only one who hears the tree falling in the forest—the only one who appears to have a problem with race—then any issue to be scrutinized lie not in the message but it in the source.

Reflection in Conclusion

I will conclude my response by reminding readers that if we are to excavate what Smith Roberts terms "the contemporary American political realities that continue to make it possible to blatantly disrespect and accuse a black woman of racism because she dared to ask the question," we should recognize that such discrimination does not need a reason. But scholars of religion have tools for understanding the way people will try to save face after doing the deed. When we refuse to marshal the histories from which we have learned, then we have failed to do our task as scholars. And it is in the mirror of such reflections that we might find "der Rassist."

Richard Newton is Assistant Professor of Religious Studies at the University of Alabama, where he serves as Undergraduate Director in the Department of Religious Studies. Newton's research focuses on scriptures as sites of identity formation, the politics of comparison, and the legacy of the New Testament. He is the author of *Identifying Roots: Alex Haley and the Anthropology of Scriptures* (Equinox 2020), Editor of the *Bulletin for the Study of Religion*, and founding curator of the social media professional development network, Sowing the Seed: Fruitful Conversations in Religion, Culture, and Teaching (SowingTheSeed.org).

References

Fields, Karen E. and Barbara J. Fields. 2014. *Racecraft: The Soul of Inequality in American Life*. New York: Verso.

Freud, Sigmund. 2017 [1933]. "The Question of Weltanschauung." In Jacques Waardenburg (ed.), *Classical Approaches to the Study of Religion*, 2nd edition, 358–365. Berlin: De Gruyter.

Hébert, Julie (dir.). 2004. "Slow News Day." *The West Wing*, season 5, episode 12. First broadcast on NBC, February 4. Retrieved www.imdb.com/title/tt0745678.

Long, Charles H. 1999 [1986]. *Significations: Signs, Symbols, and Images in the Interpretation of Religion*. Aurora, CO: The Davies Group.

McLuhan, Eric. n.d. "Why is the Title of the Book 'The Medium is the Massage' and Not 'The Medium is the Message'?" Retrieved from www.marshallmcluhan.com/common-questions.

Moore, Alan, and Dave Gibbons. 2008 [1986–1987]. *Watchmen*. New York: DC Comics.

Müller, Max. 1867–1875. *Chips from a German Workshop*. London: Longmans, Green, and Co.

Murphy, Tim. 2007. "Religionswissenschaft as Colonialist Discourse: The Case of Rudolf Otto." *Temenos* 43(1): 7–27. https://doi.org/10.33356/temenos.4604

Newton, Richard. 2017. "Signifying Theory: Toward a Method of Mutually Assured Deconstruction." In Aaron W. Hughes (ed.), *Theory in a Time of Excess: Beyond Reflection and Explanation in Religious Studies Scholarship*, 37–46. Sheffield: Equinox Publishing.

Newton, Richard. 2020. *Identifying Roots: Alex Haley and the Anthropology of Scriptures*. Sheffield: Equinox Publishing.

Nye, Malory. 2019. "Decolonizing the Study of Religion." *Open Libraries of Humanities* 5(1). https://doi.org/10.16995/olh.421

Omi, Michael, and Howard Winant. 2015. *Racial Formation in the United States*, 3rd edition. New York: Routledge.

Smith, Jonathan Z. 2004. *Relating Religion: Essays in the Study of Religion*. Chicago, IL: University of Chicago Press.

White, Hayden. 1987. *The Content of the Form: Narrative Discourse and Historical Representation*. Baltimore, MD: John Hopkins University Press.

Wolcott, Harry F. 2004. "The Ethnographic Autobiography." *Auto/Biography* 12: 93–106. https://doi.org/10.1191/0967550704ab004oa

Wolcott, Harry F. 2005. "The Art of Discretion." In Harry F. Wolcott, *The Art of Fieldwork*, 2nd edition, 229–259. Oxford: AltaMira Press,

Zimmer, Ben. 2018. "The Origins of the 'Globalist' Slur." *The Atlantic* (March 14). Retrieved from www.theatlantic.com/politics/archive/2018/03/the-origins-of-the-globalist-slur/555479.

Part III

Gender and Sexuality

Chapter 12

This Field Which Is Not One/The Body Is Smart: Rethinking Theory in the Study of Religion

Megan Goodwin

This paper was first delivered on the lands of the Ute, Cheyenne, and Arapaho people, all the more reason for us to recognize the fraught political terrain and violent material effects of "religion." As queer poet Alix Olson reminds us: every theory has a human price, and you gotta watch how your god is used.

* * *

Once upon a time at an annual meeting of the American Academy of Religion, a straight white male friend/colleague and I—both of us Americanists—found ourselves in attendance of three or four back-to-back panels in a single day. By the end of the third (or fourth) panel and *en route* to receptions (imagine this as a Sorkinesque walk-and-talk, except in this scene I am supporting my own work and not the Important Work of a Great Man), he turned to me and said: "I figured it out. You ask questions in every session, except those questions are actually all the same question."

He was not wrong, Reader. The question is this: what about gender? What about sexuality?

(I think it's important to clarify that when I ask this question, I don't mean "what about ladies? What about queers?" Or rather, I don't *just* mean that. I mean "how does your work, which purports to be about religion and the people or do it (or not), fail to account for the people with bodies who are doing that religion (or not)?)

I could only respond, "Friend, I swear to god: the minute they start asking themselves my question, I will ask about something else."

So, imagine my delight when Brad Stoddard invited me to address this very question with you all today—not just the question of gender and sexuality *in* the theorization of religion, but gender and sexuality *as* the theorization of religion. To some extent the charge of this workshop is impossible: there is no meaningful discussion of gender or sexuality that does not also center race, or class, or ability, or documented status, or mode of religious belonging, or recognize all these categories as comprising but not exhausting "politics." It must also be said that asking a white cis able-passing woman, however queer in however many ways, runs the very real risk of centering whiteness, ability, cisgender identity, and too many other positions of privilege as unmarked, inevitable, and universal. As queer trans writer Parker Molloy tweets every night: "I tried my best today. I'll do it again tomorrow."

We in the academy owe our articulation of identity as imbricated bodily realities and limits to a Black woman scholar, Kimberlé Crenshaw, who first offered the term intersectionality. In rooms where religion and sexuality are theorized, some scholars have proposed a post-intersectional mode of inquiry (which, as Traci West has offered, does not discard but meaningfully complicates the intersectional model). But since I'm still asking the same damn question every year in sessions of every single national meeting, I can confidently say that scholars of religion are not done with intersectionality, nor is intersectionality done with them.

For folks unfamiliar with the term, let's refer to a poor queer white woman scholar, Dorothy Allison, and her theorization of intersectionality (though she does not use the term). In "A Question of Class," Allison opines, "What I know for sure is that class, gender, sexual preference, and prejudice—racial, ethnic, and religious—form an intricate lattice that restricts and shapes our lives, and that resistance to hatred is not a simple act. Claiming your identity in the cauldron of hatred and resistance to hatred is infinitely complicated, and worse, almost unexplainable" (Allison 1994: 23). And yet Black women, Indigenous women, women and men and gender non-conforming and non-binary people of color, queer people, poor people, disabled people have worked for decades to explain how and why centering those identities matters, and demonstrated a thousand ways that the world (and, for our purposes, the academy) hates them—hates us—for trying.

It is for this reason that the politics of citation are so crucial in the theorization of religion, or any production of knowledge, for that matter. As professional killjoy Sara Ahmed insists in "Making Feminist Points," "citation [is] a rather successful reproductive technology, a way of reproducing the world around certain bodies" (Ahmed 2013). Ahmed draws our attention to the "selective history" of disciplines, to the "techniques of selection" that make "certain bodies and thematics core to the discipline, and others not even part" (ibid.). When we talk about "the founders" of religious studies, when we limit "theorists" of religion to thinkers who identify themselves as such or who have been historically recognized as such by the academy, we participate in the violent and hateful exclusion of those already too often violently and hatefully excluded beyond the academy.

In *Living a Feminist Life* (2016), Ahmed calls for a radical feminist politics of citation, through which "we acknowledge our debt to those who came before; those who helped us find our way when the way was obscured because we deviated from the paths we were told to follow" (Ahmed 2016: 15–16). This paper is a performance of radical feminist citational politics. If we must choose politics or theory, then let us, with Ahmed, choose politics and "be glad [we are] not doing theory!" (ibid.: 8). But her work shows it's possible to do both. "Think of this," she urges us. "Those of us who arrive in an academy that was not shaped by or for us bring knowledge, as well as worlds, that otherwise would not be here. Think of this: how we learn about worlds when they do not accommodate us. Think of the kinds of experiences you have when you are not expected to be here. These experiences are a resource to generate knowledge... We use our particulars to challenge the universal" (ibid.: 9–10). This is the charge, then: to use our particulars to challenge the universal.

I am indebted to so many scholars—space invaders, Ahmed would say, in the academy and in theory, because they refer to the "wrong texts" or ask the "wrong questions" (Ahmed 2016: 9)—who have shaped and are shaping the conversation about what it is to study religion. I especially want to acknowledge that three Black scholars—Nyasha Junior, Ed Curtis on behalf of the *Journal of Africana Religions*, and Kayla Wheeler—have directly informed my thinking on these matters, largely through our interactions on Twitter. And given the pivotal role Twitter is now playing in the production and dissemination of knowledge about religion, I also want to use this space to consider where the theorization of religion happens.

On that note: in March 2018, in response to an extensive Twitter thread calling for quotes about religion paired with animated GIFs, Islamic Studies scholar Kayla Wheeler asked for suggestions of women of color theorists of religion, as most of the responses so far were quoting white men (Wheeler 2018). Kecia Ali (2018) was the first to propose Zora Neale Hurston and Tomoko Masuzawa. Nyasha Junior (2018) cited Ntozake Shange: "i found god in myself & i loved her / i loved her fiercely" (Shange 2010: 63). Several others proposed Jasbir Puar. Annette Yoshiko Reed (2018) raised an important point: that in asking this question, we need to think about who gets recognized as a theorist, and whether recognition as a theorist requires that the work be (imagined as) universalizable. Today, I propose that theorizing religion is (or should be) less a call to consider what religion is than a call to consider what religion does, and here I am indebted to Carole Cusack's insightful formulation of this question in *Invented Religions* (Cusack 2010). Theorizing religion, of course, includes considerations of whose cultural work counts as religion—here we are all of us indebted to Masuzawa—but also whose thinking about religion is worth centering, worth, as we like to say, taking seriously (Masuzawa 2005). Every piece of writing about religion offers a theory of what religion is and what it does; we should expand our definitions of theory accordingly.

Let me say that again, because it's important. (I'll pause here to note that Ilyse Morgenstein Fuerst helped me clarify this assertion.) *Every piece of writing about religion offers a theory of what religion is and what it does.* That the author does not identify themselves as a theorist—that the academy has not encouraged them to view themselves as a theorist, because they are not limiting their theorization of religion to abstract and universalized statements of how religion works—does not invalidate their theories. Encouraging certain kinds of scholars—especially those in certain kinds of bodies, bodies marked as gendered, or sexualized, or raced, or classed, or disabled—to declare loudly that they are *not* theorists, that they do not "do theory," is an exercise in colonizing the academy, in privileging normative voices and bodies. Limiting theory to something only certain kinds of scholars do, rather than recognizing theory as the very premise of scholarship, claims theory as the special province of those legible to the academy as capable of "doing theory." Theories—and theorists—of religion have by and large exculpated themselves of needing to account for the specificities and intimate and explicit violences of gender, of sexuality, of race, of class, of ability, of the thousand things that make up the people who do religion.

If that is theory, then with Sara Ahmed, let us rejoice and be glad that we are not "doing theory." But rather than cede that territory to normative voices and normative bodies, let us hone our definition of theory to privilege scholars who have to work so much harder to do this work, whether or not they are confessed theorists of religion.

This paper reimagines a field of religious studies radically reoriented to center the theorizations of religion offered by Black women, women of color, queers, and other thinkers from marginalized backgrounds. Please note: I am not (merely) calling for scholars of religion to cite more Black women scholars, more queer/trans/GNC/NB scholars, more poor scholars, more scholars of color. Certainly we must ask ourselves why such scholars are seldom found on prosem syllabi or on lists of the "founders" of religious studies (Curtis 2018a). As Ed Curtis challenged: "Religious studies scholars, please don't tell us that you can't include Black women in your 'theory of religion' course. Or that there were are no foundational Black women in the academic study of religion. Only your racism prevents their inclusion" (Curtis 2018b). This tweet was accompanied by a photo of Zora Neale Hurston, who worked with Franz Boaz and Margaret Mead at Columbia, and whose groundbreaking ethnographic research on Vodou and African American folk religions in *Go Tell My Horse* seldom finds its way onto theory syllabi. For more on Hurston's contributions to the study and the theorization of religion, I'll refer you to the *Journal of Africana Religions*, and particularly their 2016 roundtable on Hurston (Curtis 2018c).

We should include Zora Neale Hurston, and Hannah Adams, and Omar Ibn Said, and other non-white, non-male, non-normative early scholars of religion in such classes. (I want to say "obviously" here, but given the composition of most of these classes, it seems this point is far from obvious to the academy at large.) That would be a good start, and to be frank, I am tempted to use the remainder of this space to just list marginalized scholars who have made invaluable contributions to the study and the theorization of religions. I have named quite a few already, and to that litany we should add Emilie Townes, Anthea Butler, Marcella Althaus-Reid, Mark Jordan, Mary Daly, Amina Wadud, Grace Jantzen, Catherine Bell, Kelly Brown Douglas, Katie Cannon, Beverly Harrison, Carol Christ, Judith Plaskow, Rebecca Alpert, Rosemary Radford Ruether, Leila Ahmed, Lila Abu-Lughod, and many others. But merely citing these scholars, adding them to an existent list of foundational thinkers, is insufficient.

Rather, I am demanding—rather stridently, if I do say so myself—that we center the work of marginalized thinkers so as to fundamentally shift the academic study of religion. This is not to suggest that the study or the theorization of religion should begin and end with these groups, but rather to propose that centering marginalized voices forces us to challenge our assumptions about normalcy, about what is worth studying, about what (and whom) we take for granted.

Whiteness, masculinity, cisgender-ness, heterosexuality could never go untroubled in a field that centers on the margins.

This requires, too, an interrogation of what kind of work might be understood as a theory of religion. The too prevalent assumption that the study of religion must be dispassionate and disembodied to be properly theoretical—that it must do its work with its underwear on, as Althaus-Reid would have said—often prevents us from taking seriously creative work, work beyond the bounds of traditional scholarship, as theorizations of religion. This is where theories of gender and sexuality might prove helpful in undertaking a germinal shift in the way we study religion.

* * *

In some ways, it seems incredible that gender and sexuality could still *be* open questions in the study of religion. I suspect my mindset here is akin to Foucault's when he told an interviewer that "sex is boring" (Foucault 1982: 229). I am so very bored with the question of how we as religious studies scholars should think about gender and sexuality, because how are we not all thinking about these categories by now? How have we not *been* thinking about them? How can a learned society like NAASR ask scholars to comment on gender and sexuality, or race, or class, or politics, as though they are discreet categories, or cutting edge topics of concern, or anything but the life's work of countless women, queers, people of color—work that will be cited, if it is cited at all, as the niche interests of the nonnormative but never as "theory?"

Despite Caroline Walker Bynum's observation in the introduction to *Gender and Religion* (published thirty-two ago in the year of someone's lord 1986) that there is no such thing as *homo religiosus*—which is to say there exists no religious being unmarked by gender; "no scholar studying religion, no participant in ritual, is ever neuter" (Bynum et al. 1986: 2)—the academy still treats gender as a marginal concern, usually the concern of those marked as having gender, which is to say women, trans, and gender nonconforming and nonbinary folks. (I offer myself in this position as exhibit A.) In a piece I wrote for *Religion Compass* a decade ago, I adapted the words of queer theory foremother Eve Sedgwick to propose that the study of religion is not merely incomplete but *damaged* if it fails to meaningfully account for sex and sexuality (Goodwin 2011: 774). And yet, here we are. Again, friends, I swear to god: when the academy starts asking itself these questions—really asking itself, rather than asking nonnormative scholars to do its homework for them—I will ask about something else. But in the meantime …

How can theories of gender and sexuality help us understand what work religion does in the world, and how does the work of theorizing religion shift when we center those who do sex or gender otherwise (as Derrida might say)? Answering these questions requires us to define our terms—and to acknowledge that these definitions are, to borrow from Linda Nicholson (1998), both ongoing tasks and ongoing political struggles.

Gender and sexuality are interrelated ways we are encouraged—sometimes on pain of death or dismemberment—to make sense of our bodies and the bodies of those around us. When we speak of gender, we speak of meaning made of the parts and (w)holes of our bodies, the cultural imperative that certain bodies are intended to make other bodies, the strange correlation of certain kinds of bodies with certain colors, or activities, or intellectual capacities, or preferences for baking and power tools. While gender and sex/uality are not reducible to one another, we cannot think gender without first thinking sex (or so Judith Butler tells us). Gender starts, not with identification of body parts, but with assumptions about what those body parts are for and what we should therefore want to do with them: which is to say, make more bodies.

We begin making sense of our bodies and the bodies of those around us by assuming heterosexual reproduction as the primary function of those bodies (this is what Adrienne Rich meant, in part, by compulsory heterosexuality [Rich 1980]; in "Gender: Being It or Doing It?," Mary McClintock Fulkerson refers to it as a "relationship of reciprocity between body, gender, and desire" [Fulkerson 1997: 192]). Critical theories of gender and sexuality propose that understanding bodies and culture begins with interrogating this assumption—by wondering how else people think about their bodies, how else it might be possible to think about bodies, what else people do with their bodies, and why, and how many more things and meanings people make of bodies than just making more bodies with them.

The Luce Irigaray essay that gave this piece its original name notes that bodies assigned femininity at birth are always imagined in relationship to—and indeed, less significant than—bodies assigned masculinity at birth. In "This Sex Which Is Not One" and throughout the corpus of her work, Irigaray demonstrates the ways language shapes the way that we think, drawing connections among religion, language, and gender (Irigaray 1985). She observes that women's bodies never signify in the absence of men's bodies, which alienates women from the bodies into which they were born. The questions we ask, the frameworks we provide, alienate those embodied Otherwise from the study of religion, by largely rejecting them as theorists of religion per se and by making them novelties rather than core components of scholarly inquiry. Irigaray charges us to make the study of religion, like the bodies of those who study it, like the language we must use to describe them, multiple, complex, abundant. She exhorts us to recognize that a study of religion that emphasizes multiplicity, indeterminacy—a study that attends to the specificity of our bodies, making the theorization of religion as rich and abundant as the bodies of those who do religion—is not incomplete. It lacks nothing.

Theorizing sex likewise requires attention and acknowledgment of multiplicity and indeterminacy. Sedgwick defined sex as "the array of acts, expectations, narratives, pleasures, identity-formations, and knowledges ... that tend to cluster most densely around certain genital sensations but is not adequately defined by them" (Sedgwick 1990: 29). Critical theories of sex began with disrupting heteronormative assumptions and challenging the regulation of bodies and pleasures by the state, by proposing that sex—and bodily pleasures more broadly—should be a topic of public concern rather than private preference, and by addressing that some sex is better (or gets treated better, as more moral, more normal, more healthy) than others.

This last bit is what Gayle Rubin refers to as the "charmed circle" of "Good, Normal, Natural, Blessed Sexuality" and "Bad, Abnormal, Unnatural, Damned Sexuality" in her germinal essay, "Thinking Sex" (Rubin 2007: 153). Most of my scholarly work has focused on the intersection of good/bad sex with good/bad religion, the assumption that those who participate in nonnormative sex acts for religious reasons must be duped or coerced into doing so, or invested in duping or coercing others—and that those who participate in nonnormative religious practices are more likely to engage in nonnormative, likely abusive sexual practices as well (Goodwin 2020).

I want to highlight some recent work by scholars of religion and sexuality, who have demonstrated the ways attending to nonnormative sex—we might say questionable sex, or at least sex that gets questioned—helps us better understand the work religion does in the world. Anthony Petro's "Beyond Accountability: The Queer Archive of Catholic Sex Abuse" (2015) reads the documented horrors of BishopAccountability.Org as queering the records of Catholic sex abuse: because the site demands public discussion of these horrible acts, because the discussion of these horrible acts transforms victims into survivors, and because this archive expands notions of queerness and religion to include "acts of abundant evil." Petro argues that we must understand Catholic sex abuse as religious abuse—this, too, is Catholicism—and that we must understand Catholic sex abuse as queer—this, too, is nonnormative sexuality. This argument does not excuse or minimize the horrors of the abuse, but rather calls scholars of religion to account for the whole spectrum (palatable or otherwise) of lived religion and sexuality.

Melissa Wilcox's vivid ethnography of the Sisters of Perpetual Indulgence in *Queer Nuns* (2018) offers the concept of serious parody as an analytical lens for the study of religion. The Sisters' work—both deadly serious and fabulously campy—troubles the boundaries between religion and secularism, queering our notions of whether we might even reasonably argue for a meaningful distinction between the two categories. Debra Majeed's accounts and analysis of polygyny among African American Muslim women blends ethics, ethnography, scriptural interpretation, and activism, asking important questions about the utility and goals of religious studies scholarship (Majeed 2015). She centers polygynous women, disrupting scholarly and cultural trends that privilege men's perspective, men's desires, men's exegeses in considerations of multiple partner marriages. Monique Moultrie's *Passionate and Pious: Religious Media and Black Women's Sexuality* (2017) applies womanist sexual ethics to her ethnographic survey of single Black churchwomen and how they "make meaning from their varied history, lived experiences, and faith perspectives" (2-3). Using the lens of womanism—a word which here means "the discipline interrogating the multilayered oppression of women of color," first coined by Alice Walker in *In Search of Our Mothers' Gardens*—shows Black women as agents in defining religion and its relationship to their own sexual acts and desires (Walker 2011: 2).

But as important as these contributions are, this work still fits comfortably within the parameters of traditional scholarship. How does the conversation shift if we look at theorizations of religion beyond—or, in the case of Anzaldúa—*on* these borders? What if we consider letters, poetry, fiction, autobiography, or even the humble tweet as the site where religion might be theorized? What if "theorist" invoked images of Indigenous women, queer Black women, Latinx farm workers, and queer Chicana women in our minds?

In the early twentieth century, the Dakota writer, educator, musician, and activist Zitkála-Šá wrote a series of personal essays for national periodicals, including the *Atlantic Monthly* and *Harper's Bazaar*. "Why I Am a Pagan" (1902) is a beautiful affirmation of her commitments to her Indigenous heritage, but also an unrepentant rejection of Christian imperialism and a subtle condemnation of the violences she suffered at the hands of white missionaries determined to "civilize" her. Claiming Pagan identity, too, interprets her Indigenous commitments *as* religion, demanding the category of religion expand to account both for indigeneity and imperial violence. (This is of course in keeping with Tisa Wenger's analysis of Pueblo practices in *We Have a Religion*, 2009.)

Audre Lorde's open letter to Mary Daly in response to *Gyn/ecology* (Daly 1978) affirms Daly's project of expanding the religious imaginary to celebrate feminine aspects of the divine. Significantly, though, Lorde calls Daly to account for conceptualizing Goddess in the image of white women, and for engaging Black women and women of color only as victims of patriarchal violence, rather than as the architects of their own religious meanings and worlds. Perhaps most pressingly, Lorde demands that Daly acknowledge that Daly's theories fail to acknowledge the material risks of being a Black woman advocating for change in the world— that gender does not exhaust Lorde's lived reality. "The white women with hoods on in Ohio handing out KKK literature on the street may not like what you have to say," Lorde (1981: 93) writes, "but they will shoot me on sight." She calls Daly—and all of us who would think religion—to address the multiplicity of bodily experience. "The oppression of women knows no ethnic nor racial boundaries, true, but that does not mean it is identical within those differences. Nor do the reservoirs of our ancient power know these boundaries. To deal with one without even alluding to the other is to distort our commonality as well as our difference" (ibid.). Our theories of religion must account for the interlocking oppressions women of color face—as Monique Moultrie's work does, as Nyasha Junior's work does, as Alice Walker calls us to do—or it will be not merely incomplete, but damaged—and damaging.

In March 1968, Cesar Chávez presented an article called "The Mexican American and the Church" at the Second Annual Mexican Conference in Sacramento, California. In this piece, Chávez details the relationship between Mexican American farm workers and the Roman Catholic Church, noting that the Protestant California Migrant Ministry had supported and advocated for workers in ways that the Catholic Church—which many of the workers themselves attended—did not. More than mere activism, Chávez's formulation of the Church *as* the people ("We ask the Church to sacrifice with the people for social change, for justice, and for love of brother ... we ask for servanthood"; Chávez 2007: 189) expands categories of religious belonging beyond church attendance or the hierarchy of the Magisterium and directly applies liberation theology to lived religious practice.

Gloria Anzaldúa's *Borderlands/La Frontera* (1987) blends poetry, history, and autobiography to offer a multilayered analysis of how Chicanx people make meaning of gender, sexuality, nationality, and religion. In "Entering into the Serpent," she highlights the hybridity of her religious upbringing, which blended Roman Catholic and folk religious elements. Anzaldúa argues for the radical materiality of her own knowledge of the divine, the materiality of divine presence in parsing her own multiple identities. "Enter[ing] into the Serpent," into the hybridity of divinity that is the figure of the Virgen de Guadalupe, is for Anzaldúa "to acknowledge ... that I have a body, that I am a body ... the body is smart" (Anzaldúa 1987: 48, 60). Her rejection of religious multiplicity as syncretism (which assumes stable and discreet religious traditions), her insistence on both hybridity and on acknowledgment of divine presence, anticipates more formal theorizations of these concepts in the field of religious studies by decades.

Finally, I want to offer a seemingly facetious example as a place where theories of religion happen. Consider this tweet:

> Roman Catholic Church: @ Mexico, stop creating weird skeleton saints!!
> Mexican Catholics: anyway this is Santa Muerte and she loves trans people
> (Tonebender 2018)

This tweet is accompanied by a photo of Santa Muerte adorned and carried through a Mexican street festival. In fewer than 280 characters, the author notes the space between the Magisterium and lived Mexican Catholicism, catalogues religious innovation and resistance, notes the connection between religious innovation and populations made vulnerable through gender and sexuality, and recognizes transgender people as agents of religious meaning making. This tweet was liked almost six thousand times and retweeted nearly two thousand times. How many of us in this room can say with confidence that our work has been read by that many people—that we've had the opportunity to shift understandings of religion on that scale? With these two sentences, this self-described asexual nonbinary xicanx geek might have had more of an impact on how the public understands religion than most of us will have in our entire careers.

There are more voices we could add here: Assata Shakur, Winona LaDuke ... frankly I think there's space to consider Pussy Riot theorists of religion. But I think I've made my point. I'll close by invoking Ntozake Shange, who once called "for a god who bleeds now, whose wounds are not the end of anything" (Shange 2016: 248). If we are to truly parse religion—this radically embodied, visceral human phenomenon—our theory must bleed, too.

Dr. Megan Goodwin is Program Director of Sacred Writes, a Henry Luce Foundation-funded program hosted by Northeastern University that promotes public scholarship on religion. Her first book, *Abusing Religion: Literary Persecution, Sex Scandals, and American Minority*

Religions, is now available through Rutgers University Press. With Dr. Ilyse Morgenstein Fuerst, she hosts and produces *Keeping It 101: A Killjoy's Introduction to Religion Podcast.*

References

Ahmed, Sara. 2016. *Living a Feminist Life.* Durham, NC: Duke University Press.
Ahmed, Sara. 2013. "Making Feminist Points." Retrieved from https://feministkilljoys.com/2013/09/11/making-feminist-points (accessed July 4, 2019).
Ali, Kecia [@kecia_ali]. 2018. 2 March. Retrieved from https://twitter.com/kecia_ali/status/969589864856457216 (accessed July 4, 2019).
Allison, Dorothy. 1994. *Skin: Talking about Sex, Class, and Literature.* Ann Arbor, MI: Firebrand Books.
Anzaldúa, Gloria. 1987. *Borderlands / La Frontera: The New Mestiza.* San Francisco, CA: Aunt Lute Books.
Bynum, Caroline Walker, Paula Richman, and Stevan Harrell. 1986. *Gender and Religion: On the Complexity of Symbols.* Boston, MA: Beacon Press.
Chávez, César. 2007. "The Mexican American and the Church." In Paul Harvey and Philip Goff (eds.), *The Columbia Documentary History of Religion in America since 1945,* 186–189. New York: Columbia University Press.
Curtis, Ed. [@JAfricanaRelig]. 2018a. 22 August. Retrieved from https://twitter.com/JAfricanaRelig/status/1032361442526330880 (accessed July 4, 2019).
Curtis, Ed. [@JAfricanaRelig]. 2018b. 22 August. Retrieved from https://twitter.com/JAfricanaRelig/status/1032232201512017920 (accessed July 4, 2019).
Curtis, Ed. [@JAfricanaRelig]. 2018c. 19 August. Retrieved from https://twitter.com/JAfricanaRelig/status/1031161289329061888 (accessed July 4, 2019).
Cusack, Carole M. 2010. *Invented Religions: Imagination, Fiction, and Faith.* Farnham: Ashgate Publishing.
Daly, Mary. 1978. *Gyn/ecology: The Metaethics of Radical Feminism.* Boston, MA: Beacon Press.
Foucault, Michel. 1982. "Afterword: On the Genealogy of Ethics: An Overview of Work in Progress." In Hubert L. Dreyfus and Paul Rabinow (eds.), *Michel Foucault: Beyond Structuralism and Hermeneutics,* 229–252. Chicago, IL: University of Chicago Press.
Fulkerson, Mary McClintock. 1997. "Gender: Being it or Doing it?" In Gary David Comstock and Susan E. Henking (eds.), *Que(e)rying Religion: A Critical Anthology,* 188–201. New York: Continuum.
Goodwin, Megan. 2020. *Abusing Religion: Literary Persecution, Sex Scandals, and American Minority Religions.* New Brunswick, NJ: Rutgers University Press.
Goodwin, Megan. 2011. "Thinking Sex and American Religions." *Religion Compass* 5(12): 772–787. https://doi.org/10.1111/j.1749-8171.2011.00316.x
Irigaray, Luce. 1985. "This Sex Which Is Not One." In Catherine Porter and Carolyn Burke (trans.), *This Sex Which Is Not One,* 23–33. Ithaca, NY: Cornell University Press.
Junior, Nyasha [@NyashaJunior]. 2018. 2 March. Retrieved from https://twitter.com/NyashaJunior/status/969605402190106624 (accessed July 4, 2019).
Lorde, Audre. 1981. "An Open Letter to Mary Daly." In Cherrie Moraga and Gloria E. Anzaldúa (eds.), *This Bridge Called My Back,* 90–93. Albany, NY: State University of New York Press.
Majeed, Debra. 2015. *Polygyny: What It Means When African American Muslim Women Share Their Husbands.* Gainesville, FL: University Press of Florida.

Mazusawa, Tomoko. 2005. *The Invention of World Religions: Or, How European Universalism Was Preserved in The Language of Pluralism.* Chicago, IL: University of Chicago Press.

Moultrie, Monique. 2017. *Passionate and Pious: Religious Media and Black Women's spirituality.* Durham, NC: Duke University Press.

Nicholson, Linda. 1998. "Gender." In Alison M. Jaggar and Iris Marion Young (eds.), *A Companion to Feminist Philosophy*, 289–297. Hoboken, NJ: Blackwell Publishing. https://doi.org/10.1111/b.9780631220671.1999.00030.x

Petro, Anthony. 2015. "Beyond Accountability: The Queer Archive of Catholic Sexual Abuse." *Radical History Review* 122: 160–176. https://doi.org/10.1215/01636545-2849594

Puar, Jasbir. 2007. *Terrorist Assemblages: Homonationalism in Queer Times.* Durham, NC: Duke University Press.

Reed, Annette Yoshiko [@AnnetteYReed]. 2018. 2 March. Retrieved from https://twitter.com/AnnetteYReed/status/969619823025115136 (accessed July 4, 2019).

Rich, Adrienne. 1980. "Compulsory Heterosexuality and Lesbian Existence." *Signs* 5(4): 631–660. https://doi.org/10.1086/493756

Rubin, Gayle. 2007. "Thinking Sex: Notes for a Radical Theory of the Politics of Sexuality." In Richard Parker and Peter Aggleton (eds.), *Culture, Society, and Sexuality: A Reader*, 143–178. Abingdon: Routledge.

Sedgwick, Eve Kosofsky. 1990. *Epistemology of the Closet.* Berkeley, CA: University of California Press.

Shange, Ntozake. 2016. "We Need a God Who Bleeds Now." In Carol P. Christ and Judith Plaskow (eds.), *Goddess and God in the World: Conversations in Embodied Theology*, 248. Minneapolis, MN: Fortress Press.

Shange, Ntozake. 2010. *For Colored Girls Who Have Considered Suicide/When the Rainbow Is Enuf.* New York: Scribner.

Tonebender, Tommy-Rae [@ellameno]. 2018. 29 July. Retrieved from https://twitter.com/ellameno/status/1023525670461140992 (accessed July 4, 2019).

Walker, Alice. 2011. *In Search of Our Mothers' Gardens.* New York: Open Road Media.

Wenger, Tisa. 2009. *We Have a Religion: The 1920s Pueblo Indian Dance Controversy and American Religious Freedom.* Chapel Hill, NC: University of North Carolina Press.

Wheeler, Kayla [@krw18]. 2018. 2 March. Retrieved from https://twitter.com/krw18/status/969552561115140096 (accessed July 4, 2019).

Wilcox, Melissa. 2018. *Queer Nuns: Religion, Activism, and Serious Parody.* New York: New York University Press.

Zitkála-Šá. 1902. "Why I Am a Pagan." *Atlantic Monthly* 90: 801–803.

Chapter 13

A Happy Headache

Emily D. Crews

Before addressing the primary content of this chapter—a response to Megan Goodwin's essay for the 2018 NAASR annual meeting panel on the theme of gender and sexuality (Chapter 12, this volume)—I would like to acknowledge the difficulty I had in writing it. That difficulty was born, one might say, of multiple mothers. On the one hand, gender and sexuality are, as Goodwin eloquently demonstrates in her chapter, difficult to think and difficult to speak in the context of a culture and a discipline dominated by normative assessments of those categories. The chapter, in particular, is difficult to address because it works on and within multiple semiotic layers, effectively and strategically deploying certain discourses, vocabularies, and silences. And finally, like so many people who might identify with the category "woman" (and so many other categories besides) the topics of this panel are ones to which—and, to be frank, *because* of which—I feel a great burden, and not only one of scholarly responsibility. As Goodwin makes clear, gender and sexuality are not simply words on a page or in the mouths of thinkers, but unstable and volatile realities we live, suffer, judge, mobilize, reject, etc. To think, talk, and write about them is at all times both a personal and political project, and one in which there is a great deal at stake.

Having acknowledged these productive difficulties of contending with Goodwin's chapter and the happy headache that has accompanied them, let us now turn to the task at hand. After providing a brief analysis of the essay, I will offer a few questions inspired by the essay itself, but which I hope might be addressed in future discussions about gender and sexuality among NAASR members.

In her chapter, Goodwin offers a trenchant critique of the field of Religious Studies: that it has historically and systematically privileged normative bodies and normative voices, and thus has taken as given the normative theories those bodies and voices have performed and produced. Goodwin argues that we in Religious Studies have treated as theory only those texts produced explicitly *as* theory and by bodies and subjectivities that hold privileged positions of enfranchisement. She writes, "Limiting theory to something only certain kinds of scholars do, rather than recognizing theory as the very premise of scholarship, claims theory as the special province of those legible to the academy as capable of 'doing theory'." Theory, then, is the domain of the few, in spite of its claims to the universal.

Some scholars who do not hold these privileged positions, she tells us, have responded to this encompassing occupation of the disciplinary landscape by rejecting theory altogether. They have rejoiced, as Goodwin says (referencing Sarah Ahmed), that they don't "do theory." But Goodwin advocates for a different approach. She writes, "Rather than cede this territory ... let us hone our definition of theory to privilege scholars who have to work so much harder to do this labor, whether or not they are confessed theorists of religion." She argues that it is necessary that we work to de-center normative theory in favor of works that are both written by and account for "the people with bodies who are doing religion," not simply the cis-gendered, straight, white, male bodies that have been understood as ideal, unmarked, and unquestionable.

Out of these ruminations Goodwin constructs what is arguably the main claim of her chapter (and I know this because she very kindly typed it in Italics): "*Every piece of writing about religion offers a theory of what religion is and religion does.*" (Make a note of that, because we're going to come back to it.) She goes on to argue that Gender and Sexuality Studies as academic enterprises have much to offer us in the process of re-orienting theory. Gender theory troubles the fundamental assumptions made about its object of study—that is, bodies and the ideas, expectations, and limits we place on them. Rather than taking for granted the primacy, normalcy, or desirability of certain bodies, rather than assuming that some bodies mean and are meant for some things and not others, gender and sexuality studies, as Goodwin writes, "wonder how else people think about their bodies, how else it might be possible to think about bodies, what else people do with their bodies and why, and how many more things and meanings people make of bodies than just making more bodies with them."

The complementary studies of gender and sexuality offer a model for Religious Studies, an invitation to question the foundational assumptions on which our field is based, and the relationship those assumptions have to bodies: right and wrong bodies, privileged and de-privileged bodies, bodies that are ignored and silenced even as they mourn and celebrate and labor and bleed. In doing so, we fulfill Goodwin's charge to us: that "if we are to truly parse religion—this radically embodied, visceral human phenomenon—then our theory must bleed, too." Bodies, then, are ultimately the hinge on which swings the gate into a better practice of doing theory, for every body.

While there are many directions my response to this chapter might take, there are three particular questions I want to ask here. The first concerns the aforementioned operation of de- and re-centering. I wonder, does this move to replace the theories of white men with what Goodwin characterizes as the thriving, living work of oft-ignored scholars replicate the same spatial, hierarchic structures of center/periphery or center/margins that are themselves the product of white, Western epistemological frameworks? Are there, perhaps, other modes of organization we could imagine that might open up a greater range of possibilities, and that might shift us into new forms of thought about theory, identity, and social formation? Might we think, for instance, of a network of overlapping and entangling perspectives, which makes some gains in the attempt to avoid the hierarchic relations bound up in the language of centrality and marginality? One potentially fruitful angle to consider might be the productive use that scholars like Chrysanthi Nigianni, Margrit Shildrick, and others in feminist, queer, and disability studies have made of Deleuze and Guitarri's notion of the rhizome, and especially the rhizomatic body (see Nigianni and Storr 2009; Shildrick and Price 2005–2006).

The second question deals with the concept of the subject position. Must one occupy a (or even a *specific*) marginalized subject position in order to produce the theory on which this newly oriented Religious Studies would be based? Would we argue that the process of centering the voices of those who have historically been forced into the margins requires the experience of marginalization? Or can one simply value, acknowledge, and speak in concert with the voices of those who *do* occupy such subject positions? What I mean to ask is, are there ideal architects of this vision of the future? Are there some whose blueprints and schematics simply are not welcome? Who is responsible for adjudicating this decision, and who is entitled to? And how do we think through the language of belonging, identity, ally-ship, and appropriation in this world to come? Borrowing from Gayle Rubin, what then are these relations by which scholars become practitioners of this new theory? To be clear, I am not arguing against the prioritization of marginalized voices over and above those that have historically dominated conversation. Rather, I am curious about how Goodwin specifically envisions the practice of "re-centering" and allyship as they are practically undertaken in the academy.

I think this second question is particularly significant in this venue. Within Critical Religious Studies, which has been taken up and made meaningful by many of the people who founded and have continued to work within the community articulated by NAASR, there has been a long and entrenched debate about the relationship between the insider and the outsider. That debate was begun and has continued, at least in part, because of the insistence that to assume that one must be an insider to a tradition, or occupy a subject position that makes that tradition legible in certain ways, privileges the internal claims of that tradition, and potentially the resulting ontologies, epistemologies, and ... I couldn't think of another ology, so let's just pretend I had one there.

The logical extension of this argument is, for instance, that Judaism is best studied by Jews, Hinduism by Hindus, etc. This discourse fails to acknowledge the flexible, multiple, and constructed nature of identity itself and places experience in the position of pride of place. If the answer to the question, "Must one occupy a specific subject position vis a vis gender to write about gender, or vis-à-vis religion to write about religion?" is "Yes," how might we square the dissonance of this move with the aforementioned inside/outside anxiety in Religious Studies? Is such a reconciliation is even possible or worth attempting?

A third and final question: is there a conflict between the two components of Goodwin's project—on the one hand, the critique of identity (both the category itself and the specific gendered, racial, and sexual identities Goodwin addresses) and, on the other, the argument for the privileging and advancing of certain scholars who occupy those identities? That is, is the act of creating a list of marginalized identities and people who claim them (or in some cases, are assigned them) contrary to—and, in fact, a re-inscription of—the very kinds of epistemological stabilities Goodwin critiques? I think it is possible that we might answer "Yes," to this question, and, if so, that we must then consider and critique such a move. However, I think it might also be worth noting the potentially productive friction between these two pieces of the project and acknowledging that, while identities of this sort *are* culturally constructed, they nonetheless have a profound impact on our lived experiences as human beings who exist in community, and so it is possible both to abjure and to uphold them. There is much more to say here—far too much for me to do justice to it in this forum—but, again, I hope that NAASR may continue to provide spaces for such conversations in the future.

By way of conclusion, I want to take seriously a modified version of Goodwin's main assertion: that all discourses about religion offer a theory of what religion is and what religion does. This is, after all, a version of a claim I have made myself, in both my own writing and especially in my classroom, where I encourage students to think about what their classifications of ideas, actions, desires, needs, etc., as "religion" or "religious" might imply or reveal. Thus, I want to ask: how might this shape my understanding of the scholarship I produce and its relationship to the network of interlocutors on whom it's based? The Nigerian immigrant women among whom I have undertaken my dissertation fieldwork would not refer to themselves as theorists of religion (or gender, for that matter), nor are they likely to be recognized as such by most people in our field. But what if the narratives they have crafted through life histories and memory work were intentionally understood *as theorization*?

I find this possibility quite persuasive for a number of reasons. It acknowledges the power and significance of these women as social actors who have agency in crafting and critiquing their own realities, and doing so at a level of sophistication that they (as women of color in situations of complex documentation statuses) are often denied. It also requires that we avoid the pat and comforting stories that assertions of agency often become—ones where "religion" feels good, where it heals wounds, and so any concern we might have about prioritizing it as our object of study becomes nullified. Instead, "religion," as it is theorized by these women, is as much a limiting as a liberating force when it acts upon and is practiced by particular kinds of bodies. It is a system of signification that makes possible certain ways of being, but prevents others.

Goodwin's proposal also helps me to think through—and maybe even around, I hope—a persistent discomfort I have felt with anthropological research and writing. I have struggled—and, in fact, continue to struggle as I write my dissertation—with the implication common in ethnographically driven scholarship that our interlocutors provide the raw materials for the production of a finished scholarly product. Language like mining, sorting, gleaning, and compiling conjure an industrial complex that is exploitative and even dehumanizing, one in which scholars control the means and modes of production, and our conversation partners become alienated from the possibilities that result from the interaction of our academic structures and their lived experiences.

What if, rather "theory" being the object that I, the scholar, must generate out of my informants' experiences, "theory" is instead the product of that interaction? What if, rather than being understood as the sole manufacturers of theory, scholars instead act as midwives, helping people with diverse bodies bring into the world an equally diverse set of possibilities?

Thank you again to NAASR for the invitation to contribute to this volume, and to Dr. Goodwin for the always valuable opportunity to question my own work and the motives that animate it. I look forward to the discussion this volume might make possible.

Emily D. Crews is a Postdoctoral Teaching Fellow at the University of Chicago, where she teaches in the Religious Studies Department and the College. She completed her PhD in History of Religions at the University of Chicago Divinity School in 2021. Her work focuses on the ways that women's reproductive bodies are linked to projects of identity construction, maintenance, and negotiation in Nigerian Pentecostal immigrant communities in the United States. In the classroom she thinks with students about categories and ideas in the study of religion through mundane phenomena like love, sororities, Jane Austen, and Alabama football (Roll Tide).

References

Nigianni, Chrysanthi, and Merl Storr. 2009. *Deleuze and Queer Theory*. Edinburgh: Edinburgh University Press.

Shildrick, Margrit, and Janet Price. 2005–2006. "Deleuzian Connections and Queer Corporealities: Shrinking Global Disability." *Rhizomes* 11–12. Retrieved from www.rhizomes.net/issue11/shildrickprice/index.html.

Chapter 14

Addressing Gender Parity in Critical Pedagogy

Tara Baldrick-Morrone

At its core, Megan Goodwin's essay (Chapter 12, this volume) addresses many of the same questions that NAASR programs for the past several years have been asking: whose field is it? What are the boundaries of this amorphous term "theory," and who polices them? In other words, "Who speaks here? With what interests?" (Lincoln 1996: 225–226). The implications of such questions are, of course, that there are those who do not speak and those whose interests are not heard. This is why I think Goodwin's use of Sara Ahmed's 2013 blog post "Making Feminist Points" is central to how we address the politics of citation, one of the most pressing issues in our field. The earliest exposure I had to this issue was Ellen Muehlberger's "Review of Biblical Literature Parity Project," a two-year project focused on tracking the gender disparities present in the *Review of Biblical Literature* (*RBL*), the Society of Biblical Literature's publication of books in biblical studies. Muehlberger's project, which took into account the genders of authors, reviewers, and editors listed in the weekly release from *RBL* from April 2013 to April 2015, produced staggering (but unsurprising) statistics. For example, the highest percentage of women to appear in an issue of the *RBL* within those years occurred on May 19, 2014, with 42.11 percent (8 out of 19 total scholars), while the lowest percentage—zero—occurred three times in 2013 (April 25, August 7, and September 27) and once in 2014 (January 29) (cf. Muehlberger 2013–2015). In total, out of the 1,650 scholars listed in 68 issues of the *RBL*, 265 were women, amounting to a little over 16 percent. The data here provide an important example of Ahmed's central point, that "citation [i]s a rather successful reproductive technology, a way of reproducing the world around certain bodies" (Ahmed 2013).

But I want to return to Goodwin's essay and her list of scholars who are too often left off the list of those who have contributed to how we study and theorize religion. Rather than attempt to replicate poorly what Goodwin has already done, and to follow Muehlberger's example, I want to explore what the politics of citation looks like in another setting. Akin to Goodwin's point about impacting how the public understands religion through the use of social media, we should also think about the impact that centering unheard voices can have on our pedagogy and in our classrooms. Studying and teaching at a public institution in the U.S. South for over six years, many of the almost 700 students I have taught represent the communities of these marginalized voices, whether along the lines of ability, race, sexuality, ethnicity, socioeconomic status, and/or gender, among other identities. For the remainder of this essay, I want to discuss how I have tried to address issues concerning the politics of citation in my Gender and Religion classroom, outlining both the successes and failures that I have experienced.

For two years, I have been the instructor of record for five different sections of REL3145, an upper-level course on gender and religion offered through Florida State University's Department of Religion. As is often the case when graduate students are asked to teach a course, I was neither given a "course-in-a-box" nor told what I should or must teach within the scope of how gender relates to religion (or vice versa). Left to decide how to approach such daunting topics, I chose to teach the course in a manner that made sense to me, one that could rely on my training as a scholar of early and late antique Christianities and my scholarship on modern interpretations of ancient sources. Additionally, I strove to avoid teaching the course as I have sometimes seen it done, that is, through the highly problematic world religions paradigm with a focus on gender issues. With these motivating factors in mind, then, I turned to Bruce Lincoln's typology of religion found in the chapter "Religion, Rebellion, Revolution" from his 2003 book *Holy Terrors*, though I made a modification: the course would consider both religions *and genders* of resistance, revolution, and counterrevolution, with useful examples that served to illuminate not only the historical situatedness of how gender and religion are defined, but also how these categories are used as devices with which social groups exercise and contest power. Instead of continuing to detail all the intricacies of my pedagogical decisions, let me give you an example from my course.

Students begin by reading two foundational texts on which the course is built: Lincoln's aforementioned chapter and Joan Wallach Scott's 1986 article "Gender: A Useful Category of Historical Analysis." One of the most important elements for the course comes from Scott's definition of gender, that it is "a primary way of signifying relationships of power (Scott 1986: 1067). Or, as she rephrases, "gender is a primary field within which or by means of which power is articulated" (ibid.: 1069). After this, students turn to the ancient world to consider Christian martyr texts, which serve as examples of religions and genders of resistance. The sources we consider are the *Martyrdom of Polycarp*, the *Letter of the Churches of Vienne and Lyons to the Churches of Asia and Phrygia*, and the *Martyrdom of Perpetua and Felicitas*. Yet before engaging with the ancient texts, we have to orient ourselves with what we can and cannot know about the realities behind ancient sources and their discussions of gender. For this, we rely on Ross Kraemer's introduction to *Women's Religions in the Greco-Roman World*, which encourages the students to see these texts as not simply reporting events as they occurred:

> We have begun to understand that socially constructed and variable ideas about gender—about what it means to be female and male—permeate ancient thought, culture, and experience so extensively that sources that appear to be about women may often instead be devices by which ancient writers, male and perhaps also female, wrote about all sorts of other concerns. Sources written by women might indeed provide important controls for those written by men, but they would not

alter this fundamental dilemma that stories about women might really only incidentally correspond to social and historical realities.

(Kraemer 2004: 5)

While Kraemer gets students thinking about the particular interests with which ancient texts are written, Candida Moss offers students a similar argument in regard to particular martyr stories: "We cannot know what the martyrs themselves thought and said; we can only get at what their biographers want us to think" (Moss 2013: 124). In general, it would appear that what those "biographers" want us to think is that gender resides not in one's body, but in one's actions and ability for self-mastery. Moreover, this mastery stems from one's identity as a Christian as opposed to the identities of ancient Jews or the so-called pagans of Rome as described by the texts. Thus, according to each martyr text, the elderly Polycarp is an epitome of Christian masculine self-mastery by refusing to cry out while being burnt alive; the manly behavior of the "vile and deformed" Blandina allows her to withstand exposure to wild animals because of her Christian identity, superseding her doubly contemptible nature as a slave and a woman; and the young Carthaginian matron Perpetua embodies what it means to be masculine by rejecting motherhood in order to act out her Christian identity through a gruesome death in the arena.

Considering the abundance of gendered images and language, not to mention the descriptions of explicitly horrific torture, these stories show us how early Christians used gender and martyrdom as markers of identity. "The memory work done by early Christians on the historical experience of persecution and martyrdom was a form of culture making," Elizabeth Castelli argues in *Martyrdom and Memory*, "whereby Christian identity was indelibly marked by the collective memory of the religious suffering of others" (Castelli 2004: 4). Likewise, Stephanie Cobb addresses the use of gender in these sources more specifically, insisting that when we consider the "textual formulation of emerging Christian group identities … the portrait of the Christian martyr that emerges from the composite picture … is strikingly masculine" (Cobb 2008: 62). Even though most of my students have never heard of these stories, they are quick to pick up on how gender identities in the texts are fashioned to cast Christian identities as superior, leading them to examine the interests involved in using gender to cast one's own group in opposition to an "other." In our discussions, oftentimes they will bring up modern parallels, indicating to me that they understand the ways in which these constructions and rhetorical strategies are used to create and contest social identities.

I am deeply indebted to the scholarship I use in class to help students understand how gender and religion are used to "signify relationships of" power. In this sense I want to return to my discussion of the politics of citation, because I do not think this point about the way in which power is articulated could be made as salient without hearing from diverse scholarly voices. To continue with the example from my own course, the makeup of scholars cited in the section on resistance includes seven women scholars and four men. And yet there are ways that I could do better. For example, many of the scholars I cite are white.

Many come from universities and educational backgrounds of prestige. As I have written about elsewhere (Baldrick-Morrone, Graziano, and Stoddard 2016), I also recognize the ways in which my situation as a graduate student, one whose area of focus lies outside the scope of the course, limits the resources and means available to teach the course in a manner that does not simply replicate the status quo. But rather than continue to treat this essay as a catalog of my pedagogical shortcomings, I want to end by thinking about why including diverse voices in our pedagogy matters by looking to Sarah Bond's public scholarship on ancient polychromy. This work has pushed classicists and those who work on the ancient world to address the idea of "lily white antiquity" that persists in the public's mind. Moreover, she encourages us to think about the future of the field: "Do we make it easy for people of color who want to study the ancient world? Do they see themselves in the ancient landscape that we present to them?" (Bond 2017). Beyond even simply wanting students to study antiquity or, in our case, theory, we should also work towards teaching scholarship that represents not only the diversity of our fields, but also the diversity of our students.

Tara Baldrick-Morrone is a Visiting Assistant Professor in the Study of Religions at Wake Forest University. Her research considers how different conceptions of an ancient Christian past influence twentieth-century American politics and legislation of abortion rights. She has published essays in books such as *Fabricating Difference* (2017) and *Fabricating Origins* (2015), and, more recently, an article in the journal *Method & Theory in the Study of Religion* titled "Power and the Reproduction of History: Twentieth-Century Histories of Abortion in the Ancient Mediterranean World" (2022).

References

Ahmed, Sara. 2013. "Making Feminist Points." Retrieved from https://feministkilljoys.com/2013/09/11/making-feminist-points.

Baldrick-Morrone, Tara, Michael Graziano, and Brad Stoddard. 2016. "'Not a Task for Amateurs': Graduate Instructors and Critical Theory in the World Religions Classroom." In Christopher R. Cotter and David G. Robertson (eds.), *After World Religions: Reconstructing Religious Studies*, 40–47. New York: Routledge.

Bond, Sarah. 2017. "Why We Need to Start Seeing the Classical World in Color." Retrieved from https://hyperallergic.com/383776/why-we-need-to-start-seeing-the-classical-world-in-color.

Castelli, Elizabeth. 2004. *Martyrdom and Memory: Early Christian Culture Making*. New York: Columbia University Press.

Cobb, L. Stephanie. 2008. *Dying to Be Men: Gender and Language in Early Christian Martyr Texts*. New York: Columbia University Press.

Kraemer, Ross Shepard. 2004. *Women's Religions in the Greco-Roman World: A Sourcebook*. New York: Oxford University Press.

Lincoln, Bruce. 1996. "Theses on Method." *Method and Theory in the Study of Religion* 8(3): 225–227.

Lincoln, Bruce. 2003. *Holy Terrors: Thinking about Religion after September 11*. Chicago, IL: University of Chicago Press. https://doi.org/10.1163/157006896X00323

Moss, Candida. 2013. *The Myth of Persecution: How Early Christians Invented a Story of Martyrdom*. New York: HarperCollins.
Muehlberger, Ellen. 2013–2015. "Review of Biblical Literature Parity Project." Retrieved from http://tinyurl.com/RBLparity.
Scott, Joan Wallach. 1986. "Gender: A Useful Category of Historical Analysis." *The American Historical Review* 91(5): 1053–1075. https://doi.org/10.2307/1864376

Chapter 15

The "Muscle Jew" and Maccabean Heroism of the Jewish Legion during World War I

Tim Langille

In responding to Dr. Goodwin's essay (Chapter 12, this volume), I'm going to discuss masculinity and the ancient imagery invoked by the Jewish Legion, who fought on behalf of Britain during World War I. In doing so, I will focus my attention on the figure of the "muscle Jew," which emerged in nineteenth-century Zionist thought and interfaced with Anglo-Jewish patriotism in the late-nineteenth and early-twentieth centuries. During World War I, British Jewish soldiers shaped the images of the "muscle Jew" through collective memories of Jewish antiquity, especially those of the Maccabees.

Goodwin's chapter asks, "what about gender?" The essay also wants us to consider intersectionality, as meaningful discussions of gender or sexuality are grounded in race, class, ability, documented status, religious affiliation, and politics in general. As my point of departure, I'll use Goodwin's point about gender being not about body parts but rather what those body parts represent and do.

The Muscle Jew in Britain

Jewish heroism during World War I was informed and shaped by the image of the "muscle Jew," which emerged from nineteenth-century Zionist thought. The term was coined by Max Nordau, a Hungarian Zionist leader, at the 1898 Second Zionist Congress in Basel, Switzerland. The "muscle Jew" was physical, strong, and formulated in response to the stereotype of the cowardly, weak, and unsoldierly Jew. Moreover, the "muscle Jew" became an aspirational figure for the future—one of physical labor, self-defense, or the antithesis of the frail, immigrant Jew of urban Europe. It was the remaking of Jewish men in the mold of Gentile men. A new embodiment wherein preconceived notions of what bodies do and represent were reimagined along both physical and ethical trajectories. Nordau's "muscle Jew" mapped on well to the goals of the Zionist movement with its emphasis on the spiritual and corporeal rebirth of the Jewish nation, its physical strength, and moral grounding. It was an expression of discipline, agility, and strength to cultivate and rejuvenate health, fitness, and nationalism in military strong Jews. For Nordau, only a united, muscular Jewish nation could push back against the growing shadow of antisemitism. Nordau's "muscle Jew" drew on Jewish antiquity for its inspiration (Presner 2007: 1–2).

According to scholars such as Sarah Imhoff (2017), Nadia Valman (1996), Todd Samuel Presner (2007), and Daniel Boyarin, the "muscle Jew" should be understood in the context of Zionism and Zionist masculinity. However, Gavin Schaffer argues that the "muscle Jew" is best understood in the context of patriotism and integration—that is, Jews presenting themselves as equals to non-Jews in physique, heroism, and military service (Boyarin 2012: 375). According to Schaffer, Anglo-Jews, as a racialized, minority community, wanted to exemplify their loyalty and bravery to the nation in the face of many British citizens who viewed Jews as unpatriotic and motivated by financial gain from the Boer War, World War I, and World War II. This desire can be seen in the British periodical, the *Jewish Chronicle* (August 7, 1914): "We know but a single cause, a single passionate desire. Our cause is the cause of England, our desire is the triumph of England with all that she has stood and stands for, so that she may overcome her enemies, and come forth from the crowning ordeal as free, great, mighty as ever." Thus, the development of the "muscle Jew" and service of British Jewish soldiers seem to have been motivated by both patriotism and Jewish nationalism.

Of course, allegations against Jews about patriotism and military service were ubiquitous throughout Europe. In Germany, for instance, some accused Jews of not fighting and dodging the draft because quick victory hadn't arrived by 1916, so the infamous Jew Count occurred that year. These accusations came from antisemitic elements within the war ministry. The results were never published after they discovered that Jews were fighting on the frontline in disproportionally large numbers. The Jew Count demoralized Jews but many asserted themselves even more to prove themselves in the war effort. However, many felt that they were being deluded at the suggestion that they were being fully embraced by non-Jewish Germans. Zionism and Jewishness displaced Germanism in some because of this count (Efron et al. 2009: 337).

In reference to Jews in Britain, it is important to mention the Jewish Lads' Brigade, which is the oldest surviving Jewish youth organization in Britain (1895). This group was informed by similar Christian movements, such as the Anglican Church Lads' Brigade (1891) and the Presbyterian Boys' Brigade (1883), which was a catalyst for the development of these youth movements at the end of the nineteenth century. In the vein of the Salvation Army, these Christian youth movements mixed Christian mission and military methods. In fact, in April 1891, the *Jewish Chronicle* published a letter from Francis Lyon Cohen calling for the establishment of a Jewish youth group, modelled on the Boys' Brigade, for the working-class youth of East London to help guide them through the formative years of the completion of school and manhood (Kadish 1995: 1–12).

Colonel Albert Edward Williamson Goldsmid, a distinguished soldier and son of two baptized Jews, brought this movement to fruition. Goldsmid was a Zionist and founder of the British branch of the "Lovers of Zion," which originated in Eastern Europe. He visited Palestine in 1883 and 1891. In 1902, Goldsmid became the president of the Maccabean Society (more on the society's name in a moment). In

1894, Goldsmid helped form the Maccabeans' Physical Sub-Committee in order to facilitate the physical development of East End Jewish youth. In an 1894/95 lecture, he advocated for the establishment of a Jewish Lads' Brigade in order to improve the physical and moral health of East End youth (Kadish 1995: 1–12). The Jewish Lads' Brigade (JLB) formed as a quasi-military group in the incubator of comparable Christian groups—that is, it was the Jewish equivalent of the "muscular Christianity" of the late Victorian Period (ibid.: 13). Importantly for this talk today, this military prowess was built on the ancient past. In the words of Goldsmid, according to *The Jewish Chronicle*, "The lads should remember the war-like deeds of their ancestors... no finer fighting race ever lived than the Jews ... The Romans were defeated more times by the Jews than by any other nation."

Importantly for this talk today, this military prowess was built on the ancient past—note the allusion to the Maccabees. In the words of Goldsmid, according to *The Jewish Chronicle*, "The lads should remember the war-like deeds of their ancestors ... no finer fighting race ever lived than the Jews ... The Romans were defeated more times by the Jews than by any other nation." This mnemonic process of heroism wasn't confined to British Jews. Other European Jews also viewed themselves as the intersection of German courage and ancient Jewish heroism. Jewish journalists drew on biblical imagery to boost the morale of German-Jewish soldiers. For instance, an Austrian-Jewish newspaper declared on Rosh Hashanah 1914 that World War I was a "holy war" for Jews as it evoked the imagery of the *Akedah*: just as Abraham was called on to sacrifice his son Isaac, Austrian Jews should sacrifice their sons to the war effort. More central to this talk, German-Jewish soldiers described themselves as modern Maccabees. A eulogy for a Berlin rabbi who died in battle stated that "German courage and Maccabean heroism came together in his worldview" (Efron et al. 2009: 334–337).

In Britain and elsewhere, sports were encouraged to facilitate discipline and fitness. Members of the JLB swam and played cricket and football (Kadish 1995: 13). In the 1890s, sports and physical fitness were seen as integral for Jewish survival and national regeneration. Even Nordau pled at the Second Zionist Congress (1898) for "the physical education of the new generation which will return to us the lost 'Muscular Judaism'" (Kadish 1995: 115). He saw sports as the bridge that reconnected future Jews to the ancient sporting and military traditions of the time of Bar Kochba in re-establishing "deep-chested, sturdy, sharp-eyed" Jews of antiquity. During the same year of the establishment of the JLB, the first Jewish sports club—the Israelite Gymnastics Club—opened in Istanbul. Others opened in Bulgaria. The Bar Kochba Gymnastics Club was established in Berlin in 1898. Soon after, a network of Jewish sports clubs connected Germany, Austria and Hungary, Turkey, Bulgaria, Poland, and Palestine. After the Sixth Zionist Congress (1903), this network came to be known as the Union of Jewish Gymnastics Clubs (Kadish 1995: 115–116). It is worth noting that "Bar Kochba" and "Maccabees" were the namesakes adopted by these Zionist gymnastics associations (Presner 2007: 3).

Of further importance to our understanding of this pervasiveness of this gendered, racialized, and nationalized identity is the role of the JLB during the Great War. 525 names appear on the JLB Roll of Honour, which represents 27 percent of the 1,949 British Jews who died serving their country. Moreover, 80% of deceased Jewish officers were JLB. According to *The British Jewry Book of Honour*, 80 of the 90 JLB officers signed up voluntarily in 1914. More central to the remainder of this talk, 10 former JLB were killed as members of the Jewish Legion in 1918 and the beginning of 1919. Most of these casualties probably died fighting the Ottoman in Palestine in the summer and fall of 1918 (Kadish 1995: 55–56).

Over the tumultuous two decades between 1898 and the end of World War I, Nordau's "muscle Jew" became an emblematic and iconic figure. Like biblical imagery, Zionism and the muscle Jew were sinews that connected Jews on both sides of the World War I battlefields and trenches. The Zionist movement brought together Eastern and Western Europeans, secular and religious, socialists and bourgeoisie Jews—it encompassed a wide-range of religious, political, and social views. The New Hebrew (person), the Land of Israel, and the Hebrew language were central to this belief system and ideology. These three elements were the key components for the New National Revival (Zerubavel 1995).

According to Sarah Imhoff, "[m]asculinity plays a starring role in the traditional story of European Zionism: The diaspora made Jews weak, hunched over, and passive, but Zionism would bring reconnection with the land and the regeneration of the strong male body" (Imhoff 2017: 180). Yael Zerubavel (1995) has shown, Zionist thought at that time was anchored in the heroism of antiquity and the collective memories of the Maccabees, Masada, and Bar Kochba were especially symbolic.[1] Within this framework, one can see how figures like the Maccabees helped shape Zionist thought, memory, and identity. In contrast to this ancient heroism is the Zionist construction of Exile as a long, dark period that was defined and exemplified by persecution, suffering, pogroms, and expulsions. The image of the diaspora Jew was one of weakness, submission, and passivity—an image rooted in antisemitic stereotypes (Imhoff 2017; Valman 1996; Zerubavel 1995). Zionism advocated active heroism over passivity and martyrdom, and figures from the past, like the Maccabees, became part of this identity.

A prime World War I example of Zionist ideologist associating Jewish soldiers with the heroes of Jewish antiquity is the figure of Rabbi Leib Isaac Falk, the military chaplain to the Jewish Legion in the British army. Falk viewed the exclusively Jewish unit as both the revival of the heroism of the ancient past and an opportunity to show loyalty and support to Britain.[2] Falk sought to connect a

---

1. Even the figure Theodor Herzl himself was tied to Jewish antiquity and represented as another Moses: the departure from diaspora was seen as an Exodus from enslavement to freedom. According to Ariel Hirschfield, "The myth of the Exodus became a powerful tool of propaganda in the first Zionist congresses but also discussed in a very serious and complex manner by the Hebrew writers of the day." Hirschfield also tells us that "Zionism activated within Jewish culture a store of eschatological tensions and provided even the most practical political acts much broader significance" (Hirschfeld 2002: 1015).
2. The case of Falk reveals the intersections between religion, the Bible, and chaplaincy during World War I. Falk catered to the communal and religious needs of his Jewish unit. He performed Sabbath and holiday prayers and supplied kosher food. He ordered candles on Hanukkah and Matzoth on Passover from Jewish merchants in Alexandria and elsewhere. He also ensured

motley crew of recruits, including his "schneiders" (Yiddish for "tailors") and the Russian-born Jews from the East End of London, Leeds, Manchester, and Glasgow who objected to the very idea of Jewish units. He did so by aligning Zionism with Britain's war objective, which included taking Palestine. He saw this effort as divine providence and the prophetic message of restoring the ancient homeland. In order to do so, Falk had to transform the pale, meek "schneiders" into "robust looking fellows with expanded chests and hardened muscles." Even Jabotinsky lamented recruiting these Easterners: "We are not Jews. We are not Englishmen. We are not men. We are tailors." Falk praised the healthy bodies and strong muscles of his unit (Keren and Keren 2008: 191). He advocated physical training and arranged boxing matches with other units. Pride in the body, pride in the nation, pride in the dreams of the restoration of Zion.

For Falk, the identity of his soldiers was tied directly to the heroic figures and events of antiquity. He saw his soldiers as direct descendants in this genealogy and lineage. In the present, they were refugees in the sanctuary of Britain awaiting the liberation of and return to Zion. Their past connection to the land shaped their heroic identity in the present. Falk saw their identity as rooted in the land and therefore recoverable. They were like a prophetic remnant awaiting return. World War I gave them access to the ancient past and the opportunity to return as the prophetic remnant. Falk's soldiers were the new Joshua and the new Maccabees. In this context, the road to the future was through the past.

It is here where Dr. Goodwin's question is pressing to my work. Her question, "how does your work, which purports to be about religion and the people who do it (or not), fail to account for the people with bodies who are doing the religion (or not)." This question, posed to my field of research, speaks directly to an intersectional scaffolding of ethnicity, race, religion, citizenship, nationality, physicality, and of course gender, identities that were purposefully mobilized by figures like Nordau and Falk to reimagine the bodies of the boys and men who aspired to be "muscle Jews" in the place of an increasingly precarious alternative that was conceptually scorned and violently dehumanized.

Tim Langille is a Senior Lecturer at Arizona State University's (ASU's) School of Historical, Philosophical and Religious Studies (SHPRS). His areas of expertise are Hebrew Bible, Jewish history, genocide studies, and trauma and memory. He is on the board of directors for both Genocide Awareness Week and the Phoenix Holocaust Association.

References

Boyarin, Daniel. 1997. *Unheroic Conduct: The Rise of Heterosexuality and the Invention of the Jewish Man*. Berkeley, CA: University of California Press.

---

that Hebrew speaking nurses were available for the wounded; established a library in Hebrew, Yiddish, and English; guided soldiers on visits to the pyramids in Egypt and the Old City of Jerusalem (Keren and Keren 2008: 188).

Efron, John, Steven Weitzman, Matthias B. Lehmann, and Joshua Holo. 2009. *The Jews: A History*. Upper Saddle River, NJ: Pearson Prentice Hall.

Hirschfeld, Ariel. 2002. "Locus and Language: Hebrew Culture in Israel, 1890-1990." In David Biale (ed.), *Cultures of the Jews: A New History*, 1011–1060. New York: Schocken Books.

Imhoff, Sarah. 2017. *Masculinity and the Making of American Judaism*. Bloomington, IN: Indiana University Press.

Kadish, Sharman. 1995. *"A Good Jew and a Good Englishman": The Jewish Lads' and Girls' Brigade, 1895-1995*. London: Valentine Mitchell.

Keren, Michael, and Shlomit Keren. 2008. "Chaplain with a Star of David: Reverend Leib Isaac Falk and the Jewish Legions." *Israel Affairs* 14(2): 184–201. https://doi.org/10.1080/13537120801900201

Levene, Mark. 1992. *War, Jews, and the New Europe: The Diplomacy off Lucian Wolf, 1914-1919*. New York: Oxford University Press.

Mosse, George L. 1977. "The Jews and the German War Experience, 1914-1918." New York: Leo Baeck Institute.

Patterson, J. H. 1922. *With the Judeans in the Palestine Campaign*. London: Hutchinson.

Rechter, David. 2001. *The Jews of Vienna and the First World War*. Portland, OR: Littman Library of Jewish Civilization.

Schaffer, Gavin. 2012. "Unmasking the 'Muscle Jew': The Jewish Soldier in British War Service, 1899–1945." *Patterns of Prejudice* 46(3–4): 375–396. https://doi.org/10.1080/0031322X.2012.701809

Watts, Martin. 2004. *The Jewish Legion and the First World War*. New York: Palgrave Macmillan.

Chapter 16

"There is No Place for the State in the Bedrooms of the Nation": The Case of Québec's Bill 21

Jennifer A. Selby

Introduction

"*Every piece of writing about religion offers a theory of what religion is and what it does,*" writes Megan Goodwin in her essay (Chapter 12, this volume) exploring what a compounded gender/religion theoretical lens offers for the academic study of religion, which she extends to "intersections with social class, disability, queerness and race."[1] Even if religion is often popularly imagined as "private" or "bedroom" matters, Goodwin shows how nation states have long been concerned with delineating religion in relation to appropriate expressions of sexuality and gender. Among other topics in her essay, Goodwin applies a "gender/religion" lens to consider representations of religious minorities in the contemporary United States. Attention to the imbrication of gender and religion reveals how representations of the sexuality of religious minorities in the US are often narrow, assuming, for instance, that these minorities are "duped or coerced" into non-normative sex because of their religiosity, including within academic treatments. With this lens in mind, Goodwin takes a state-down approach, leaning on the Foucauldian adage that states are especially attentive to the regulation of sexuality, for it is within these discourses that "the disciplinary and the regulatory, the body and the population, are articulated" (Foucault 2003: 252). Thus, despite a comment made by then-Canadian Prime Minister Pierre Elliott Trudeau in 1967 that "there is no place for the state in the bedrooms of the nation,"[2] the state manages the religious and gender politics of its citizens, whether in the public sphere or in the bedroom. Related to this point, political secularism can be interpreted as a tool of governmentality, insofar as it justifies white secular politics.

In my brief response, I aim to extend this gender/religion lens, applying it not to a "religious" context, but to a "secular" one. This exercise is premised on my assumption that the secular is necessarily tied to religion. From top-down state-based perspectives, scholars have long considered how the secular is invoked to delimit and define "religion" (see Asad 2003; Hurd 2012; Selby, Barras,

---

1. Goodwin attributes this quotation to Ilyse Morgenstein Fuerst.
2. Pierre Elliott Trudeau's comment followed revisions to the Criminal Code of Canada to decriminalize "homosexual acts."

and Beaman 2018). Like religion, the secular is not a fixed concept. Elizabeth Shakman Hurd (2012: 955) usefully defines political secularism as "a contingent series of legal and political claims and projects that are deeply implicated in the definition and management of religion" (see also Asad 2011; Fadil 2011). I also assume that, despite their relationality, the secular can be examined in its own right, as similarly including a range of social and physical dispositions that also relate to sex and gender. For this brief intervention, my point is that like religion, the secular functions as an expeditious mechanism to bolster desirable social versions of sexuality, whether more formally by the state or more informally through social norms, sometimes called "secular embodiments" (Amir-Moazami 2013). I therefore seek to slightly reformulate Goodwin's maxim to test the idea that "every piece of writing about *secularism* offers a theory about what religion is and how it relates to gender."

I consider this maxim in relation to a popular[3] state-based articulation on secularism, religion and gender in contemporary Québec, Canada. I ask: What does a 2019 Québécois law that curtails the visibility of religious signs tell us about religion and gender? I take a gender/religion lens to analyze this June 2019 law titled, "An Act Respecting the Laicity of the State," or "Bill 21." Methodologically I draw upon discourse analysis of the 16-page, 32-article governmental bill and ethnographic data from fieldwork with Montréal-living interlocutors of Algerian origin.[4] For the sake of brevity, I describe some of the impacts of the application of article 6 of the law for one of my 89 interlocutors in Montréal, "Zohra," a University of Montreal undergraduate student completing her education degree. As we will see, Article 6 prohibits individuals in positions of authority, including public school teachers, from wearing religious symbols on the job. I show how this secularism bill has narrow versions of both religion—as encapsulated in those symbols rendered "conspicuous"—and of gender—in how it curtails the professional lives of religiously visible women. For these reasons, I conclude we should be wary of Bill 21's liberatory promises in relation to gender/religion.

Bill 21 in Québec, Canada

Since 2010, four provincial bills[5] have been proposed by different political parties in Québec, Canada in attempts to "solve" the province's "reasonable accommodation" problem. The so-called problem of accommodation unofficially refers to the province's increased religious and racialized population since the 2000s,

---

3. Polling data suggest that 64% of Quebeckers support the law, particularly those who are Francophone (see http://angusreid.org/quebec-bill-21-religious-symbols).
4. These interviews are part of a broader seven-year SSHRC-funded transnational ethnographic project examining Algerian marriage migration to France and Québec.
5. Two of these bills (Bills 62 and 21) have passed through the province's legislature, of which one (Bill 62) was stayed in December 2017 on the grounds that it could be injurious to Muslim women. The primary contents of Bill 62 have been folded into Article 8 of Bill 21, so that its being stayed is no longer significantly relevant for discussion.

and officially refers to a 2007 commission and 2008 report commissioned by the provincial government that surveyed accommodation requests deemed problematic titled, *Consultation Commission on Accommodation Practices Related to Cultural Differences*. Even if making up less than 3 percent of the population and very few lodged accommodation-related complaints, the mediatization around the report has centered around Muslims (Brodeur 2008; Sharify-Funk 2010; Rousseau 2012; Bilge 2013; Barras 2018). Following a six-month inquiry, its two authors, Gérard Bouchard and Charles Taylor, released a 310-page report. This report included 13 pages of recommendations, including one that judges, Crown prosecutors, prison guards and police officers refrain from wearing any religious attire or symbols on the job; Bouchard and Taylor (Brodeur 2008: 271) did not include teachers and health care professionals in this recommendation. Both Bouchard and Taylor have formally critiqued Bill 21, saying that it goes against their vision of secularism in Québec (Fletcher 2019b).

Eleven years later, Bill 21 was introduced by the province's majoritation *Coalition Avenir Québec*'s (Coalition for Quebec's Future or CAQ) Minister of Immigration, Diversity and Inclusiveness (since tellingly renamed the Minister of Immigration, Francisation and Integration), Simon Jolin-Barrette. The bill passed with a 73–35 margin in June 2019. The law, an "Act Respecting the Laicity of the State," aims to affirm laicity in the province in ways that include prohibiting the wearing of religious symbols for government employees in positions of authority (Article 6). While not my focus here, the bill also requires those seeking government services to have their face uncovered (Article 8), a clause largely impacting Muslim women who might don a full-face veil. Those who have their faces covered for medical reasons (including when regulated amid the global COVID-19 pandemic) or to do their jobs are exempt from these rules. In response to concern with Article 6 for already-employed public school teachers, the CAQ introduced a grandfather clause that allows already employed teachers to hold the same job, at the same institution.

In addition to these practical matters, Bill 21 also amends the provincial Charter of Human Rights and Freedoms so that all persons must "maintain proper regard for state laicity" (Quebec National Assembly 2019: 2).[6] To protect it from challenge, Premier François Legault invoked a notwithstanding clause, allowing Bill 21 to override sections of the Canadian Charter of Rights and Freedoms (which explicitly entrenches rights related to freedom of religion and conscience) for a five-year period.[7] This move has been critiqued by a number of rights groups

---

6. Note also its introduction of the notion of "laicity." It is no accident that the preferred neologism is "laicity", effectively positioning the bill alongside French state legal articulations of secularism, including its 2004 law prohibiting "conspicuous" religious signs in schools and government offices and its 2011 law prohibiting full-face niqabs in the public sphere (see Selby 2014).

7. The invocation of the notwithstanding clause has been read by some pundits as an expression of sovereignty, in counter response to federal versions of religious rights. Bill 21 positions Québec as distinct "nation" based on its legal system, its differing social values, history, and attachment to "laicity."

including the Canadian Bar Association, who argued that the clause blocks Bill 21 from challenges of "violations of fundamental rights" (cited in Valiente 2019). Defending the government's decision to use the notwithstanding clause, Jolin-Barrette responded in the press that "the National Assembly [the Québécois provincial legislature] rather than the courts is the appropriate place to make a choice as fundamental as the secularism of the state" (cited in Peritz 2019).[8] A key component of the rationale for this model of laicity builds on a narrow definition of religion and how it relates to gender, as we will see in the next two sections.

On How Bill 21 Understands "Religion"

> A religious symbol ... is any object, *including* clothing, a symbol, jewellery, an adornment, an accessory or headwear, that (1) is worn in connection with a religious conviction or belief; or (2) is *reasonably considered* as referring to a religious affiliation.
> (Bill 21, Article 6; Quebec National Assembly 2019: 7; my emphases)

In this section, I consider how this bill promoting Québécois laicity manages religion through religious symbols. I am particularly interested in two facets of its conceptualization of "religion": first, how the bill focuses on "religious symbols" as expressions of religion in the public sphere (among individuals in positions of authority), a point I interrogate from a Foucauldian perspective (following Asad 1983, 2004). And second, how in ignoring questions of Indigeneity, Bill 21 reflects a continuing Christian colonial stance in its call for a "Québec nation." The CAQ's silence on the 2015 federal Truth and Reconciliation recommendations is notable. In this section, when considering the category of religion in this bill, I seek to analyze its focus on symbols and its silence on questions of Indigeneity.

Religion as Apolitical

In the first place, we must notice how the CAQ appears to take full advantage of the ambiguity and malleability of symbols. Bill 21 does not explicitly define what constitutes a "religious symbol," which is its target to assure laicity. Article 6 outlines that these symbols are "any object including clothing, a symbol, jewellery, an adornment, an accessory or headwear, that (1) is worn in connection with a religious conviction or belief" (see above). The "including" caveat is notable and leaves the possibilities intentionally expansive. In contrast to the description of symbols, the bill includes greater specificity in who it means by "persons in authority," devoting two appendices (or "schedules") of four pages (one quarter of the report) to include an exhaustive list of those individuals included under the purview of Article 6. The lack of clarity on symbols is also notable in contrast

---

8. The appeal launched by the National Council of Canadian Muslims and the Canadian Civil Liberties Association in July 2019 failed. A second appeal, that included four groups, was attempted in October 2020 (see more on the content of their appeals in Dabby 2020).

to the "Charter of Values" or Bill 60 proposed (and not passed) in 2013 by the Parti Québécois, which was far more expansive in its prohibition of "conspicuous" religious symbols among all public employees (Quebec National Assembly 2013). Alongside the Charter of Values, the Parti Québécois promoted a widely circulated pictogram that made clear which symbols were considered conspicuous and which were not.

We might be surprised that this bill did not include a similar chart, but Bill 21's ambiguity around what should be included makes its application more forceful. It effectively collapses religiosity into visual symbols. A headscarf—the primary foci of the bill and its debate—can thus never be read as a statement of fashion, or national belonging, or tradition, or modesty or habit because it is positioned as self-evidently religious.[9] Symbols are thus conceived as stable and uniform in their representation. The bill shapes this "headgear" so that the garments are uniquely "religious," and therefore necessarily problematic.

Foucault's thinking on power is helpful in conceptualizing the politics in the Bill's focus on symbols. Taking a Foucauldian approach that underscores the presence of power, Talal Asad (1983: 238) famously critiqued Clifford Geertz's work to "formulate a universal, a-historical definition of religion", showing the explicit politics laden in his understanding of symbols. Like Bill 21, Geertz's theory rests on understanding religion through signs and symbols. Geertz's "Religion as a Cultural Symbol" (1973: 80) conceptualizes religion as a "system" of symbols that serve to capture the "moods" and "motivations" central to creating an "aura of factuality" for those who engage them. Geertz's definition has been celebrated for its breadth, but also critiqued for its conceptualization of symbols as self-evident and apolitical, as Asad does. For both Geertz and in Bill 21, symbols are easily identified and interpreted. They are free from shifting politics and meanings. They are uniform in their significance and meaning. In other words, like for Geertz, Bill 21 positions symbols as reflecting the "essence" of religion.

Yet, clearly determining whether a symbol is "religious" or "cultural" is not a neutral assignation. Article 16 of the Bill notes that the province's religious and cultural past must be protected and not subject to its disciplinarity (Quebec National Assembly 2019: 6). Echoing this statement, the Premier of Québec and leader of the CAQ, François Legault, makes a category distinction and notes how some "religious" symbols cannot be read as such given their cultural meanings in the province. In a news conference following the provincial election (before the passing of Bill 21), Legault explains: "We have to understand our past ... In our past we had Protestants and Catholics. They built the values we have in Quebec. We have to recognise that and *not mix that with religious signs*" (BBC News 2018;

---

9. This understanding of religion counters the very broad definition of religion largely accepted through the Supreme Court of Canada with the *Syndicat Northcrest v. Anselem* case (2004). In this case, the court positioned religion as a personal or subjective freedom and, as such, the Orthodox Jewish claimant did not need to ground his claim in an objective religious obligation, requirement or precept to order to invoke the freedom of religion protection in the Canadian Charter of Rights and Freedoms.

my emphasis). Lori G. Beaman's (2012) work on religious and cultural symbols in Québec and Italy charts how religious symbols deemed as reflecting Québec's "cultural heritage," like a large illuminated Christian cross on Mount Royal a high point in the center of the city of Montréal, are rendered by the state (and majoritarian population) as benign by becoming representations of "culture." To be fair, following the passing of Bill 21, a contentious cross centrally hung in the provincial National Assembly has been relocated from its position of privilege. Still, it is clear from Legault's comments that the province's "culture" is Christian. The ambiguity of the description of symbols in the Bill allows for these protections of those determined as cultural rather than religious ones. A more radical reading might conclude that Bill 21's restrictions of some (ambiguous) symbols does not apply to those holding long-standing power in the province.

The ambiguity of categorization and of politics has engendered debate following the bill's passing on the question of the visibility of "religious" tattoos, assuming they can be clearly categorized as religious (see Barras and Saris 2021 for more on the limited legislation of the visibility of tattoos in Québec). When asked whether they would be included in the prohibitions on religious symbols in Bill 21, the Minister who introduced the bill, Jolin-Barrette, replied that those who choose to conceal their religious symbols— including tattoos—will not be subject to "a morning strip search" (Jolin-Barrette cited in Authier 2019). Jolin-Barrette imagines that tattoos are surely more easily concealed than other symbols. They might be more difficult to distinguish because of their perceived greater individualization or that they are more readily privatized (Barras and Saris 2021). Put differently, "religious signs" must be "visible," "conspicuous" and are imagined as removable in ways that permanent tattoos are not.

The question of religious tattoos on the bodies of individuals in positions of authority also brings up the question of choice, insofar as the removability of symbols is conceptualized in Bill 21 in a Protestant version of free choice and will. The implicit message, therefore, is that veils, yarmulkes or turbans (as freely chosen garments) can "reasonably" be removed (for critiques on the use of reason in relation to accommodation, see Barras et al. 2018). Ahmed Sahi (2019) interrogates this presupposition in the Canadian context, saying that from his perspective, "the veil is not a religious symbol, it is a tenet of faith. It is not a piece of cloth, it is a deep-seated conviction. And choosing to wear it or not, is not a wardrobe decision; it is a question of conscience." Saba Mahmood (2009: 273) has similarly argued that the hijab is often understood as external to its wearer, which then renders divine duty or religious prescription as external to a woman's "choice" to wear it (see also Barras and Saris 2021). With this reasoning, expressions of religion can be modified or limited because they are only representations of the sacred. The imagined removability of "headgear" thus speaks to how religious symbols are pushed to an imagined private sphere and, as such, the state can remove them in public. These presuppositions mean that some symbols should be surveilled. And some should not.

Post-bill questioning by the media further clarified the ambiguity of these categorizations. For instance, when asked if dreadlocks are included in the ban,

Jolin-Barrette noted: "No. [Dreadlocks are] part of the body. Scarves some African women wear? Only if they are religious. Tattoos? No problem. On the skin." This parsing raises the question of Hasidic women, of which there is a sizable population in Québec's largest city. Presumably because one of their religious symbols—a wig worn on a shaved head—is not clearly conspicuous in ways that are imagined as "religious," they will escape state surveillance, like people with dreadlocks.

Unlike the 2004 French law restricting so-called conspicuous signs in public schools and government offices, the CAQ has been also ambiguous on which disciplinary measures will be enforced on those who do not comply with Article 6. When pressed, Jolin-Barrette responded that those who do not comply with the rules will receive "court injunctions." For now, no special group—like that created to protect language rights with Bill 101 (where the notwithstanding clause was also invoked)- has been created (cited in Fletcher 2019a). Still the threat of job loss has arguably greater legs than its enforcement.

In sum, the ambiguity of the "religious symbols" in this Bill is no accident, particularly when we compare Bills 21 and 60, the latter of which focused on barring conspicuous religious symbols but was far clearer on which religious symbols were allowed (because they were "small") and which were banned (as "overt and conspicuous"). In contrast, Bill 21's "including" renders the list far more expansive, open to public sanction, and thus more readily self-enforced.

Religion as Ahistorical

In the second place, religion in Bill 21 is ahistorical, insofar as Québec's history of colonialism is erased from the document's very brief characterization of the history of the province. Granted, it is not a bill written with concern for questions of Indigeneity, but it refers several times to a history of distinctiveness in order to argue for a "laicity" as part of the "nation" of Québec. This omission is not surprising insofar as the three other bills proposed to censure religious signs in Québec since the 2008 Bouchard–Taylor commission have not included this past or present either. The Bouchard–Taylor commissioners' final report addresses this non-inclusion, noting that due to its vastness and complexity, the "Aboriginal question" was not included in the government mandate (or as a directive from First Nations or Inuit groups) to address accommodation (Brodeur 2008: 34). Critiquing this omission, Bruno Cornelier (2016: 81), for one, has argued how Gérard Bouchard's preferred intercultural model (as recommended in the report to replace Canadian multiculturalism; Brodeur 2008: 269) positions Indigenous populations as a minority to be invited to the Eurocentric state, but never as foundational. Bouchard and Taylor note a Québécois "multicultural crisis" imploring the settler majority to reconcile itself to the presence of immigrant others (ibid.: 243), in which Indigenous peoples are presumably included but are never named. Schaefli and Godlewska (2014: 228) similarly argue how this absence of Indigeneity in the BT Report works as a "mechanism through which colonial logic is reproduced and settler continuity ensured."

This tone relates to Bill 21 passed eleven years later. Tellingly, in response to the omission, Jolin-Barrette's press secretary noted that "Bill 21 is not intended for Aboriginal people" whose school commissions (where self-identified Indigenous teachers work) are part of a distinctive legislative regime. The press secretary seems to implicitly assume Indigenous people would not hold other positions of authority, like those imaged in Schedules 1 and 2 of the Bill (2009: 11–14), in only including this example. Moreover, because the bill does not take Québec's history of colonialism, Indigeneity or conversion into account, it is unclear whether an Indigenous identifying person working in a public school who might wear a Christian cross (sometimes an expression of Indigenous spirituality) would be sanctioned or not. This question is particularly pertinent given how the Truth and Reconciliation recommendations (particularly recommendations 48 and 49; Truth and Reconciliation Commission of Canada 2015: 9) call for a greater inclusion of Indigenous symbols and rituals in the Canadian public sphere as gestures toward reconciliation.

Lastly, the omission of any acknowledgment of Indigeneity or settler histories reminds us how the problem of "religion" here focused on symbols is individualistic insofar as it focuses on problematic religiosity as evident in religious symbols worn by individuals. Such a focus allows for an erasure of how the Bill makes no gesture to respond to obstacles to reconciliation like structural racisms in ways the TRC does far more effectively. These points of purposeful exclusion of structural obstacles are echoed in the Bill. The CAQ has denied that Bill 21 can engender harm, whether anti-Semitic, xenophobic, racist, Islamophobic or other. In responding to questions on symbols and the purview of the Bill, Jolin-Barrette takes a "colorblind" approach, noting that the Bill does not intend to target any one religious group: "it's applied to all religions. It applies to all Christians" (cited in Lau 2019). Similarly, in response to an Islamophobic incident occurring in the capital city's central mosque following the passing of the Bill, Legault noted that "you will always have, unfortunately, some racist people." Jolin-Barrette emphatically echoed that "there is absolutely no link between what happened [at the Québec City mosque] and Bill 21." However, social scientific data show that Legault and Jolin-Barrette are wrong: anti-Muslim sentiment is on the rise in Canada and is highest in the province of Québec (Wilkins-Laflamme 2018). A number of agencies in Québec, including *Justice Femme*, an organization providing legal support to women, have reported an escalation in both verbal and physical hate crimes at the time of debates on Bill 21 (Abedi 2019). A number of women who wear hijab who work in the French language school district of Montréal have already removed their hijabs in order to keep their jobs (LeClair 2019). In sum, Bill 21's ambiguity on religious symbols and erasure of Indigeneity show how laicity is neither neutral nor apolitical.

On How Bill 21 Understands "Gender"

Bill 21 borrows from a common refrain in political *laïque* discourse: that protecting secularism protects women's equality (Quebec National Assembly 2019: 5–6; see also Selby 2014 and Scott 2018). In this section I apply Goodwin's gender/religion lens to the experience of one cis-gender woman, a self-defined Muslim and newcomer of Algerian origin living in Montréal, "Zohra," and the effects of Bill 21 on her life.[10] Doing so highlights blind spots and violence implicit in Article 6 that especially impact her as a woman who is racialized, a new immigrant whose French accent is not Québécois, as poor, and a Muslim who wears hijab. An intersectional approach as encouraged by Goodwin reveals Zohra's vulnerability to the machinations of this version of laicity. I met Zohra, 35, a half-dozen times in July and August of 2018 and 2019, through her aunt, who I had also interviewed and had met through a mutual friend. The timing of our meetings meant that we spoke about her experiences as a teacher-trainee before and after the passing of Bill 21 in June 2019. Zohra is quick-witted and self-assured. Her sparkling brown eyes and easy smile make her very likeable. Zohra married "Samir" twelve years ago. Together they have three children: a daughter, aged 7, and two sons, aged 4 and 3.

Zohra chose to migrate to Montréal and not France because of her hijab and her dream of becoming a high school math teacher; she knew the two would not mix if she had migrated to France. As she explains:

> I first submitted my immigration request [in Algiers] in 2008 and I arrived here [in Montréal] in 2015. It was a slow procedure where I was asked repeatedly for my papers and to confirm that I was working in Algeria, that it was a permanent position and that the job was linked to my university degree. But I was really motivated!

Zohra completed university studies in Algiers in math and finance and secured a "good job" at a bank in the business district. Despite its stability and good pay, she describes her worry and dismay at the internal corruption to which she was privy. She enjoyed close ties with her nearby extended family, but began dreaming of a life elsewhere. Samir needed to be convinced. He had misgivings given the expense to apply, the long wait (for them, seven years), the cold weather, and his sense of duty to care for his divorced mother. In addition, Samir had an engineering diploma and knew it would likely not be recognized in Québec. They both had cousins who had migrated to Montréal who warned them about the difficulties of finding good work. Still, Zohra said she worked for years to convince

---

10. Zohra is a pseudonym. All translations from French are my own. I recognize the methodological limitation of referring to only one of my 89 interlocutors from this study, but do so for brevity. It should go without saying that Montrealers of Algerian origin are ethnically, religiously, politically, and socio-economically diverse and hold disparate views on Bill 21, both supporting and condemning it (few of my participants were neutral on the subject). Their often personal experiences with Islamism-related terrorism in Algeria the 1990s was a factor in their position on visible religious signs in government offices in Québec.

Samir and, once their eldest daughter born, he agreed. In our first meeting in their two-bedroom apartment in a brick low-rise building in the Cartierville neighborhood north of Montréal, Zohra stressed proudly that the Canadian officials at their in-person immigration interview in Tunis noted the rarity of their immigration request in that she was the primary applicant and not he. Zohra is the primary breadwinner in their family.

Zohra and Samir arrived with permanent residency, but their settlement in Québec has been challenging. Samir was denied a degree equivalency certificate for his Algerian diploma and begrudgingly—especially in the winter months—has secured full-time shift work as a parking lot attendant. Zohra learned she was unexpectedly pregnant when they arrived, which stalled her plans to enroll in the four-year education program at the University of Montreal. Now, three years in, Zohra has just over a year of studies and internships to complete the last year of her bachelor of education degree. But, because she wears hijab, even if she is "grandfathered" into University of Montreal's educational program and will be allowed to graduate because of the CAQ concession, debates around Bill 21 have fostered a climate where racist remarks circulate, as in two of her internship replacements. One senior teacher recently reported her "foreign" accent as a problem in her final report. Zohra also says she is regularly expected to complete "demeaning" cleaning or custodial jobs in classrooms, which she suspects might be related to her hijab. Most significantly, Zohra's hijab will now bar her from employment in the province's public education system post-graduation.

In this context, given her positionality, Zohra now faces a dilemma that I see as capturing how this laicity law frames gender/religion: should she stay in Montréal, renouncing her newfound emotionally and financially expensive education degree and try to find work in one of the city's four private Islamic schools? Should she leave the field and seek work in the private sector? Or should the family leave their rental apartment and move to Gatineau, QC (a city that neighbors Ottawa, Ontario where the provincial law is not applicable), where they can still live in French, hopefully find provincially subsidized daycare spots, and see if she can find work teaching in Ottawa? Samir is not tied to his job, but they have family and other friend supports in the city and province-subsidized childcare for their two sons. Zohra considered settling in Ottawa before they migrated because she could do an education degree there in 2 years instead of 4. But, when she realized she was expecting and that her baby son had received a state-subsidized daycare spot, she and Samir chose to stay in Québec. She now regrets this decision. She has found thinking about her family's future now debilitating.

In sum, while the CAQ promotes Bill 21 because of how it imagines laicity as the absence of certain religious signs and how this neutrality protects women's rights, in not seeing its implications from a "gender/religion" lens, the CAQ ignores the violent implications for racialized religious women who are now excluded from positions of authority (and, while not my focus, for those who wear niqab, from engaging with the state in any capacity). For now, Zohra pushes on to complete her degree amidst heightened tension about the undesirable "religiosity" of her hijab.

Conclusion

In this response I have endeavored to apply Goodwin's proposed gender/religion lens to a June 2019 law passed in Québec, Canada, "An Act respecting the laicity of the State" (or Bill 21). From a Foucauldian biopower perspective, Goodwin's focus on how the contemporary US government manages gender/religion sheds light on how religiously visible and conservative women, especially those like Zohra who are racialized, newcomers, poor and who wear a "conspicuous" religious sign, are especially vulnerable to state surveillance. I have read the law as a document that, following my spin on Goodwin, is "about secularism [and] offers a theory about what religion is and how it relates to gender."

I have argued that Bill 21's focus on "religious symbols" as reflecting religious beliefs and practices is problematic in relation to the province's purported neutrality, as is its erasure of Indigeneity as part of the "Québécois nation"'s past and present. Michel Foucault's work on governmentality and "biopower" further usefully flags why the Coalition Avenir Québec political party has invested so many resources into passing this 2019 law. The bill's symbols' *sui generis* apolitical characterization positions them as coercive and all-consuming, so that Zohra's headscarf is understood as necessarily reflecting unwanted "religion" in a public school, and not a number of other values (itself an assumption, as Mahmood (2009) reminds us, that the symbolism of the garment can be separated from how she understands her faith). This view offers further ammunition for the state to surveil racialized minorities. Moreover, imagining symbols as stable and unchanging does not reflect the ways that people actually "live" their religious lives. Lastly, not all "religious" signs are categorized by the state as such. Some are problematic and religious and must be surveilled and sanctioned. Others, related to an imagined "Christian-Protestant" past are deemed cultural and protected so that a large cross on the Montréal skyline remains inconspicuous. The CAQ's dismissal of religious tattoos sheds further light on the power dynamics laden in determining those symbols that are conspicuous and those that are not. Together, this vision of religion particularly entrenches visibly religious women, who like Zohra may hold more conservative views on sex, as unagentic and as undesirable citizens.

The absence of Indigenous concerns in these discussions of laicity in the province of Québec is perhaps not surprising given how the 2008 Bouchard–Taylor report sets the scene for later iterations by annexing the "Aboriginal Question" from its mandate. But amnesia around Québec's colonial past replicates a colonial-era logic of protecting foreign women from their patriarchal religious families and the state from these values that we see in the Bill's implicit characterization of gender.

So, in response to Goodwin, let's remember bodies in our theorization on religion and the secular. And in the case of Bill 21, let's see this law in contemporary Québec for what it does: It might be about erasing religious and racial difference in the public sphere. Or curbing racialized immigration. Or increasing the state's disciplinary apparatuses through better equipping the state's disciplinary arm.

As I read it, Bill 21 cunningly allows the state to discipline certain bodies while bolstering a "nation" that effectively silences Indigenous pasts and present. In sum, reading it through a gender/religion lens as Goodwin suggests makes evident that Bill 21 is *not* about fostering neutrality.

Jennifer A. Selby is an Associate Professor of Religious Studies and Political Science and affiliate member of the Department of Gender Studies at Memorial University of Newfoundland and Labrador. Her ethnographic-based research examines secularism in contemporary France and Canada, with attention to Muslim life and gender. Selby is the author of over 40 articles and book chapters, co-author of *Beyond Accommodation: Everyday Narratives of Muslim Canadians* (UBC Press, 2018), author of *Questioning French Secularism: Gender Politics and Islam in a Parisian Suburb* (Palgrave MacMillan, 2012), and co-editor of *Debating Sharia* (with A. Korteweg, University of Toronto Press, 2012) and *Producing Islam(s) in Canada* (University of Toronto Press, 2022). In addition to her work on the executive of the Canadian Corporation for Studies in Religion, Selby is co-chair of the Anthropology of Religion section for the American Academy of Religion.

References

Abedi, Maham. 2019. "Muslim Women in Quebec Facing Increased Hate Amid Bill 21 Debate: Advocates." *Global News* (May 15). Retrieved from https://globalnews.ca/news/5274699/muslim-women-quebec-hate-incidents/

Amir-Moazami, Schirin. 2013. "The Secular Embodiments of Face-Veil Controversies Across Europe." In Nilüfer Göle (ed.), *Islam and Public Controversy in Europe*, 83–100. Farnham: Ashgate Publishing Company. https://doi.org/10.4324/9781315589930-7

Asad, Talal. 1983. "Anthropological Conceptions of Religion: Reflections on Geertz." *Man* 18(2) (June): 237–259. https://doi.org/10.2307/2801433

Asad, Talal. 2003. *Formations of the Secular: Christianity, Islam, Modernity*. Stanford, CA: Stanford University Press.

Asad, Talal. 2011. "Thinking about the Secular Body, Pain, and Liberal Politics." *Cultural Anthropology* 26(4): 657–675. https://doi.org/10.1111/j.1548-1360.2011.01118.x

Authier, Philip. 2019. "Religious Symbols: Quebec 'Convinced We Have Found the Right Balance'." *Montreal Gazette* (March 29). Retrieved from https://montrealgazette.com/news/quebec/religious-symbols-quebec-to-table-secularism-bill-caq-will-propose-moving-crucifix

Barras, Amélie. 2018. "Reasonable Accommodation." In Catherine Holtmann (ed.), *Exploring Religion and Diversity in Canada: People, Practice and Possibility*, 183–205. Cham: Springer. https://doi.org/10.1007/978-3-319-78232-4_9

Barras, Amélie and Anne Saris. 2021. "Gazing into the World of Tattoos: An Invitation to Reconsider how we Conceptualize Religious Practices." *Studies in Religion/Sciences Religieuses* 50(2): 167–188. https://doi.org/10.1177/0008429820926988

Barras, Amélie, Jennifer A. Selby, and Lori G. Beaman. 2018. "Rethinking Canadian Discourses of Reasonable Accommodation." *Social Inclusion* 6(2): 162–172. https://doi.org/10.17645/si.v6i2.1443

BBC News. 2018. "Canada Politician Says Crucifix "Not Religious Symbol." *BBC News* (October 12). Retrieved from www.bbc.com/news/world-us-canada-45842471

Beaman, Lori G. 2012. "Battles over Symbols: The 'Religion' of the Minority Versus the 'Culture' of the Majority." *Journal of Law and Religion* 28(1): 67–104. https://doi.org/10.1017/S0748081400000242

Bilge, Sirma. 2013. "Reading the Racial Subtext of the Québécois Accommodation Controversy: an Analytics of Racialized Governmentality." *Politikon* 40(1): 157–181. https://doi.org/10.1080/02589346.2013.765681

Brodeur, Patrice. 2008. "La commission Bouchard–Taylor et la perception des rapports entre 'Québécois' et 'musulmans' au Québec." *Cahiers de recherche sociologique* 46: 95–107. https://doi.org/10.7202/1002510ar

Cornelier, Bruno. 2016. "Interculturalism, Settler Colonialism, and the Contest Over 'Nativeness'." In Michael R. Griffiths (ed.), *Biopolitics and Memory in Postcolonial Literature and Culture*. Farnham: Ashgate, 77–102. https://doi.org/10.4324/9781315563060-4

Dabby, Dia. 2020. "Le western de la laïcité: regards juridiques sur la Loi sur la laïcité de l'État." In Leila Celis, Dia Dabby, Dominique Leydet, and Vincent Romani (eds), *Modération ou extrémisme? Regards critiques sur la loi 21*, 239–254. Québec: Presses de l'Université Laval. https://doi.org/10.2307/j.ctv1h0p3qj.19

Fadil, Nadia. 2011. "Not-/unveiling as an Ethical Practice." *Feminist Review* 98: 83–109. https://doi.org/10.1057/fr.2011.12

Fletcher, Raquel. 2019a. "Opposition Accuses Quebec Government of Slyly Amending Bill 21 to Create 'Secularism Police'." *Global News* (June 17). Retrieved from https://globalnews.ca/news/5397908/opposition-quebec-government-bill-21-secularism-police.

Fletcher, Raquel. 2019b. "Both Authors of Bouchard–Taylor Report Speak Out against Quebec's Secularism Bill." *Global News* (May 8). Retrieved from https://globalnews.ca/news/5255638/bouchard-taylor-report-authors-quebec-secularism-bill.

Foucault, Michel. 2003. *"Society Must Be Defended": Lectures at the Collège de France, 1975–1976.* Ed. Mauro Bertani and Alessandro Fontana. Trans. David Macey. New York: Picador.

Foucault, Michel. 2008. *The Birth of Biopolitics: Lectures at the Collège de France 1978–1979*. Ed. Michel Senellart. Trans. Graham Burchell. New York: Picador.

Geertz, Clifford. 1973. "Religion as a Cultural System" In Michael Lambek (ed.), *A Reader in the Anthropology of Religion*, 57–76. Oxford: Blackwell.

Hurd, Elizabeth Shakman. 2012. "International Politics after Secularism." *Review of International Studies* 35(5): 943–961. https://doi.org/10.1017/S0260210512000411

Lau, Rachel. 2019. "'Quebec Will Always Be Open': Immigration Minister Defends Religious Symbols Bill." *Global News* (April 1). Retrieved from https://globalnews.ca/news/5118381/quebec-immigration-minister-defends-secularism-bill.

LeClair, Anne. 2019. "Teachers Removing Religious Symbols Proves Bill 21 is a 'Good Law': Education Minister." *Global News* (September 18). Retrieved from https://globalnews.ca/news/5920646/teachers-religious-symbols-bill-21-education-minister.

Mahmood, Saba. 2009. "Religious Reason and Secular Affect: An Incommensurable Divide?" In Judith Butler, Saba Mahmood, Wendy Brown, and Talal Asad (eds.), *Is Critique Secular? Blasphemy, Injury and Free Speech*, 64–100. Berkeley, CA: The Townsend Papers in Humanities. https://doi.org/10.1525/california/9780982329412.003.0003

Peritz, Ingrid. 2019. "Quebec Launches Hearings on Controversial Secularism Bill." *The Globe and Mail* (May 7). Retrieved from www.theglobeandmail.com/canada/article-quebec-launches-hearings-on-controversial-secularism-bill.

Quebec National Assembly. 2011. Bill n94: An Act to Establish Guidelines Governing Accommodation Requests within the Administration and Certain Institutions.

Quebec National Assembly, Canada, February 24. Retrieved from www.assnat. qc.ca/en/travaux-parlementaires/projets-loi/projet-loi-94-39-1.html.
Quebec National Assembly. 2013. Bill n60: Charter Affirming the Values of State Secularism and Religious Neutrality and of Equality between Women and Men, and Providing a Framework for Accommodation Requests. Quebec National Assembly, Canada, November 7. Retrieved from www.assnat.qc.ca/en/travaux-parlementaires/ projets-loi/projet-loi-60-40-1.html.
Quebec National Assembly. 2017. Bill n62: An Act to Foster Adherence to State Religious Neutrality and, in Particular, to Provide a Framework for Requests for Accommodations on Religious Grounds in Certain Bodies. Quebec National Assembly, Canada, October 18.
Quebec National Assembly. 2019. Bill n21: An Act Respecting the Laicity of the State. Quebec National Assembly, Canada, June 16. Retrieved from http://m.assnat.qc.ca/en/ travaux-parlementaires/projets-loi/projet-loi-21-42-1.html.
Rousseau, Louis, ed. 2012. *Le Québec après Bouchard-Taylor: Les identités religieuses de l'immigration.* Québec, QC: Presses de l'Université du Québec.
Sahi, Ahmed. 2019. "Quebec's unthinkable Bill 21." *Maclean's* (April 9). Retrieved from www.macleans.ca/opinion/quebecs-unthinkable-bill-21/#:~:text=The%20veil% 20is%20not%20a,is%20a%20question%20of%20conscience.
Schaefli, Laura and Anne Godlewska. 2014. "Social ignorance and Indigenous exclusion: public voices in the province of Québec, Canada." *Settler-Colonial Studies* 4(3): 227–244. https://doi.org/10.1080/2201473X.2013.866514
Scott, Joan Wallach. 2018. *Sex and Secularism.* Princeton, NJ: Princeton University Press.
Selby, Jennifer A. 2014. "Un/veiling Women's Bodies: Secularism and Sexuality in Full-Face Veil Prohibitions in France and Québec." *Studies in Religion/Sciences Religieuses* 43(3) (September): 439–466. https://doi.org/10.1177/0008429814526150
Selby, Jennifer A., Amélie Barras, and Lori G. Beaman. 2018. *Beyond Accommodation: Everyday Narratives of Muslim Canadians.* Vancouver: University of British Columbia Press.
Sharify-Funk, Meena. 2010. "Muslims and the Politics of 'Reasonable Accommodation': Analyzing the Bouchard-Taylor Report and its Impact on the Canadian Province of Quebec." *Journal of Muslim Minority Affairs* 30(4): 535–553. https://doi.org/10. 1080/13602004.2010.533451
Truth and Reconciliation Commission of Canada. 2015. "Calls to Action." Retrieved from http://trc.ca/assets/pdf/Calls_to_Action_English2.pdf
Valiente, Giuseppe. 2019. "Canadian Bar Association Calls on Quebec to Drop Notwithstanding Clause from Bill 21." *The Canadian Press* (April 4). Retrieved from https:// globalnews.ca/news/5130720/canadian-bar-association-quebec-religious-symbols.
Wilkins-Laflamme, Sarah. 2018. "Islamophobia in Canada: Measuring the Realities of Negative Attitudes Toward Muslims and Religious Discrimination." *Canadian Review of Sociology* 55(1): 86–110. https://doi.org/10.1111/cars.12180

Part IV

Class and Economy

Chapter 17

Regulating Religion to Maintain the Status Quo

Suzanne Owen

Introduction

Marx, Durkheim, and Weber can be found on most syllabi for teaching method and theory in the study of religion. They are known for their theories on class and economy, but, for the most part, they have been regarded as historic and of limited relevance for analyzing "religion" in society today. While Weber connected religion to class and economics explicitly, and Durkheim analyzed how social cohesion and deviance uphold the norms of a society, it is Marxian theories I wish to explore through a reconceptualization of Antonio Gramsci's notions of hegemony and consent to show how class exerts influence on the state regulation of religion, which supports the status quo and minimizes dissent.

In his book *Hegemony*, Robert Bocock notes that the concept was latent in Marx but, since the working class did not overthrow capitalism, Marxist theorists turned to Althusser, though his concept of "power was statist—located in the state and its constituents such as the army, police and church—the repressive or ideological state apparatuses" (Bocock 1986: 16). In contrast, Foucault's concept of power was diffuse, internalized, but it underestimated impositions by the state. Although he wrote ahead of the other two, Gramsci's idea of hegemony came in for a revival as it contained elements of both static and diffuse concepts of power and also allowed for individual agency for changing the status quo.

While Gramsci did not analyze the role of religion in depth, apart from stating that "religion" was a tool of the ruling classes, his concept of hegemony as applied to the state regulation of religion can reveal how the ruling classes suppress minorities while also keeping the dominant religion in its place—it must remain uncritical of the state to receive political support to maintain its position in society.

As a case study, the remodeling of Pagan groups in the U.K. to conform to legal models of "legitimate religion" as they attempt to gain public recognition reveals how the state regulation operates today where "other" religions become subservient lesser versions of the religion of the ruling classes. Some Pagans groups are thus caught between (at least nominally) retaining a counter-cultural position and conforming to state notions of "civilized religion," unless by forming alliances, they shift the position of the state. In a limited sense, Pagan groups have done that to push governmental bodies to broaden their concepts of religion.

In the U.K., the systemic discrimination of Paganism is, in particular, illustrative of the suppression of dissent as it has been a constant critic of dominant notions of religion and regarded as deviant by the Church. The case of The Druid Network (TDN), in particular, also provides an example of how "prevailing concepts of religion are extended, challenged or rejected" (Beckford 2003: 3) if the state deems the group to be acceptable and non-threatening.

Gramsci on Hegemony

Antonio Gramsci (1891–1937) was a Sardinian-born socialist and founding member of the Communist Party in Italy. Imprisoned by Mussolini's Fascists in 1926, Gramsci wrote over 30 notebooks (between 1929 and 1935) and around 500 letters to friends containing his political and philosophical ideas and analyses. In 1935, he was moved to a hospital in Rome on health grounds but was unable to recover from his multiple ailments and died in 1937.

Gramsci's use of the term hegemony refers to the power dynamic of the ruling elite, who maintain their preferences as the norm, becoming the dominant expression in society through consent where people internalize the view as their own or as common sense. Thus "the concept of hegemony is linked with a complex set of claims about what could be a coherent viewpoint on the world. ... only a coherent world-view, a well-rounded philosophy and related morality, could be hegemonic" (Bocock 1986: 17). As this becomes the status quo, other views are marginalized. However, Gramsci's ideas are not systematic, scattered as they are throughout the *Prison Notebooks*, but of crucial importance is the legal and educational institutions for exercising hegemony, through which, as Craig Martin puts it: "the state 'educates' the citizenry into consenting to its regulations" (Martin 2010: 91; see also Bocock 1986: 29; Gramsci 1971: 259).

While Marxist ideology saw the social classes as opposed to each other and economically determined, Gramsci observed that the state operates through class alliances. A union of political, intellectual, and moral leadership creates the hegemony of the ruling classes (Mouffe 1979: 179). Hegemonic apparatuses include schools, churches, the media, architecture, and even the names of streets through which ideology is produced and diffused in the superstructure of civil society. Through these, the ruling classes create the favorable conditions for their expansion. As Jon Simons puts it:

> Such leadership requires an ideology or conception of the world that operates in art, law, economic activity, and life in general, and which is a coherent version of common sense beliefs about the world and human relationships. Hegemonic rule thus means that subordinate social classes consent, at least implicitly, to live according to everyday beliefs that legitimate capitalist social order.
> (Simons 2015: 1624)

It is not through the imposition of a worldview but a diffusion of it so that each subject thinks it is their own view.

Gramsci concluded that the class which was able to articulate the interests of other social groups as its own was best placed to exercise hegemony (Notebook 4). To overturn the hegemony, he thought an education system could develop counter-hegemonic ideas among the working classes, especially those he termed organic intellectuals, and to give voice to the subaltern or excluded members of society to critique the status quo. A new alliance of different social groups whose interests are aligned could create a counter-hegemonic bloc, with its own conception of the world, before seizing power (Simons 2015). This means hegemony is inherently unstable—alliances between classes can change—opening up the possibility of challenge from subordinate groups to create a counter-hegemony (Barker and Jane 2016: 77).

Jim Collins (cited in Barker and Jane 2016: 79) rejected Gramsci's notion of hegemony because culture is heterogeneous—fragmented—due to the impact of immigration, ideas of ethnicity, gender, youth cultures, and so on. Yet I think their impact is, at the end of the day fairly limited when you observe who is still in power. Perhaps it is because of culture's heterogeneity that groups remain isolated, and thus the status quo is never seriously challenged. Those that do gain acceptance and a certain level of power must resemble the ruling classes in dress and manner.

Likewise, marginal groups that want to become accepted as "religions" must resemble in several ways the dominant religion, and yet be content with a status a little below that religion in terms of social and political influence. In the U.K., the Church of England is as much the state as the state is the Church of England. Twenty-six bishops, known as the Lords Spiritual, as opposed to the Lords Temporal, serve in the House of Lords—no other church has this privilege, not even the Church of Scotland or the Anglican Church in Wales.[1] The General Synod of the Church meets every five years to consider legislation, but any decisions they make are subject to veto by the Parliament. The Queen remains the Supreme Head of the Church of England and inaugurates the opening session of Parliament.

And while the Queen's role as Supreme Head of the Church of England is mainly symbolic, the Church of England is still very much representing the elite ruling classes. Other groups who have gained recognition as "legitimate religions" according to various laws in England and Wales can be regarded as lower-class religions. This model was replicated in India, for example, where Brahmans were enabled as the elite class and other groups were marginalized.

Religion as Apolitical

In Marxist theories, religion is part of or a tool of the state apparatus, yet it does not always do so willingly. There had been occasions when Rowan Williams, the former Archbishop of Canterbury, at times challenged government policy but was

---

1. This distinction was in earlier times between nobles and clergy. The latter were at one time more dominant until Henry VIII dissolved the monasteries.

told to shut up. It was viewed as transgressive for an archbishop to make a political comment because it was assumed religion should be apolitical (Martin 2010: 109). In some ways, this is because the state itself is standing in for the church.

As meanings and practices are presented as universal truths by the ruling classes, Gramsci (1971: 349) likened the state to how "religion" operates: it provides moral codes of behavior "in the secular sense of a unity of faith between a conception of the world and a corresponding norm of conduct." In Europe, by privatizing religion to limit the influence of churches, the state substitutes the church in providing moral codes and a worldview. Naomi Goldenberg (2015) argued that religions operate as vestigial states but, in reading Gramsci, it seems it is states, at least in modern Europe, that operate like religions, or rather churches.

However, the framing of religion as a private matter has put churches and similar bodies in a strange situation as subordinate or vassal states. While it may seem that the Protestant emphasis on faith reduces a church's relevance, its secondary emphasis on good deeds allows a church to remain public as a charity "for the advancement of religion." In England and Wales, they are forced into this peculiar existence, between being defined as concerned with private matters of "faith" while serving the public good, because if a church or similar body were to become wholly privatized, they would cease to be a religion *in law*. If they have an income, they would need to be regulated under corporate law.

Regarding this separation of private/public, Talal Asad (1993: 47) noted that:

> [T]he characterization of religion as matter of "belief"—which on the surface appears to be a private, interior matter—is part and parcel of a discursive regime that hopes to "privatize" religion. This sort of definition of religion is far from arbitrary; it was the result of a process in which political forces defined belied as something "private" and "interior" in order to reinforce privatization and toleration of Protestant sects after the wars of the Protestant Reformation. It is not a neutral use of the word religion, but one with a political goal.

This also characterizes the political philosophy of John Locke in his *A Letter Concerning Toleration*, which both Craig Martin and Russell McCutcheon discuss in relation to the emergence of the category of religion. When Locke likens the separation of church and state to "heaven and earth," he makes this division seem "natural rather than normative" (Martin 2010: 120; citing McCutcheon 2003: 239). This is a fiction hiding the imposition of a particular view as universal.

Connected to the view that religion is "apolitical" is how the state maintains its hegemony through legislation and the harnessing of the media and education to create the public view that religion (or "true religion") is essentially benign and thus non-threatening to the state. There is an apparent contradiction, as Craig Martin says, between the view of religion as "private and generally harmless" and the view that it is "violent, authoritarian, and essentially tribal ... thus special measures are required to keep them in place (Martin 2010: 112–113). Yet, those recognized as religions are by their very nature "political," but of an acceptable kind that either furthers state interests or can be tolerated up to a limit. Druidry might be a case in point—members of TDN engage in a range of Druid-inspired political activity to protect the environment or ancient monuments. Their support for tree planting is listed as a public benefit but it could also be viewed as an acceptable form of eco-activism.

Charity Law as Replicating the Hegemony

It is interesting to examine how groups negotiate criteria for religion as defined by public bodies in order to highlight both the problems with defining religion and how the state marginalizes groups that do not fit their criteria by denying them access to certain benefits. Not only is conforming to state definitions of religion a challenge for groups, but, according to legal scholar Matthew Harding (2014: 2), "in charity law we find the state marking out certain purposes as 'charitable' according to contested conceptions of the good and then extending legal privileges to the citizens who pursue those purposes." In this way, the state domesticates religion for its own purposes, such as promoting social cohesion in communities.

Charity registration is the primary means for a group to gain recognition as a religion in England and Wales. Charity law replicates the hegemony by categorizing religion as non-political, non-economic, and for the "good" of society. In regulating religion, it suppresses dissent and discourages heterogeneity in groups applying to be recognized as a religion. This categorization of religion keeps it out of the political sphere because it generally views religion as a private matter centered on beliefs. Yet, as groups must also prove their "religious" activities are for public benefit, it domesticates those regarded as religions by forcing groups to conform to liberal Protestant Christian values, including contested notions of "good" religion. This raises important questions about the way religion is framed as promoting the good according to liberal values (Harding 2014: 2).

The Charity Commission is a non-ministerial government department that regulates charities within the limits of the Charity Act. Although part of the civil service, it is independent of ministerial influence (Pocklington 2015: 138) and governed by a board with members who have links to financial services, economics, social enterprise, and law. These are the types of people defining and interpreting "religion." According to the Charity Act of 2006, which had applied to the 2010 TDN application, a religion can involve a belief in more than one god; and a religion which does not involve belief in a god.[2] This is because exceptions were made for "religions of antiquity," such as Buddhism, though this did not include Pagans, ancient or modern. In fulfilling such criteria, groups reproduce normative

---

2. Charity Act 2006: section 3(1)(c) of the 2011 Act. Religion is defined in section 3(2)(a). This was updated in 2011 in light of the TDN case to "the belief system involves belief in a god (or gods) or goddess (or goddesses), or supreme being, or divine or transcendental being or entity or spiritual principle, which is the object or focus of the religion (referred to in this guidance as 'supreme being or entity')" (Charity Commission 2011: Annex A).

Christian understandings of what constitutes the "core essence" of religion based on belief and worship (Owen and Taira 2015: 94).

In English law, at least, religion appears to be conceived as *sui generis*—the view that religion is somehow unique and so it gets a unique status in law, in distinction to politics, education, and so on. This categorization relies on the distinction between "religion" and "secular" and perceives them as having different functions in society (e.g. a "religious" activity is "non-political"). By treating religion as a special category, the Charity Commission has made life complicated for itself, especially when it insists that the activities must also be religious in nature.

Another problem with religion in English law, according to David Pocklington, is that it "is sometimes treated with reference to individual beliefs," as in individual court cases of discrimination, "or in terms of collective beliefs and practices, as in charity registration" (Pocklington 2015: 134). So, while the Church of Scientology is regarded as religious by some bodies, such as HM Revenue and Customs, it is not by others, such as the Prison Service or Charity Commission. In some cases, the criteria for one is met, while it is not met for another. Again, with Scientology, they met the criteria for religion "for the purposes of the Places of Worship Registration Act 1855" (after it went to the Supreme Court in 2013) but were still not able to satisfy the Charity Commission criteria, particularly when defining worship practices (ibid.: 139).

As this chapter was being prepared, the National Secular Society in the U.K. published a document arguing for the removal of the "advancement of religion" as a charitable purpose because it "is based on the outdated presumption that religion is inherently a good thing" and that "religion can be a source of tension and conflict, and a significant driver of harmful social division" (National Secular Society 2019: 4). It also says that there are "religions" that do benefit society but presumably they could register as a charity under a different purpose. Toward the end of the document, it also asks if charity regulators are best placed to define "religion" as many would argue that it is not within the remit of a governmental department to wrestle with this philosophical question" (ibid.: 36). It then provides a case study of the Pagan Federation despite the Census recognizing Paganism in its list of "other religions." The document also examines briefly the cases of the Church of Scientology and the Temple of the Jedi Order, which also failed in their applications, as well as the difficulties encountered by "closed" groups, such as the Plymouth Brethren.

Pagan Challenges to the Hegemony of Religion

Peter Edge devotes a whole chapter to Pagan groups in his book *Legal Responses to Religious Difference* (2002). He says, "organizational and epistemological norms of many Pagans pose a problem for legal institutions and doctrines predicated on a less diffuse approach to spirituality and religion" (ibid.: 351). "Additionally, there is a strong commitment to non-hierarchical, non-proscriptive structures in many Pagan communities" (ibid.: 355). Charity law supports non-democratic organization with top-down authority structures (this has affected Quakers, too). However, while some Pagans have a history of counter-cultural engagement, this does not always mean an absence of top-down authority structures. In Druidry, the Loyal Arthurian Warband (LAW) are counter-cultural, often confronting the state in order to defend the environment, ancient monuments, and human remains, and led by an authoritative figure, King Arthur Pendragon. LAW is also an example of Druid-inspired political activism.

In Charity Law (and elsewhere), the notion of "belief," too, is hierarchical (vertical) rather than democratic/horizontal—groups must demonstrate collective worship practices of a transcendent deity. The Pagan Federation, who failed in their applications for charity registration, respects diversity of belief and practice, but that makes it "not a religion" according to the Charity Commission. The problem for Pagans is they usually set out to challenge norms, not to conform to them, which leaves them in a quandary when seeking registration as a religion. For TDN, on the other hand, they succeeded in blurring the boundary of what counts as the object of religion and gained charity registration in 2010 once the commissioners were able to accept that "Nature" could be regarded as a "supreme being or entity" (see more about the TDN case in Owen and Taira 2015). Though the definition of religion used in charity law was only extended rather than changed, Pagan groups more than most have the opportunity to challenge the "religion" category.

After its success with charity registration, TDN next challenged the membership criteria for the Inter Faith Network U.K., which represents "established" groups, after they were initially rejected in 2012. They succeeded two years later when both TDN and the Pagan Federation were able to become members (while the latter is still without charity recognition as a "religion"). Through Inter Faith participation, Pagan groups become part of the establishment and undoubtedly conform to established notions of "religion," albeit an expanded one. In the end, there is greater acceptance of Pagan groups, but hegemony of religion (as a liberal Christian idea) remains.

Conclusion

In charity law, religion is seen as essentially different from secular activities and something that contributes to the public good as long as its activities are non-political, non-economic, and relate to things transcendent. This serves to domesticate religion by pushing groups to conform to a liberal Protestant Christian definition of religion. If a group does not fit the criteria, it will not gain any state protection or benefits and remain marginal and powerless. Why else have a separate category of religion in the first place? This enables the ruling classes, which in the U.K. includes the Church of England, to maintain their position of influence in society while making sure other groups remain weak as second-class religions or not religions at all.

Suzanne Owen obtained her PhD from the University of Edinburgh and published her thesis as *The Appropriation of Native American Spirituality* (Continuum 2008). She is currently Reader in Religious Studies at Leeds Trinity University in the UK researching indigeneity in Newfoundland and British Druidry.

References

Asad, Talal. 1993. *Genealogies of Religion: Discipline and Reasons of Power in Christianity and Islam*. Baltimore, MD: John Hopkins University Press.

Barker, Chris, and Emma A. Jane. 2016. *Cultural Studies: Theory and Practice*, 5th edition. London: Sage.

Beckford, James A. 2003. *Social Theory and Religion*. Cambridge. Cambridge University Press.

Bocock, Robert. 1986. *Hegemony*. Chichester: Ellis Horwood.

Charity Commission for England and Wales. 2011. *The Advancement of Religion for the Public Benefit*. Liverpool: Charity Commission for England and Wales.

Edge, Peter W. 2002. *Legal Responses to Religious Difference*. The Hague: Kluwer Law International.

Goldenberg, Naomi. 2015. "The Category of Religion in the Technology of Governance: An Argument for Understanding Religions as Vestigial States." In Trevor Stack, Naomi Goldenberg, and Timothy Fitzgerald (eds.), *Religion as a Category of Governance and Sovereignty*, 280–292. Leiden: Brill. https://doi.org/10.1163/9789004290594_013

Gramsci, Antonio. 1971. *Selections from the Prison Notebooks*. Ed. and trans. Quintin Hoare and Geoffrey Nowell Smith. London: Lawrence and Wishart.

Harding, Matthew. 2014. *Charity Law and the Liberal State*. Cambridge: Cambridge University Press.

Martin, Craig. 2010. *Masking Hegemony: A Genealogy of Liberalism, Religion and the Private Sphere*. London: Equinox.

McCutcheon, Russell. 2003. *The Discipline of Religion: Structure, Meaning, Rhetoric*. London: Routledge.

Mouffe, Chantal. 1979. "Hegemony and ideology in Gramsci." In Chantal Mouffe (ed.), *Gramsci and Marxist Theory*, 168–204. London: Routledge.

National Secular Society. 2019. *For the Public Benefit? The Case for Removing "Advancement of Religion" as a Charitable Purpose*. London: National Secular Society.

Owen, Suzanne, and Teemu Taira. 2015. "The Category of 'Religion' in Public Classification: Charity Registration of the Druid Network in England and Wales." In Trevor Stack, Naomi Goldenberg, and Timothy Fitzgerald (eds.), *Religion as a Category of Governance and Sovereignty*, 90–114. Leiden: Brill. https://doi.org/10.1163/9789004290594_006

Pocklington, David. 2015. "Quasi-Law and Religion." In Russell Sandberg (ed.), *Religion and Legal Pluralism*, 133–149. Farnham: Ashgate.

Simons, Jon. 2015. "Hegemony." In Michael T. Gibbons (ed.), *The Encyclopedia of Political Thought*, 1624–1625. New York: John Wiley & Sons.

Chapter 18

A Gramscian Inversion: Hegemony in Theory and in Practice

Thomas J. Carrico, Jr.

... it is one more example—as if one were needed—of the contradiction that is the essence of ideology: that between theory and practice, lofty ideals and grubby dealings.

(Lincoln 2018: 83)

... we must, on my reading of the evidence, stand Gramsci's analysis of hegemony upside down in at least one respect.

(Scott 1990: 91)

Introduction

In Suzanne Owen's essay "Regulating Religion to Maintain the Status Quo" (Chapter 17, this volume) she argues that, through specific political and legal mechanisms, the English state creates and enforces a definition of religion that benefits religious groups that are in line with dominant social, political, and economic ideologies. She analyzes these mechanisms through the lens of Antonio Gramsci's notion of hegemony: "the power dynamic of the ruling elite who maintain their preferences as the norm, becoming the dominant expression in society through consent where people internalize the view as their own or as common sense." It follows that, through the production of such a "status quo, other views are marginalized." England's charity laws and state-sanctioned organizations, like the Inter Faith Network U.K., allow those in power to remain in power by sorting subordinate groups[1] into those whose stated beliefs and behaviors align with dominant interests and those that do not. The former groups receive benefits while the latter groups are ostracized.

---

1. Denis LoRusso raises a particularly important issue in Chapter 20 of this volume: namely, whether (or how) Gramsci's theory of hegemony is relevant with regard to contests between religious groups. Given that his theory of made sense of economic class interests and contests between dominant economic groups and subordinate economic groups, LoRusso astutely asks "how might the economic standing of members in subordinate religious groups impact the processes of state sanctioning that Owen seeks to analyze?"

The Charity laws accomplish these objectives in two ways: first, they reinforce the definition of religion as "essentially different from secular activities *and* something that contributes to the public good as long as its activities are non-political and non-economic and relate to things transcendent" (emphasis mine). The crux of the matter lies not only in the first movement, recognizing a group as non-secular group, but offering benefits only to those groups that demonstrate their disengagement from the politico-economic order. This thereby defines "the public good" as a commitment to disavow challenging dominant social, political, and economic systems. By rewarding subordinate groups that are, or are willing to become, more behaviorally and ideologically in sync with those in power, those implementing English Charity Laws maintain or enhance a hierarchical social arrangement by coercively recruiting subordinate groups.

On Owen's reading, this illustrates the pervasiveness of hegemonic control—dominated groups participate in their own domestication and willing acquiescence to dominant values and ideologies. In short, Owen uses her case studies to illustrate a social arrangement wherein groups that would normally seek to challenge social hierarchies end up participating in, and reinforcing, those same inequalities. But the social contests are rarely that simple. Noting that Gramsci's conception of hegemony is scattered throughout the *Prison Notebooks*, it is worth reflecting on the material scattering of hegemonic authority as well. Like class, gender, race, and citizenship, hegemony is a singular term that points towards a complicated social reality. Hegemonic control is rarely as straightforward as "dominant group coerces subordinate group." This manipulation involves legal and governmental apparatuses, access to the means of enforcing one's control, a system of social, cultural, and economic rewards and punishments, and a system of beliefs and definitions that justifies, naturalizes, or valorizes this arrangement—an ideology. But it also entails strategy and resistance and the agency of both dominated and dominant group members; in other words, the policies of dominant groups may not reflect an accurate description of subordinate groups, even when the subordinate groups adhere to these policies.

While it is tempting to take these types of documents as evidence of a dominant ideology and agreement to these policies as agreement with that ideology, ideological interpretations of hegemonic domination rarely tell the whole story. Owen makes a point that Gramsci's theory of hegemony moves away from Louis Althusser's "statist" conception of ideology and towards a more diffuse theory of social control. In what follows, this chapter will examine prominent critiques of this ideological emphasis in order to argue that, while attempting to move beyond a statist conception of ideology, the framework of Owen's argument does not leave enough room for antihegemonic protest, subversion, and resistance. By collapsing a theory of hegemonic control of thought into historical examples of hegemonic control of policy, this approach is unable to account for informal critique of the status quo, the agency of subordinate groups, and the material production of analytical categories.

The Ideology of "Ideology"

Owen situates "hegemony" as a sort of synthesis between an overly broad, Foucauldian thesis of "power" and Althusser's narrowly policy-driven, "statist" ideology antithesis. Her essay, though, seems to take positive elements from each theory, eradicating their shortcomings. Particularly with regard to ideology, Owen's essay relies heavily on the idea that the state is the sole agent in the administration of charity law. This is more in line with an Althusserian conception of ideology that runs throughout the piece. On Althusser's reading, each individual is born into a set of relationships not of their own making. Althusser further argues that this external set of structures and relationships, these social formations, provide an individual with an identity as opposed to their identity being something fixed, internal, or essential. These social formations, though, benefit some people and not others; they are characterized by inequality. Following Marx,[2] Althusser recognizes that those who benefit from this inequality have a vested interest in maintaining the status quo. In order to do so, dominant groups are buttressed by the repressive apparatuses of the state like police forces and armies as well as ideological apparatuses of the state, like, in this case, institutions that define and enforce a particular conception of religion or any other set of ideas that justify or explain why this unequal arrangement is necessary, natural, or beneficial (Althusser 1970).

The subordinate groups are categorized, sorted, evaluated, moralized, and either integrated or ostracized depending on the will of the state and the state's system of definitions. Owen concludes her chapter by stating that "through Inter Faith participation, Pagan groups become part of the establishment and undoubtedly conform to established notions of "religion," albeit an expanded one. In the end, there is greater acceptance of Pagan groups, but hegemony of religion (as a liberal Christian idea) remains." While Owen's essay illustrates the participation of Pagan groups in the structures of the establishment, it is a leap to suggest that they undoubtedly conform to established notions of "religion," or dominant ideology more generally.

The problems with this type of approach, assuming that official markers of domination indicate universal assent to dominant ideology, are twofold. First, it assumes the primacy of analytical categories—the concept of religion is first defined, and then used to sort people according to a definition. Second, and related to the first, the people who have been sorted are then characterized by a homogeneity of thought—all members of a group are in agreement with the official position of the group. Not only are social groups the site of disagreement, discord, and competition, but categories are the result of this disagreement, discord, and competition and not applied in a top-down manner, originating in the thought of the powerful and bequeathed to the dominated classes. While some social agents are better situated to benefit from particular definitions, these social categories are the site of social struggle. Further, official records and policies serve to obscure

---

2. For an overview of the development of "Ideology" as a conceptual tool, see Eagleton (2007).

these competing interests and conflicting viewpoints by offering unified definitions and structures that do not reflect the complicated and unstable reality of social interaction.

Creating Categories

Althusser sought to render a "philosophical" reading of Marx, discerning a methodology and a set of categories essential to Marx's conception of history as a productive dialectic between groups competing over material interests.[3] The production of scholarly categories, however, is merely a distinct mode of social production: in addition to producing categories and definitions, the scholastic mode of production imbues these categories with a degree of objectivity buttressed by his class position. By creating a degree of separation between scholar and object of study, this process has the tendency to begin with ideas and situate society accordingly.[4] In a blistering critique of Althusser's works, E. P. Thompson argues in *The Poverty of Theory* that Althusser's study is too far removed from the objects of his analysis to be of much use. Discussing the concept of "consciousness," Thompson states:

> Obviously, consciousness, whether as unselfconscious culture, or as myth, or as science, or law, or articulated ideology, thrusts back into being in its turn: as being is thought so thought also is lived—people may, within limits, live the social or sexual expectations which are imposed upon them by dominant conceptual categories.
>
> (Thompson 1978: 12)

Thompson is concerned that Althusser is more engaged in playing word games with scholastic categories than he is with attending to the historical production of categories like class. But also with ideology, when human agents assess their social situation, they may or may not adhere to behavior consistent with the dominant ideology. But the question of behavior is different from the question of belief, acting in accord with the dominant ideology, or not seeking to challenge it, is different from acquiescing to an idea. Further, it takes more than state legislators to construct a category.

For Thompson, it isn't that concepts like class and ideology are useless, but they are not merely concepts. They are part and parcel of historical processes. He concludes his magnum opus, *The Making of the English Working Class,* by commenting on a parliamentary report that utilizes philosophical categories. Thompson comments that [the working class] "met Utilitarianism in their daily lives, and they sought to throw it back, not blindly, but with intelligence and moral passion.

---

3. See, particularly, Althusser and Balibar (2009).
4. Bruno Latour (2005) refers to this method of analysis as a "sociology of the social" – an analysis of a socio-categorical word game (the concept of "society") that masquerades as an analysis of material reality.

They fought, not the machine, but the exploitative and oppressive relationships intrinsic to industrial capitalism" (Thompson 1964: 832). Class isn't a category into which social agents can be placed. For Thompson, social class is what occurs when social agents are born into specific economic conditions and come to the realization that they have interests that align with the interests of some people and are different from others. So while Althusser sought to develop a philosophy of dialectical materialism, Thompson sought to develop an understanding of class grounded in human interaction amidst material reality.

This is the type of differentiation that would greatly enhance Owen's essay. What would it mean to view the Pagan groups as "throwing back" a concept of religion to the dominant classes? To recognize that this is a group with their own interests finding ways to articulate and work towards a common set of goals *against* or *in spite of* the religious state or stately religion? Owen addresses the relationship between religion and state, suggesting that, through definition and enforcement, religions can act as states and states as religions. Naomi Goldenberg has recently examined the interaction between religion and state, arguing that the confluence of religion and state, institutionally and theoretically, "has always involved a mystification of male dominance and a consequent anxiety about women in relation to that dominance" (Goldenberg 2019: 333). In other words, while definitions of religion and its maintenance as a category are connected to state power, this power and these definitions have relevance beyond the maintenance of a solely religious, or Christian, hegemony. What, then, are the economic impacts of this particular arrangement of religion and the state with regard to maintaining an antagonistic relationship between upper and working classes? Between wage labor and capital? How does the shifting definition of "public good" in the charity laws and institutions "mystify" class antagonisms? What are the possibilities of rebellion and how might religion's association with state power delimit those possibilities? This leads to the second problem with discussing ideological manipulation as unanimous subscription to dominant patterns of thought—namely, it is difficult, if not impossible, to firmly link action with intellectual ascent to dominant modes of thought, *especially* in contexts characterized by inequality.

Obscuring Dissent

The view of ideological domination as a relatively simple, top-down manipulation of each individual consciousness is a widespread reading of Gramscian hegemony that James Scott is at pains to move away from. He states:

> we must, on my reading of the evidence, stand Gramsci's analysis of hegemony upside down in at least one respect. In Gramsci's original formulation, which has guided most subsequent neo-Marxist work on ideology, hegemony works primarily at the level of thought as distinct from the level of action...It is this dominated consciousness that, Gramsci claims, has prevented the working class from drawing the radical consequences inherent in much of its action.
>
> (Scott 1990: 91)

This is in line with Owen's application of the Gramscian notion of hegemony—not only are the dominated groups "in the thrall of hegemonic social thought," to borrow Scott's phrasing, these groups are therefore unable to reach the revolutionary conclusions that would lead them to overthrow this bondage. They also willingly reproduce the conditions necessary for their own domination. Scott, however, argues that the disconnect between dominated action and dominated thought is most pronounced outside of the public sphere, where the consequences for rebellion are lessened. Scott concisely illustrates this dynamic through an Ethiopian proverb that serves as the book's epigraph: "When the great lord passes, the wise peasant bows deeply and silently farts" (Scott 1990: v). While the public actions of this wise peasant indicate reverence, respect, and adherence to dominant ideology, the flatulence evinces rebellion. Similarly, Owen illustrates that pagan groups "bow deeply," but there is not room for the accompanying dissent.

However, there does not need to be any outward sign of dissent to suggest that beliefs and actions may not exactly correspond. Nicholas Abercrombie and Bryan S. Turner rightly criticize this link between belief and action as a faulty "ruling ideas model" of society (Abercrombie and Turner 1978). They argue that, generally, subordinate classes do *not* share the same assumptions, categories, and definitions as the ruling classes. In fact, due to the means of disseminating a dominant ideology, and the lack of motivation to question it, the ruling classes tend to adhere to the dominant ideology while the subordinate classes see it as a justificatory tool that doesn't hold up to material reality and yet it is not the only method of ensuring conformity. Scott summarizes this dynamic, stating:

> it is therefore more accurate to consider subordinate classes less constrained at the level of thought and ideology, since they can in secluded settings speak with comparative safety, and more constrained at the level of political action and struggle, where the daily exercise of power sharply limits the options available to them.
> (Scott 1990: 91)

In other words, the hegemony of religion may serve as a justification for enforcing the status quo, but it does not describe the attitudes of all agents subject to the hegemonic group.

To return to Owen's essay, while the inclusion of Pagan groups does extend the state's definition of religion and, therefore, the implementation of hegemonic power. It is worth dwelling on the questions of whether, and to what extent, The Druid Network has changed. What resources are available to ascertain whether their adherence was an acquiescence to state power or a counterhegemonic strategy to advance the group's interest? If the group did change their practices, then how can we as scholars look for evidence regarding the group's attitude towards this arrangement? As social agents seek to contest dominant categories of thought and action, what role does scholarship play in reifying or challenging those categories? How do the dominant definitions of religion (that it is separate from political and economic life and works to maintain the public good) gloss over, ignore, or obscure expressions of dissent? To return to Goldenberg's link of the ideological to the practical, where do these categories and definitions intersect with practical, economic restrictions on subordinate classes?[5] To connect with the other categories in this volume, how does this dominant expression (and legislation) of religion impact race and ethnicity (Newton, Chapter 6), gender and sexuality (Goodwin, Chapter 12), and citizenship and nationality (McVicar, Chapter 1)?

Concluding with Dissenters/Dissenting from Conclusions

In closing, there is a substantial difference between acquiescing to the status quo through one's public actions (in this case, applying for recognition as a religious charity) and acquiescing to dominant justificatory schemes by taking them at face-value as truths. By way of example, in England, the late nineteenth century saw the demise of the extremely popular "lucifer" matchstick industry. This was the first mass-produced matchstick, an invention that revolutionized any process that required fire or heat. A formerly arduous task, creating flame, was now as simple as striking a match on any rough surface. The industry had been at least somewhat in the public consciousness since the 1830s due to poor labor conditions, mistreatment of workers, as well as a jaw disease particular to this industry caused by exposure to phosphorus. These issues reached a social climax in July of 1888 at the Bryant and May factory, one of England's largest matchstick manufacturers, when 1,400 female laborers went on strike. In June of that year, Annie Besant wrote an article called "White Slavery in London" that critiques working conditions at Bryant and May, especially when compared to increasing returns for shareholders (Besant 1888). Ensuing scholarship about this episode tended to treat it as a result of one prominent activist's work or as a relatively minor strike in broader labor histories.

In this case, the actions of the subordinate class of matchstick workers ("matchgirls") were at odds with the dominant interests of factory owners and shareholders. However, by focusing on Besant's efforts, it seems they were unable, or unwilling, to rebel until publicly chastised by an upper-class revolutionary. Many treatments saw them as pawns of competing dominant groups—socialists and capitalists. So whether they worked or rebelled, they were only doing so by sharing in one or another dominant ideology. In her 2009 work, *Striking a Light: The Bryant and May Matchwomen and Their Place in History*, Louise Raw argues that their involvement in the strike was much more substantial—both behaviorally and ideologically. Raw argues that this was a worker-envisioned and worker-led strike and uses letters, registers, and oral histories from relatives of matchstick workers to support her claim. This type of research is a time-consuming process and is, in some ways, methodologically problematic, but it is an effective example of using scholastic resources to center a research project on the lives and work of lower class, female laborers. These sources point towards the way that some

---

5. See also McCutcheon (2005).

social agents, like Besant, the shareholders of Bryant and May, or academic historians, are able to record and have recorded their lives and works in print while others are not. It isn't that hegemony and ideology are irrelevant, it is just that they indicate the way that economic factors allow some to record, reproduce, or otherwise enforce their interested set of norms. This is not the same as universal acceptance of those norms, despite what public actions may suggest.

Conversely, there were matchstick workers who did not join the labor unions, did not join the strike, and continued to show up for work. Nellie McDowell, for instance, was a child laborer in the industry at the end of the nineteenth-century when worker revolts were at their most prominent. Nellie met Muriel Lester, a Christian philanthropist from the upper class, in the early twentieth century, eventually joining to spearhead efforts towards a vision of Christian pacifism. Seth Koven uses their relationship as "loving mates" (Koven 2014: 134) to explore inter-class dynamics, sexual attraction, charity, and revolutionary Christian thought in England at the turn of the century. What is particularly relevant for the present volume is Nellie's continued employment in the matchstick industry despite exploitation and the threat of disease. Nellie's labor invites the ruling ideas model of social action wherein she earnestly believes in, or at least supports, the dominant ideologies that cast "matchgirl" as her natural lot. Koven argues that not only is there little evidence of Nellie's attitude or worldview, her motivation to continue laboring in this industry is far from simple. Koven argues:

> She put job security before worker solidarity. In this respect, she resembled the vast majority of women workers in late-nineteenth- and early-twentieth-century Britain, who were neither trade unionists nor members of labor and socialist political parties...they are often lumped together into a vast inert body of metropolitan toilers whose supposed passivity Frederick Engels lamented; in Gareth Stedman Jones's influential formulation, such apolitical men and women bartered away class-conscious politics for cultural autonomy from bourgeois meddling.
> (Koven 2014: 17)

In other words, Nellie's submission to employment in this industry was a choice that could have been informed by an awareness of her options rather than an obliviousness toward her own agency brought about by ideological manipulation. Koven continues, though, stating:

> the more deeply I researched Nellie's working life in the match industry, the less evidence I found that she was radicalized by it...in light of the profound insecurity of her childhood experiences as a Poor Law half-orphan ward of the state, Nellie used her keen intellect and strong work ethic to ensure economic security for herself and her family. Her choices, rooted in the logic of family life and pride in her own labor, require no apology, although they certainly invite explanation and analysis.
> (Koven 2014: 132–133)

Her case involves ideological manipulation, to be sure, and her participation in the industry certainly helped reproduce the conditions necessary for the exploitation of workers; but this does not tell the whole story. Rather, her whole story points towards the practical restraints on her agency or to the way her experience of poverty informed her attitude towards the costs and benefits of socio-economic protest and political dissent.

I have argued that dominant ideologies are simply one element of a social milieu and do not hold universal explanatory value but rather point towards the practical constraints on and possibilities of challenge and rebellion against the status quo. The question of why a group may adhere to behaviors, categories, and definitions that benefit the status quo are more appropriately matters of practice than matters of thought. Finally, in closing, it is worth returning to Gramsci in order to examine the role that intellectuals play in reproducing hegemonic norms. He argues that "all men (sic) are intellectuals…but not all men (sic) have in society the function of intellectuals" (Gramsci 2000: 304). Gramsci defines intellectuals as those who exert the intellectual functions of giving the group "homogeneity and awareness of its own function not only in the economic but also in the social and political fields" (ibid.: 301). Traditional intellectuals, however, produce an account of history as unified, an account of intellectual activity as separate from material class struggles, and accounts of analytical of categories that dress up the interests of the ruling class with objectivity, necessity, and moral value. In order to critique, or even bring to light, the dynamics of class struggle inherent in intellectual activity, it is necessary to attend to the role of economic structures that undergird all categories of scholastic critique. Owen has shown that this is necessary with the category of religion, but the use of the concepts of ideology and hegemony ought to be included as well.

For this reason, scholars have a research imperative to focus on the complexities of group dynamics and struggles for and against power. Likewise, scholars have a pedagogical imperative to draw attention to the ways that universities are structured to communicate and naturalize class distinctions—from the material reality of new buildings and technologies to the ideological role of titles, scholarships, and prestige, we need to pay attention to the markers of class distinction to which we conform in our university settings. By emphasizing adherence to the dominant ideology as a, perhaps the, defining characteristic of hegemonic control, an ideology-focused, Althusserian Marxist approach risks producing an intellectual picture of social contests that is abstract enough to not only obscure the material conditions of social life but also to dismiss the agency of the dominated. At best this is an incomplete analysis, at worst this approach is complicit in the domination it attempts to critique.

Thomas J. Carrico, Jr. is a PhD candidate at Florida State University's Department of Religion. Focusing on the matchstick industry in Victorian England, Carrico's dissertation examines the social, political, and economic constraints on moral reasoning, especially in response to industrial disease. Carrico has published work in Method Today: Redescribing Approaches to the Study of Religion (2018), has entries forthcoming in London's East End: A Short Encyclopedia (2022), and serves as the pastor of Finley Memorial Presbyterian Church.

References

Abercrombie, Nicholas, and Bryan S. Turner. 1978. "The Dominant Ideology Thesis." The British Journal of Sociology 29(2): 149–170. https://doi.org/10.2307/589886

Althusser, Louis. 1970. "Ideology and Ideological State Apparatuses." Trans. Ben Brewster. Retrieved from www.marxists.org/reference/archive/althusser/1970/ideology.htm (accessed July 1, 2019).

Althusser, Louis, and Étienne Balibar. 2009. Reading Capital. Trans. Ben Brewster. London: Verso Press.

Besant, Annie. 1888. "White Slavery in London." The Link 21 (June 23). Retrieved from www.mernick.org.uk/thhol/thelink.html (accessed July 1, 2019).

Eagleton, Terry. 2007. Ideology: An Introduction. London: Verso Press.

Goldenberg, Naomi. 2019. "Revisiting BISFT Summer School 2006, Harriot-Watt University, Edinburgh, 'What's God got to do with it?—Politics, Economics, Theology'." Feminist Theology 27(3): 329-338. https://doi.org/10.1177/0966735019834003

Gramsci, Antonio. 2000. The Antonio Gramsci Reader: Selected Writings 1916–1935. Ed. David Forgacs. New York: New York University Press.

Koven, Seth. 2014. The Matchgirl and the Heiress. Princeton, NJ: Princeton University Press.

Latour, Bruno. 2005. Reassembling the Social. Oxford: Oxford University Press.

Lincoln, Bruce. 2018. Apples and Oranges. Chicago, IL: University of Chicago Press.

McCutcheon, Russell. 2005. Religion and the Domestication of Dissent. New York: Routledge.

Raw, Louise. 2009. Striking a Light: The Bryant and May Matchwomen and Their Place in History. New York: Continuum International Publishing Group.

Scott, James. 1990. Domination and the Arts of Resistance. New Haven, CT: Yale University Press.

Thompson, E.P. 1964. The Making of the English Working Class. New York: Random House.

Thompson, E.P. 1978. The Poverty of Theory and Other Essays. London: Monthly Review Press.

Chapter 19

The Druid Network as a Capitalist Success Story: or, Why The Druid Network's Charity Status is Beside the Point

Neil George

If I call this a capitalist success story, I mean it not as classic rags-to-riches propaganda, but rather a tale of potential dissent being quieted in the name of ever-greater profits for those best positioned to exploit capitalist modes of production, thereby making future dissent even more difficult. I have no interest in dismissing the achievements of The Druid Network (TDN) as irrelevant, yet my interests lie first and foremost in the question: Who benefits? The most obvious answer is TDN, who gained tax benefits as well as apparent social capital. Their gains, however, were not without costs, and they were certainly not the only ones to gain. Focusing on the stated goal of "advancement of religion" has the potential to conceal the "circulation of power" at work in the charity approval process. In this regard, we require a broader view that sees the Charity Commission, TDN, and their respective adherents as having been socialized members of society whose concerns/interests were shaped by that society long before they ever interacted in this context. It was not random that TDN members would consider and/or desire charity status, let alone to do so under the auspices of the "advancement of religion."

Craig Martin has argued in *Capitalizing Religion*, "discourses on individual religion tend to envision individuals in isolation, rather than as subjects interpellated and thereby brought into existence through ideologies and discourses; as such, they block structural analysis by obfuscating the extent to which subjects in a capitalist system are determined by social norms outside their control" (Martin 2014: 5). I have no desire to conflate "individual religion" with Druidry, despite the existence of individualistic and anti-institutional ideas present within the Druidic community, evidenced within Owen and Teemu Taira's treatment of the TDN case elsewhere, which highlighted the reactions of some Druids against the label "religion," with some preferring philosophy, spirituality, or some other term, believing "religion" to diminish the importance of individual experience (Owen and Taira 2015). This anti-institutional/dogma stance can be seen clearly on TDN's website, where a disclaimer can be found that reads: "The views put forward within these pages are voices of individuals within the Druid community and those who touch it. They do not represent the entirety of Druidry, nor do they necessarily represent the views of The Druid Network nor its members. There exists a wide spectrum of opinions within Druidry and, while some views expressed may be rich sources of inspiration, there may also be views that cause offence to others" (TDN 2020). Regardless then of any other similarities or differences, Druidry and "individual religion"/spiritual but not religious employ similar rhetorical divisions regarding institutionalized religion and private experience, which generates a discourse among insiders that can fall prey to the problems pointed out by Martin.

The criticism leveled by Martin is one that seems to hold some truth for Owen. At times, in her essay "Regulating Religion to Maintain the Status Quo" (Chapter 17, this volume), Owen seems to present the druidic/pagan community and/or TDN as would-be counter-cultural or counter-hegemonic agents foiled by the Charity Commission's rules that turn them into a Protestant-lite tradition. In this telling, the Charity Commission is presented as being deeply rooted in the hegemonic interests of the elites/status quo. At the same time, TDN is left undertheorized, leaving the impression that they are acting/existing almost entirely outside of society and its regimes of socialization prior to their decision to pursue charity status under the guise of "advancement of religion." This places a great deal of interpretive power in the hands of the Charity Commission, for whom it can mean almost anything at all, since neither "advancement" nor "religion" have a particularly stable meaning, which does not even account for the exemptions the Charity Commission granted when they wanted to call a group religious that did not meet the criteria, as Owen notes they did for Buddhism.

TDN succeeded, not because they conformed themselves to any Protestantized definition of "religion," but because they played the game secular rhetorical game with sufficient proficiency. Much like arriving at the door of an old speakeasy where a section of the door could slide or swing open and a password offered for admittance, TDN showed they were "on the level." In meeting the Charity Commission's admission requirements, this does not mean that they will advance "religion," while avoiding economic, political, or other public realms deemed taboo. Such goals are impossible. Craig Martin has rightly held that any firm religion/state separation is untenable, and that the rhetoric of separation functions to mask the workings of hegemony (Martin 2010). Instead of perfect separation, what we see is a separation that is at best selectively enforced in ways that are intended to maximize support while minimizing dissent. Seeking and achieving charity status may be usefully seen as an oath of allegiance that grants benefits and incentivizes continued good behavior.

As much as there are various ways that TDN, as a group permitted to "produce and distribute ideology, to produce conditions of persuasion, to socialize subjects into regimes of normalization and privilege, and so on," is necessarily, if often covertly, political, TDN's website openly advocates political behavior in a section title "The Dissenting Druid." This section highlights possible expressions of Druidry's long history of activism, including "funding an environmentalist pressure group, or joining a green political party." This is not an explicit endorsement of the Green Party of England and Wales, which coincidentally saw its first Member of

Parliament in 2010, the same year TDN was granted charity status. That said, in a country that votes using First Past the Post, encouraging or at least permitting smaller groups to vote for parties/candidates that are not top contenders, vote splitting, can have serious political benefits for some of their opponents.

TDN members have been socialized into the same systems of production as the members of the Charity Commission. These are economically, politically, etc. interested individuals who were taught how to be good citizens/capitalists prior to applying for charity status, and, at the very least, for those born in Britain or other "Western" countries, they have been learning these lessons from childhood. The desire for charity status is a representation of those interests. They are not indifferent to tax exemptions or potential social standing that might be achieved by such recognition. They did not approach these debates over whether or not TDN was a "religious" organization unaware of the "World Religions paradigm," "spiritual, but not religious," "philosophy, not religion," religion as private/individual, sex scandals, religious violence, abortion rights, televangelists, crusades, interfaith networks, British history, the internet, etc. Debates among Druids as to whether they were a "religion," a "philosophy," "spirituality," a "way of life," a "practice," or something else were not unique to them, and reflect the messiness of socialization, but also a hegemonic system that had so thoroughly socialized them that their allegiance to the status quo was a fait accompli. Class interests structured the language of the debate. Whatever differences you may wish to draw between religion/spirituality/philosophy, and I do not wish to make any strong or universal distinctions, because I see them as rhetorical devices, not meaningfully distinct categories, these categories do not in and of themselves make individuals or groups more or less capitalist, more or less counter-hegemonic, counter-cultural, or capable of challenging norms.

TDN did not succeed in "blurring the boundary of what counts as the object of religion" because that boundary was always blurry. This blurriness was the result not only of a disconnect between the Charity Commission's criteria and reality, not only because they made exceptions for any organization they considered worthy, but also because the religion-secular dichotomy was built to be blurry, so as to create "malleable limits that make almost anything possible to say" (McCutcheon 2007: 191). Thus, while we can certainly credit TDN was pushing for an expanded definition of "religion," this change is more about the legitimacy of the charity system than it is about legitimizing future applications by druids, pagans, or others who have hitherto been less officially connected to the apparatuses of the state.

The success of TDN in expanding the official definition of religion used by the Charity Commission was a victory for elite interests. To draw on McCutcheon's argument from *The Domestication of Dissent*, the capacity of TDN or any other group to challenge hegemonic systems is curtailed when they accept that there is something about themselves, what they believe and/or practice, that is meaningfully distinct from the realm called "politics." In other words, "The fiction of [apolitical] faith thus makes selves more governable" (McCutcheon 2005: 95). This does not require identification as a religion. This does not require identification as a charity. Internalizing this fiction comes prior to pursuing, obtaining, and maintaining charity status. It is worth reconsidering the role played by the Charity Commission in securing consensus around the "secular" status quo, as the way they dole out or withhold privileges likely has more to do with, to use the language of commerce, customer retention than it does with growing their clientele. Further, it is worth viewing the Charity Commission as part of the hegemonic structures whereby elite preferences are conflated with those of the working/middle classes. The economist Thomas Piketty has argued that "In most countries, tax benefits for giving mostly favor the rich, whose preferences in charity, culture, arts, education, and sometimes politics are de facto subsidized by less well-to-do taxpayers," which "grant[s] the rich greater say in defining the public good" (Piketty 2020: 512, 1021). The same system that may be seen to offer some perceived legitimacy to TDN as an official charity, whose relatively small income yields fairly small tax breaks can use TDNs charity status to legitimize further the same system, which gives massive tax breaks to the wealthiest members of society, tax breaks that contribute to the underfunding of public services and an increased tax burden on the working/middle classes.

Increased access to charity status, such as through the "expanded" definition of religion that resulted from TDNs efforts, does little to solve the class imbalances in the charity system, and may even serve to further entrench them. To draw on the work of the philosopher of science Thomas Kuhn, scientific paradigm shifts require not only a new theoretical framework, but a critical mass of anomalous data that the regnant theory cannot explain. One of the reasons why the Charity Commission has granted exceptions to certain groups is that the legitimacy of its entire system would be cast into doubt if one or more of the so-called "world religions," such as Buddhism, could not meet the threshold of "religion" for charity purposes. For Kuhn, there needs to not only be a plausible new system, but sufficient reasons to abandon the current system. By making exceptions and by modifying the definition to be more inclusive, the Charity Commission is minimizing anomalous data. There may even be a case to suggest that granting charity status to TDN may add to the perceived reasonable of denying charity status to other groups. After all, will they not expand their criteria when presented with a compelling case?

Bruce Lincoln (1989: 165–166) has argued that rhetorical battles over anomalous data are of great importance to the scientific community for their potential implications to social, structural, economic, etc. concerns that exceed the purely theoretical. The same undoubtedly holds true here. The Charity Commission is run by people who are not disinterested in the legitimacy of their work and the systems it supports. I have no idea whether or not the members of the Charity Commission consciously approached the TDN case with these issues in mind, but it is clear that the Charity Commission operates in ways that naturally tend toward reinforcing its own charity systems as well as broader hegemonic systems.

Protestantism's status as a benchmark for participation in the structures of many "secular" nation states, undoubtedly one part cultural narcissism, was bound up with the rhetoric of secularism from the beginning. Despite prior discourse on church–state separation from the likes of Thomas Jefferson and John Locke, "religion" largely only took on its modern meaning in the latter half of the nineteenth century, which made possible the religion-secular dichotomy that so successfully marginalizes "religion" in discussions of the "secular" fields of economics, science, politics, etc. It is no coincidence that the so-called conflict between science and religion, the world religions paradigm, and the World Parliament of Religions (possibly the first notable interfaith gathering) all appeared in the same timeframe, or that they were all seen through what might be called a secular Protestant lens. They were all discursive tools useful for securing hegemonic authority. Nor is it surprising that the early twentieth century saw Max Weber argue for the unique role Protestantism played in advancing capitalism and Robert K. Merton that Protestantism played a similar role in the history of science. Not only can Protestantism easily be co-opted to a discourse of individual faith that mirrors secular interests, the Protestantization of secular rhetoric helped protect against charges of atheism in the nineteenth century when secularism had to overtly appear religious.

Assuming any strong comparison between the haves and have nots among the "religions" in England and Wales is problematic. Even if in some hypothetical future the Church of England was disestablished and saw plummeting attendance rates, TDN would still bear little resemblance to what remained barring dramatic changes to their structures and fortunes. The Church of England is well-positioned to continue as an elite institution firmly invested in the status quo, not just because of their establishment as state religion, which has helped, but because they are a major player in and exploiter of current systems of capital. A 2017 article in *The Guardian* revealed a striking picture of the Church as not only immensely wealthy (£7.9 billion in investable assets), but a key player—and a very successful one at that—in the investment market, yielding a 17.1 percent return in 2016, well above the market average and outperforming some of the most successful hedge funds over many years. Undoubtedly their 26 seats in the House of Lords help them to protect those privileges. The Church of England sees more revenue pass through their accounts in a single year than TDN might end up seeing in a century. It may then be problematic to claim, as Owen does, that, "Through Inter Faith participation, Pagan groups become part of the establishment," except insofar as it may help solidify their complicity in the capitalist enterprise. After all, interfaith networks are overtly designed to socialize individuals/groups into a specific view of good/bad religion that is overtly capitalist/secular, a sort of "common core" approach to religion weighted towards the dominant tradition(s), which is to say, primarily Protestantism. Indeed, using the same term to describe both TDN and the Church of England benefits the Church more than it benefits TDN. There has never been a level playing field—charity status and interfaith networks were never designed to change that—and suggesting that TDN is now part of the establishment has the potential to conceal important power dynamics that meaningfully separate TDN from those with power and masks the ways that interfaith networks serve to marginalize groups like TDN.

Hegemony is pervasive. TDN did not sell out to hegemonic interests by seeking charity status, but in doing so, they did further support the broader structures that maintain those interests. Their active and passive involvements with the maintenance of those structures predate their deliberations over whether or not to seek charity status, and all druids, pagans, and indeed all members of society, insofar as they are involved in the society, tend to reproduce those structures in countless, often small, ways. Hegemonic structures are often best preserved by making them part of the taken-for-granted fabric of society rather than something to which individuals must consciously subscribe. Certainly, Owen is right to highlight the ways that class and economic interests can be concealed through the use of language, both in how words are defined as well as which words are used in the first place. Even so, Owen's discussions of how "good deeds" allow "religions" to "remain public" seem to take the focus off of the circulation of power involved in the hegemonic control of language, whereby the public and public good are all reflective of elite interests. Charity status did not make TDN part of "the establishment," but may have served to further marginalize it, especially insofar as it participated in interfaith networks. If TDN sees itself as counter-cultural, counter-hegemonic, or otherwise embracing a tradition of dissent, there is no reason to think that presenting themselves to the Charity Commission in Protestant-like language or accepting the benefits of charity status will change the difficulty level of what has always been nearly impossible—unmasking and combatting hegemony. It is never easy to speak truth to power when, in some sense, power controls truth.

Neil George is a doctoral candidate (ABD) in the Humanities at York University. His research focuses on discourses of science, religion, and the secular.

References

Lincoln, Bruce. 1989. *Discourse and the Construction of Society: Comparative Studies of Myth, Ritual, and Classification.* New York: Oxford University Press.
Martin, Craig. 2010. *Masking Hegemony: A Genealogy of Liberalism, Religion and the Private Sphere.* London: Equinox.
Martin, Craig. 2014. *Capitalizing Religion: Ideology and the Opiate of the Bourgeoisie.* New York: Bloomsbury.
McCutcheon, Russell T. 2005. *Religion and the Domestication of Dissent, or How to Live in a Less than Perfect Nation.* Sheffield: Equinox.
McCutcheon, Russell T. 2007. "'They Licked the Platter Clean': On the Co-Dependency of the Religious and The Secular." *Method and Theory in the Study of Religion* 19: 173: 199. https://doi.org/10.1163/157006807X240109
Merton, Robert K. 1938. "Science, Technology and Society in Seventeenth Century England." *Osiris* 4: 360–632. https://doi.org/10.1086/368484
Owen, Suzanne, and Teemu Taira. 2015. "The Category of 'Religion' in Public Classification: Charity Registration of the Druid Network in England and Wales." In Trevor Stack,

Naomi Goldenberg, and Timothy Fitzgerald (eds.), *Religion as a Category of Governance and Sovereignty*, 90–114. Leiden: Brill. https://doi.org/10.1163/9789004290594_006

Piketty, Thomas. 2020. *Capital and Ideology*. Trans. Arthur Goldhammer. Cambridge, MA: The Belknap Press of Harvard University Press.

Weber, Max. 2001. *The Protestant Ethic and the Spirit of Capitalism*. Trans. Talcott Parsons. New York: Routledge.

Chapter 20

Who's Afraid of Class Analysis? Rethinking Identity and Class in the Study of Religion

James Dennis LoRusso

The relationship between religion and political economy has perplexed and propelled the academic study of religion since its genesis during the modern period. Early on, Max Weber anchored the nascent discipline of sociology around this nexus. In his most important influential work on the topic, he asserted that religion, specifically Puritan theology, could explain a great deal about the nature of the world—particularly the economic domain—we inhabit. *The Protestant Ethic and the Spirit of Capitalism* challenged assumptions about this relationship, or rather lack thereof. Orthodox Marxism rejected religion as an "opiate," an element of the superstructure that engendered a false consciousness in the proletarian, justifying their exploitation at the hands of capital. The real action, in contrast, unfolded not around the speculative systems of belief but the material conditions of society. "The history of all hitherto existing society," Marx had declared in the *Communist Manifesto*," is the history of class struggles," a conflict between social classes for control over the means of production (Marx 2002: 3). Weber instead countered that the roots of the modern capitalist system lay in religion itself, in the theological innovations of the Protestant Reformation.

My point here is that Weber gifted the study of religion a framework through which scholars could explore meaningfully the nexus of religion, class, and the modern socioeconomic order. Suzanne Owen pursues a similar end in her essay (Chapter 17, this volume), asking what we can learn about religion in a particular context if we apply a neo-Marxist lens. Aligning with Marx's *opiate* hypothesis, she argues that the state regulation of religion "supports the status quo and minimizes dissent." Specifically, Owen appeals to the concept of *hegemony* as articulated in the works of Italian dissident and "neo-Marxist" Antonio Gramsci in order to make sense of the marginalization of religious minorities in the contemporary U.K. These groups, she suggests, "remodel" themselves to comport with the legal "definitions" of religion in order to gain the advantages of state recognition and protections. Ultimately, because Protestant Christianity enjoys a place of privilege with state and society, minority religious groups, in this case neopagans, effectively become "subservient lesser versions of the religion of the ruling classes." Overall, Owen offers a compelling account of how state power domesticates religious groups by goading them into an unwelcome isomorphism, lest they remain branded as illegitimate religions before the law.

Even though I do find Owen's argument illustrative of the pressures facing minority religious groups, I want to suggest that her application of hegemony requires a significant revision of Gramsci's usage of the term. I will argue, in fact, that it represents such a radical departure from neo-Marxist concerns that no longer should we consider it class analysis in any meaningful way. Rather, Owen repurposes a Gramscian critique of *class exploitation* to illuminate a case of *religious discrimination and marginalization*. Although class exploitation and religious discrimination designate modes of power, domination, and social control, these modes and the theories designed to unmask their operation are not interchangeable parts. Instead, I shall argue, scholars must attend to the distinctions between these categories. "Class" is not simply another marker of identity like one's religion, and "religion" is not simply a proxy for class hierarchies in a society. In her chapter, Owen comes dangerously close to conflating these two analytics precisely because she has not sufficiently theorized "class" in the first place. In the process of detailing the limits of Owen's argument, I hope to consider what a more fully developed sense of class analysis might reveal about the neopagan struggle for state legitimacy.

Before moving to my critique of Owen's reading of Gramsci, it is vital that we understand the terrain she maps. Owen explains a social situation in which neopagans reside on the outskirts of mainstream religions. They constitute a minority of identifiable religious groups, and as we shall see, even referring to them as a distinct "group" reflects some of the concerns to which Owen points. For reasons that might be self-evident, Protestant Christianity occupies a privileged place in the U.K., both formally and informally. The liberalization of the religious landscape in the modern period has failed thus far to loosen the entanglement of the state and state church. The Church of England continues to represent the prototype for how the majority of the population imagine religion. From an informal perspective, its practices, structure, and theology provide the baseline for how all other religious groups are received. Likewise, the formal privilege of Anglicanism means that the legal framework through which the state regulates religion has been shaped in relation to the Church and in turn, Anglicanism itself, and therefore religion more generally, has been molded through formal governance. State and state church are mutually constitutive. The apolitical and civic orientation of Protestantism in the U.K. unfolded in tandem with the rise of the nation-state as a means of asserting the authority of the state over what had been a religious domain steeped in discord and even violence. The domestication of religion and its relegation to private concerns facilitated the emergence of a strong centralized government.

As Owen observes, the state sustains this domesticated character of religion in a couple of ways. First, it requires religions to present themselves as apolitical, remaining "uncritical of the state to receive political support and to maintain its position in society." Second, through the Charity Commission, religious groups must demonstrate their commitment to "serving the public good" in order to gain recognition as a legitimate religion and therefore avoid regulation "under corporate law." While this arrangement may accord closely to the contours of

Protestantism, it, Owen asserts, has a chilling effect on religious groups, namely neopagans, whose beliefs, organizational structure, and aims may not comport to these expectations. All in all, Owen suggests that this regulatory regime sustains the hegemony of the state and hegemonic place of Protestant Christianity as the "dominant religion" or "religion of the ruling classes."

These governing strategies present unique challenges for neopagans simply because they resist conformity to this dominant paradigm (although Owen uses "Paganism," I prefer the term "neopaganism" to emphasize its relatively recent genesis as a new religious movement). Neopagan groups, according to Owen, deliberately organize in a "counter-cultural" fashion, often preferring non-hierarchical organization and to "set out to challenge norms, not conform to them." Thus, baked into the very ethos and structure of many neopagan groups are basic ingredients that antagonize the status quo of a Protestant hegemony. This leaves neopagan groups with a devil's bargain. On the one hand, they can "remodel" themselves in order to seek the advantages of recognition from the authorities like the Charity Commission, H.M. Revenue and Customs, or the Prison Service, and risk relinquishing central elements of pagan religiosity and identity. Or, on the other hand, retain their core identity as counter-cultural and operate in the shadows of formally recognized religious groups without the dignity of public acknowledgment. In either case, Protestantism preserves its hegemony and these minority groups "become subservient lesser" religions. Whether inside or outside the boundaries of state-defined religion, they become the victims of a discriminatory regime.

Owen, therefore, employs Gramsci's notion of hegemony and consent in a particular manner. Hegemony refers to the *fact* of Protestantism's dominate position within the state and the state's complicity in the reproduction of this situation. Smaller or less-resourced religions have little choice but to offer their *consent* to this state of affairs. In the end, the interests of the dominate religion and the state are served since they remain essentially indistinguishable. On its surface, this explanatory model proves quite convincing. Clearly, minority religious groups *do* face discrimination and risk marginalization at the hands of state regulation, and certainly Protestant Christianity *does* enjoy monopolistic advantage. However, the question we must ask is not whether these processes occur but rather whether they represent the kind of social repression theorized in neo-Marxist theory, or are they something else altogether?

To begin with, we need to clarify Gramsci's concerns when he develops his theory of hegemony and consent. For him, these interrelated concepts resolve a very specific dilemma with which Marxists were wrestling at the turn of the twentieth century: *if orthodox Marxism accurately explained the inherent contradictions of the capitalist system, then why, in light of the increasingly visible ways in which capital exploited working people, had the much heralded proletarian revolution failed to manifest?* To answer this query, Gramsci, like other "neo" Marxists, reassesses the presuppositions of Marxist orthodoxy. He challenges the assumption that the superstructure represents a mere echo of the material base upon which society is constituted. Classic Marxism envisioned the social order through a strict lens of historical materialism and cultural norms or attitudes as distorted reflections of economic relationships. From this perspective, bourgeois society relies on the "false consciousness" represented in culture, which under the conditions of capitalist exploitation will inevitably erode as "class consciousness" arises among the proletarian masses. For our purposes, it also should be noted that orthodox Marxism says very little about religion beyond the oft-cited remark from *A Contribution to the Critique of Hegel's Philosophy of Right* (Marx 1970: Introduction) in which Marx writes, "religion is the sigh of the oppressed creature, the heart of a heartless world, and the soul of soulless conditions. It is the opium of the people." Again, Marx characterizes religion not as an agent of oppression but rather its expression, as a cultural manifestation symbolizing the suffering of an exploited working class.

Gramsci revises these precepts to acknowledge that, in fact, the superstructure, too, serves as a mechanism—in addition to the state's enforcement of the private-property regime—through which bourgeois dominance is upheld. "The doctrine of hegemony," he writes, is "a complement to the theory of the state-as-force" (Notebook 10, paragraph 12).[1] In Notebook 8, Gramsci further emphasizes this point. In tandem with the state-sponsored repression found in schooling and law, "a multitude of other so-called private initiatives and activities tend to the same end—initiatives and activities which form the apparatus of the political and cultural hegemony of the ruling classes" (Notebook 8, paragraph 179). This is a remarkable departure from prevailing Marxist theory because it imbues culture with the power to perpetuate the false consciousness of the working classes. Moreover, it is a key to understanding Gramsci's conception of *consent*. Consent, according to Gramsci, arises spontaneously, "given by the great masses of the population to the general direction imposed on social life by the dominant fundamental group; this consent is 'historically' caused by the prestige (and consequent confidence) which the group enjoys because of its position and function in the world of production" (Notebook 12, Section 1). Therefore, *hegemony* and *consent* comprise two inextricable processes whereby the bourgeois material interests are dispersed to the masses via the cultural authority of the ruling classes. The exercise of this cultural hegemony garners the "spontaneous" consent of the masses to their own perpetual exploitation. In hegemony and consent, Gramsci finds the answer he is looking for, the reason why a proletarian revolution has yet to emerge.

Owen's reading of Gramsci rightly suggests that hegemony is maintained when the ruling class can successfully represent its particular interests as the general interests of society, but she errs in its application to the case study. First, hegemony operates *in coordination with* state action. This may appear as a minor point, because after all, in the U.K. context, the Church of England is positioned as both a public *and* a cultural institution. However, according to Gramsci, hegemonic

---

1. All citations from the works of Antonio Gramsci in this essay can be found in *The Antonio Gramsci Reader* (Gramsci 2000). However, the in-text citations refer the reader directly to the original location of the material in Gramsci's writings.

authority remains distinct from state authority because the former relies not on legal repression but *persuasion*. "The apparatus of state coercive power which 'legally' enforces discipline on those groups who do not 'consent' either actively or passively. This apparatus is, however, constituted for the whole of society in anticipation of moments of crisis of command and direction when spontaneous consent has failed" (Notebook 12, Section 1). In other words, consent obviates the need for legal enforcement. Therefore, when Owen describes the legal regime to which marginal religious groups like neopagans must assent or face marginalization, she is not talking about *consent* in the Gramscian sense at all. Instead, Owen redefines consent not as willing assent to the cultural norms but the reluctant submission to state coercion, which for Gramsci is an altogether distinct form of repression. Because the central drama of Owen's account occurs between neopagan struggle for equality and state regulation of religion, consent as already "failed" and the dynamics of cultural hegemony and consent simply fail to apply.

In addition to this problematic usage of consent, Owen's analysis only makes sense if one abandons one of the fundamental social ills that Marxists and neo-Marxists alike are attempting to resolve. Gramsci is concerned with explicating the strategies and structures that permit a ruling elite to diffuse its interests to the masses and subsequently anticipate the means by which this injustice might cease. "The fact," he asserts in the socialist weekly *Il Grido del Popolo*, "is that only by degrees, one stage at a time, has humanity acquired the consciousness of its own value and won for itself the right to throw off the patterns of organization on it by minorities at a previous period in history" (January 29, 1916). However, is Owen describing an identical situation here? Are the struggles of neopagans representative of a general struggle of the masses to "throw off" the oppression of a ruling minority? This correspondence seems thorny, at best, and perhaps even confounds the logic of class analysis at worst. In fact, Owen effectively inverts the framework of neo-Marxist theory to fit the case study. Here, a minority religious group is subject to the prevailing norms of the majority, what Owen refers to interchangeably as "the dominant religion" or "liberal Protestant Christianity." Departing substantially from Gramsci's project, we are no longer considering how an elite minority solicits the consent of the masses but rather how the state coerces marginalized groups to conform to the preferences of the majority. Rather than an account of class exploitation, Owen offers an example of state-sponsored religious discrimination.

Of course, Owen does classify "liberal Protestant Christianity" as the "religion of the ruling classes," so perhaps she is suggesting that neopagan groups are representative of and therefore a proxy for the proletarian masses. Certainly, it might be fair to say that Protestant Christians are overrepresented among the ruling elite, and it might be fair to say that the Protestant institutions wield an inordinate degree of cultural authority. In the U.S. context (with which I am more familiar), we can witness this disparity in the fact that the National Cathedral in Washington DC is affiliated with Episcopal Church, part of the global Anglican Communion, despite Episcopalians representing a tiny fraction of the adult population (1.2%), according to a report from the Pew Research Center (2014).

Undoubtedly, the Episcopal Church in the United States is not representative of the masses, although it exerts influence well beyond its scale. However, the problem of overrepresentation is distinct from the problem of class struggle. The former signals *disparities* within the existing class structure, whereas the latter recognizes the inherent inequality of the structure itself. Focusing on disparities addresses an altogether different problem than that which (neo-)Marxist critique seeks to explain. If the yearned-for telos of Marxist ideology is the disruption of the inequalities of class-based society, then the goal of what Adolph Reed, Jr. labels "disparitarianism" is the distribution of inequality equally across all social groups, for all groups to achieve statistical parity (Mackaman 2019). Of course, tracking disparities can be a useful tool for discerning the persistence of social injustices (I will refer to statistical inequalities later as a part of my argument), but it is a distinct exercise from neo-Marxist analysis. Each are effectively observing the same situations through different lenses. Although in many instances of scholarship on religion, one often becomes conflated with the other. Religious groups are not surrogates for social classes because they are rarely homogenous. Rather a range of class positions comprise a given religious group, and therefore to suggest that any particular religious group exerts hegemony (via the state as Owen suggests or otherwise) over others sidesteps the central concerns of Gramsci.

Before proceeding along this line of argument, however, I wish to pause and ponder the following question: if religious groups are not "classes," then who are the neopagans to whom Owen refers? Although the evidence remains elusive because neopagans resist traditional quantitative measures (formal membership, clearly defined organizational boundaries, etc.), the existing data suggests that their composition transgresses the boundaries of class divisions. According to the 2011 U.K. Census, slightly more than eighty-thousand individuals identified as Pagan, Wicca, or Druid (Source: Office of National Statistics). They are eclipsed not only by Protestant Christians, but Muslims, Buddhists, and even adherents to "Jedi" religions. Therefore, in terms of sheer size, neopagans comprise only a small portion of the self-identified religious population in the United Kingdom. Lewis and Tollefsen (2014: 65) observe that women comprise a sizable majority of neopagans as a whole. However, it should be noted that men outnumber women in Druid groups more than two-to-one (ibid.), suggesting that gender plays an important role in the formation and organization of different neopagan orientations. Furthermore, neopagans—those who self-identified as Pagan, Wiccan, Witchcraft, or Druid—report educational levels slightly higher than the national population, 21.3 percent and 18.4 percent having attained a bachelor's degree respectively (Lewis et al. 2016: 100). Yet, this compares to the approximately 15.0 percent of self-identified Christians with a college degree. Further demographic information on the racial, political, and occupational composition of neopagan groups would be helpful but were not readily available, therefore what we can learn from this data is quite restricted. Still, we *can* infer from this data that neopagan groups exhibit a slight female majority and educational levels slightly higher than the general population. More significant for our purposes, however, is the remarkable disparity between college-educated neopagans and their counterparts among Christians. Clearly, placed alongside Christians, neopagans occupy a relatively privileged position in terms of education, and from this we *might*, in the most modest sense, expect this to extend to their relative economic positions as well.

These data complicate Owen's characterization of neopagans as marginalized by reminding us that religious advantage does not readily translate into class privilege, and vice versa. In terms of their class position, therefore, it would be hasty to identify neopagans with the kind of oppressed multitudes in Gramsci's framework. In fact, given that modern Wicca emerges not among the urban proletariat but rather among suburban, educated populations during the early twentieth century, a proper Gramscian approach might classify it as a product of the liberal bourgeoisie. Its emphasis on counter-cultural values and practices, and its rejection of rigid organizational structures reinforce as they purport to resist liberal bourgeois notions of individual autonomy and subjectivity. Consider, for example, that the vast majority of pagans—between 75 and 80 percent—practice in solitude, outside any group affiliation (Lewis and Tollefsen 2014). Neopaganism is not practically oriented towards solidarity or collectivist resistance to the capitalist status quo but more closely resembles the highly privatized, individualistic "spiritual" movements that, as I and others have argued elsewhere, reflect and reinforce the interests associated with neoliberal capitalism (Carrette and King 2004; Wood 2007; LoRusso 2017).

I am not suggesting that all adherents to Wicca or Druidism are privileged, only that these groups resist easy categorization according to Marxian conceptions of class. My point is not to dismiss or undermine their very real struggles for recognition and legitimacy or the existential perils that minority religious groups face daily, but rather to acknowledge the difference between two but often interrelated forms of social oppression: on the one hand, discrimination against marginalized social groups, and on the other, the subjugation of the exploited masses. Owen's conflation of these two modes reflects broader trends in the academic study of religion to treat class as a marker of identity like religion and to impose Marxist or neo-Marxist theories of class analysis onto social contexts for which they were not designated. Class and economy certainly play an important role in the construction of religion, but they cut across these formations and vice versa. The fact that some socioeconomic elites are likely self-identified neopagans challenges scholars of religion to explore how broader class interests are asserted or contested within and around these neopagan groups. As Owen notes, the state apparatus charged with regulating religion—the Charity Commission and H.M. Revenue and Customs—is "governed by a board with members who have links to financial services, economics, social enterprise and law." What might we glean from these linkages from a proper application of Gramsci? In her chapter, Owen takes us only halfway to class analysis. She states that these "types of people ... reproduce normative Christian understandings of what constitutes the 'core essence' of religion based on belief and worship." Again, Owen persuasively illustrates how dominant norms result in discrimination against groups that fail to conform, but she demonstrates neither how these "normative Christian" assumptions themselves reflect ruling class preferences nor how these preferences bolster and sustain the power of elites in "financial services, economics, social enterprise, and law."

Class analysis, particularly from a Gramscian perspective, acknowledges that elite interests (i.e., control over the means of production) *masquerade* as "Protestant values." Their imposition by the state is not an end in itself, but a means to service the material interests of the bourgeoisie. In other words, it is not the consent of neopagans that cultural hegemony requires but rather the way in which ruling class hegemony gets expressed through "liberal Protestant Christianity" and consequently elicits the "spontaneous consent" of the multitudes who tacitly internalize its values. The inculcation of Protestant norms bonds the working class to elite preferences and therefore operates as a tool for capitalist exploitation. This is how hegemony and consent presumably work!

All in all, I do not wish for readers to take my criticisms out of proportion. I find Owen's intervention timely, important, and substantively sophisticated. My critique is solely theoretical. Scholars of religion must attend to the distinction between *theory-building* and *theory-using* in their redescriptive endeavors. The theories we deploy in our analyses are not wholly abstract models to be imposed on our data in order to "see what happens" when we apply them. They come to life in and through the researcher's pursuit of insight. Gramsci sought answers to specified limitations in the explanatory purchase of orthodox Marxism and thus, he explicitly drew on existing Marxist concepts (hegemony) and built a new theoretical device to account for a bounded range of social phenomena. Owen accomplishes a similar undertaking. She draws on neo-Marxist theory to develop a novel theoretical framework to illuminate the struggles of neopagans in the U.K. context. The only misstep, from my perspective, is not owning up to the theory-building in which she is engaged. Instead of an application of Gramsci's theory, Owen has provided readers with her own theory of hegemony and consent, influenced by neo-Marxist perspectives but drastically retooled in order to reveal modes of domination otherwise unavailable to us. Owen only needs make her theoretical innovations explicit.

Still, I remain convinced that were Owen to admit these innovations, she would likewise have to acknowledge that she is no longer pursuing class analysis. Her work joins recent scholarship in religion seeking to give voice to historically marginalized or ignored social groups, but, like much of this research, it either eschews class altogether or reduces class to simply another marker of social identity, without any further consideration of how it might operate in unique ways, often at cross purposes from religious identity, race, gender, etc. When we conflate class position with identity, we lose the opportunity to decipher the complex social tapestry to which these elements contribute. In the U.S. context, for example, we should remember that the New Deal coalition, which established the welfare state and laid the foundation for political liberalism in the latter half of the twentieth century, succeeded only because it left Jim Crow and racial oppression intact. Strengthening the American (white) "working class" only came at the cost of excluding others. Conversely, the rolling back of this same welfare state over the last four decades has occurred by gaining the spontaneous consent of a white working majority through the sustained marginalization of others who do not conform to a nostalgic image of a Christian America, be they African Americans, members of the LGBTQ community, or immigrant populations classified as "illegal." If anything, my call to acknowledge this distinction between class and identity, between exploitation and discrimination, can only enrich our scholarship in what are, for many vulnerable populations today, troubling and dangerous times.

James Dennis LoRusso currently serves as Vice President of the North American Association for the Study of Religion. He is a former Associate Research Scholar in the Center for the Study of Religion at Princeton University, USA and is the author of *Spirituality, Corporate Culture, and American Business: The Neoliberal Ethic and the Spirit of Global Capital* (Bloomsbury, 2017).

References

Carrette, Jeremy, and Richard King. 2004. *Selling Spirituality: The Silent Takeover of Religion.* New York: Routledge.

Gramsci, Antonio. 2000. *The Antonio Gramsci Reader: Selected Writings 1916–1935.* Ed. David Forgacs. New York: New York University Press.

Lewis, James R., and Inga Bårdsden Tollefsen. 2013. "Gender and Paganism in Census and Survey Data." *Pomegranate: The International Journal of Pagan Studies* 15: 1–2. https://doi.org/10.1558/pome.v15i1-2.61

Lewis, James R., Sean E. Currie, and Michael P. Oman-Reagan. 2016. "The Religion of the Educated Classes Revisited: New Religions, the Nonreligious, and Educational Levels." *Journal for the Scientific Study of Religion* 55: 1. https://doi.org/10.1111/jssr.12246

LoRusso, James Dennis. 2017. *Spirituality, Corporate Culture, and American Business: The Neoliberal Ethic and the Spirit of Global Capital.* London: Bloomsbury Academic.

Mackaman, Tom. 2019. "An Interview with political scientist Adolph Reed, Jr. on the New York Times' 1619 Project." Retrieved from www.wsws.org/en/articles/2019/12/20/reed-d20.html.

Marx, Karl. 1970. *A Contribution of the Critique of Hegel's Philosophy of Right.* Trans. Annette Jolin and Joseph O'Malley. Cambridge: Cambridge University Press. Retrieved from www.marxists.org/archive/marx/works/1843/critique-hpr.

Marx, Karl. 2002. *The Manifesto of the Communist Party.* New York: Penguin.

Pew Research Center. 2014. "Religious Landscape Study." Retrieved from www.pewforum.org/religious-landscape-study.

Wood, Matthew. 2007. *Power, Possession, and the New Age: Ambiguities of Authority in Neoliberal Societies.* New York: Routledge.

Chapter 21

Definition, Comparison, Critique

Johan Strijdom

For its 2018 conference, under the title "Critique in Context," NAASR selected a number of key categories in the study of religion, among them Class and Economy, and invited potential contributors to submit questions and issues that they would consider crucial under this theme. The plan was that someone would write and distribute in advance a paper on these keywords, to which a few people would respond.

Not knowing at that stage who would write the main paper or what the focus of such a paper would be, I proposed a number of questions based on my reading of David Chidester's exploration of the economy of religion and the religion of economy, from his first phenomenological descriptions of ethical patterns of economic exchange in *Patterns of Action* (1987), through his critical examination of the intersection of religion and capitalism under colonial conditions in *Savage Systems* (1996a), to his analysis of the theme after 2000 in American popular culture in *Authentic fakes* (2005), and post-apartheid South Africa in *Wild Religion* (2012).

I would therefore like to respond to Suzanne Owen's contribution (Chapter 17, this volume) by foregrounding a few issues, primarily on the basis of Chidester's persistent exploration of the key categories of religion and economy over the past 30 years. I will structure my comments under three overlapping headings, focusing on definition, followed by briefer remarks on comparison and critique.

Definition, to loosely paraphrase J. Z. Smith (2018: 88), aims to keep things out, to delimit, to make clear what it is that we want to single out for analytical attention.[1] Defining or giving content to a concept in order to render it useful for analysis, an etic or second-order step, Smith (2004) further held, should necessarily *not* coincide with emic or first-order concepts. Should that become the case, he

---

1. In discussing his pedagogy, particularly the importance of designing a syllabus, Smith (2018: 88) emphasizes that he begins with definitions of terms in the title of a course to indicate the complexities of what the class will study. This crucial orientation includes a definition of the term "definition" itself, whose function in Smith's view is to "limit" what we study and to "keep out" things that we do not study, "to get as few things as possible on the table, but let them be the best examples of the species that you can get on the table," in brief, quoting Edward Bellamy, to "[enclose] the wild with a fence."

famously argued, we would be like Borges's cartographers whose maps eventually coincided with the territories, leaving them without jobs.[2]

Defining key concepts in the study of religion and giving them theoretical depth, Chidester (2013: 6) too maintains, offers us our best hope to produce innovative insights into the academic study of religion. Broadening the concept of "religion," he came to include not only the conventional religions, indigenous religions, and new religious movements, but also forms of popular culture that function like religions.[3] At the basis of his expanding notion of religion has been his appropriation of Durkheim's definition so that any beliefs and rituals that unite a group can be considered a religion, although with added critical attention to the boundaries and hierarchies that such formations entail.

In *Religion: Material Dynamics* (2018: 3), Chidester emphasizes, however, that defining religion and giving the concept theoretical depth for analytical purposes is *not* the prerogative of academics alone. "Not merely the product of scholarly inquiry, 'religion', he says, "has been produced in a diverse array of human engagements, including politics, legislation, public discourse, and popular culture, which have rendered the term as not only meaningful but also powerful in

---

2. In Smith's (1995, 2004: 134, 204, 208, 221) view, "nativists" who insist on the reproduction of emic or insider categories on the basis of the uniqueness or incommensurability of their cultures, not only reject the legitimacy of translation from one culture to another, but also the possibility of comparative research as such within the human, cultural and social sciences. Their conservative model remains at the level of paraphrase, and condemns us "to live in the world of Borges's Pierre Menard, in which a tale must always be identically 'twice-told,' where a word can only be translated by itself" (Smith 2004: 372). Smith (2004: 209) illustrates its uselessness for critical thinking from Borges's parable "Exactitude in Science" (where the cartographers who make their maps coincide with their territory are left without jobs), arguing instead that it is precisely the gap between map (analytical category) and territory (emic category) that creates the space necessary for producing surprising insights.

3. See particularly Chidester (2005) for this broadening of the concept of "religion." Chidester has contributed to the genealogy of the concept by showing how Christianity (particularly Protestantism) was used as norm in nineteenth-century colonial South Africa to first deny that indigenous Africans had religion and then to acknowledge that they had religion, but categorizing it as a "savage" form of religion at the bottom of an evolutionary ladder which justified a civilizing mission (notably in Chidester 1996a). An important turn came with phenomenologists of religion, such as Gerardus van der Leeuw, who abolished the evolutionary model and argued that "primitive" and rational mentalities were universal and equally valid (cf. Strijdom 2018). Chidester (1994) appreciates the phenomenological aim to identify recurring patterns in religion, but critiques phenomenology in so far as it obscures and mystifies hierarchical power relations. Instead of abolishing the term "religion," as proposed by some scholars of religion (e.g., Fitzgerald 2000), Chidester (2005) retains it and gives it a broader content than in conventional definitions, by appropriating Durkheim's definition with the additional foregrounding of inclusions and exclusions, as well as hierarchies, that are legitimized, maintained, or challenged by means of religious beliefs, practices and institutions. Chidester's broadening concept of "religion" differs markedly from J. Z. Smith's (2018: 88–89) more limited one: "[Definitions are] not generous, they're not 'you all come'—that's what screws up most definitions of religion. You hear about some funny something or other and say, 'Oh my god, I gotta change the definition to let the Society of Boot-Strap Lickers and Worshipers into my definition.' 'No keep them out!'"

the world." He considers as exemplary Nicolas Howe's analysis of the effects that definitions of the term "religion" in U.S. law have had on indigenous claims to sacred land.

Reading Owen's chapter, I understood her argument to be developing along similar lines, in the sense that she shows us what real effects the definition of "religion" in British law, as private faith (non-political and non-economic) *and* public good (charity for the good of society), has had for pagan groups, in subjecting them to the dominant political order and giving them a secondary status to the Church of England. The British state, by means of *inter alia* its laws, educational system, and privileging of the dominant religion creates, diffuses, and maintains a hegemonic discourse that suppresses dissent.

Owen importantly notices that the definition of religion in British charity law, as a matter of private faith as well as for the public good, has a Protestant genealogy. Now, what might be important, I would like to suggest, is to relate this definition in British law to definitions of religion in the imperial study of religion. David Chidester (1996a, 2000, 2005: 9, 50–51, 2014, 2018) has shown not only how the Protestant emphasis on faith has influenced definitions of religion in imperial religious studies (a bias now to be corrected by foregrounding material mediations of religion), but has also left a legacy of evolutionary ranking of religions (a bias to be corrected by giving indigenous religions, alternative or new religious movements, and popular culture that functions like a religion, the same recognition as the acknowledged world religions). Might it, in other words, be helpful to relate the definition of "religion" in imperial religious studies to that in contemporary British law in order to understand its function in creating hegemonies, normalizing hierarchies, and subjugating certain groups?

I now turn from the concept of "religion" to definitions of "economy" as the term that NAASR asked Owen to reflect on and invited us to comment on, by taking Chidester's exploration of the intersection between the two categories as inspiration for my comments. As in the case of "religion," Chidester (2008) eventually developed, theorized, and applied a broad definition of "economy."

In his earliest comparative work on ethical patterns across religions, in a chapter on *Economics*, Chidester (1987: 246–269) still used the term "economics" in a narrow sense as the exchange of goods and services among humans. He identified, described, and interpreted two contrasting modes of exchange of goods and services by making use of crucial theorists of each mode: for reciprocal exchange, Mauss's (1954 [1925]) appreciation of reciprocal sharing among indigenous peoples was a primary reference, including a paragraph on "charity" in modern times as a mode of exchange in which goods are given away; for modern capitalism aiming at accumulating wealth and maximizing profit, Adam Smith (1977 [1776]) and Karl Marx (1976 [1867–1894] were primary references (with Adam Smith arguing for, and Marx against, this mode of exchange). He emphasized that economic exchange in traditional societies was an integral part of society, religion, and politics, whereas the separation of these categories was a Western invention that needed to be overcome in our attempts to understand societies as *total* systems.

In this early interpretive exploration of modes of exchange, Chidester refrained from taking a normative stance. In the 1990s, however, he became more critical about phenomenological descriptions of religious phenomena that mystify power relations or underemphasize their contestations (Chidester 1994), and maintained that political oppression and economic exploitation under Western colonialism, in which imperial Religious Studies was complicit, should be exposed lest this horrible history be perpetuated (Chidester 1996a,[4] 2009 [2000]).

It is particularly in his work since 2000, *Authentic Fakes* (2005) and *Wild Religion* (2012), that Chidester explores the analytical possibilities of a broader definition of the concept of "economy" as referring to both material and symbolic exchanges. He uses the terms "fetish" and "cargo" to analyze the capitalist exchange of material objects under colonialism, in American popular culture[5] and in post-apartheid South Africa, in contrast to alternative communal exchanges. If Adorno (2001 [1944]) theorized popular culture as oppressive, Chidester holds that Benjamin (2008 [1939]) helps us further in appreciating the creative agency of subjects as consumers under such conditions. Importantly Chidester (2008, 2018) now holds that the term "economy" should no longer be taken in the limited sense of material exchanges only, as used by professional economists who design models to minimize material losses and maximize material profits. The term should instead be employed in the broader sense in which cultural theorists have for a long time done by deploying economic terms and models to analyze also the exchange of *symbols* in cultures to produce sacred surpluses (notably by Bourdieu 1977), or to emphasize the sacrifice and destruction of accumulated wealth and energy as crucial to sacred practices (notably by Bataille 1985 [1933]). In applying the theorized terms "economy" and "religion" in a broader sense to case studies, he concludes, it is experimenting with the inversion of the terms "economy of religion" and "religion of economy"[6] that might offer the best hope to produce innovative knowledge in the field of religious studies.

In reading Owen's contribution, I noticed, of course, her opening statement that although Marx, Durkheim, and Weber's theories of society, class, and economy feature prominently in religious studies, they are in her view of limited analytical value today. She proposes to explore the Marxian theory of Gramsci instead, whose concept of "hegemony" she briefly compares with Althusser and Foucault's concept of "power." If Althusser conceptualized "power" in a "statist" way (i.e., as imposed by the state on subjects) and Foucault theorized "power" in a more diffusionist way (i.e., as diffused through educational, religious, legal,

---

4. *Empire of Religion* (Chidester 2014) as a sequel to *Savage Systems* (1996a) describes the threefold mediation in the formation of imperial theories of religion. In so far as "economy" is discussed, the focus is on capitalist exploitation (i.e., "economy" in a more restricted sense).

5. The argument is already evident in Chidester (1996b, 2003), but further elaborated in Chidester (2005).

6. In the latter case, Benjamin's (1996 [1921]) view of capitalism as religion serves as important reference for Chidester (2008, 2018: 6, 93), who analyzes the 1956 animated cartoon *Destination Earth* to illustrate the way in which it symbolized capitalism as utopia and communism as tyranny within the context of America's Cold War.

military, etc., means), Gramsci not only considered both views in his concept of "hegemony," but also foregrounded the potential of subjects to resist as agents. Owen then sets out to apply this concept to British charity law, showing how its definition of "religion" has impacted on pagan religious groups, and how these groups have in turn also effected a broader definition of "religion" in British law.

The term "economy," however, is not defined or given sufficient theoretical depth in her discussion. It is mentioned in passing as part of the state's definition of "religion" as a private affair (i.e., as "non-political and non-economic," as well as serving the public good as a "charity"). My suggestion is that Owen's contribution to the theme of the keywords "class and economy" might benefit by further elaborating a definition of "economy," giving it theoretical depth, and applying it to her case study of "charity," which is certainly pertinent to an analysis of the intersection of "religion" and "economy."

After these suggestions on definitions and theories, I conclude with two much briefer suggestions on comparison and critique.

Comparison, in spite of its abuses in dehumanizing, evolutionary theories of imperial religious studies (as has been shown by Chidester 1996a, 2000, 2014), remains a foundational strategy in the academic study of religion. By juxtaposing historically contextualized case studies that illustrate a key concept, J. Z. Smith (2004: 29, 197) argued, we might see anew the one case study in light of the other and revise our understanding of the concept itself.

Owen's argument on the effects of the definition of religion in charity law on pagan groups, as illustrative of the intersection of religion and economy, is located in the U.K. I wonder, as a challenge and a program, whether J. Z. Smith's thesis on the value of disciplined comparison to shed new light on an important issue can be demonstrated by comparing the definition of "religion" in U.K. charity legislation and its effect on pagan and new religious movements to keep it under control of the state, with U.S. systems, or with systems from the global South.

Lastly, the term "critique," from Greek *krinein* "to judge," has been used in the West to refer among other things to a doctor discerning a critical illness, a philologist doing textual criticism, a historian stratifying historical layers in texts, but also to philosophers arguing about ethical norms. Although prominent scholars of religion have maintained that the academic study of religion should limit itself to a historical critical analysis of religious texts and/or a phenomenological description of the entangled histories of religious movements, critical social theorists (e.g., Marxists, feminists, critical race theorists, post-colonialists) have argued that so-called "neutral" descriptions are often blind to asymmetrical power relations, and that a moral responsibility rests on academics to change the world for a better future. Chidester, as I mentioned above, in his early work offered not simply descriptions of religious phenomena and patterns, but included in his interpretation critical theories as well (e.g., Marxist theories on religion and economics to interpret the intersection between these fields). In the 1990s, however, he took a clear stance against the role of the dominant religion under colonialism and apartheid, as well as the complicity of religious studies, in systemic capitalist exploitation. After 2000, he seemed to have reverted to phenomenological descriptions and interpretations of different patterns of economic exchange without taking an explicit moral stance.

My concluding question in responding to Owen's chapter concerns precisely this: Is her use of Gramsci intended only to *describe* how the state normalizes subjugation and maintains hierarchies, or is there a normative judgment, a moral imperative, here—to create counter-hegemonies, whether in the academy or in marginalized groups such as the pagans?

Johan Strijdom is Professor of Comparative Religious Studies at the University of South Africa, Pretoria. In his research he focuses on religious nationalism and violence, critiques of indigenous religious claims and practices, and critical approaches to material mediations of religion. These areas are analyzed in a comparative and historically nuanced way, by elaborating a critique of class, gender and ethnic power relations from a postcolonial location in the global south. He is currently editor of the *Journal for the Study of Religion*, which is the official journal of the Association for the Study of Religion in Southern Africa.

References

Adorno, Theodor. 2001 [1944]. *The Culture Industry*. London: Routledge.

Bataille, Georges. 1985 [1933]. "The Notion of Expenditure." In A. Stoekl (ed.), *Visions of Excess: Selected Writings, 1927-1939*. Minneapolis, MN: University of Minnesota Press.

Benjamin, Walter. 1996 [1921]. "Capitalism as Religion." In Bullock, M & MW Jennings (eds.). *Walter Benjamin: Selected Writings, Vol 1: 1913-1926*. Cambridge, MA: Harvard University Press.

Benjamin, Walter. 2008 [1939]. *The Work of Art in the Age of its Technological Reproducibility, and Other Writings on Media*. Cambridge, MA: Harvard University Press.

Bourdieu, Pierre. 1977. *Outline of a Theory of Practice*. Cambridge: Cambridge University Press.

Chidester, David. 1987. *Patterns of Action: Religion and Ethics in a Comparative Perspective*. Belmont, CA: Wadsworth.

Chidester, David. 1994. "The Poetics and Politics of Sacred Space: Towards a Critical Phenomenology of Religion." *Analecta Husserliana* 43: 211-231. https://doi.org/10.1007/978-94-011-0846-1_15

Chidester, David. 1996a. *Savage Systems: Colonialism and Comparative Religion in Southern Africa*. Charlottesville, VA: University Press of Virginia.

Chidester, David. 1996b. "The Church of Baseball, The Fetish of Coca-Cola, and The Potlatch of Rock 'n Roll." *Journal of the American Academy of Religion* 64(4): 743-765. https://doi.org/10.1093/jaarel/LXIV.4.743

Chidester, David. 2000. "Colonialism." In Willi Braun and Russell T. McCutcheon (eds.), *Guide to The Study of Religion*. London: Continuum.

Chidester, David, 2003. "Cross-cultural Religious Business: Cocacolonization, McDonaldization, Disneyization, Tupperization, and Other Local Dilemmas of Global Signification." In Jennifer I. M. Reid (ed.), *Religion and Global Culture: New Terrain in the Study of Religion and the Work of Charles H. Long*, 145-166. Lanham, MD: Lexington Books.

Chidester, David. 2005. *Authentic Fakes: Religion and American Popular Culture*. Berkeley, CA: University of California Press.

Chidester, David. 2008. "Economy." In David Morgan (ed.), *Keywords in Religion, Media and Culture*, 83–95. New York: Routledge.
Chidester, David 2009 [2000]. "Situating the Programmatic Interests in the History of Religions in South Africa." In Rosalind Hackett and Michael Pye (eds.), *IAHR World Congress proceedings Durban 2000. The History of Religions: Origins and Visions*. Cambridge: Roots and Branches.
Chidester, David. 2012. *Wild Religion: Tracking the Sacred in South Africa*. Berkeley, CA: University of California Press.
Chidester, David. 2013. "Postgraduate Students Producing Knowledge." *Journal for the Study of Religion* 26(1): 5–7.
Chidester, David. 2014. *Empire of Religion: Imperialism and Comparative Religion*. Chicago, IL: University of Chicago Press.
Chidester, David. 2018. *Religion: Material Dynamics*. Oakland, CA: University of California Press.
Fitzgerald, Timothy. 2000. *The Ideology of Religious Studies*. Oxford: Oxford University Press.
Marx, Karl. 1976 [1867–1894]. *Capital*, 3 volumes. New York: International Publishers.
Mauss, Marcel. 1954 [1925]. *The Gift*. New York: Free Press.
Smith, Adam. 1977 [1776]. *An Inquiry into the Nature and the Causes of the Wealth of Nations*. Chicago, IL: University of Chicago Press.
Smith, Jonathan Z. 1995. "Emic/Etic." In Jonathan Z Smith (ed.), *The HarperCollins Dictionary of Religion*. New York: HarperSanFrancisco.
Smith, Jonathan Z. 2004. *Relating Religion: Essays in the Study of Religion*. Chicago, IL: University of Chicago Press.
Smith, Jonathan Z. 2018. "The Dean's Craft of Teaching Seminar (2013)." In Willi Braun and Russell T McCutcheon (eds.), *Reading J. Z. Smith: Interviews and Essay*, 85–110. Oxford: Oxford University Press. Also available at www.youtube.com/watch?v=RRDLBCTrJug (accessed July 28, 2019).
Strijdom, Johan. 2018. "'Primitive': A Key Concept in Chidester's Critique of Imperial and Van der Leeuw's Phenomenological Study of Religion." *HTS Theological Studies* 74(1): 1–6. https://doi.org/10.4102/hts.v74i1.4797

Chapter 22

The Public Good Requirement

Suzanne Owen

The last time I had given much thought to the topics of class and economy was while I was an undergraduate student. When I was invited to present a paper on class and economy for the annual meeting of NAASR in Denver, I thought it a good opportunity to become more familiar with the work of Gramsci. I had thought to explore Max Weber's association of types of religion with the class system or Karl Marx's critique of the collusion of religion with the oppressors of the working classes. However, I had little new to say on these matters.

For several years I had been researching charity registration cases involving Pagan groups (capital P to denote the modern movement). As I was reading Gramsci's ideas of hegemony and consent, I could see how they might relate to how charity law works to maintain the status quo in U.K. society. It occurred to me that Gramsci's work could have something to say about the hegemonic alliance of the state and the established church in the U.K., suppressing dissenting views in order to maintain the status quo. In 2018, as I was writing my paper for the conference, the U.K. was experiencing the fall-out of the Brexit referendum. The Conservative Party's strategy has been to remain in power at all costs by appealing to white nationalists and other groups considered on the right wing of politics. The Church of England, sadly, were gagged (according to some clergy) in the run up to the December 2019 general election, accepting (grudgingly perhaps) their role as "non-political." It is this constraint of religion that connects to how charity law works, and I wanted to explore the implications of this. Therefore, I acknowledge that this moved the topic away from directly engaging with class and economy and more toward church and state.

In his response to my chapter, Thomas J. Carrico Jr. (Chapter 18, this volume) makes several fine observations such as the implication that "the public good" commits a group to disengage from the political-economic spheres of activity and thus they participate in their own domestication. As Carrico remarks, "Hegemonic control is rarely as straightforward as 'dominant group coerces subordinate group.'" When he says, "While some social agents are better situated to benefit from particular definitions, these social categories are the site of social struggle," this is why Pagan groups make interesting cases as we see the tensions being played out in the discussions among members of Pagan groups and in the decision documents of the charity commissioners. Indeed, the documents obscure internal disagreements, which is why Teemu Taira and I had included a section on Druid responses to the charity registration of The Druid Network (TDN; Owen and Taira 2015: 104–107), which showed not only that the trustees themselves needed convincing that Druidry could be regarded as a religion, but that a number of members and Druids outside the organization were in disagreement about this categorization. A few had also accused TDN of becoming part of the establishment. For the trustees of the latter, they may have thought that this was no bad thing as it they thought it might bring more respect for Druidry.

In response to Carrico's comment that "it takes more than state legislators to construct a category," I'd never meant to imply that the state creates the category of religion, but that the definition the charity commissioners use is based on social conceptions of religion modelled on Protestant Christianity. There is little evidence that they consult scholarly definitions, though scholars do provide supporting statements to the charity commissioners on behalf of groups making applications, but more in advocating how a group conforms to the charity definition rather than challenging the definition itself. In terms of what would it look like if a Pagan group "threw back" a definition of religion, TDN did do this to a certain extent, although in the end they had only managed to push the commissioners to expand their definition of religion rather than alter it (Owen and Taira 2015: 112). There might have been an opportunity for the Pagan Federation to push them further, but I understand that this group will no longer try to register under the "religion" category after their last one was rejected in 2012 (Owen 2018: 280). I'm not entirely sure I understand Carrico's view that "there does not need to be any outward sign of dissent to suggest that beliefs and actions may not exactly correspond." I question whether this is really dissent if not public or acted upon. Would private rebellion lead to a change in the status quo?

Neil George (Chapter 19, this volume) notes the "broader view that sees the Charity Commission, TDN, and their respective adherents as having been socialized members of society whose concerns/interests were shaped by that society long before they ever interacted in this context." This doesn't contradict what I've written. TDN and the Charity Commissioners have both inherited a view of "religion" along Protestant Christian lines, which has served the elite members of society more than others. The disclaimer that TDN does not represent all Druids was no doubt prompted by some critical comments from other Druids about their registration as a charity for the advancement of religion. They are just one Druid organization, though the only one so far to register as a charity. The page about the "The Dissenting Druid" was added in the summer of 2020, long after I'd written my paper. It lists environmental activism and similar interests but is not a call to political activism but rather a call for research input to chart the links between Druidry and dissent both historically and more recently. The tone of this piece suggests that they are aware that they cannot organize political protests themselves but can only write about other Druids doing it.

I don't think it changes my argument to recognize that many Druids follow the pattern of individualized religion or that members employ a distinction between institutional and privatized experience as this fits the Enlightenment project to relegate even institutions labelled as "religions" to the non-political sphere, despite the impossibility of it—an institution is by its very nature political. Indeed, as Craig Martin (2010) indicates, the religion/state separation is untenable. When George says "TDN succeeded, not because they conformed themselves to any Protestantized definition of 'religion,' but because they played the same secular rhetorical game with sufficient proficiency," I don't see it as a "but" but as an "and." The type of secularism found in the U.K. might be considered "Protestant Christian secularism" after all. George recognizes this, too: "Not only can Protestantism easily be coopted to a discourse of individual faith that mirrors secular interests, the Protestantization of secular rhetoric helped protect against charges of atheism in the nineteenth century, when secularism had to overtly appear religious." Regarding TDN's membership to the Inter Faith Network, they may have gained a place at the high table, but members of the Church of England sit at its head.

In Dennis LoRusso's response (Chapter 20, this volume), he recognizes that the argument I'm making is that state regulation of religion supports the status quo and minimizes dissent and thus domesticates religion. This can be borne in mind when reading his critique as I believe that this point still stands, although I have veered away from addressing class and economics along the lines of Max Weber or neo-Marxists, as I'd initially intended. I became more interested in ideas of hegemony more broadly as I was writing my paper while class and economics became side-lined, apart from making an analogy between social classes and the hierarchies of groups recognized as "religions."

As I mentioned, it was while reading Gramsci's different descriptions of hegemony that led me to see the analogy with state regulation of religion. It should be pointed out that Gramsci makes reference to the Catholic church spreading its worldview through secular alliances (see Chino 2020). It was this that led me to understand the processes in England whereby the state recognizes religions under certain restrictions (their activities must be for public benefit) and limitations (they must fulfil certain criteria modelled on Anglican Christianity). I agree with LoRusso's view that I had begun with a different starting question from Gramsci—he was asking why the proletariat had failed to revolt, which led to his theory that consent arises spontaneously. Instead, I perhaps wondered why minority religions had not challenged the processes for recognition significantly. In LoRusso's summation of my view, "Protestantism preserves its hegemony and these minority groups 'become subservient lesser' religions."

LoRusso, though, says I had erred on a couple of points: "First, hegemony operates *in coordination with* state action. This may appear as a minor point, because after all, in the U.K. context, the Church of England is positioned as both a public *and* as cultural institution. However, according to Gramsci, hegemonic authority remains distinct from state authority because the former relies not on legal repression but *persuasion*." I would not say hegemony is "separate" but rather emerges out of the alliance between institutions such as the state and church as well as cultural bodies adopting this persuasion in order to maintain their positions. Those working for the British Broadcasting Corporation (BBC) have occasionally needed to be persuaded more forcefully. A counter-hegemony would require a different alliance. The application of legal repression is through persuasion, in this case on what constitutes a "religion." Charity Commission is an advisory non-departmental public body that, I would argue, relies on consensus through various consultations with its members and the public (we are seeing this currently with regards to revising religious education in schools).

LoRusso also argues that I've redefined Gramsci's view of consent: "Instead, Owen redefines consent not as willing assent to the cultural norms but the reluctant submission to state coercion, which for Gramsci is an altogether distinct form of repression. Because the central drama of Owen's account occurs between neopagan struggle for equality and state regulation of religion, consent as already "failed" and the dynamics of cultural hegemony and consent simply fail to apply." As members of U.K. society, Druids and Pagans have been socialized to accept a Protestant definition of religion and had left it largely unchallenged apart from broadening the notion of deity. Therefore, I read Gramsci with the question of what does hegemony and consent tell us about the way the category of religion operates in a particular society? LoRusso argues that individual Druids and Pagans might not be members of an oppressed class, but this is irrelevant in terms of how religion is regulated in the U.K. Yes, this departs from Gramsci's aims regarding class struggles because I've applied the concepts elsewhere. However, only the Church of England bishops are members of the ruling classes (in that they have seats in the House of Lords)—no other group recognized as a religion has this privilege.

When LoRusso says, "the problem of overrepresentation is distinct from the problem of class struggle," I wonder how would Gramsci analyze "religion" as part of a hegemonic elite? As he does not address religion beyond the Catholic Church, I'd thought to apply his ideas creatively to a particular case. I would have liked to have seen LoRusso provide a different example that might more faithfully apply Gransci's ideas of hegemony and consent in relation to religion in the U.S. context. He mentions the influence of the Episcopal Church relative to its size but dismisses it as far as class struggle is concerned. Nevertheless, what is its place in the alliance that forms the ruling elite? In pointing out that religions are not classes (not even analogously), or that Pagans are more educated on the whole compared with Christians, LoRusso narrows the potential of Gramsci's ideas for an analysis of hegemony. However, I appreciate that I have "retooled" Gramsci's ideas of hegemony to illuminate a different problem from the one he was addressing and that this ought to have been made more explicit in my paper.

Johan Strijdom (Chapter 21, this volume) brings in David Chidester, whose work I admire. Chidester's book *Savage Systems* (1996) was useful in my Ph.D. studies on the appropriation of Native American spirituality, particularly as Native Americans had been denied "religious" rights by colonizers and settler governments. Chidester's view that "religion" is "[n]ot merely the product of scholarly enquiry," at first appears to counterargue against J. Z. Smith's claim that "religion is solely the creation of the scholar's study" (Smith 1982: 11)—a scholar creates the category, even if they do not define it explicitly, because there is no data "out there" corresponding to religion (unless the discourse is the data).

As Strijdom notes, I've developed my argument along these lines. And like Chidester, I think the Protestant assumptions have influenced definitions of religion. As Strijdom states, this "left a legacy of evolutionary ranking of religions." When "monotheism" is assumed to be the "truth," Protestant colonizers, lawmakers, etc., both deny certain groups rights on this basis and remodel them to fit their criteria for religion (e.g., the creation of the "High God" in indigenous societies—see Cox 2014). One way of examining the implications of these assumptions is by analyzing particular case studies within a particular political context. The process for charity recognition of religion can then be compared with processes in other contexts, such as the U.S. Presumably non-Protestant states would have their own assumptions, though as Chidester and other have shown the Protestant creation of "religion" has been applied in many global contexts through colonization and imperialism.

In answering Strijdom's final question, I would say I am describing how the state (as an alliance of government, church, and media) maintains the status quo. When I asked myself what a counter-hegemony would entail, I put forward possibilities, not a judgement or imperative. However, the description itself can influence conceptual changes beyond the academy. The scholar, too, is often pressured to make normative claims or to push through an agenda for change. This is apparent in the additional requirement to the Research Excellence Framework in the U.K. where scholars have to provide evidence of the public impact of their research in order to receive any financial support from the government. This is then embedded in the research design—"pathways to impact"—which, in the humanities and social sciences, can in some cases end up taking the form of advocacy or activism or it makes explicit that what we study can act as a legitimizer and affect public assumptions.

Suzanne Owen obtained her PhD from the University of Edinburgh and published her thesis as *The Appropriation of Native American Spirituality* (Continuum 2008). She is currently Reader in Religious Studies at Leeds Trinity University in the UK researching indigeneity in Newfoundland and British Druidry.

References

Chidester, David. 1996. *Savage Systems: Colonialism and Comparative Religion in Southern Africa*. Charlottesville, VA: University Press of Virginia.
Chino, Takahiro. 2020. "Gramsci's Critique of Croce on the Catholic Church." *History of European Ideas* 46(2): 175–189. https://doi.org/10.1080/01916599.2019.1653352
Cox, James. 2014. *The Invention of God in Indigenous Societies*. Durham: Acumen.
Martin, Craig. 2010. *Masking Hegemony: A Genealogy of Liberalism, Religion and the Private Sphere*. London: Equinox.
Owen, Suzanne, and Teemu Taira. 2015. "The Category of 'Religion' in Public Classification: Charity Registration of the Druid Network in England and Wales." In Trevor Stack, Naomi Goldenberg, and Timothy Fitzgerald (eds.), *Religion as a Category of Governance and Sovereignty*, 90–114. Leiden: Brill. https://doi.org/10.1163/9789004290594_006

Owen, Suzanne. 2018. "The Problem with Paganism in Charity Registration in England and Wales." *Implicit Religion* 21(3): 268–281. https://doi.org/10.1558/imre.38296

Smith, Jonathan Z. 1982. *Imagining Religion: From Babylon to Jonestown*. Chicago, IL: University of Chicago Press.

Index

Note: italic page numbers indicate figures; numbers containing *n* refer to notes.

Abbott, Greg 25
Abercrombie, Nicholas 192
accommodation problem 163–164
ad hominem arguments 80–81, 81*n*5
Adams, Hannah 138
Admiralty Law 12, 13, 14, 20
Adorno, Theodor 216
Africa 84*n*9, 102, 115, 214*n*3
African American scholarship 80, 118–119, 138
  see also Black women scholars
African Americans 19–20
  Dolezal's identification as 109
  police shootings of 23
  and Trump 112, 130
  see also Black women; Combahee River Collective; MSTA
Africana Religions, Journal of 137, 138
agency 109, 149, 188, 194, 195
Ahmed, Sara 120, 121, 136–137, 138, 147, 151
Al Jazeera 32, 33, 39
Albanese, Catherine 113–114, 118
Alcindor, Yamiche 112–113, 120, 129–130
Algeria/Algerian immigrants 163, 163*n*4, 170–171
Ali, Kecia 137
Allison, Dorothy 136
Althaus-Reid, Marcella 138, 139
Althusser, Louis 179, 188, 189, 190, 195, 216
Altman, Michael J. 80
American Academy of Religion 3, 81*n*5, 135
American religious history 113–121, 124
  and conflict/contact models 115–117
  and consensus model 113–115, 116, 117, 118
  counternarratives of 118–120
  and Native Americans 114, 117–118
  and structural racism 118

Anderson, Benedict 55, 62
Anderson, Victor 77
Anglican Church 157, 181, 205, 208, 222
Anglo-Saxons/-Americans 114–115, 116
anthropology 9, 9*n*1, 80
anti-racism 103, 125
anti-Semitism 20, 96, 97, 129, 157, 159
anti-tax movements 20, 22
Anzaldúa, Gloria 142
Arabic language 96
archives 9, 9*n*1
Arkansas 20
"Arms Permit" cards 20–22, *21*
Aryan myth 93, 94, 96–97, 103
Aryan Nations 20
Asad, Talal 166, 182
Asia 94, 102, 102*n*2
Asiatic ethnicity/identity 15, 16*n*8, 18, 32, 57
Attie, Eli 123
Austria 158
authority 44
Avalos, Natalie 117–118
Axial Age 84*n*8, 85, 88, 101

Baird, Robert 113, 114, 115, 117, 118
Bangladesh 33, 37
baptismal certificates 25, 51, 57, 59, 62
Baptists 24, 25, 57
Bar Kochba 158, 159
Barkun, Michael 13
Baton Rouge (Louisiana) 19
Beach, Henry L. 20
Beaman, Lori G. 167
Beckford, James A. 180
Bellamy, Richard 43, 48
Benjamin, Walter 216, 216*n*6
Besant, Annie 193
BI (Bureau of Investigation) 15–19, 15–16*n*7

Bible App 61
Biblical Literature, Society of 151
biblical studies 93, 97–98, 124, 125, 127–128, 151
Bill 21 (Québécois law) 163–173
  and accommodation problem 163–164
  ambiguity around religious symbols in 165–168
  and Bouchard-Taylor report (2008) 164, 168, 172
  and Canadian Charter of Rights and Freedoms 164–165
  and Christian symbols 167, 172
  and colonialism 165, 168, 169, 172
  colorblind approach of 169
  and cultural symbols 166–167
  and dreadlocks 167–168
  and gender 170–171, 172, 173
  and hijab/niqab 164, 164n6, 167, 169, 170, 171
  impacts of 172–173
  and Indigeneity 165, 168–169, 172
  and laicity 164, 164nn6, 7, 165, 169, 171, 172
  and power/governmentality 162, 165, 166, 172
  and religious symbols 167, 168, 172, 173
  and school teachers 163, 164, 169, 170–171
  and tattoos 167, 172
  and Truth and Reconciliation Commission 165, 169
biological essentialism 114, 115, 116
biometric data 63–64, 68
biopolitics 69–70
birth certificates 9, 24, 24n15, 37, 50, 57, 59
Black activism 15, 23, 55
Black Identity Extremism 23
Black women 109, 113, 125, 130, 141, 149
Black women scholars 128, 136, 137, 138, 141–142
Blandina 153
Boaz, Franz 138
Bocock, Robert 179, 180
bodies 55, 60, 63, 64, 65, 68, 83, 95, 107
  and religious studies scholarship 135, 136, 137, 138, 139–140, 143, 146, 160
  and religious symbols 167, 168, 172, 173
  rhizomatic 148

Bodin, Jean 52
Bond, Sarah 154
Bopp, Franz 96
borders/boundaries 44–45, 108, 141–142
Borges, Jorge Luis 74–77, 80, 81n5, 124, 214, 214n2
  The Garden of Forking Paths 74–77, 87
  Three Versions of Judas 74–75, 83, 100
Bouchard, Gérard 164, 168
Bourdieu, Pierre 109, 216
bourgeoisie 159, 207, 210, 211
Boyarin, Daniel 157
Boys' Brigade 157
Brexit 220
Briggs, Katharine Cook 92–93
Briggs Myers, Isabel 92–93
Britain (U.K.) 157–160, 204
  charity laws in *see* Charity Commission; charity laws
  and Church of England *see* Church of England
  and H.M. Revenue and Customs 184, 206, 210
  matchstick industry in 193–194
  Paganism in *see* Paganism
  Research Excellence Framework in 224
  state religion in 181–182
Bryant and May 193–195
Buddhism 183, 198, 209
Buddhism and violence 4, 31–32, 34n2
  and Buddhist history/literature 34, 35
  and cyclical time concept 35, 38
  and politics 38–39
  and religious essentialism 35, 36, 39–40
  and true/false religion dichotomy 33
Bundy family 23
Bureau of Investigation (BI) 15–19, 15–16n7
bureaucracy 9, 13, 14–15, 49
  alternative 18, 25, 26, 56
Burman ethnic groups 36–37
Butler, Judith 140
Bynum, Caroline Walker 139

Canada
  Charter of Rights and Freedoms 164–165, 166n9
  Charter of Values (Bill 60, 2013) 166168
  secularist law in *see* Bill 21

Truth and Reconciliation Commission 165, 169
capitalism 93, 104, 179, 191, 197, 201, 204, 206, 210, 215, 216n6
cargo cults 14
Castelli, Elizabeth 153
category and religion 2–5, 10n2, 67, 104–107
   and hegemony 182, 183, 185, 187, 189, 191, 199
   and politics 167, 190, 192–193
   and race 113, 114, 116, 123, 126
   see also classification; definitions of religion
Catholicism/Catholics 47, 116, 141, 166, 222, 223
   in Mexico 142–143
Cavanaugh, William T. 51
Charity Commission 183, 184, 185, 197, 198, 199, 200, 205, 206, 210, 220, 221, 223
charity laws 182, 183–184, 185, 187–188, 189, 197–202, 215, 217, 220, 224
Chávez, Cesar 142–143
Chicanx people 143
Chidester, David 213, 214–215, 214n3, 215–216, 216n4, 217–218, 223, 224
Christian Identity movement 20
Christian martyrs 152–153
Christianity
   early 93, 96, 97, 98, 102, 102n2, 152–154
   fundamentalist 23, 24, 50, 57
   "muscular" 158
   in U.S. 57, 58, 68, 69
   youth movements of 157
Church of England 181, 186, 201, 205, 207, 215, 220, 222, 223
citation 118, 128
   politics of 136, 151–154
Citizen's Law Enforcement and Research Committee (CLERC) 20
citizenship 4, 31, 32, 33, 43n1, 67–68, 160, 193
   alternative 58–59, 64–65
   antistatist see sovereign citizen movement
   autonomous 26
   and bodies 55, 60, 63, 64, 65, 68
   and difference 55
   digital 56, 60–64, 68

   fragility of 23, 43, 55
   heavenly/earthly dual 57, 58–59, 60, 61, 62, 68
   and materiality/bureaucracy 9, 25–26, 55–56, 60, 62, 65, 68
   and rights 48, 49
   and Rohingya Muslims 32, 33, 34, 34n1, 36
   and undocumented children 24–25, 26, 50–51, 52
Civil Rights Movement 23, 119
class 4, 77, 104, 136, 138, 156, 162, 204, 210, 216
   and hegemony 179, 180–181, 182, 190–191, 199, 223
   and neopagans 210
   see also working class
classification 3
   racial/colonial 84n9, 107, 108, 110
   religious 33, 126, 149
CLERC (Citizen's Law Enforcement and Research Committee) 20
Cobb, Stephanie 153
Coleman, Cedric 80
Collins, Jim 181
colonialism 36, 47, 64, 69, 76–77, 84n9, 102, 214n3, 216, 217
   and missionaries 142
   and religious studies 102, 115
   and religious symbols 165, 168, 169, 172
   and sovereign citizen movement 13–14, 42
colorblind approach 169
Combahee River Collective 78–79, 81n5, 104, 109–110, 119, 126–127
common law 12, 13, 20
community 84n7, 87, 97, 183
   imagined see imagined communities
   political 45, 48
comparison 213, 217
conflict/contact models 115–117
conscientious objectors 18, 18n9
consciousness 190, 191
consensus model 113–115, 116, 117, 118
consent 179, 180, 187, 206, 207–208, 211, 223
"Constitutional Arms Permit" cards 20–22, 21
Cooper, Frederick 110

Copernican turn 77, 100, 102
counter-conducts 70
counter-hegemony 181, 184–185, 188, 191, 192, 198, 199–200, 202, 218, 222–223, 224
counterhistories 118–120
court filings 11, 42
Covenant, Sword, and Arm of the Lord 20
Covid-19 pandemic 1, 164
credit ratings 9, 22
Crenshaw, Kimberlé 79, 136
crimen oscuro see dark sin/skin
Critical Race Theory 78, 217
critique 213, 217–218
cultural appropriation 82
cultural criticism 78
culture 81, 82, 83–84n7, 95, 214, 216
    and digital media 55, 56, 60, 61–62, 63, 65, 68
    and gender/sexuality 137, 140
    heterogeneity of 181
    and race 116, 128–129
    and religious symbols 166–167
    and state system 45, 46, 48
Cunningham, Lillian 92
currencies, homemade/non-government 11, 42
Curtis, Ed 130, 138
Cusack, Carole 137

Daly, Mary 142
dark sin/skin 74, 75, 75n2, 77, 81, 100–101, 113, 124
Davis, Alison Tyner 116, 118
de Certeau, Michel 82
definitions of religion 10n2, 166, 182, 183, 185, 187, 189, 213–215, 213n1, 214n3, 217, 224
Deleuze, Gilles 69, 148
Derrida, Jacques 25–26, 50, 139
Deuteronomy 108
Dew, Spencer 14, 14n6, 19n11
Dhammapada 34
Diamond, Jared 87
Dick, Philip K. 101
Diener, Alexander C. 44–45
digital media 57–58, 60–64, 68
    and biometric data 63–64, 68
    and bodies 60, 63, 64, 68
    and heavenly/earthly citizenship 58–59
    and imagined communities 60, 62
    and materiality 56, 60, 61–63, 63n11
    and memory 56, 63
disciplinary regimes 69, 101, 162
documentation *see* paperwork
Doktorvaters/Doktomaters 73, 74, 103
Dolezal, Rachel 109
Dorsey, Charles 75
dreadlocks 167–168
Drew Ali, Noble 19
drivers' licences *11*, 12, 42
Druid Network, The *see* TDN
Durkheim, Emile 85, 179, 214, 214n3, 216

economy 4, 179, 210
    political 60, 102, 204
    of religion 213, 215–217
Edge, Peter 184–185
education 181, 182, 209, 210, 215, 223
    and religious symbols 163, 164
Efron, John 158
Egypt 94
Emre, Merve 93
Engler, Steven 3, 83–84
Enlightenment 81, 82, 100, 221–222
Episcopalians 208–209, 223
ethnic cleansing *see* Rohingya Muslims
ethnic studies 102–103, 125–126
ethnicity 4, 77, 84n7, 88, 93, 160, 193
    in Myanmar *see* Rohingya Muslims
    and race science 116
    and resistance to state power 18, 19n11, 56, 57
ethnography 138, 141, 149, 163, 163n4
    auto- 127n1
etymology 94–95
evangelical Christianity 23, 68, 69, 114
    see also Life.Church

Falk, Leib Isaac 159–160, 159–160n2
Fanon, Franz 77, 87, 102
FBI (Federal Bureau of Investigation) 15, 20, 22, 55
    and Black Identity Extremism assessment 23
    see also BI
feminism 78, 136, 148, 217
Ferraris, Maurizio 25–26

Feuerbach, Ludwig 93
financial crisis (2008) 13
Fitzgerald, Timothy 2n3, 85–86
Florida 80, 152
Floyd-Thomas, Juan M. 118–119
folklore 94, 96, 98
Foucault, Michel 69–70, 83, 139
    and power 162, 165, 166, 172, 179, 189
France 46, 76, 163n4
Frankfurt School 84
Frazer, James George 14, 26, 42, 84
Freud, Sigmund 129
Fulkerson, Mary McClintock 140

Garden of Forking Paths, The (Borges) 74–77, 87
Gardiner, Mark Quentin 83–84
Geertz, Clifford 166
gender/sexuality 4, 4n6, 135–143, 146, 193
    and the academy 136, 137–138, 139
    and agency 109, 149
    and Black women scholars 128, 136, 137, 138, 141–142
    and bodies 135, 136, 137, 138, 139–140, 143, 147, 156
    and Christian martyrs 152–154
    and identity 135–136, 143, 148–149, 152–153
    and marginalized scholars 138–139
    and Mexican Catholicism 142–143
    and politics of citation 136, 136–137, 151–154
    and power relations 152, 153
    and queer religious scholarship 135, 136, 138, 141
    and re-orienting theory 137–138, 143, 146–148, 149–150, 151
    and religious symbols 170–171, 172, 173
    and secular context 162–163
    and sex 140–141
    and subject position 148
    see also masculinity
Genesis 94
German Romantic tradition 93–98, 125, 127
Germany 84, 92, 158
    Jew Count in (1916) 157
Gibbons, Dave 128
globalism 105, 113
Godlewska, Anne 168

Goldenberg, Naomi 182, 191, 192–193
Goldschmidt, Henry 104
Goldsmid, Albert Edward Williamson 157–158
Gordon, Colin 69, 70
Goston El-Bey, Verdiacee Tiari Washitaw Turner 19
governance 45, 46–48, 69
    in medieval period 46–47
    political/social 47
governmentality 69–70
Gramsci, Antonio
    and consent 179, 180, 187, 206, 207–208, 223
    and hegemony 180–181, 182, 188, 191–192, 195, 204–212, 216–217, 218, 220, 222
    as neo-Marxist 191, 204–205, 206–207, 208
Greece 94, 96
Green Party 198–199
Grewal, Zareena 16n8
Grimm Brothers 93, 94
Groeschel, Craig 62
Grosby, Steven 45–46
Guitarri, Felix 148

Hagan, Joshua 44–45
Haraway, Donna 78, 79
Harding, Matthew 183
Harré, Rom 49
heavenly citizenship 57, 58–59, 60, 61, 64, 68, 69
Hebrew 95, 96
hegemony 179, 180–181, 184–186, 187–195, 207–208, 216
    and charity law 183–184, 220
    and consciousness 190, 191
    and consent 179, 180, 187, 206, 207–208, 211
    counter- *see* counter-hegemony
    and definition of religion 182, 183, 185, 187, 189, 191, 199
    and ideology *see* ideology
    and intellectuals 195
    and matchstick workers' strike example 193–195
    and Protestantism 200–201, 204, 205, 206, 208, 222

Hellenism 94, 96, 97
Herberg, Will 116
Herder, Johann Gottfried 93, 94, 95, 96
heterosexuality 104, 139, 140
Hickman, Jared 105
hierarchies
   and authority 44
   of citizenship 57, 62
   social 107–108, 109, 110, 188
hijab/niqab 164, 164n6, 167, 169, 170, 171
historiography 85, 114, 116, 119
history
   and citizenship 58
   counter- 69–70
   and Marx 190
   and Myanmar 32, 36
   and nation 45, 55
   of religions 73–74, 94–98
   as temporal/terrestrial 106
   and tropes 73
H.M. Revenue and Customs 184, 206, 210
Homer 96
homeschooling 24, 25, 57, 58
Howe, Nicolas 215
Hughes, Aaron 2n2, 80
human rights 37
humanities 9, 224
Humboldt, Wilhelm von 96
Hurd, Elizabeth Shakman 163
Hurston, Zora Neale 80, 137, 138

Ibn Said, Omar 138
Ibrahim, Azeem 38–39
identification abuse 24–25, 57
identity 31, 46, 55, 63, 70, 135–136, 160
   Christian 115, 125, 153
   and class 205, 210, 211, 212
   embodied 55, 60, 63, 64
   and imagined communities 56, 62
   marginalized 135–136, 143, 148–149, 151–152
   Moorish 15, 16n8, 18, 23, 56–57, 64
   national *see* national identity
   racial 109
   religious 19n11, 20, 34
   "strawman" 13, 14, 20, 22
identity documents 38, 55, 57
   alternative 22–23
identity politics 78–79, 104

ideology 180, 187, 188, 189–190, 191, 192, 193
   and agency 194, 195
imagined communities 55, 55n, 56, 56n2, 57, 62
   private 60
Imhoff, Sarah 157, 159
immigration 23
India 94, 96, 181
indigenous people 84, 114, 117–118, 142, 214n3, 215, 224
   and religious symbols 165, 168–169, 172
   see also Native Americans
Indo-European languages 94, 94n2, 95
Instagram 4, 58–59, 61–62, 92
Inter Faith Network U.K. 185, 187, 189, 222
interfaith networks 199, 201, 202
intersectionality 79, 136, 156, 160, 162
Ireland 125
Irigaray, Luce 140
IRS (Internal Revenue Service) 22, 23
Islam 56, 64, 163n5, 164, 209
Islamophobia 169
Israelite Gymnastics Club (Istanbul) 158
Italy 167, 180

Jackson, Richard 49–50
Jaspers, Karl 84, 103
Jedis 184, 209
Jefferson, Thomas 201
Jerryson, Michael 31, 35, 38
Jewish Chronicle 157, 158
Jewish Lads' Brigade (JLB) 157–158
Jewish Legion 156, 159
Jews/Judaism 96–97, 116, 166n9, 168
   see also anti-Semitism; "muscle Jew"
Jim Crow laws 15, 18, 55, 64, 211
John's Gospel 57
Johnson, Sylvester 9
Johnston, Les 26
Jolin-Barrette, Simon 164, 165, 167, 168, 169
Jones, William 94, 94n2
Joyce, James 79
Judaism *see* Jews/Judaism
Judas Iscariot 74, 84, 100, 101
Jung, Carl 92
Junior, Nyasha 137

kalpas 35
King, Richard 81–82, 100
kinship 45, 46, 78
Koven, Seth 194
Kraemer, Ross 152–153
Kuhn, Adalbert 94, 94n3, 96
Kuhn, Thomas 200

Lahu people 36–37
land disputes 10–11, 23, 125
language 93, 94–95, 96, 97, 140, 149
    rights 168
Latour, Bruno 10n2, 43, 190n4
law 107–108, 182, 215
    charity 183–184
    and religious symbols *see* Bill 21
    resistance to *see* sovereign citizen movement
law enforcement 11, 13, 15, 18, 20–23
LAW (Loyal Arthurian Warband) 185
Legault, François 164, 166, 167
Lewis, James R. 209
liberation theology 143
license plates 12, *12*, 62
licenses, alternative *11*, 12, 22–23
Lidell Hart, B.H. 76
Life.Church 57–59, 60–62, 64, 68
    and digital media 60–61
    and heavenly citizenship 58–59, 60–61, 64
    and politics 58–59
Lincoln, Bruce 2n3, 86n10, 106, 107, 151, 152, 187, 200
Lion's Roar (online magazine) 34, 39n5
literacy 86–87
Locke, John 52, 59–60, 182, 202
Loeser, Charles E. 12
Long, Charles 5, 87, 116, 118, 119–120, 129
Long, Gavin E. 19
Lopez, Donald 35
Lorde, Audre 142
Louisiana 20
Loyal Arthurian Warband (LAW) 185
Luke's Gospel 108

Ma Ba Tha 38, 39
McAlister, Elizabeth 104
Maccabean Society 157–158
Maccabees 156, 158, 159
McCutcheon, Russell 3, 3n4, 4, 39–40, 73, 81n5, 182, 199
McDowell, Nellie 194–195
McLuhan, Marshall 124
magic 14, 23, 26, 42, 43
Mahmood, Saba 172
Majeed, Debra 141
marijuana 108
Martin, Craig 180, 182, 197, 198, 222
martyrdom 152–153
Marxism 59, 85, 179, 181, 189, 190, 195, 210, 211, 215, 216, 220
    neo- 191, 204–205, 206–207, 222
masculinity 139, 153
    see also "muscle Jew"
Masuzawa, Tomoko 137
matchstick industry 193–195
material culture 94
    digital 56, 60–62, 63, 65, 68
Matthew, Gospel of 97, 108
Mauss, Marcel 215
MBTI (Myers-Briggs Type Indicator) 4, 92–93
Mead, Margaret 138
Mead, Sidney 118
media 32, 33, 38, 68, 180, 182
medieval period 45, 46–47
meditation 82
Meisenhelder, Susan E. 80
memory 56, 63
Merton, Robert K. 201
Metta Sutta 34
Mexico 142–143
minority religions 113, 117, 118, 162, 204–205
    see also Paganism
Miranda warning cards 22, 22n12
missionaries 142
Missouri 20
Molloy, Parker 136
monotheism 105, 224
Montana Freemen movement 13
Montréal (Canada) 163, 169, 170–171, 172
Moore, Alan 128
Moore, Lawrence 116
Moorish identity 15, 16n8, 18, 23, 56–57, 64
Moorish Science Temple 10
    and Washitaw Nation 19

Moorish sovereign citizenship 11, 14
    see also MSTA
Morgenstein Fuerst, Ilyse 137, 162
Mormons 23, 116
Morris, Christopher W. 43, 44, 45, 46, 47, 48
mortgages 20
Moss, Candida 153
Moultrie, Monique 141, 142
MSTA (Moorish Science Temple of America) 56–57, 59, 62, 64
    paperwork tactics of see Nationality Cards, MSTA
Muehlberger, Ellen 151
Müller, Friedrich Max 84, 93, 94, 96, 102, 127, 127n1
"muscle Jew" 156–160
    and Jewish diaspora 159, 159n1
    and Jewish history 156, 158, 159, 160
    and Jewish Lads' Brigade 157–158
    and patriotism 157
    and sports 158, 160
"muscular Christianity" 158
Muslim women 163n5, 164, 170
Myanmar
    Constitution (1974) 37
    democratisation of 37
    ethnic groups in 36, 37
    military in 36–37, 38–39, 68
    see also Rohingya Muslims
Myers-Briggs test 4, 92–93, 127
myth 94–96, 97

NAASR (North American Association for the Study of Religion) 2, 5, 67, 123, 125, 139, 146, 148, 149, 150, 151, 213, 215, 220
naming, discourse of 79, 84, 104, 105, 106
nation 45–46, 129
    alternative 56, 64, 65
nation-state 45, 46, 59, 67–68, 69, 70
    and Protestantism 200–201, 204, 205, 206
    and sexuality 162
national identity 63, 64, 65, 193
    American 56, 57, 60, 64, 115, 116, 117–118, 129
National Secular Society 184
nationalism 33, 57, 93, 95, 113

Nationality Cards, MSTA 15–19, 17, 20, 57, 62, 67
    and draft 18
    and federal agents' attitudes 15–16n7
    and Moorish identity 18
    as national security threat 15
    and racial segregation 15, 16, 18
    state regulation of 18–19
Native Americans 13–14, 19, 114, 117–118, 119, 135, 223
nativism 13–14, 26, 42, 56, 113, 214n2
Nazis 84
neopaganism see Paganism
Nevada 23
new religious movements 206, 214, 215, 217
New Testament 93, 97, 98
Nicholson, Linda 139
Nigerian women 149
Nigianni, Chrysanthi 148
niqab see hijab/niqab
Nongbri, Brent 52, 59–60, 84n9
Nordau, Max 156–157, 158, 159, 160
Nye, Malory 83

Ocampo, Victoria 76
Oklahoma 57–58
Olson, Alix 135
Omar, Ilhan 64
Omi, Michael 102, 125
Order, the 20
Orientalism 82n6, 94, 102
Orsi, Robert 3
Ottawa (Canada) 171
Owen, Suzanne 197, 220–221

Pagan Federation 184, 185, 221
Paganism 142, 179–180, 182–183, 209–211, 215, 223
    and charity law 183, 184, 197, 206, 217, 220–221
    and counter-hegemony 184–185, 191, 192, 198, 199, 199–200, 202
    and definition of religion 185, 191, 199
    demographics of 209–210
    and Inter Faith Network U.K. 185, 187, 189
    and LAW 185
    see also TDN
Palestine 46, 157, 158, 159, 160

"paper terrorism" 11–27, 42, 49, 50
　magical model of 14–15, 23
　and property liens 11, 13, 14, 20, 22
　and SPC 20
　and SPC/CLERC 20–22, *21*, 23
　and "strawman" identity 13, 14, 20, 22
　tactics of 11–12, 13
　and undocumented children 24–25, 26
　and Washitaw Nation 20, 26
paperwork 9–27, 42, 55, 60
　alternative legal 11–12, 14–15, 56, 57, 59
　nonlegal 25
parallel universes 1–2, 1n1
passports 12, 42
patriarchy 104, 119, 128, 172, 191
patriotism 57, 156, 157
Pauline Christianity 97, 98
Pennington, Alecia Faith 24–25, 26, 43, 50, 52, 57
　and heavenly/earthly citizenship 58, 59
Perpetua 153
personality tests 92–93, 98
Petro, Anthony 141
phenomenology 81, 213, 214n3, 216, 217–218
philology 88, 94, 96, 97, 217
Philpott, Daniel 44, 45, 46–47, 47n3, 48
Piketty, Thomas 200
Plymouth Brethren 184
Pocklington, David 184
police officers *see* law enforcement
political activism 198–199, 221
political communities 31, 35, 39, 40, 45, 48
political sovereignty 43, 44, 48
politics 4, 38
　and racism 112–113, 120, 124
　and religious studies 97, 128
　and religious symbols *see* Bill 21
　see also religion and state
Polycarp 152, 153
positioning instruments, religion/race as 109–110, 127
power 9, 31, 36, 38, 39, 49, 50, 52, 102
　Foucauldian 162, 165, 166, 172, 179, 189, 216–217
　and gender 152, 153
　and governmentality 69–70
　hegemonic *see* hegemony
　and imagined communities 60

　and race 78, 78n4, 120
　and religious studies and race 78, 79, 80, 85, 87, 102, 104, 105, 106
　and religious symbols 166, 172
　resistance to 13, 25, 43, 56, 62, 68
　statist 179, 188, 204, 216
Presner, Todd Samuel 157
Prometheus 94, 94n3
property liens 11, 13, 14, 20, 22, 42
Protestantism 58, 102, 166, 185, 214n3, 221, 222, 224
　and American religious history 113–114, 115, 116, 117, 118
　and charity 182, 183, 205–206, 215
　and hegemony 200–201, 204, 205, 206, 208, 211
　see also Life.Church
Puar, Jasbir 137
public good 182, 185, 188, 191, 200, 220
　and charity laws 205

Quakers 185
Québec (Canada)
　Algerian immigrants in 163, 163n4, 170–171
　Islamophobia in 169, 171
　religious symbols bill in *see* Bill 21
queer religious scholarship 135, 136, 138, 141

race 4, 15, 23, 31, 33, 39, 42, 55, 64
　category of 113, 114, 116, 123, 125, 193
　and religious studies *see* religious studies and race
　as social construct 109, 116
　see also ethnicity
race science 116
racecraft 124, 125
racialization 83, 102, 116, 125
racism 10, 42, 78, 113–121
　in American politics 112–113, 120, 129–130
　in American religious history 113–118
　and counterhistories 118–120
　in religious studies 82, 93, 95, 97, 113, 120–121, 125, 138
　see also white nationalism/supremacism
Rand, Ayn 78
Rassist, der 81, 83, 87, 88, 124, 130

Raw, Louise 193
Reed, Adolph , Jr. 209
Reed, Annette Yoshiko 137
religio 51
religion
    as category *see* category and religion
    defined *see* definitions of religion
    and essentialism 3, 31, 35, 36, 39–40
    evolutionary model of 214n3, 215, 217, 224
    and job advertisements 2n2
    and national identity 57, 65
    privatized 52, 52n6, 64, 182, 210
    as racialized category 39n6
    and social objects 26
    as transcendent/eternal 107, 108
    true/false dichotomy 33
    ubiquity of 4
    and violence 31, 32, 33, 34–35
religion and state 48, 50–52, 68, 69, 179–186
    and belief/faith 180, 182, 183, 183n2, 184, 185
    and charity status *see* Charity Commission; charity laws
    and hegemony *see* hegemony
    and political activities 182–183
    and private/public separation 182, 197
    and public good 182, 185, 188, 191, 200
    separation between 182, 198, 201, 222
    see also Bill 21
religionsgeschichtliche Schule 97, 127
Religionwissenchaft 73, 83, 87, 88, 96, 100, 102, 124, 127n1, 129
religious fundamentalism 23, 24, 50, 56, 57, 62
religious pluralism 52n6, 59, 69, 114, 117, 118
religious studies 2–4, 73–88
    and categories 2–3, 4
    and data 3
    and gender/sexuality *see* gender/sexuality
    handbooks/guidebooks 3–4
    method/theory in 3, 5
    racism in 82, 93, 95, 97, 113
religious studies and race 76–78, 80–88, 101, 123–130
    and American religious history *see* American religious history
    and Axial Age 84n8, 85, 88, 101
    and Borges 75, 76–77, 81n5, 100
    and citation practices *see* citation
    as co-constituent categories 104–107
    and Combahee River Collective 78–79, 81n5, 104, 109–110, 119, 126–127
    and conflict/contact models 115–117
    and consensus model 113–115, 116, 117, 118
    and Copernican turn 77, 100, 102
    and dark sin/skin 74, 75, 75n2, 77, 81, 100–101, 113, 124
    and discourse of naming 79, 84, 104, 105, 106
    and disruption 101, 125, 126
    and ethnic studies 102–103, 125–126
    and ethnological amnesia 84, 93
    and fetishization 93, 95, 96, 101, 102
    and gender/sexuality *see* gender/sexuality
    and German tradition 93–98, 125, 127
    and identity politics/intersectionality 78–79, 156, 160
    and literacy/scriptures/canons 6–7, 85
    and maps 83–84, 85, 86, 214, 214n2
    and marginalized scholars *see* gender/sexuality
    and positioning 109–110, 127
    and power 78, 79, 80, 85, 87, 102, 104, 105, 106
    and reflexive turn 123
    and signification *see* signification
    and tropes 5, 73, 83, 85
    and World Religion Paradigm 84, 85, 86, 88, 100, 102
religious symbols 163–173
    Bill 21 definition of 165–166
    dreadlocks 167–168
    hijab/niqab 164, 164n6, 167, 169
    and school teachers 163, 164
    tattoos 167, 168, 172
Remarque, Erich Maria 75
Research Excellence Framework 224
resistance movements 31
    see also sovereign citizen movement
rhizomatic body 148
Rich, Adrienne 140
Rig Veda 94

Rohingya Muslims 31–34, 46, 67–68
    and Buddhism 31, 33, 34
    and citizenship 32, 33, 34, 34n1, 36
    and cyclical time concept 35, 38
    disenfranchisement of 37
    labelled as terrorists 33, 34
    and media 32, 33, 38
    political causes of persecution of 38
    and politics/ethnicity 31, 32
    and religious studies teaching 32–33, 34–35
Romantic tradition 94–98, 127
Rosenthal, Randy 34, 35
Rubin, Gayle 141, 148

Sahi, Ahmed 167
Sandoval, Chela 78
Schaefli, Laura 168
Schaff, Philip 113, 114–115, 117, 118
Schaffer, Gavin 157
Schlegel, F. 94
science 73, 200, 201
science fiction 1–2, 1n1
science of religion *see Religionwissenchaft*
Scientology 184
Scott, James 187, 191, 192
Scott, Joan Wallach 152
scriptures 85, 108
secularism 162–163, 165, 184, 200–201, 222
    and gender 171
Sedgwick, Eve 139, 140
Segal, Robert 3
segregation laws 15, 18
Selective Service 15, 15n7, 16n7, 18
Setepenra, Cosmo Ausar 19
sex 140–141, 162
sexuality *see* gender/sexuality
Shange, Ntozake 137, 143
Sharot, Stephen 85–86, 87, 88
Sheriff's Posse Comitatus (SPC) 20–22, 23
Shildrick, Margrit 148
signification 5, 80–83, 85, 86, 87, 88, 101, 102, 104, 129
    and American religious history 118, 119, 120
    and gender/sexuality 149
Simons, Jon 180
Sioux Ghost Dancers 13–14
Sisters of Perpetual Indulgence 141

slavery 115
Sliders (TV series) 1, 4
smartphones 58, 61
Smith, Adam 215
Smith, Jonathan Z. 10n2, 33, 83, 84, 87, 127n1, 214n3, 217, 223
    on canons 87
    on definition 213–214, 213n1, 214n3
Smith, Leslie Dorrough 2–3, 3n
social difference, and religious studies 77–78, 80, 81, 84, 84n8, 85, 87, 106, 117, 125
social media 61, 151
    see also Instagram; Twitter
social objects 10n2, 26, 43, 51
social order/ordering 45, 104, 108, 109, 124, 206–207
sociology 85, 204
South Africa 213, 214n3, 216, 217
southeast Asia 31, 32, 35, 37, 68–69
sovereign citizen movement 9–27, 42–43, 49–50, 55–56, 67
    and Admiralty Law 12, 13, 14, 20
    and common law 12, 13, 20
    and driver's licences 11
    and governmentality 70
    and land disputes 10–11, 23
    and magical model 14–15, 23
    as nativist movement 13–14, 26
    and "paper terrorism" *see* "paper terrorism"
    proto-form of *see* MSTA
    and religion/politics 31, 32
    and religious studies 13–14
    and social objects 26, 43
    and "strawman"/"flesh-and-blood" identity 13
    tactics of 11–12, 13
    and terrorism 49–50
    and undocumented children 24–25, 26, 50–51, 52, 53, 57
    and U.S. Constitution 12
    and Washitaw Nation 19–20, 26
sovereignty 19–20, 24, 42, 68, 164n7
    political 43, 44, 48–49
    see also state sovereignty
SPC (Sheriff's Posse Comitatus) 20–22, 23
squatting 13
Sri Lanka 35

Stack, Andrew Joseph 23
state sovereignty 43–53, 43n1
   and authority/law 44, 48, 50, 52
   challenge to *see* sovereign citizen movement
   external/internal 48, 52n6
   fragility of 50, 52–53
   and governance *see* governance
   internal 52
   and kinship 45, 46
   and materiality 49
   and nation 45–46, 55
   and religion 48, 50–52, 68
   sovereign citizen challenge to 49–50
   and territoriality *see* territoriality
   and terrorism 49–50
   ubiquity of 43–44
   and Westphalian settlement 37, 47–48n3, 52n6, 69
Stausberg, Michael 3
Stoakes, Emanuel 39
Stoddard, Brad 135
Stollar, Ryan 57
"strawman" identity 13, 14, 20, 22
surveillance 18n10, 22, 69
   and religious symbols 167, 168
Suu Kyi, Aung San 37, 37n4

Taira, Teemu 197, 220–221
Taiwan 125
tattoos 167, 168, 172
tax filings 13, 20, 22
   see also anti-tax movements
Taylor, Charles 164, 168
Taylor, Mark C. 3–4
TDN (The Druid Network) 180, 182–183, 185, 192, 197–202
   anti-institutional stance of 197–198
   and charity law 183, 183n2, 197–202, 221
   and definition of religion 199, 200
   and Inter Faith Network 185, 222
   and political activism 198–199, 221
teachers 163, 164
territoriality 44–45
   as constructivist 45
   and governance 45
   and nation 45–46
terrorism 10, 33, 34, 49–50, 83, 170n
   see also "paper terrorism"

Texas 24–25, 50–51, 57, 58
Thailand 35
theory of mind 93
Thomas, Scott 51–52
Thompson, E.P. 190–191
Three 6 Mafia 80
Three Versions of Judas (Borges) 74–75, 83, 100
Tiele, C.P. 84
Tollefsen, Inga Bårdsden 209
tropes 5, 73, 83, 85, 120, 123
Trotsky, Leon 48
Trudeau, Pierre 162
Trump, Donald 33, 108, 112–113, 120, 129–130
Turner, Bryan S. 192
Twitter 128, 137, 138, 143

United States (U.S.)
   and American identity 56, 60, 64, 116, 117–118
   Christianity in 57, 58, 68, 69, 208–209, 212
   citizenship in *see* sovereign citizen movement
   Constitution 12
   Episcopalians in 208–209, 223
   immigrants in 55
   Indigenous people of *see* Native Americans
   IRS in 22, 23
   Jim Crow laws in 15, 18, 55, 64, 211
   MBPT in 92, 93
   minority religions in 113, 117, 118, 162, 217
   and New Deal/welfare state 211–212
   religious history of *see* American religious history

Valman, Nadia 157
Volk 94, 95, 95n7, 96, 97, 127

Walker, Alice 141
Wallace, Michele 104
Washington, Fredrix Joe 19n11
Washitaw Nation 19–20, 19n11, 26
Watts, Isaac 75
Weber, Max 85, 179, 202, 204, 216, 220, 222
Weisenfeld, Judith 9

welfare state 211–212
Weltanschauung 129
Wenger, Tina 142
Wessinger, Catherine 13–14
West, Tracy 136
Westphalia, Treaty of (1648) 47, 47–48n3, 69, 70
Wheeler, Kayla 130
White, Hayden 73, 129
white nationalism/supremacism 15, 20, 23, 42, 102, 104
    and Brexit 220
    and Trump 112–113, 120, 129–130
Whiteness 78, 78n4, 139
Wicca *see* Paganism
Wilcox, Melissa 141
Wilde, Oscar 75
Williams, Rowan 181–182
Williamson, George S. 96, 98
Wimbush, Vincent 77
Winant, Howard 102, 125
Wirathu, Ashin 38

Wolff, Robert 44
womanism 141
women, religiously visible 163, 168, 170–171
women scholars 146, 151
    see also Black women scholars
working class 179, 181, 190–191, 193–194, 200, 209, 211, 220
    and false consciousness 204, 207
world religions paradigm 84, 85, 86, 88, 100, 102, 199, 201
World War I 75–76, 156, 157, 158–160, 159–160n2

yoga 82, 82n6
youth movements 157, 158
YouTube 24
Yusuf, Imtiyaz 34n1, 37

Zerubavel, Yael 159
Zionism 156–157, 159, 159n1, 160
Zitkála-Šá 142